DON'T WORRY 'BOUT
THE BEAR

DON'T WORRY 'BOUT THE BEAR

From the Blues to Jazz, Rock & Roll and Black Sabbath

Jasper, a tremendous supporter and a really good guy.

Jim Simpson with Ron Simpson

Jim Simpson

BREWIN BOOKS

BREWIN BOOKS
56 Alcester Road,
Studley,
Warwickshire,
B80 7LG
www.brewinbooks.com

Published by Brewin Books 2019

© Jim & Ron Simpson 2019

The authors have asserted their rights in accordance with the Copyright, Designs and Patents Act 1988 to be identified as the authors of this work.

All rights reserved. No part of this publication may be reproduced, stored in a retrieval system, or transmitted in any form or by any means, electronic, mechanical, photocopying, recording or otherwise, without the prior permission in writing of the publisher and the copyright owners, or as expressly permitted by law, or under terms agreed with the appropriate reprographics rights organization. Enquiries concerning reproduction outside the terms stated here should be sent to the publishers at the UK address printed on this page.

The publisher makes no representation, express or implied, with regard to the accuracy of the information contained in this book and cannot accept any legal responsibility for any errors or omissions that may be made.

A CIP catalogue record for this book is available from the British Library.

ISBN: 978-1-85858-700-4

Printed and bound in Great Britain by
Hobbs the Printers Ltd.

CONTENTS

	Foreword	vii
	Preface	ix
1	Early Years	1
2	Locomotive On The Tracks	21
3	On A Mission From Dog	40
4	From Earth To Black Sabbath	54
5	Sabbath Bloody Sabbath	72
6	Sabbath: The After-Party	82
7	Blues And The Bear	90
8	Not So Foolish As I'm Badly Dressed	110
9	Goin' To Kansas City	130
10	Making Tracks	140
11	Jazz City UK	155
12	Lady Sings The Blues	176
13	Humph: Our Leader	195
14	The Boss Is Home	209
15	There's No Business In Show Business	219
16	King Pleasure And The Biscuit Boys	239
17	Marbella: Fiesta And Fiasco	255
18	The Midem Years	274
19	Jagger, The Killer And The Prettiest Man In Rock And Roll	286
20	In The Confident Hope Of A Miracle	301
	Appendix 1: Discography	311
	Appendix 2: Bands That Appeared At Henry's Blueshouse	314
	Appendix 3: American Bluesmen Toured / Recorded By Big Bear	316
	Appendix 4: Events Organised By Big Bear Music (Partial List)	318
	Acknowledgements	319
	Photo Credits	320
	Index	321

FOREWORD

The entertainment industry is full of the most diverse of people from the mega famous to nondescript individuals whose influence can be obvious or hidden, slight or momentous, no matter what their standing in the consumers' awareness.

Jim Simpson is not a name that is too familiar outside the City of Birmingham, but his influence is quite remarkable. It began in the early sixties when as a musician, manager, promoter and entrepreneur he was responsible for the ups and downs of many well-known bands and artists.

Jim has been around the music scene in Birmingham for over 60 years. Not an actual Brummie, he has nevertheless carved himself a place in the hearts and minds of the citizens of the City who know him as the indefatigable dynamo who is responsible for the history of many of its renowned musical legends, places of entertainment and of course the world famous Birmingham Jazz Festival.

This book is not what you would call an autobiography, more a collection of stories and events that have shaped the comings and goings of the famous and the almost made-its. His love of Blues and Jazz directed him eventually into the less popular of the musical genres, but the satisfaction he has derived from the involvement is there for all to see.

Jim drops names like no other, all quite legit, all quite genuine. How on earth he remembers them all is very impressive. Here you will find the low down on bands like Black Sabbath, musicians of the stature of Humphrey Lyttelton, singers such as Val Wiseman, clubs and venues that have been extremely influential and of course Big Bear Records, his own record label and prized heritage.

Jim writes with brutal honesty, a light touch of genuine humour, incredible recall, and a quiet modesty, which all makes for a darn good read and a record of our times from the early sixties to his present day activities. All very impressive!

Jasper Carrott

PREFACE

Don't Worry 'Bout the Bear is the musical memoirs of Jim Simpson over a career of well over 50 years in the music industry. His memory for events, in some cases dating back to the 1940s, is prodigious, but not always precise: rather like Eric Morecambe with the Grieg Piano Concerto, all the facts, but not necessarily in the right order. My role has been to check and arrange the facts, but the words and opinions are all Jim's.

The arrangement of the book needs some explanation. How do you arrange the memoirs of someone who at the same time was running a club, touring American bluesmen, managing bands and working as a photographer/journalist? Not chronologically, that's for sure: stories would become impossibly tangled together. So, after the opening chapter takes Jim to the brink of his musical career, each chapter is thematic. The order of the chapters is, as far as possible, loosely chronological, but many of them cover the full 30 year-plus span of a festival, a band or an event. There is some inevitable overlap, but we have tried to achieve some sort of logical separation.

Of course you can simply ignore the logic and enjoy the unlikely, but true, stories.

Ron Simpson

Don't Worry 'Bout The Bear is the title of a song written, performed and recorded by Doctor Ross on the Big Bear album *Doctor Ross, The Harmonica Boss.*

Chapter 1

EARLY YEARS

I must have been 11 years old before I became aware that Jack Teagarden was not really my uncle.

For years, when asked how I first became aware of jazz, I would make this spurious claim. It was actually not without some foundation in truth as I, and my younger brother Ron, grew up to a soundtrack of Louis Armstrong, Bing Crosby, Jack Teagarden and the other jazz greats, in a house where our father spoke their names with such familiarity that it became perfectly natural to hear him refer to Teagarden as 'Uncle Jack'. This was a man who remembered seeing Fats Waller, fortified by a bottle of gin, sitting in with Nat Gonella at Sherry's Ballroom in Brighton. Among his other memories of the 1930s was the first musician he ever saw appear on stage in a theatre in a lounge suit, not a dinner jacket – the great tenor sax player, Coleman Hawkins.

It had not always been this way. Born in 1938 to a Swansea-born schoolteacher mother and a Scots painter and decorator father, I was left, thanks to the demands of war, with nothing but female company.

After Mom graduated from Birmingham University, she moved to London and took up a teaching post with Westminster Council. I suspect that her love of theatre had a lot to do with that decision. In later years she told me that she would have preferred working in a theatre box office to teaching which I never took seriously, but you can never be sure. My parents met outside Charing Cross Station when Mother was selling the *Daily Worker*. She was one of the many clear-thinking people who subscribed to the anti-Fascist Communist ideal in the mid-1930s, only to have their beliefs totally shattered when Stalin signed the non-aggression pact with Nazi Germany in 1939.

At the time the Spanish Civil War was seen as an opportunity to crush Fascism and thousands of British men, intellectuals and working-class, joined the fight in Spain as part of the International Brigade. Their passages were facilitated in Britain by the Communist Party and the Independent Labour Party and I believe that there was every good reason to support that cause.

My parents had been married for nearly a year when I was born, but, while I was still an infant, Dad went off to fight Nazi Germany, leaving Mom teaching in London and looking after me. Soon her school, plus Mother and me, were shipped off en masse to Brighton in the first wave of evacuees, before returning when the anticipated air raids didn't materialise. And then they did and the school was again evacuated, this time to Exeter. When Hitler enlarged his bombing campaigns to include Exeter, Westminster Council evacuated the school to Bromsgrove in Worcestershire, only 10 miles from Mom's parents' home in Halesowen.

I remember our Christmas there, in a pub in a canalside village close to Bromsgrove, when Mom was upset that the only Christmas toy available in the shops was a set of miniature railway signals. I remember expressing great pleasure and excitement on receiving this, not actually because that's what I felt, but because I somehow understood how important it was to comfort my mother.

Mom did the logical thing and applied to be transferred from Westminster to Worcestershire Council. We moved to her mother's house and she started teaching in Halesowen which she did for the rest of her working life. For the last 25 years she was Head of Stourbridge Road Infants School which is still referred to by many local people as Mrs. Simpson's. Even now I meet people who were taught by her and they all seem to remember it with great pleasure. I spent many a year involved in one way or another with Halesowen Town Football Club (its ground, coincidentally, next to the school) and mother, well into retirement, was invited to a function there. It was great to see the queue of hard-bitten football officials lining up to speak to her. When Club Chairman Ron Moseley shook her hand, he asked if she remembered him. 'Of course,' she said. 'You're Ron Moseley. How's Derek Beasley? Does he still get nose-bleeds?' at which Ron collapsed in laughter. Derek, his boyhood pal, by then Chairman of Halesowen Harriers Football Club, was waiting a little further down the line.

Thus it was that, when my soldier father returned on leave, I was being raised in the company of women, none of them noted for her love of jazz. My mother and I lived with her mother, next door were Auntie Amy and her daughters Flora and Muriel and in the next door but one bungalow lived the spinster sisters Aunts Flo and Minnie. I received far more attention than is good for a child of that age, but there was worse. Incorrectly assuming in me an early liking for country music, they made that my entire musical diet. To this day I wake up in a cold sweat to the imagined sound of Montana Slim 'The Yodelling Cowboy' singing *When the White Azaleas Start Blooming.*

Rescue was at hand when my father came back on leave, saw with horror what his (then) only son was being subjected to, climbed into the attic and came back

1. Early Years

with box after box of 78 rpm shellac records, with the names Louis Armstrong, Coleman Hawkins, Fats Waller and, of course, Jack Teagarden. Salvation!

Dad was a singer. Leaving school in the Royal Burgh of Dysart in Fife, where the obvious choice of employment for a man was between the pit and the fishing, he began work in a butcher's shop, hated wading through blood and opted for an apprenticeship as a painter and decorator. He travelled daily by train, across the Forth Bridge, to Edinburgh where he worked for the old-established firm of Dobie & Son. This is where he discovered jazz and where he first had a singing engagement.

Subsequently – I suspect, lured by the music – he took the bold step of moving to London where he took a job with a top Mayfair painting and decorating firm before seeking singing auditions. He sang with bands throughout the West End and recorded *Blue Prelude* – not an easy song – and *Waltz of the Gypsies*. They still sound good.

What convinced Dad to shelve his singing career was actually the moment when he might have made the big breakthrough. He obtained an audition with the well-known songwriter/bandleader Billy Reid, a regular Decca recording artist who topped variety bills throughout the country. Sadly no one seemed very interested in listening to Dad sing. Billy left him in the charge of his star singer and then-partner, Dorothy Squires, who in turn was, as Dad said, 'all over Billy like a rash'. Her rudeness was a lifelong memory for Dad who quite understood when, in later life, she gained as big a reputation for her court appearances as for her singing. He walked out of the audition, leaving behind his ambition to be a professional singer.

With war imminent, Dad was assigned as foreman to the Rolls Royce Derby factory in charge of a group of painters camouflaging the factory roofs. Although this was designated a reserved occupation and protected from military service, when war broke out he volunteered, initially joining the Fife and Forfar Yeomanry. The Scots are like that, they never forget their roots, though he delighted in referring disrespectfully to the regiment as 'The Knives and Forks'.

A tank regiment, the Fife and Forfar were absorbed into the 3rd Royal Tank Regiment and shipped out to the Western Desert on active service against Rommel's Panzer Divisions. He told of the convoy bound for Egypt having to take a circuitous route to avoid U-boat activity, even spending a few days in Rio de Janeiro en route to Cairo. He saw plenty of action with only one UK leave in six years. In later years he preferred to recall managing the battalion football team while convalescing from wounds in Alexandria. With the team containing such stars as Wilf Mannion of Middlesbrough and England cricketer Jim Laker, his career as a football manager was highly successful, if fairly brief.

At the end of the war his regiment was deployed to Palestine, then in turmoil in the last days of the British Mandate. As a result he was not demobbed until

1946 whereupon he rejoined the family in Halesowen and set up his own painting and decorating business which he ran till his retirement.

But, really, Dad was a singer.

When I was 10, I bought my first record, Pee Wee Hunt's *12th Street Rag* on Capitol, a *Billboard* chart-topper which spent no fewer than 32 weeks in the charts – imagine a jazz record doing that! I drove the family mad; it was never off the turntable. It wasn't long before my brother Ron, some four years my junior, began to share my fascination with jazz and we would spend hours poring over the latest reviews in jazz magazines and listening to the late-night broadcasts of Willis Conover on *Voice of America.*

By then we had moved to Old Hill, near neighbours to the Grand Theatre, later more famous as the Plaza Ballroom, then home to a weekly-changing variety show, featuring dancers, singers, acrobats, ventriloquists, the occasional (and, by today's standards, very tame) strippers – and, far too often for our taste, a famous boy soprano from Cradley Heath singing *Ave Maria.* Our favourite act was the comedy/jazz band Freddy Mirfield and his Garbage Men which, I learned later, had once contained such future jazz greats as John Dankworth, Freddie Randall and Bruce Turner.

This was our introduction to live theatre. Mother rarely missed an opportunity to see the weekly shows and Ron and I were the immediate beneficiaries. Our early theatre experience didn't stop here, with trips to Dudley Hippodrome to see Laurel and Hardy, Abbott and Costello, Chico Marx, Harry Secombe and, as Captain and Mate in *Dick Whittington*, Morecambe and Wise.

A watershed moment came in 1952 when Mother took me to see American blues artist Big Bill Broonzy at Birmingham Town Hall. Broonzy, actually, was not what he seemed. Previously a slick, really hip Chicago guitar man, he was taken under the wing of Yannick Bruynoghe, a Belgian blues fanatic who arranged appearances and recording sessions throughout Europe and later co-wrote *Big Bill Blues*, Broonzy's autobiography. The catch, because there always is one, was that he required the City Slicker to adopt the primitive persona of a rural Mississippi bluesman, even down to the dungarees. This Broonzy took to with alacrity. Not that he was a charlatan; he was actually a fine blues guitarist and singer who delivered a first-class performance. The support band for Big Bill that night was Mick Mulligan's Magnolia Jazz Band whose singer was a wild, young, track-suited and extremely effete George Melly.

I don't know what inspired my mother to take me to a blues performance, but it was a significant moment, though it was many years before I realised just how significant.

1. Early Years

There was an odd footnote to the concert. I read a review in the following week's edition of the *Melody Maker* and learned of dramatic events outside the Town Hall. A group of uncouth Brummie youths had given Broonzy a difficult time during his solo vocal and acoustic guitar performance. This some of Mulligan's band found disrespectful. So much so that, at the end of the band's set, Mulligan, drummer Stan Greig and a couple of others were seen chasing audience members down New Street, bent on revenge.

I think I had gone to the concert to enjoy Mick Mulligan more than Broonzy. I had heard nothing prior to that to prepare me for Big Bill's music. However, confused, mesmerised and bewildered as I was, Big Bill Broonzy had opened my eyes to the blues. The problem now was knowing where to look next. There wasn't very much blues around just then, either in clubs or on the radio.

At this time, though, I was going to jazz clubs in Birmingham – mostly, the Old Crown in Digbeth. To get to the upstairs room where the gig was, you had to walk along a passage past a hatch through which a young woman served the outdoor customers. I would be wearing short trousers, so I wasn't supposed to be there on licensed premises. I used to wait till the hatch was closed and the barmaid was serving somebody at the bar, then I would scuttle past and upstairs, sit quietly at the back and fondly imagine no one could see I was there. Many years later, during the Jazz Festival, we were doing a 24-hour version of *Honeysuckle Rose* non-stop to raise money for charity. One of the musicians who came along was a drummer called Ron Burnard who had played regularly in the band at the Old Crown. He delighted in telling me that all the band used to look out for the kid in short trousers who reckoned that no one could see him. Apparently I was the source of much amusement to the band.

School Music lessons taught me nothing about jazz, and in fact very little about anything except sleeping silently through the music teacher's piano recitals, but I did manage to found a jazz club and run it for some time. The supposedly scurrilous nature of the music meant that I was unable to get permission to meet to play records after school one day a week unless one of the masters was present to assure moral probity. Of course none of the masters wanted to stay behind longer than necessary, but eventually our English teacher, David Henschell, agreed and our jazz club was operative. Our main source of jazz on the radio was Kenny Baker's *Let's Settle for Music* on Thursday evenings. Later I was to work many times with Kenny, but my first memory of him is Friday mornings at school with a group of friends swapping views on the previous night's programme which was essential listening as far as we were concerned.

Don't Worry 'Bout The Bear

My brother and I were regular attenders at the annual Ideal Homes Exhibition in Bingley Hall, not because we were interested in the latest Ercol furniture, but because Sid Phillips' Band appeared there every year. That must have been quite a tough gig. Each of the bands there would play maybe 30 or 45 minutes, then have an hour or so off, then return and so on throughout the day. It meant they had to be there all day – and that meant we were, too. I remember being very taken with the band's glamorous singer, Betty Miller (my earliest crush – or was that June Allyson as Glenn's wife in *The Glenn Miller Story*?) and trumpet star Kenny Ball. On record the Sid Phillips Band can sound a bit mannered, but it was a fine band, all good players who knew how to swing.

There were plenty of good big bands on the scene in the 1950s, including the one led by Sid Phillips' brother Woolf, and plenty of theatres and cinemas to stage Sunday concerts, together with Humphrey Lyttelton's regular visits to Birmingham Town Hall.

By 1955 I had left school and was working at Lewis' store in the City Centre which gave better access to Birmingham's jazz clubs – and then I discovered rhythm and blues! Next to the Locarno was a milk bar with a juke box which is where I first heard Wynonie Harris' *Bloodshot Eyes*. This was the missing link back to Big Bill Broonzy and I started listening to more of the old blues guys then as well as my newly discovered rhythm and blues.

Then it was 1956 and I was liable for National Service. In one way the timing was unfortunate as, at that time, the Musicians' Union ban on visiting American bands had just been lifted and suddenly it became possible to see the Basie and Ellington bands each year – sadly, I was to be out of the country! My brother managed to hear most of them so I got first-hand reports which, of course, increased my frustration at not being there. However, before I joined up, I was able to catch the first tour for 25 years of the greatest of them all, Louis Armstrong, with his All Stars.

In the early 1930s Dad had first heard the Louis Armstrong Orchestra. Now I was with him, my brother Ron and June Griffiths, the butcher's daughter, at the Embassy Sportsdrome in Walford Road for Louis' return with the All Stars. The band, without Satch, were onstage noodling through *Sleepytime Down South*, when suddenly, about four feet behind my right ear, came the most beautiful sound – Louis Armstrong's trumpet. I was on an aisle seat as Louis made his entrance and amazingly (for me, at least) the photographer from the *Birmingham Mail* caught the moment – and there I was, with Dad, Ron and the butcher's daughter, on the next day's front page, with Louis Armstrong.

Ironically, that photograph has been published several times in recent years when I have been identified, as Managing Director of Big Bear, by a ring round my head.

Louis Armstrong, Ron and me.

Sadly they have ringed the wrong person! I'm the one behind him gazing in awe at Armstrong's trumpet or, more probably, checking what mouthpiece he was using.

A wonderful evening in every way, although it was also strange in its barn-like boxing arena setting and the unusual opening act, the great one-legged tap dancer Peg Leg Bates who had lost a leg at the age of 12 in an accidental encounter with agricultural equipment. Peg Leg was amazing, spinning on his good leg while tapping with the other, turning somersaults that would do credit to a two-legged man, all delivered with obvious enjoyment and a huge grin.

Many years later I was talking to Humphrey Lyttelton about Peg Leg. Humph shared my enthusiasm for the dancer, but told me that he toured with him on the Scottish leg of the Armstrong tour. Apparently, after his show, Peg Leg would sit on his own in a corner of the dressing room weeping with pain. That's so sad, but it's grand that Peg Leg was blessed with such an indomitable spirit.

I never met Peg Leg, but I had a surprising telephone encounter with his townsfolk many years later when I was researching the subjects for the Birmingham-based suite, *Swinging Down Broad Street*. One of the numbers featured the appearance of Louis and Peg Leg at the Sportsdrome and somehow I found the phone number for a Peg Leg Bates Community Centre in Fountain Inn, South Carolina. The phone was answered by a cheerful female voice who informed me that, in South Carolina, that very day was designated Peg Leg Bates Day! There's also a Peg Leg Bates Highway, incidentally.

On my application form for National Service, I had put down, in order of preference, the Royal Tank Regiment (because of my dad, I wanted to be a tanker), the Royal Marines and the Parachute Regiment, so quite naturally I ended up in the Royal Air Force! I was disappointed, but that quickly changed. I had a very good basic training, it was the same as in the Army and I'd been a very keen member of the Army Cadet Force at school, so I knew it all – and, on occasion, that could be a problem.

I incurred the wrath of one weapons corporal by sailing through a demonstration of emergency drills on a Bren gun. On wet lunch-times in the Orderly Room at school we had practised these procedures blindfold as a game. Now, of course, I had been expected to flounder and give the corporal an opportunity to unleash his foul-mouthed fury. When I sailed through the drill with the swagger that only comes with total confidence, instead of giving me a pat on the back or even a brisk 'Well done', the corporal exploded. Pushing his face right up to mine, nose to nose, he yelled, 'Don't you ever fucking come near any of my fucking lessons again!'

And he meant it! What to do for the remaining weeks of the course? Fortunately another corporal had the answer, 'Get yourself a clipboard and paper and walk around a bit. Stop for a cup of tea at the NAAFI now and then, but remember to look like you're busy.'

Then it came to choice of trades. As a National Serviceman you had a limited choice and no guarantee of getting your preference; if you signed up for three years, the choice was wider and the certainty greater. And that is how I ended up in the RAF for three years, in Air Traffic Control at Gibraltar for two and a half of those years. Two and a half years that prompted a lifelong love of Spain and also advanced my musical career.

We all volunteered for posting to the Middle East Command, at this time the scene of the Suez Crisis: I remember thinking there was only one better posting, the Liaison Office in Washington, DC, but that would have been too much to hope for. As it happened, my posting only took me as far east as Gibraltar and I fell in love with the place at once. It was December, but I could feel the heat rising from the ground the evening I got off that terrible old Hastings aircraft.

It wasn't long before the RAF turned me into a bandleader. I had bought my trumpet in a second-hand shop when I was 15 or 16. I remember I put it proudly on the bedside table when I went to bed. Dad came in late and, as I was pretending to be asleep, I saw him fingering the valves and lifting it towards his lips. He didn't play it, of course, but he was fascinated by it – probably, rather less

1. Early Years

Night duty at RAF Gibraltar control tower.

fascinated later by my early attempts at practice! I didn't really do a lot with it at first, tootled along to a few records at home, never had a lesson, but importantly I took it with me to Gibraltar in the RAF.

After a few weeks somebody heard me playing and shortly afterwards I was summoned to see the Station Commander. 'Would I like to form a station band?' They'd got all the instruments, they'd got a rehearsal room, but they hadn't got a band. I prevaricated, but I already knew another trumpeter, Paddy Bruton, a good player, so I got him involved and formed a jazz band. We immediately had somewhere to rehearse and, on the occasions the station band had a gig, my jazz band took over and no one seemed to notice.

At that time I did not know enough tunes and my reading was painfully slow, but I worked hard at my reading and also learnt tunes in a most unorthodox fashion, by following Paddy's fingering. We recruited other musicians from the Seaforth Highlanders who were the garrison regiment for much of my time on The Rock, including Dave Fimister who played trumpet and piano with the band,

and after demob became a stalwart of Dundee's East Side Jazz Band, playing trumpet. For some reason we called ourselves the Riverside Jazz Band, though there's no river anywhere near Gibraltar. We had plenty of work at the honky-tonks such as the Universal and the Trocadero along Main Street: when the American Sixth Fleet came in, we worked every night. I think we made an entertaining noise, playing Chicago-style jazz, and Dave Fimister could listen to the radio and chat to us while writing out the chords to the music he was listening to. Walking down Main Street with me and Johnny Morris, another trumpet player trained at Kneller Hall, Dave heard a car horn. 'A flat!' he proclaimed. Johnny held the note, rushed into the Garrison NAAFI and hit A flat on the piano – sure enough, there it was! Dave was a really remarkable musician: although he didn't practise and had no lip as such, he played with a flair and swagger that put the rest of us to shame. But he never seemed to care about his talent: every week he'd pawn his trumpet, then redeem it a few days later – or not, he was quite capable of turning up for a gig without his instrument.

Chas Hounslow, our clarinettist, had a bad habit of going AWOL and being brought back in chains and put in prison. Fortunately I had a good relationship with the Squadron Leader, so, when we had a gig, he let me sign Chas out like an item of equipment. We always brought him back, usually the worse for wear.

We played a regular Sunday gig on the ferryboat across the bay to Algeciras. I remember our guitarist, Jim Smith, who would sit on a metal chair. Perched on a high deck, the chair would vibrate ever nearer to the side of the ship. We watched eagerly, but he never went over. A newspaper cutting shows Jim working his way across the deck as the band plays and records the band's name as the Kansas City Seven – not a name I recall using at that time, but curiously prophetic.

We used to go on tours of the nearby Spanish villages – never very far – and one time I had an embarrassing experience at a Patio Party in La Linea. I hadn't taken my trumpet, so I asked to borrow one. I had never heard of a key-change trumpet! It had a lever to change key, the owner had set it for A and I thought I was in B flat as usual – I never did manage to adjust!

For the last 15 months or so I was on Gibraltar I had my own jazz programme on Radio Gibraltar, with a tiny allowance for buying records: the first I bought was *Robbins' Nest* and *The Hucklebuck* by Buck Clayton. I even wrote a column for the RAF *Roundel* magazine – or, rather, I didn't. Somehow my grammar school education had managed to convince me I couldn't write, so the subject material was sent back to my younger brother in England and turned into an article by him. Since then I have realised that my mother was right when she told me, 'If you can say something, you can write it.'

Our regular gig on the Gibraltar-Algeciras ferry – Chas Hounslow on clarinet.

Finally Gibraltar came to an end. I was the longest-serving RAF man on The Rock. I should have served the normal 18 months tour, but because I was in Air Traffic Control I was in close touch with the office that scheduled return flights and I would say, 'Move my name down to the bottom of the list.'

Life in Gibraltar was never dull and I was reluctant to leave a place with so much going on. The beach was barely a two-minute stroll from the barrack block, the town maybe 15 minutes away and the neighbouring Spanish town, La Linea de la Concepcion about half an hour. I've never been so well off, comparatively, that is. Eventually my RAF pay reached over £7 a week, meals, accommodation and clothing came free, compared with the average worker's wage in La Linea of £5. In my later months on The Rock I was able to take a room in La Linea – I'm still not sure if that contravened any RAF regulation.

Working in Air Traffic Control in Gibraltar was in itself an adventure with the only road to the Spanish border crossing the middle of the runway which meant we had to signal the lowering of barriers every time we had an aircraft movement. There was an occasion, not on my watch, when a Canadian Air Force T33 lost radio contact and, instead of following procedure, flying the length of the runway at 500 feet rolling the aircraft and waiting for a green Very light, the pilot simply took it upon himself to land without warning. The road was open, traffic was crossing and a Spanish workman, riding his bicycle, was decapitated by the aircraft's wing.

The road wasn't our only external hazard, far from it. Both ends of the runway ended at the sea, so there was no run-off area, and the Western half of the runway was surrounded by sea on all sides. To further complicate matters, The Rock, standing some 1,398 feet, was more or less adjacent to the runway and, when the winds picked up, created significant turbulence to the threshold at the Mediterranean end.

We regarded T33 fliers in general, be they Canadians or Americans, as cowboys. Incidents involving the T33, also known as the Lockheed Shooting Star, were many and varied. When any aircraft came in on final approach, we always instructed the pilot, 'If your wheels are not firmly on the ground by the 500 yard bar, you are to take overshoot action.' The T33 flyboys often ignored this instruction and more than once ended up on the beach or in the sea.

When US aircraft carriers came into Gib, it was customary for their aircraft to take off from the carrier some 30 minutes away and fly onto our strip as part of a landing exercise. This was often a recipe for confusion, but my worst experience was when USS *Forrestal* came into port. It started with an RT call from one T33 asking permission to land. As they flew in across the bay, we realised that he was speaking on behalf of the entire ship's complement of aircraft, some ten flights, each of three aircraft. The real problem was where to stack them as Gibraltar has no perimeter or taxi tracks to relieve pressure on the runway. There was no alternative to parking the first arrivals tightly at the runway's end and stacking up the following T33s in as close order behind them as possible. By the time we had got them all down, we found that we had filled about 30 per cent of the entire runway. Later we laughed about it, but it was pretty tense at the time and we took it as some sort of an apology when the US Navy pilots brought us a case of whisky into the control tower when they came to file their flight plans prior to departure.

Things didn't always end so well. The 224 Squadron Coastal Command was our resident squadron and flew Shackletons. My trombone player, Ken Powers, was a Navigation Sergeant on one of the Shacks taking part in the RAF's annual showing off to the locals as part of the Battle of Britain Day display. In 1957 his Shack simulated a low-level anti-submarine run, roaring down the length of the runway at speed with bomb doors open at maybe 250 feet, much to the excitement of the crowds of several thousand lining the runway.

Probably having too much fun, the pilot, Flight Lieutenant Bluett, radioed to inform us that he was going to repeat the procedure with the starboard outer engine feathered to demonstrate the aircraft's capability when partly disabled. We relayed the information to the clearly impressed crowd and waited for the Shack to reappear from behind The Rock. The Shackleton's hydraulics are operated by the power generated by the two starboard engines, so, when just short of the runway threshold, the starboard inner failed, Bluett found himself in all sorts of trouble. Unable to gain height because of the loss of power or to lower his wheels because of the hydraulics failure, he belly-flopped his huge aircraft on the runway at quite a speed. The Shack squirmed from right to left, avoided plunging into the crowd and gradually came to a grindingly loud halt just short of the runway's end. As it slowed, a figure was seen jumping from the aircraft and sprinting back up the runway. 'I bet that's Ken Powers,' I remarked, and sure enough it was, putting as much distance as he could between himself and the stricken Shack for fear it might explode.

I think they classed it as a Grade 7 wreck and we were all mightily impressed when they flew in an RAF Beverley, dismantled the Shackleton and flew this huge aircraft back to the UK for repair. Amazingly, it was returned to action at Gibraltar some six months later.

We had our share of hooligan fliers and they were usually a lot better at it. One of our Air Traffic Control officers was a former World War II Spitfire pilot who enjoyed a reputation, both for his wartime exploits and his taste for alcohol – hence his nickname Flight Lieutenant 'Pissy' Parsons. I wasn't present at the conversation in the Officers' Mess when Parsons was ribbing some visiting American Navy pilots for what he perceived as their lack of flying skills. They flew the Walrus amphibian aircraft which, while not as large as the RAF Sunderland flying boats, were still pretty big and very cumbersome. Parsons insisted that aerobatics could be performed with any aircraft, even the Walrus, which they heartily disputed.

The upshot was that the following morning Parsons, totally without permission other than that of the Walrus crew, took their aircraft out over the bay and dramatically demonstrated the Falling Leaf, not the sort of aerobatic manoeuvre to be attempted in such a workhorse of an aircraft. Thus Parsons clearly maintained his legendary status for years to come.

It's probably the same now in the armed forces and certainly back then it was pretty much unknown for officers to fraternise with other ranks. Most officers maintained a chasm between the ranks, though Flight Lieutenant Parsons was one of the chaps who would instigate drinking in La Linea. However, our Squadron Leader, who during a night shift discovered that we shared a mutual interest in the running of bulls, used to arrange to meet me in an out-of-the-way La Linea bar to go to bull fights in La Linea, Algeciras or San Roque, and one time we drove together to Sevilla for the corridas at the famous La Maestranza.

So there I was, finally leaving after two and half years. I knew everyone, I was involved in everything, I couldn't walk down the street without meeting friends. When I was due to go back to the UK to be demobbed, because I was already missing Spain so much, I said, 'See you in a couple of days' – and I did. But, when I came back from England, I found out that I was on the outside. Suddenly no one was saying, 'Come for a drink!' or 'Let's go for a swim!'. And I still don't know why. Maybe it's that I was an outsider because I was no longer subject to the same stiff rules as everyone else. But suddenly I didn't know Gibraltar any more and after two or three days I went back to Spain.

It was the summer of 1959. I was back home with the family, though not in a familiar setting as they had moved house from Blackheath to Halesowen in my absence and the unfamiliar setting added to the awkwardness of getting to know my parents all over again. In almost three years I had only seen them for two weekends, and that was during the first three months of my service. I guess that I had gained a bunch of life experiences when away and been involved in things they could not easily imagine. The awkward phase was short-lived and we all piled into Dad's ageing Daimler Majestic shooting brake and set off for a holiday in Fife.

The roads were clear, the sun was shining and we made good time – as far as Nottingham when the Big End went. Big Ends, whatever they are, went quite often in those days and my father always seemed peculiarly unlucky in that respect. Undeterred as always, Dad asked the garage mechanic which was the nearest seaside place, was told Skegness and promptly booked a cab to take us there.

I fear that the two weeks we spent in Skegness suited me rather better than it did the rest of the family. It was the summer of Cliff Richard's *Living Doll* and the town was living up to its tagline 'Skegness is so bracing!' It was the playground of the youngsters of Nottingham and the East Midlands and they came to town by the busload.

I felt rather guilty asking my parents if they minded if I stayed on for a couple of weeks after our holiday. They couldn't have been happy, as we were still in the process of getting to know each other again, but they were nice enough not to raise any objections.

So I needed a job. My landlady knew the folks who ran the local dairy, effected the introductions and that was the beginning of my short, but eventful, career as a milkman. The dairy was based on a disused airfield – which provided an irresistible temptation to race the milk floats. I found myself sacked before my two weeks trial was up, something to do with cornering too quickly in my loaded milk float and depositing a pile of milk crates and smashed bottles on the ground.

1. Early Years

I next worked for Skegness Foreshore Council, renting out deck-chairs and erecting wind-breaks, but at least I had the opportunity to handle the donkey rides. The donkeys were a pleasure to work with: they knew the routines exactly, so all I had to do was go along with them. The highspot of the day was herding the six donkeys from their field to the beach. I would ride my bicycle behind them, smacking my stick on the handlebars to attract their attention and shouting what I hoped were helpful instructions. However, the donkeys knew far better than me what was required and all went well until the morning when we approached a pedestrian crossing just as three large ladies decided to cross. It was chaos. Trotting donkeys and shouting ladies inextricably mixed together. Despite appearances there was no actual contact – the donkeys were far too savvy to let that happen – but, as we resumed our journey towards the beach, I was followed by a barrage of abuse from three extremely irate ladies. I never did work out why they thought their presence on a pedestrian crossing would prompt a donkey to give way.

The most coveted seasonal job in Skegness was as a beach photographer for Wrates, but few got to sport the trademark multi-coloured striped blazers. Fortunately I was one of them, though I was rather sad to walk out on my donkeys. Alfie Wrate had a thriving business, with up to 30 photographers on patrol in high season. A photographer would work independently for up to two hours at a time before the cycling supply man came along with fresh film and to take the exposed film to base. Wrates had a Free See Service which meant the photographer took his shot and handed over a numbered ticket which the customer took to the Pier after a certain time had elapsed – and bought or rejected the photograph.

The photographer's basic pay of £1 a day was supplemented by a sales commission and, as peak season passed, Alfie would systematically lay off photographers based on their sales figures, so good sales were doubly important. I soon found that, unless you had gambler's luck, there was no point in simply shooting a large quantity of photographs. Instead I concentrated on families with children or dogs or young couples, taking carefully posed photographs that they would really want to own.

I also made full use of a plentiful supply of props that Wrates had available, but which most photographers ignored: a full-sized stuffed lion, fortunately on wheels; a selection of toy monkeys and dogs; and my favourite, a five and a half stone bear which kids found irresistible. In the morning, when I had lugged it half the length of the promenade, I would take a break at a café on the pier. The husband of the café owner ran an adjacent Guess Your Weight stand – and this was the deal. I would go in, order teas for me and the bear (which came free) and take a seat. When trade got slack, they would call up my bear, make a song and dance about guessing his weight, weigh him on the machine, precisely 'guess' his weight and build up an Edge – fairground talk for gathering a crowd.

Some 30 years later, in conversation with tenor saxophonist Martin Winning, then with King Pleasure and the Biscuit Boys, I found that we shared a Skegness connection. His parents ran a café on the pier with a Guess Your Weight stand – and they remembered me and my bear. My first connection with the animal that has presided over my music business for 50 years was so successful that, with the bear's help, I ended up as the sole remaining Wrates photographer that year and was then taken on as Alfie's official photographer in a Barnsley department store, taking photographs of a reluctant and vicious Santa and his rather cowed young customers. I have no idea why this Father Christmas took on the job, for the money, I suppose, because he was a grumpy, ill-mannered old bugger who clearly hated children. They must have sensed this because, he told me, the neighbourhood kids delighted in tormenting him. He told me that they would habitually nick his garden gate by lifting it off its hinges and dump it further up the street. He confided to me that he had sorted out that problem by fixing razor blades on the underside of the gate top so the kids would cut their fingers!

So it was Christmas Eve before I finally went home and resumed the mercifully painless process of re-acquainting myself with my family, although, looking back, it was probably a little insensitive of me to bring Derna, a young lady of my acquaintance from Barnsley, with me.

The following summer I was back in Skegness, having spent the intervening months working at Clancey's factory, half a mile from home in Halesowen, grinding tappets and valve guides, whatever they are, to earn enough money to spend some months in Spain and then doing just that. On my return to Skegness I was properly prepared, took along my trumpet and immediately formed a band. We hit dizzying heights very quickly, entering Skegness Carnival on a Wrates Photography float and picking up Seventh Prize. A farm lady herding some very handsome pigs came sixth. Even more meaningfully, we entered the Weekly Talent Show at the Embassy Ballroom and were offered a regular Wednesday residency, a handy showcase for picking up other gigs.

The big music event of that summer was held a few miles up the coast at the Derbyshire Miners Welfare Centre in Ingoldmells. Despite the uncool name the venue had a splendid gig room, nice stage and PA, but sadly no audience to speak of, not even for the wonderful Humphrey Lyttelton Band.

I had a sort of preview of the show earlier in the day when in my role as street photographer I snapped Humph's pianist and bassist, Ian Armit and an extremely glum Pete Blannin, on the way to a dental appointment for Blannin. Back in those days the concept of painless dentistry was unheard of.

The alto saxophone player in our band was a mild and quiet Cambridge graduate named John Slater. Our bass player was fellow-Wrates photographer Derek Rideout from Nottingham whose girlfriend Gwen worked in the processing department at Wrates. Then, to everyone's surprise, probably braced by the Skegness air, Derek switched girlfriends mid-season. On the night of the Humph concert, Derek's new amour was being her usual possessive self which meant he was unable to go to the show. Gwen, unsurprisingly, was in need of a night out and I was in need of transport, so I borrowed John Slater's distinctive bright yellow bicycle and, with Gwen perched on the handlebars, set off for Ingoldmells. The band was sensational and the audience – Gwen, me and the other nine – had a great night. We cycled back to her flat; excited by the music, we had much to talk about before I fell asleep on her settee.

Alfie Wrate's finest, celebrating their triumph at the Skegness Carnival. (L-R) Dude Rideout, unknown, John Slater and JS in someone else's top hat.

Back at the studio the next morning, I found Derek unusually taciturn. Eventually he said he wanted to ask my advice on a personal matter. Apparently, following an argument with his new love, he had got up at dawn and gone over to Gwen's, probably seeking solace, only to find she was in a relationship with John Slater. Derek knew that it was him as his very recognisable yellow bike was parked outside. I didn't feel it appropriate to enlighten him.

My second Skegness season was also my last. As I prepared to return to Spain, John Slater, who had never been abroad, was in a state of excitement at the prospect of spending a few months in Greece. I used every argument to persuade him to come to Spain with me, but to no avail: he was set on Greece. At the end of the summer I flew to Malaga. After a week or so shambling down the coast, I took the elderly local bus into Gibraltar. Clearing customs, the bus lurched towards the city and, as it rounded the Casemates roundabout by the terminus, I saw, sitting on the fountain wall, engrossed in staring at one of his shoes, none other than John Slater! Staggered by the coincidence, I raced over with the biggest and most enthusiastic of Hellos. 'Look at my fucking shoe, it's ruined,' he said. No hello, no expression of surprise or pleasure, but that's saxophonists for you.

With Autumn gone as well as my remaining funds, I activated my return flight ticket. This time I settled permanently in the Birmingham area and looked for a proper job, though over the years I still seized every opportunity to return to Southern Spain. My first job at this time was in the offices of Shelton's metal works in Halesowen.

Birmingham's music scene back in the early 1960s was rocking on at least three separate fronts in a way that it probably never did before and certainly hasn't done since. The Beat Boom was in full flow, captured as it developed on the pages of Dennis Detheridge's indispensable monthly magazine, *Midland Beat*. The underground blues scene was populated by some fine players and a tremendous singer named Roy Everett or Joe Taylor or even Roy Taylor, his real name. On the jazz front it felt like 1930s Harlem, with jam sessions breaking out like a rash and top level players everywhere. What sustained this gathering of talent can be traced to the dance halls of which there were seven or eight in the vicinity, each with a resident orchestra of maybe 16 pieces and a support band of six to eight musicians. Professional musicians the length and breadth of the country came to take work in Birmingham's dance halls and, just like most big band musicians, all they wanted to do in their down time was find a jam session with like-minded souls. The musical instrument shops became informal social clubs for musicians to meet and talk about music, instruments, gig opportunities and the latest record releases. Not all of them were jazzers, of course, but there were enough to make it hard to get a blow at the many jam sessions.

1. Early Years

The most prominent jam session of the time was the Sunday lunch session at a pub called The Chapel. Here the big guns would gather and only the very best players could get a knock. It was a wonderful atmosphere, a room packed with musicians listening to other musicians and almost no civilians, as top tenor sax man Mike Burney used to classify non-musicians. It was also a great education and a sobering reminder of what a young musician had to aspire to.

Ex-John Dankworth trumpeter Dougie Roberts, when he felt so inclined, was one of the stars, but for many of us the most eagerly awaited confrontation was between two tenormen, the Scot Joe Patterson and local boy Mike Burney, two totally contrasting styles, but players of the highest order.

My mother was ever so slightly impressed when I told her I was going to The Chapel on a Sunday, but she knew there would be a catch in there somewhere – and me and my mates always said that we were off to Kansas City because that's what it felt like. The Chapel was where I first got to know Mike Burney, the start of a friendship that lasted until his death in 2014.

I had realised a while back that I needed to be in the City, so I decided I would have to give up my steady, but extremely boring, job at Shelton's. My first application, for the post of photographer at the College of Technology, now Aston University, was made more in hope than expectation. I had brushed with photography since childhood. My maternal grandfather had been an enthusiast, processing his own work, and Mother consistently took good photographs throughout her life and was pretty much single-handedly responsible for recording our family history.

En route to photographing Birmingham from above.

Since early teens I had been using a primitive camera until my parents sent the money for me to buy a more sophisticated piece of equipment, a Zeiss Ikon, for my 21st birthday, when I was in Gibraltar. There I became a prolific photographer, taking advantage of the wonderful light of Andalucia. I had had my first taste of serious (i.e. paid) photography with Wrates in Skegness, but, though I knew my way round a camera, I had absolutely no formal qualifications – which the college would surely insist on.

In interview I was questioned in embarrassing detail about my lack of qualifications, so I was in no doubt I would be rejected. But I had not known that the Head of Photography, David Hunt, a decent man and also a jazz-loving trumpet player, was not much of a photographer himself and also bereft of any qualifications. The last thing he wanted was to have some technical whizz working for him who might just undermine his own position. With this stroke of luck I unexpectedly found myself in paid employment as a photographer as well as picking up money from jazz gigs on trumpet – much of which went on lessons with Dougie Roberts.

Being based in the City, with daytime access to a telephone and all the new contacts made at jam sessions and from hanging around music stores, put me in the right place to form a band.

Chapter 2

LOCOMOTIVE ON THE TRACKS

The first step in forming a jazz band at the College of Technology was to convince the President of the Students' Union, one Jeff Rooker, later a respected politician, now Baron Rooker of Perry Barr, that a regular Wednesday evening jazz club would be a benefit to student life and that the resident Saturday dance band was well beyond its sell-by date. Having done that, I had two regular gigs a week to offer musicians and pretty quickly had the band in place. Embarrassingly I chose the name The New Magnolia Jazz Band, overlooking the fact that it was a typical name for a Trad band which we definitely were not. Stylistically we could probably be categorised musically as Kansas City Swing and eventually we did make the name change to the Kansas City Seven.

We opened at the newly named Tek City Jazz Club in 1962. The Students Union Refectory was a nice room, with a capacity of 200, but with an adjacent room available that took another 600. We had three college students in the band: guitarist Speedy Shuttleworth, trombonist Gordon Davidson who has become my longest-standing friend, and Liverpudlian Ken Dickinson. Ken played alto saxophone and went on to build a reputation as one of the country's finest provincial jazzmen, predominantly with Liverpool's Blue Magnolia Jazz Band – nice to know that the Magnolia survived in one form or another.

Jamaican Sleepy Reid was our fine double bass player. He didn't drive and depended on me for transport for himself and instrument. Looking back, it's hard to believe that we routinely managed to get him, me and a double bass into a tiny Morris Minor. The drummer was one Biz Twiby, a young man with matinee idol looks and an impeccable and unshifting sense of time. The piano player was the nearly professional Lazy Ade Fendick, a man of prodigious talent with both the repertoire and the girth of Fats Waller. The line-up was completed by a most attractive singer, Carol Mills, known to all as 'The Bilston Budgerigar' – but mostly to Gordon Davidson!

The Magnolias at work: Phil Ward (clarinet), Ken Dickinson (alto sax), Gordon Davidson (trombone), JS.

My band was resident, but we brought in guest bands whenever they were available. Humphrey Lyttelton was the first name on the team sheet, but we also presented Bruce Turner's extremely under-rated Jump Band, the Alex Welsh Band, Kenny Ball's Jazzmen – all the usual suspects! We also hosted top visiting Americans such as Wild Bill Davison and, clearly a precursor of what was to come, I organised a series of blues presentations. We featured that great one-man band Jesse Fuller, the Lone Cat, whose compositions included the evergreen *San Francisco Bay Blues*; the finest of the hotshot young Chicago guitarslingers of the time, Buddy Guy; and the New Orleans piano master and former prize-fighter Champion Jack Dupree who, for some reason, was then based in Halifax, Yorkshire. Actually it wasn't so unlikely – fairly predictable, really – it was a woman, the same reason (different women) that saw him also reside in Copenhagen, Zurich, Stockholm and, finally, Hanover.

Jesse Fuller was the first one-man-band I had ever seen close up and he was tremendous – and a very funny man. He sang, played guitar, had a chest rack with harmonica and kazoo, and supplied his own bass lines with a contraption that he had constructed using part of a piano frame, pedals and bass strings. He called it a 'Fotdella' and when I asked why, he gave his smiley, squinty look and said,

2. Locomotive On The Tracks

'Because I hits it with my foots and it goes della, della.' His tour manager told me that, when they were set to play Dublin on that tour, Jesse hadn't been allowed to take his Fotdella on the flight, much to his disappointment. When they had a four day break, mid-tour, apparently Jesse was nowhere to be found. Feeling that he hadn't given his proper show to the Dublin audience, he had simply taken off, via train and the overnight car ferry, to Dublin, set up, unannounced, in one of the city's squares and performed to passers-by. I do wonder if anyone actually knew who or what they were listening to.

Buddy Guy, now the Grand Old Man of Chicago blues, still is one of the greats. A musician of impeccable taste, stunning technique and a complete understanding of the blues, he came up at a time in Chicago when there seemed to be more bluesmen there than you could shake a stick at: Jimi Hendrix, of course, Hubert Sumlin, Jimmy 'Fastfingers' Dawkins, Matt 'Guitar' Murphy, Jimmy Rogers from Muddy Waters' Band. But Buddy was always the one that cut it for me. While he

Buddy Guy, now the Grand Old Man of Chicago Blues, pictured in Birmingham in 1964.

Don't Worry 'Bout The Bear

was in Birmingham, I took Buddy into the University photographic studio for some fairly formal portraits with the guitar giant looking distinctly dapper, even Ivy League-ish, complete with a neat tartan bowtie.

My tenure at the Tek City Jazz Club came to an unexpected end (to me, at least). It was the time of the Beat Boom and I received a summons to a meeting of the executive committee of the Students' Union where I was informed that jazz was no longer considered to be a suitable music for students. The Union had decided to replace our gigs with a Beat Club, the first session to feature an emerging group from Liverpool called The Beatles. They showed me the posters, complete with the deliberate 'ea' misspelling. 'The Beatles!,' I snorted as I departed. 'They'll never get anywhere with a name like that!'

I wasn't just going to skulk away into the night. The club had a good following, so we crossed the street to the Warwick Castle pub and continued where we had left off. I was enjoying playing with my band, now known as The

Keith Harris, JS and John Kiernan at the Warwick Castle.

2. Locomotive On The Tracks

Kansas City Seven, though none of us at that time had been further west than Weston-super-Mare. The capacity in the upstairs room at the Warwick Castle was on the small side, but we made it work financially. My brother Ron handled the door while I took care of the band.

Our reputation grew, other musicians came along to sit in and the audience built so that the room was usually full to capacity. When our piano player – by that time the West Indian Ron Daley who bore a remarkable resemblance to Count Basie – couldn't make it, a 15-year-old kid from Erdington sometimes depped for him. He was a stunning player, by the name of Steve Winwood, and not one of us had any idea he could sing! The sitters-in were many and various. I was particularly knocked out by the trumpet playing of Joe McIntyre, a real swash-buckler, who had come along with Pete Hodge, both of the Harry Gold Band.

After some time my alto saxophone player, Ken Dickinson, completed his studies and returned home to Liverpool. It was with some temerity that I invited the illustrious Mike Burney to join on tenor saxophone – and to my surprise and delight he said yes. I never saw the sense in not going for the best musicians available, a policy I have always stuck with. I figured that I had to have a band where I was the least accomplished musician, an objective I achieved with ease on many an occasion.

The first night that Mike played with the band was, I determined, going to be a good one. I put in a lot of trumpet practice, including the invaluable long-note exercises I had learnt from Humphrey Lyttelton, and I even bought a new shirt. Mike turned up just in time to get his horn out of its case, do his warm-ups and enquire about the title and key of the first number, just leaving me to count up to four. We were off! It was as if he had been with the band forever.

I chatted with Mike during the intermission and after the show was thrilled beyond belief when he invited me to hang out with him at New Street. Now New Street was the City Centre's main thoroughfare, so I had visions of a jam session, maybe girls or even a milkshake or two. Who could tell? So Mike bought a couple of four-packs from the Warwick Castle bar and we set off, him leading, for I knew not what.

When we got to New Street, I was a little surprised that we found ourselves in the railway station and then settled down on a bench, cracking open the beers. It all became a little clearer when Mike took out a note-book, began to scan what appeared to be a railway time-table and announced that the 12.05 from Crewe appeared to be running late. We sat there, me afraid to talk about music for fear of disturbing his concentration on trains until 2 or 3 in the morning, with Mike meticulously noting details of all the train movements and letting out yelps of pleasure every time a train roared past us in an unidentifiable (to me, at least) blur.

My favourite Blueshounds line-up at the Tower Ballroom in borrowed pink jackets: (l-r) JS, Graham Gallery, John Kiernan, Mike Burney, Duncan Swift, Roy Dutton; (front) Roy Everett.

In time the band outgrew the Warwick Castle and went on the road, now with a remarkable singer named Roy Everett. Actually it was Roy Taylor, but he considered that too ordinary. He shouldn't have worried, his talent was anything but ordinary. His rough, tough, blues-rooted vocals fitted the band's Kansas City Swing and the band, now known as the Blueshounds, was becoming a force to be reckoned with.

I had, almost without realising it, been managing the band, by default as there was no one else to do it. We had an approach from ITB Management whose main client was the eminently successful Ian Campbell Folk Group, whose music was nothing like ours, but whose status we aspired to. The boss of ITB didn't like the band name and offered us a list of alternatives, all of which we declined, but finally he approved our counter-offer of Locomotive, so that's what we became.

2. Locomotive On The Tracks

Ian Campbell, incidentally, produced four sons only one of whom is not, nor ever has been, the lead singer with UB40. His name is David Campbell and he sings folk and protest songs; his brothers are Ali, Robin and Duncan.

The management deal proved totally unsatisfactory, running for two weeks before we decided that their ambitions for the band fell way short of what we were capable of.

But the name stuck. Locomotive.

Locomotive was a hard-working band, once going through June, July and August without a night off. Most Friday nights were a double, maybe an out-of-town gig in Stoke and the 3 am slot at The Flowerpot, just across the street from Digbeth Police Station. How the thin blue line never wised up to the not strictly above board goings-on on their doorstep is anybody's guess.

Musically Locomotive was always a good band, though stylistically, with their swinging jazz and blues repertoire, they were nowhere near in step with the then current popular music. Birmingham music was going through another purple patch, the Brum Beat era. I always contend that Birmingham is the Rock 'n' Roll Capital of the UK and in 1964 the *Midland Beat* paper estimated that there were over 500 rock groups in the city. In that year the Spencer Davis Group, featuring Pete York, a drummer poached from Locomotive, signed for Island Records and the Moody Blues were formed with recruits from four top Birmingham groups. And many more were following in the footsteps of the pioneering Modernaires, with groups as diverse as the Rockin' Berries and the Applejacks breaking through nationally in 1964.

The Flamingo in Redruth, Cornwall, was a venue that had a special relationship with Locomotive and we would always add a date there whenever we played Devon or Cornwall. It was a particularly good place to play, with an always enthusiastic and invariably capacity audience, and, as a motel, accommodation was provided on site – a welcome change from having to search deserted streets in an unfamiliar town for digs.

But I had a personal reason for my special affection for The Flamingo. My maternal great grandfather Samuel Bryant was born in Camborne, near Redruth, and worked with his father as a blacksmith before getting the call to the ministry at a revival meeting when he was 18. He went on to become one of the most distinguished Primitive Methodist circuit ministers, always operating in the West Country or South Wales. One of his last ministries was in Gorseinon, Swansea, before he retired to Camborne where he died in 1923.

In The Flamingo's bar after a show, I was served my beer in a pint glass bearing the name Gorseinon Working Men's Club. To this day, however unlikely

An early line-up of Locomotive: (back) JS, Rick Storey, Monk Finch, Pete Allen; (front) Mike Kellie, Danny King, Chris Woods.

it may be that a Primitive Methodist preacher of that time would go for a pint, I like to believe that the Reverend Samuel nicked this glass from the bar on the eve of his retirement to Cornwall. I explained this to the bartender who told me he had no idea where the glass came from, it had been there longer than he had and I might as well take it as it was no use to him. 52 years on I still have (and use) my favourite glass.

    Many musicians believe that they are on a crusade in the name of good music and we were no exception, often getting unreasonably annoyed in the face of anything we deemed to be musically offensive. Often our vitriol would be aimed at what we considered to be particularly trashy pop music – most particularly with the big sellers which dominated the airwaves. Why, we probably reasoned, would radio waste precious time on musical rubbish when they could be airing the Count Basie Orchestra, Jimmy Rushing, Louis Armstrong, Billie Holiday, or even us?

    On one occasion I overstepped the mark just a little on a bus taking us from Ostend to Knokke in Belgium where we were set to appear on a television show.

2. Locomotive On The Tracks

The object of my ire was Marty Wilde, appearing on the same show and guilty in my mind of perpetrating an utterly crass single in *Abergavenny* which was charting all over the place. My mutterings of discontent probably began on the short flight from Southend and might just have been fuelled by a restorative beverage or two. The other band members urged me to go and speak to Marty if I felt that strongly about it. I could, they said, share my thoughts with Marty and we could discuss the matter like grown men. I must have found the suggestion irresistible as soon I was rolling around on the bus floor with Marty, each of us trying half-heartedly to find the space to throw a punch. Looking back, it's pretty clear that neither of us was much good at scrapping or had much intent to hurt the other. I remember that we were both quite polite to each other for the rest of the weekend.

As a postscript, *Abergavenny* was the last of Marty Wilde's string of big hits, so I can still kid myself that I had something to do with bringing the public round to my way of thinking.

There were a lot of great UK venues during the 1960s, but for me the most exciting was Jeff Kruger's Flamingo Club downstairs from the Whiskey-A-Go-Go on Wardour Street. Our first time at the Flamingo was in support of Georgie Fame and the Blue Flames in the mid 1960s when they were at their peak and as cool an outfit as could be found anywhere. Every Friday and Saturday the Flamingo sessions were split in two, the first finishing at 11.00, the second starting at midnight. Both the feature band and the support would play two sets in each session, making for a pretty long night, but it was never a chore. We delivered some of our best performances there supporting Fame, Zoot Money's Big Roll Band, Chris Farlowe and the Thunderbirds or The Animals with Alan Price, but the hottest band at The Flamingo was the American Herbie Goins & the Nightimers – red hot, always an inspiration!

We played The Flamingo pretty regularly every five or six weeks. It was a natural fit for our seven-piece and we were moved up to feature band. However, not every band member has warm memories of the club. Singer Norman Haines, in search of something to relax him on the road back to Birmingham, made a clandestine purchase in the adjoining alley at around 4 in the morning, boarding the van triumphantly brandishing his purchase, wrapped in silver foil. It had cost him most of his gig money and his extreme disappointment was thoroughly understandable when he opened the packet to find…a small stone!

Locomotive built and maintained an enviable reputation for producing excellent musicians who went on to make their name in the business. I was again happy to be the least talented member of the ensemble. There was a downside to this policy. If you want to hold on to your musicians, then book mediocre talents; if you book the best, there is always a realistic prospect that they will be headhunted, not necessarily by a better band, but by one that has already found success.

Baritone saxophone player Brian 'Monk' Finch was a lovable oddball, lovable, that is, to those who knew him well, but probably exasperating to those who knew him *really* well. To those who knew him less well, he was simply puzzling! He had a wild sense of humour and a ferocious anger that would dissolve into an embarrassed grin as quickly as it had erupted.

The only person I knew who could handle him properly certainly wasn't me – I was just the bandleader – but his wife. Her technique was to respond to him in his own wild manner. I would often go to Sunday lunch at their Kings Heath flat. She was an excellent cook and local musicians would often angle for an invitation. After I had been unable to prise Monk away from the pub at a reasonable time for several Sundays running, we returned – late again! – to a memorable homecoming. Monk's wife had served his and my food on plates to which she had attached those old-fashioned wire devices which folk used to display posh plates on the wall. Sure enough, she had put our lunches on display on the wall! The potatoes, meat and Brussels sprouts sliding gently down the wall in a river of gravy might have been viewed as modern art, but Monk studiously retrieved most of the unappetising mess, served me and proceeded to scoff his with apparent relish. I was unable to do the same, but would have paid good money to listen in on the conversation that must have taken place after I left.

As a kindergarten band Locomotive produced a fine line of drummers. I love the story Mike Kellie told me about a U.S. tour of British rock musicians. He was a fine drummer who after Locomotive went on to play with the VIPs (later Art), then Spooky Tooth. A Brummie, he became a leading session drummer who worked a lot with Steve Winwood. He was in a New York hotel room sharing a bottle of something with fellow-drummers John Bonham and Carl Palmer when they realised that they had all been drummers with Locomotive. If only Pete York and Bob Lamb had been there, it would have been the full set.

Tenor saxist Chris Woods joined Steve Winwood and Traffic, guitarist Dave Pegg went to the Ian Campbell Folk Group and then Jethro Tull and Fairport Convention, trombonist Duncan Swift joined the Kenny Ball Band on piano and tenor man Mike Burney had a contrasting career with the Syd Lawrence Band and Roy Wood's Wizzard.

The vocals were handled at first by Roy Everett, one of the UK's finest blues voices who retired early to concentrate on his greengrocery business. He was followed by Danny King, an extraordinary singer possessed, in my opinion, of the most pure English pop voice of all – think Jackie Wilson! Danny had everything,

Locomotive circa 1966 at Birmingham Town Hall: (l-r) JS, Monk Finch, John Barry, Pete Hodges, Pete Allen; Rick Storey and Mike Kellie (both hidden).

except for the desire or the need to take his career further. Dave Mason did a short stint with the band, then came Londoner Pete Hodges.

    The next singer to join the band, doubling on Hammond organ, influenced the band in a significant change of style. Norman Haines held down a day job behind the counter at a small independent record store on Smethwick High Street. With the band's star players now scattered far and wide, anchorman and baritone saxophone player Monk Finch having gone so far as emigrating to Australia, I began to feel that the band's trademark swing and blues were not being delivered with the earlier conviction. For reasons of economy the horn section was reduced to trumpet and tenor sax and the guitar was dropped, leaving Locomotive as a five-piece.

    Norman's vocals came from the school of Georgie Fame and Alan Price. The Smethwick record store clientele was pretty much exclusively West Indian – and so was the music. Their speciality was importing 45s and singles from the Islands which meant that we, particularly Norman, became familiar with the sounds of Jackie Mittoo, Young Growler and Desmond Dekker.

Locomotive of 1967 plumbed new depths of bad sartorial taste with (top to bottom) Norman Haines, JS, Joe Ellis, Billy Madge and [R] Mooney Mazzone.

2. Locomotive On The Tracks

With Norman Haines in the band, we prepared to go back into the recording studio, after the fiasco of a first attempt some years previously. At that time Polydor Records had come calling with the offer of a recording audition. Generally speaking, in those days a recording deal was a rare thing and not something we seriously contemplated. To this day I am appalled by the rank amateurishness of our approach. I borrowed the band bus from the Concordes – in a previous life it had been an ambulance – and arranged for the band to meet at 9.00 am at Zella Studios where we had previously recorded our demo. Half of the band arrived on time, others drifted in over the next hour or so, but come 11.00 am bass player Graham Gallery had still not shown up.

Tempers were fraying by the minute and things were getting fractious with Monk Finch demanding we leave without Graham. I was trying to work out how we could do the recording without the bass when Graham rolled up, all smiles and oozing his usual charm while explaining to his fellow-band members that, had he been on time, we couldn't have departed for London anyway as the pubs didn't open until 12 o'clock and nobody could reasonably expect us to drive all that way without a crate of beer on board. He refused to depart without the beer, Monk was screaming at Gallery and Mike Burney, who had been on time, was increasingly feeling that actually a glass or two of beer might settle his nerves. Meanwhile I was spitting blood while reminding myself that, if I said what I was thinking, I might be left with only half a band to fulfil a busy datesheet.

We set off hopelessly late, encountered heavy traffic – to be expected in those pre-M1 days – and arrived shame-faced at the Polydor studio to be turned away by two grim-faced security men. Somehow we found ourselves, beer stocks replenished, careering round Hyde Park Corner in our ambulance with Mike Burney playing the A/B emergency call on his tenor and Graham Gallery pissing out of the vehicle's sliding door.

This was not quite the last show that Graham Gallery played with the band. He was actually a stunningly good player, later in demand by such big names as Tom Jones and Engelbert Humperdinck, but his career was curtailed by his alcoholism. He had his moments in the sun. Once he proudly showed me a splendid photograph of him looking sharp as a tack, leaning proprietorially on a gleaming pink Rolls Royce which he claimed he had bought for cash received as royalties. He then hit on me for £40 in order to properly slake his thirst. Graham was a tremendous bass player, and a really intelligent, companionable and thoroughly likeable human being. Like too many others his weakness for drink brought about his premature end.

For this next foray into the world of recording I was determined that we would be rather more ordered. Tony Hall, a pioneer and popular DJ on Radio

Luxembourg and formerly the producer of such top jazz musicians as Ronnie Scott and Tubby Hayes on the short-lived Tempo label, had just set up his independent promotion and production company, imaginatively titled Tony Hall Enterprises. THE, which numbered Dusty Springfield, Jimi Hendrix and Joe Cocker among its clients, was supported by leading publishing house Essex Music. Essex, headed by the man who was to become my favourite music industry mogul, David Platz, at that time had publishing for Elton John, The Rolling Stones and other significant acts. Tony would headhunt a promising band or singer, sign them to THE for recording and to Essex for publishing. Essex would pay recording costs and supply a producer, then Tony and David would seek a release deal, at which point Tony's expertise as a song plugger would swing into action to help chart the release.

Tony Hall first heard Locomotive at the Flamingo Club. He liked the band and wanted to work with us, but he didn't like the rock steady and ska material we had added since Norman joined the band. But he did like our soul ballad, *A Broken Heart*. We signed the band to THE and Essex Music and Tony got to work on his recording company contacts. The major CBS Records, now Sony, had just launched their new CBS Direction label with the Chambers Brothers hit, *The Time Has Come Today*, and they were wide open to new talent.

Time was booked at the CBS studios in Theobalds Road and their producer Johnny Hawkins was assigned to the project. We were to cut two titles: *A Broken Heart* and a B-side for which I nominated the band's take on Dandy Livingstone's Jamaican hit, *Rudy, a Message to You*.

Learning from my earlier mistake, I got the band down to London the previous evening which left us with time to kill the next morning as we weren't due in the studio until 2.00 pm. Wandering round the musical instrument stores on Charing Cross Road, I found a valve trombone which would have been quite a rarity in Birmingham. Pitched in B flat, just like a trumpet, with identical fingering, it seemed made for me, so I had little choice other than to make the purchase. However, despite the similarities, it was quite a different beast to play, requiring a different embouchure and the production of a lot more air in order to fill the horn. But it handled nicely and satisfied a common need of most musicians – the acquiring of new instruments!

As we trooped into the studio, Johnny Hawkins' eye fell on the bulky case in my hand. 'What's that?', he demanded, although I suspect he already knew the answer. I explained and his enthusiastic response was to say we would use it on the B-side. I immediately protested that in no way could the valve trombone be dragooned into active service in my hands. For Heaven's sake, we'd only just met!

2. Locomotive On The Tracks

Of course Johnny's will prevailed, though unsurprisingly we had to simplify the original trombone part more than somewhat. I think we probably got away with it, as ten years later The Specials had a hit with exactly the same Dandy Livingstone song – complete with trombone figure!

A Broken Heart gained a bunch of radio plays which helped the band's profile, but didn't fare too well when it came to sales which is probably why CBS Direction didn't take up their option and set Locomotive free.

In the meantime at a rehearsal for a hometown gig in the notorious Cedar Club, we were going through possible material for the next potential single when Norman said to me that he had written a neat new song that would be appropriate for a B-side. This turned out to be *Rudi's in Love*. We ran it through and it struck me straightaway that it might just be the hit song we had been looking for.

Tony Hall in the meantime had hooked up the band with EMI Parlophone, a significant label to be associated with. So we shared our news, his that he had a deal, mine that we had a hit song. On the subsequent wave of euphoria I don't think that Tony or David Platz had the time or the inclination to consider the ramifications of introducing the rock steady repertoire, but it's certainly something that I discussed long and hard with myself. What would be the effect of a white band from Brum sounding authentically Caribbean, particularly with Norman's spot-on version of a true Rude Boy, on all those Locomotive fans who over the years had been fed a diet of Kansas City swing and blues with plenty of jazz solos?

But the chance of maybe, just maybe, getting ourselves a hit record swung it for me – a hit is a hit, after all.

The demonstration disc, recorded at Birmingham's Zella Studios was a good one, with a nice feel, but spikier and more West Indies than the smoother and silkier version that Gus Dudgeon produced with such care in Abbey Road Studio One; his version just screamed out 'Radio 1!' from the very first play.

When EMI released *Rudi's in Love* in the UK, it charted for eight weeks, reaching a high of Number 25 – not quite the heights we had hoped for, but enough to justify release across Europe, with similar chart success. There was an instant boost to bookings and touring enquiries, with a significant increase in fees.

However, any thought that it would be plain sailing proved optimistic in the extreme. There was a significant audience for West Indian music out there. Many promoters, club owners and audiences, impressed by the frequent radio play of the single, assumed, not unnaturally, that the band that recorded this warm, friendly dance record was made up of West Indians. Many were visibly – some audibly – disappointed when they saw the band with no Caribbean presence at all; nor was the repertoire wall-to-wall ska and rock steady. The British black audience were discerning – no doubt about that – and they were accustomed to the performances of Desmond Dekker, all non-stop action and feel-good music.

Frankly, in comparison, Locomotive's live performances were drab. Anticipating the as-yet-undefined next chapter in the band's repertoire, the heavier, moodier Norman Haines compositions were put into the show and Locomotive became unrecognisable as the band that had thrived on the road for all those years. No attempt was made to put on a show, nor even to appear on stage dressed in other than street clothes.

I still question why I allowed a good band to drift into shabby oblivion and it is hard to pinpoint the precise moment when it all started to go bad. I know now – and in my heart I probably knew then – that I should have resisted the musicians' pressures to cut down to a five-piece from the original seven. Their 'claim' that they needed the extra cash that a reduced line-up would bring should have been countered by an insistence on smartening up the band's appearance, attitude and performance and ensuring that the band's repertoire was decided by what the audience would like to listen and dance to, not what the musicians wanted to play for their own satisfaction. Realistically the changes could only have been made by cancelling a sizeable, though visibly dwindling, date sheet, releasing two or three fine musicians and building back to the seven-piece with a charismatic singer and a band that rocked.

And that, I'm sorry to say, would not have been possible without the commitment and support of Tony Hall, EMI and the rest.

As it was, Tony remained convinced of the creative genius of Norman Haines and happily went along with everything he suggested. I felt committed to the rhythm team of bassist Mick Hincks and drummer Bob Lamb who throughout the descent into chaos remained steadfast and played impeccably.

At about this time I increasingly began to feel that holding down a day job, flexible as it was, and remaining the only non-full-timer in the band, Norman having left the record shop, was becoming just a bit too much. I also missed the sense of fun enjoyed in the earlier line-ups and the belief that we were on a crusade, proud of the level of musicianship and entertainment that we delivered. At the age of 30 I wasn't jaded, but I wanted more from my music and trying with little success to make a five-piece sound like seven wasn't how I wanted to spend my time.

So I stopped playing with Locomotive, retained management of the band, quit my job at the (by now) University of Aston and got out more, to see what musical talent there was out there.

The first thing to take care of was the follow-up to the success of *Rudi's in Love*. The second single is always considered critical, it's where groups consolidate their fan base – or lose it. As it happened, we did the latter. Spectacularly.

2. Locomotive On The Tracks

Norman Haines had written what would have been termed, back then, 'a progressive rock ballad', a style epitomised by Procul Harum's *A Whiter Shade of Pale*. Unfortunately *Mr. Armageddon* hadn't the same depth or weight. Tony Hall backed Norman's enthusiasm for the song as the follow-up single and I found myself outvoted. I figured that our new-found audience would find it a leap too far from the robust rock steady/ska of *Rudi* to the angst-ridden doom of *Mr. Armageddon*, fashionable as it might have been at the time. Sadly my fears proved well founded. *Mr. Armageddon*, despite an initial burst of radio plays, probably a testament to the song-plugging ability of Tony Hall, disappeared without trace.

Prior to the ill-fated *Armageddon* decision I had cheerfully proceeded with what I thought would be a good follow-up to our one hit. With Christmas on the horizon, and wishing to continue following the career of lovable rogue Rudi, I had returned to Zella Recording Studios in Birmingham and recorded *Rudi the Red-Nosed Reindeer* coupled with a hokum ska version of *White Christmas*. The latter featured the first, and probably only, vocal by Bob Lamb who later produced UB40 and graced the rhythm section of the fine Steve Gibbons Band. In recent years Bob has resided in Thailand where, we are led to believe, he enjoys a most convivial life-style.

So what was I to do with a finished master-tape? The logical way forward was to form a record company and release the single. I floated the idea to David Betteridge, the head of a leading independent record label, Island Records. He liked the record and offered me a straightforward distribution deal. I gave his offer my serious consideration for probably five seconds – and we were in business!

The first thing we needed was a name for the label. I had learned from several sources that the broadcaster John Peel had a party piece where he adopted a bear-like shamble which he fatuously claimed was an approximation of my gait and referred to me as the Big Bear from Birmingham. Actually I had always had a soft spot for bears and in fact counted among my closer male friends a Himalayan Sun Bear who lived in Dudley Zoo and was known to me as Gene Sedric.

It was a done deal; Big Bear Records it was. For the time being *Rudi the Red-Nosed Reindeer* was its only release, but Big Bear was launched on its career of 50 years and counting. With Christmas 1968 looming, I quickly needed a logo, so I turned to John Creasey and Associates, a classy design company in Birmingham, and paid £25 for a design. That bear looked somewhat familiar, I thought, but maybe that was a good thing.

So, in October 1968, Big Bear Records' first release, *Rudi the Red-Nosed Reindeer*, billed as by Steam Shovel, saw the light of day. It carried the number TR 635 of Trojan Records, a subsidiary of Island, as there had been no time to create and integrate a new numbering system into the Island Records catalogue.

The single was rushed out in time for Christmas and enjoyed a few radio plays, though we lacked the high-powered plugging of a Tony Hall. Nevertheless we sold a respectable 4,500 units in the UK and subsequent annual Yuletide re-releases grossed over 18,000, a good return on the small initial investment.

However, the most striking response came from a London-based lawyer representing no less than the Walt Disney Corporation. They were concerned that our bear bore more than a passing resemblance to their Baloo the Bear which, with hindsight, I can see was a perfectly reasonable observation. So I went back to John Creasey clutching Walt's missive, only to be told that, yes, they had based their creation on Baloo, but they had added extra hairs to avoid any infringement of copyright, and so I was not to worry. But, with Walt's demand that I should 'cease and desist' ringing in my ears, that is exactly what I did. The replacement logo – the work of a different designer – has served Big Bear Music well for 50 years with no hint of intervention by film studios or movie moguls.

Meanwhile, back with Locomotive, with all of us smarting at the sudden disappearance of our original fan base, something approaching panic had set in, not least with Tony Hall. He was determined to try to reinstate his hitmakers and bulldozed through a decision to record and release an out-and-out cheesy pop track, *Never Gonna Let You Go*, which, of course, totally missed the mark with our ska-hungry audience. The ongoing Locomotive album was completed in a desultory fashion, with nobody fully subscribing to it. *We Are Everything You See* was released in 1970 to mixed reviews. The band was by then more or less split down the middle, with Norman Haines, Bill Madge and Mick Taylor bent on developing their doom/gloom/rock repertoire and the rhythm team of Mick Hincks and Bob Lamb favouring a return to more robust material.

The inevitable split came when Norman left the band to form the prophetically named Sacrifice which lasted long enough to produce one single, *Daffodil*, but fell foul of Parlophone on the matter of the band's name. Parlophone took exception to Sacrifice as a name and released the single as by the Norman Haynes (*sic*) Band. By the time the Tony Hall-produced album, *Den of Iniquity*, was issued, it was officially the Norman Haines Band. Though its dark progressive sound has met with interest on a more recent re-release, initial sales were not good and in 1972 the Norman Haines Band disbanded. After one more solo single, so far as I know, his recording career came to an end and he returned to work as a BT engineer, alongside running his Norman Haines Bluskool.

Locomotive, with new recruits Keith Millar and John Caswell, effectively the line-up that soon became The Dog That Bit People (band names were changed with confusing frequency in those days), inherited the EMI recording contract, quickly producing the excellent, but ill-fated single, *Roll Over Mary*. This initially garnered enthusiastic reviews from the then influential music weeklies *Melody Maker*, *New Musical Express*, *Sounds*, *Record Mirror* and *Disc*. Unfortunately a writer for a national daily wrote a damning piece based on a total misunderstanding of the lyrics which she said made improper suggestions regarding the behaviour of Mary Magdalene. Suddenly the single was pulled by every radio playlist, no doubt leaving the journalist delighted that her piece had such a far-reaching effect and believing the good old principle that one should never let the truth get in the way of a good story.

Now gigging with a settled line-up, the band was going down well enough with audiences, but doing little more than going through the motions delivering a repertoire that did not fit well with their abilities. The audience for the band had never fully recovered from the confusion caused by the overnight shift of style.

It was clear that the band was not delivering the level of music that they were capable of and so I felt obliged to step back and make the difficult decision to put the band out of its misery and call it a day on The Locomotive.

The band had, in one form or another, been at the centre of my musical activity for some eight years, most of my adult life. The sense of missed opportunities was overwhelming. I still regret that I never recorded The Locomotive in its pomp, with Roy Everett or Danny King, Chris Wood or Mike Burney, John Bonham or Mike Kellie.

Borrowing the name from a short story by American writer James Thurber, we re-christened the band The Dog That Bit People and tailored the repertoire to the musicians' abilities in songwriting and performing. The result was a remarkable set of new songs rooted in country rock. EMI agreed to keep the band on their Parlophone imprint and invited me to produce the album in the near-legendary Studio Two in Abbey Road. Although I had produced a bunch of stuff in local studios, always financed by myself, this was my first time in a First Division studio with responsibility to others to deliver the goods. The presence of George Harrison in the control room for most of the first day could have been diverting, but, looking back, we were so involved with getting the music exactly right that I did little more that give him a hello and say as he left that I hoped he'd enjoyed our music. I don't recall his response, if there was one.

The media reviews were enthusiastic, one of them, by Jerry Gilbert in *Sounds*, so complimentary that it led to a lengthy personal friendship, but that was the end of the Dog's recording career, except for a single the same year, coupling *Goodbye Country* with *Lovely Lady*. Perhaps I had too many distractions as a manager to devote the time to them that the band deserved.

Chapter 3

ON A MISSION FROM DOG

With more time on my hands, I was able to get out and listen to bands and very soon I got lucky with a young, extremely musical blues band from Lichfield. It was a time when there were more blues bands around than you could shake a stick at and most of them played the same repertoire, even dressed the same.

Bakerloo Blues Line, later shortened to Bakerloo, were nothing like that, but I wasn't prepared to spend the rest of my life explaining that to cynical venue owners. I figured that, if we created a showcase for them to demonstrate and attract an audience, we would have an edge to build on. The Crown Hotel in Station Street had seen better days, but this was the blues and a battered, down-home feel might well be just what we needed. The gig room had a capacity of 180 with a good high stage, large adjacent bar and – luxury of luxuries – a good-sized, private and lockable dressing room. On top of all that there was a separate lounge, if that doesn't give too smart an impression, where I decided to show films from 7.30 until the support band went on at 8.30 when we reverted to silent movies featuring the likes of Buster Keaton.

So I booked every Tuesday night at a rental of £5 which the landlord Tom Pickering agreed to waive if the bartake reached a certain level. Admission was four shillings and sixpence (22½ pence), with an annual subscription of a shilling (5 pence). I decided to name the club after a particularly glamorous Afghan hound who lived next door to me, so Henry's Blueshouse it was, with the strapline, 'Tuesdays is Bluesdays'.

Not for the last time in my life I would wake in a panic, imagining just the band, me and an empty room on opening night. So, again as so often in the years to come, I over-promoted. Leaflets appeared in a rash all over the city; I probably leafletted the audiences exiting all the concerts in Birmingham for five or six weeks beforehand; I got onto the radio talking about the blues and playing recordings; there were posters in every record store and university common room; newspapers and monthlies featured the new venture – so one way or another I seriously over-did things!

3. On A Mission From Dog

On the night I really got my comeuppance. Tom agreed that I could admit 200 people, but that left at least the same amount outside, complaining. I walked the queue, apologising to all and asking them to please try again next week.

In retrospect we had enjoyed the best possible promotion for the venue. The word spread and we must have gone four or five weeks before we had less than a sell-out night. Most importantly, Bakerloo Blues Line rocked their socks off. If only we had had albums to sell, their future would have been so much different.

Back in those days, despite the number of gigs played by any good band, nobody sold records on gigs. Records were bought in record shops which were plentiful. That was all part of a totally different music scene where everything was more formal and specialised. It would never have crossed the mind of a working band that they could make and market a record on their own. That was the sphere of big companies who had studios, skilled producers and marketing and distribution departments, and bands and their managers pursued the Holy Grail of 'getting a record deal'. The idea of trying to record a hit record, using your bedroom as a studio or even your small neighbourhood recording studio, would have seemed ludicrous – almost sacrilegious. Oddly, as it transpired, in the case of Bakerloo, it was delays by one of the major record companies that led directly to this tremendous band's premature demise. But that was yet to come.

Melody Maker referred to Henry's Blueshouse as the first and best progressive music club outside of London. Nice to think that folk considered the blues to be progressive – and Henry's Blueshouse was certainly to justify the B-word in its title.

Bakerloo held down the headline spot for the first four weeks, which was the plan, then took off to play other towns, to return triumphant to their roots every six weeks or so. Amazingly the plan worked and for a while Bakerloo's return was always met with a sell-out audience.

One very special booking was veteran Mississippi bluesman Arthur Big Boy Crudup who wrote the early Elvis Presley hit *That's Alright*, one of a long list of fine blues songs by Crudup. Unsurprisingly this was another sell-out, but for the first time I witnessed the dedication of the real blues lovers, with people travelling from as far away as Manchester and Bristol. Crudup was the first of many bluesmen to play Henry's, including former John Lee Hooker sideman Eddie 'Guitar' Burns; the King of Louisiana Swamp Blues and former star of Excello Records Lightnin' Slim; the itinerant Texas guitar man Curtis Jones who actually lived on the road in as much as he didn't have a place to call home; guitarist J.B. Hutto from South Carolina; the one-man blues band from Tunica, Mississippi, Doctor Ross; the phenomenal acoustic guitar player Larry Johnson from Atlanta,

Champion Jack Dupree, a regular at Henry's Blueshouse.

3. On A Mission From Dog

Georgia; Moses 'Whispering' Smith, harmonica giant from Jackson County, Mississippi, and Henry's regular Champion Jack Dupree.

Much later Henry's was to be the venue for the opening performance of the very first of Big Bear's tours of American bluesmen. The King Biscuit Boy, a formidable harmonica player and singer from Toronto, Canada, played his first – and last – European shows at the club. At the time, for reasons that will later become clear, I was planning to locate and contact American bluesmen who I felt were neglected back home in the States. They deserved the opportunity to come over to Europe and play for a whole new audience to whom they were legends who had somehow got lost in the mists of time. The planning was already advanced for the first tour set for Autumn 1972 when I had a call from Paramount Records executive Ralph Mace, well known in classical music circles, but rather out of his depth with the Blues. His New York office had scheduled a European album release by Richard Newell, who had been given the nickname of the King Biscuit Boy by singer/bandleader Ronnie Hawkins, and they had guaranteed the artist a European tour to promote the release. Ralph had been charged with making that happen. The always active British blues mafia had got wind of my tour plans and someone – I'm told it was that great fountain of blues knowledge Mike Leadbitter – urged Ralph to contact me. This was very much in Mike's personal interest, of course – he just wanted to have a lot more blues around than there was at the time in this country.

Ralph called and agreed to fly Richard in, supply leaflets and promo albums, while I was to pay Richard a weekly salary, employ backing musicians, fix transport and sell the show to venues throughout the UK and Europe. As manager of Locomotive I had appropriate experience and contacts, but had never before had the obligation to fill almost every night with a show. Any night off incurred hotel and living expenses without income, so unsurprisingly I went into my usual panic mode and over-sold the tour.

The result was 45 performances in 42 days in four countries, including three radio and two television appearances which pretty much set the standard for Big Bear's upcoming blues tours. I rented the electric piano from Jeff Lynne and hired Birmingham musicians because they didn't make a fuss, just got on with the job and played impeccably. The musicians were mostly members of the Idle Race, a legendary local combo, and the band was billed as such.

The tour was a success and there's still a piece on YouTube from a television show in Hamburg. Richard Newell, an affable and intelligent man, was blues dynamite and did all that was asked of him. It was a gruelling tour for everyone, but I felt it was harder on Richard than the rest of us. His family was wealthy, his father owned a chain of fish and chip shops across Canada, and I don't think he had ever had to work this hard before. He arrived looking slightly chubby, but went home weeks later looking lean and mean and much more rock'n'roll. Sadly, Richard's later career suffered from his alcohol abuse and he died in 2003, aged only 58.

Henry's Blueshouse continued successfully despite my involvement in the King Biscuit Boy tour. Among the bands that played the small upstairs room over a pub were Status Quo, Rory Gallagher and Taste, Thin Lizzy, Jethro Tull, UFO, Judas Priest, Supertramp, Chickenshack, The Groundhogs and Ten Years After.

The much-missed one-man blues band from Lichfield, Duster Bennett, was a regular and always a good draw. On his early appearances, before he could drive, his mother would chauffeur him to Henry's in her Morris Minor Traveller. I became a close friend of Duster; we would spend a lot of down-time together talking about the blues and playing records. After Henry's closed, he seemed to distance himself, though I never knew why. I would book him whenever I could, but we were never to be close again.

The much-missed Tony "Duster" Bennett, a Henry's Blueshouse favourite and Britain's finest one-man blues band.

3. On A Mission From Dog

The last time we met was at one of my Birmingham Town Hall promotions, this one featuring the legendary Memphis Slim, supported by Duster. He and I talked only when necessary; otherwise he kept his distance. He died that night when his Transit van crashed on the way home to Lichfield. I still miss him and often ponder what I did to alienate him.

I've read a lot about Led Zeppelin playing at Henry's, but in fact they never did. Robert Plant, whom I had known for ages, and John Bonham, who had played in Locomotive, were friends of mine and would often show up for a drink and to listen to the music. On several occasions they would sit in with the band or take part in jam sessions. I can only guess that is where the Zeppelin myth came from.

Ex-Bonzo Dog Roger Ruskin Spear was another pal and I enjoyed every time I was able to present his wacky Kinetic Wardrobe, though I don't pretend that I understood everything he was doing any more than the audience did. It was always a risk when it came to attracting an audience, but I never regretted booking that riveting, but not always comprehensible, manic genius.

Naturally Big Bear's own bands made their contribution to the life of Henry's Blueshouse. It's probably fair to say that Moseley was Birmingham's hippie suburb. There was certainly a whiff of cannabis in the air and it was home to writers, poets, painters, designers – and musicians. Looking back, I would nominate as the archetypal Moseley band the quirkily-named Tea & Symphony. Quirky is probably the most appropriate adjective to use about the band itself, winning by a short head from weird, bizarre, outrageous, anarchic and certifiably insane! I suppose I would have to say their music was rooted in folk, although the blues were in there somewhere. They were not the most technically gifted of musicians, but nobody could deny that they were highly original and totally individualistic and that they wrote and performed songs that entertained and gave flight to thought.

I can't say that they were ever a major attraction, but they built up their own band of devotees throughout the country, sold a decent number of albums and, at one time, seriously threatened the pop charts. Again through David Platz at Essex Music I signed Tea & Symphony to EMI's underground label Harvest Records. Gus Dudgeon handled production duties and the album, the appropriately-titled *An Asylum for the Musically Insane*, was unleashed on a wholly unsuspecting public. Unsurprisingly, the reviews might be referred to as mixed, but one thing for certain was that none of the reviewers were ambivalent; no one sat on the fence.

A similar split in reaction greeted the second album *Jo Sago* which must have been one of the very first concept albums. It told the story of a black man living on

Tea & Symphony: a floating personnel, the nucleus of the band (Nigel Phillips, Jef Daw and James Langston) all wearing hats.

Moseley's Ladypool Road. This remarkable recording, again produced by Gus Dudgeon, was of limited sales potential, but that's never a reason for not recording good music.

What might have happened, but didn't – Tea & Symphony getting in the Top 20 charts – would have been the musical equivalent of Halesowen Town Football Club winning the FA Cup. The band broke their golden rule and recorded as a single someone else's song, Procul Harum's *Boredom.* Produced by the usually successful Gus Dudgeon and with Tony Hall working his radio promoting magic the single reached the rarefied heights of the BBC Radio One Chart, received significant airplay, but failed to sell in numbers.

I still get a good feeling when I think of the legacy left by James Langston, Jef Daw and Nigel Phillips; this was much more than music to smoke dope to. The band was always a pleasure to be with, but inevitably a nightmare to do business with. Typically, one Friday they were booked to play an important show at Bristol University – important, because gigs on the campus circuit were plentiful, decently paid, with seriously interested audiences. So a phone call from the social

3. On A Mission From Dog

secretary asking why the band hadn't made the 4pm soundcheck started alarm bells ringing. No mobile phones in those days, so I called Jef Daw's home number to find out what time the band had left, and to my consternation Jef answered the phone with a 'Hiya Baby, how you doin'?' This was around 5pm, the performance was due to start at 8pm with the audience allowed in at 7pm.

That was in Bristol.

They were in Birmingham.

He was clearly as high as a kite. His response to my somewhat agitated queries about what the hell he was doing still in Moseley was a serene, 'Cool it, Man, relax, take it easy.' In hindsight, that was probably the first sign of a rift in our relationship.

Jef died at an impossibly early age on a French beach taking a glass of red wine after a relaxing swim, pianist Nigel Phillips has been playing piano and teaching in Birmingham seemingly forever and singer James Langston, who was my buddy in the band, is currently living in Cornwall, sadly not in the best of health.

Locomotive drummer Bob Lamb, Jef Daw of Tea & Symphony and Locomotive bass player Mick Hincks on the set of Süddeutscher Rundfunk television in Stuttgart.

Tea & Symphony also played another role at Henry's, that of backing band for visiting bluesmen, under the name of The Shuffling Hungarians. I must own up that the name was my suggestion and that I borrowed it from that doyen of New Orleans piano professors Henry Roeland Byrd, also known as Roy Byrd or Ever Loving Henry, but most often as Professor Longhair, which shortens to Fess. I figured that he had so many names that he wouldn't miss just one.

Brewers Droop hailed from High Wycombe, were fronted by the ebullient Ron Watts and featured fine musicians in guitarist John McKay and accordionist and pianist Steve Darrington. I got to know Ron through his weekly blues promotions at London's 100 Club – which I always considered to be the finest blues venue in the UK. Ron would book every blues attraction that I offered him, the audiences were knowledgeable and large in number, and most importantly, it was where the Blues Mafia would hang out. On blues nights you could bet on Mike Leadbitter propping up the bar, deep in conversation with Mike Rowe and Simon Napier of *Blues Unlimited* magazine, Cilla Huggins of *Juke Blues* and the rest of the crowd. Many a quest to locate obscure American bluesmen started off at the 100 Club and I could always depend on generous blues media coverage for any of the Big Bear blues activities.

One time an unusually animated Ron Watts called to tell me about a band that he had featured at the 100 the previous evening. They were going to be the next big thing, he said, they were sensational and they already had a healthy fan following who spat at the band. And the band spat back at the audience. And then the band threw chairs at the audience. All apparently, in the name of entertainment. The band only knew enough songs to play one 25 minute set, but trust him, said Ron, they were great, and looking for a manager.

I told him that he hadn't quite sold the concept of the band to me, but with my curiosity aroused by his conviction and insistence I agreed to come and see the band. Unsurprisingly, they were The Sex Pistols and equally unsurprisingly they really were entertaining and did rock on in a musically inept manner, but no way would I consider them for Big Bear, they couldn't even play properly! I imagined what a nightmare it would be trying to prise an acceptable performance out of them in the recording studio, and gave Ron an unequivocal no. Of course, it never occurred to me to use studio session musicians backing the band's vocals, as EMI did ultimately. Looking back, I reckon that I might just have got off lightly.

Ron's band, Brewers Droop, did seem to have borrowed some of the Pistols' anarchic tendencies. Besides the band's name which might possibly be considered not to be in the very best of taste, there was also the introduction of the polystyrene, four-foot-long phallus which some people did find mildly disconcerting.

3. On A Mission From Dog

It has to be said that, as far as the less easily offended were concerned, Brewers Droop played extremely well, delivered some fine performances and, in the words of our press release at the time, 'Brewers Droop always have a ball. Take care. Next time it might be yours.'

The music was a neat balance between Cajun, with Steve Darrington's accordion to the fore, and rocking rhythm and blues, with John McKay's spiky guitar the feature. With Ron, Steve and John individually taking care of the vocals and the hefty rhythm team of bassist Malcolm Barrett and drummer Bob Walker kicking the whole thing along, the band built up a good date-sheet, toured Holland and Belgium and landed a record deal with a major label, RCA Records.

The album was produced by Tom McGuinness of McGuinness Flint and was entitled, appropriately, *Opening Time*. Tom did a grand production job and smoothed off many of the rough edges, though a couple of moments of anarchy slipped through, notably in the songs *I Can See Your Public Bar* and *If You See Kay Tonight*.

There followed a charming (if that's a word I'm allowed to use when referring to The Droop) accordion-based Zydeco single, *Louise*. A special moment, after a long drive on a roastingly hot day, was arriving in a small Belgian village where they were playing *Louise* repeatedly through speakers strung on lamp-posts.

In those straitened times, when the band played the Midlands and the North, my then wife, the ever-hospitable Kate, would place five mattresses in the living room and they would sleep head to foot across the entire room. The toughest part was waking them, but I found a way. I would sneak in, turn up the level through my big Tannoy speakers and give them Harold Betters' Sue Records single, *You Can't Sit Down*. Ron Watts blamed me for what he said was a lifetime of hatred for trombones.

The band, by this time featuring the precocious talents of Mark Knopfler, later recorded a second album, again appropriately named, this time *The Booze Brothers*, for Red Lightnin' Records. Despite the presence of Knopfler and – on one track – Dave Edmunds who also produced, the album, recorded in 1973, didn't see the light of day until 1989.

Mark's spell with Brewers Droop ended after a few months when an incident at the Nag's Head in High Wycombe, the band's regular haunt, prompted him to leave. When the sound man jumped on stage and manhandled Steve Darrington, the piano player, onto the floor, that was enough for Mark.

They were a handful to manage, but life with Brewers Droop could never have been called dull. Perhaps a letter I wrote at the time to RCA Records will give a flavour of what it was like.

Don't Worry 'Bout The Bear

Andy Hoy
RCA Records
50 Curzon Street
London
W1Y 8EU

6th June 1973

Dear Andy,

Brewers Droop have changed the name to just 'Droop' and are going to be superstars and have cleaned up their act (slightly) and have mislaid their polystyrene phallus and now have a blue inflatable one and have cleaned up their act (honest) and have given up drinking and have just started drinking again and 'Louise' is going to smash and make Dave Edmunds famous and Droop had a trouser-dropping competition at High Wycombe's Nags Head on Saturday and lots of guys took off all their clothes and one girl fainted and the Droop roadie gotten beaten up by some greasers and Ron Watts feels more like the ringmaster of a Three-Ring circus than a Rock singer and we're Drooping to the Polar Festival in Finland on July 7th and Jazz Bilzen in Belgium on August 17th and Ron Watts is still married and why ain't we on the front page of Mirabelle and we're recording again at Rockfield Studios for a week from June 11th and Dave Edmunds still producing and............ goodbye

Jim Simpson

Later on there were two other Big Bear bands that featured at Henry's Blueshouse, but unfortunately neither of them managed to get a toe-hold on the national touring circuit, though we secured record deals for both and individual members survived and made their mark with other significant bands.

When Olav Wyper, label boss at Phonogram's Vertigo label, was headhunted by RCA to set up their underground label Neon Records, he set about building up a stable of artists. Probably figuring that lightning can in fact strike twice, and remembering that his major successes during his short spell at Vertigo had been two Black Sabbath million-selling albums, Olav contacted me about up-and-coming bands I was involved with. I told Olav about the Coventry-based Indian Summer which I had been booking into the early venues that Sabbath had played.

3. On A Mission From Dog

They were Henry's regulars, good musicians, all four singing, with a heavy band sound based around the keyboards of lead singer Bob Jackson. All of the material was self-penned and maybe they needed a little more work in that department.

Olav brought his RCA team to see the band at Henry's and immediately offered me a deal. Olav did it right, bringing in producer Rodger Bain who had worked on the Black Sabbath albums and hiring the well-rated Trident Studios in London. It was a nice production. In retrospect maybe the arrangements should have been cut down in length and the whole thing tightened up, but it's so much easier to comment way after the event. Indian Summer is still remembered and respected, with *Record Collector* magazine issuing a double-vinyl album of the band in 2016 and Bob Jackson and drummer Paul Hooper having notable careers in music, both with the Fortunes, Bob also with Badfinger and The Searchers.

Going back to the band that had been the first to feature at Henry's, fate had not treated Bakerloo kindly. After the most promising of starts and the initial enthusiasm of EMI Harvest, the band began to wonder if they had ever recorded that album. For reasons that never became clear, either to me or the band, EMI Harvest continually delayed the release date; I didn't let it lie, applying almost daily pressure to Tony Hall to get things moving. As it was, it took some eight months from completion of recording to the album reaching the shops.

In that time the band had continued to gig throughout the country, clocking up the miles and building a following. A regular and successful gig for Bakerloo was at the Marquee in Wardour Street. They played it first as support to Jon Hiseman's Colosseum and quickly returned as headliners. This time Jon Hiseman was in the audience. We should have anticipated it, but didn't, so it came as a body-blow to the band, and to me, when Clem Clempson, the mainstay of the band, handed in his notice, quit and joined Colosseum with whom he worked right up until the band's final concert in 2015.

I really believe that, if we could have got the album released to ride the wave of their growing popularity, the band would have stayed together and become a major force in British blues. Clem later played with supergroup Humble Pie and has taken his rightful place as one of the great British rock/blues session players. He is still active today, working out of Germany with his own band which sometimes features former colleague Chris Farlowe.

The original line-up of Clem, Terry Poole and John Hincks had survived John's departure, replaced initially by my old drummer, and chum to this day, Pete York, later by Cozy Powell and, later still, by Keith Baker. With the departure of Clem, both Terry and Keith quit and I was left with a full datesheet to fulfil, so recruited an excellent guitarist Adrian Ingram, a storming young musician with an astonishing technique. Adrian didn't sing, so we brought in singer Alex Boyce as well as a new bass player and drummer. By now the style of the band was naturally developing and we decided a new name and a new character were needed to step away from the wreckage of Bakerloo.

This was to be Hannibal, with the addition of Cliff Williams on tenor saxophone and Hammond organist Bill Hunt, later of Electric Light Orchestra and Wizzard. I negotiated an album deal with B&C Records who released the eponymously-titled album produced by the ubiquitous Rodger Bain at Island Studios. The album was largely ignored by the media. Again I feel it was well played, but was let down by undistinguished self-penned repertoire, but back then everyone was writing their own material, a large proportion of which was pretty forgettable. Of course, it's laudable and creative to write your own songs, but there's no point in recording them unless they are strong as well as being original.

Whatever, Hannibal sank without trace and Adrian Ingram moved on to Yorkshire to work as a lecturer in jazz guitar at Huddersfield Technical College and Leeds College of Music, writing many books and articles on the subject and venturing out from time to time to play jazz dates and terrify other guitarists.

The former members of Bakerloo went on to make their mark on the music scene. Terry Poole and Keith Baker left Bakerloo to form Anglo-Canadian power trio May Blitz, but left before the band recorded. Keith went on to play drums with Supertramp and Uriah Heep, while Terry joined the Graham Bond Organisation, then Vinegar Joe. Detailing the later achievements of Pete York, Cozy Powell and Clem Clempson would take a chapter in itself. But I just can't help wondering what this talented group of musicians could have achieved if Harvest had managed to schedule the release of their album before terminal disillusion set in.

Fast forward to the present. The Crown Hotel, home to Henry's Blueshouse and much more, stands empty and rotting since 2014. It is apparently owned by Tokyo-based developers who – surprise, surprise! – want to build more apartments above, around and behind the pub. They did have building permission which has currently lapsed, but apparently it is the work of moments to reinstate.

But there is an alternative.

In 2013 I put forward a proposal to Birmingham City Council to preserve the Crown Hotel and to convert it into what the city needs, and certainly deserves, as the UK Capital of Rock 'n' Roll: a Rock and Roll Museum. Although the building is dilapidated, if viewed through squinty eyes the main bar does have characterful vintage fitments that would scrub up nicely. The idea was to open the main bar from dawn to midnight, from breakfast to supper, serving traditional food and traditional ales to a soundtrack of recordings of Brum's great bands. The history of the music would be available in the lounge. The 1st floor gig room, where Henry's held sway, would be reopened – remarkably that fine stage is still in place. What was the dressing room would become the recording control room – and what band would not want to record in the very room that has been graced by legends? The second floor was originally five hotel rooms and they would be reinstated as a boutique hotel with a difference. The rock and roll bedrooms would be named after Ozzy Osbourne et al.

The location is splendid, across the street from the American Steps into New Street Station. What better position for a major, and exceptionally cool, visitor attraction?

There is a further footnote regarding the Crown Hotel. Rock and roll it might be to many, but it had other lives before that. In the Brum Beat era it hosted up to nine performances a week, every evening plus Saturday and Sunday lunch-times, but it also enjoys a place in the history of folk music as the venue where the first live folk album was recorded in this country. The recording was arranged by Topic Records which was wholly owned by the Communist Party. The artists recorded included the famous Birmingham-based folksters, the Ian Campbell Folk Group, and the legendary International Brigade veteran of the Spanish Civil War, Bob Cooney.

Yet another footnote to the Henry's saga occurred in March 2019 when, after a short break of some 50 years, the headlines ran, 'Henry's Blueshouse Rides Again'. Carried away on the wave of euphoria generated by the need to celebrate 50 years of Big Bear, we launched Henry's Blueshouse at the Bull's Head, a splendid traditional pub at the centre of Birmingham's entertainment sector.

Pre-gig, journalist Stuart Constable grilled me on what I could remember about the launch of the original venture, High Wycombe's hooligan blues giants The Shufflepack well and truly took care of business as far as the sell-out crowd of serious bluesers was concerned, and some of us, including Ian Ward, leader of Birmingham City Council, and Marc Reeves, managing editor of the *Birmingham Mail*, *Birmingham Post* and *Sunday Mercury*, sat around after hours listening to early Big Bear blues recordings. So, once again, Tuesdays is Bluesdays hereabouts.

Chapter 4

FROM EARTH TO BLACK SABBATH

The original membership book for Henry's Blueshouse shows John Michael Osbourne and Anthony James Iommi as early members at the princely cost of one shilling (5 pence) a year. They became regulars, we got talking, they told me that they were in a blues band, that I should call them Ozzy and Tony, that their band was called Earth, recently name-changed from the Polka Tulk Blues Band. Sometimes they brought the other band members, Terry Butler, known as 'Geezer', and Bill Ward.

After a while they asked if they could play the intermission spot at Henry's. They were such serious folk that I had no hesitation in offering them a date. The fee for the intermission bands was £5, but the guys in Earth asked if they could have a Henry's Blueshouse T-shirt each instead of a fee. No problem there.

The first time that Earth played Henry's was to support Ten Years After, a big attraction at the club, so the boys got to play in front of a full house that night, and they played well, succeeding in the tough job of winning over an audience that was there specifically to see another band.

The support slots kept coming and a real Earth fan group was emerging, so, when the band asked me to manage them, I acceded with alacrity. The Earth datesheet at that time was pretty blank, but they already had a following in the Carlisle area and the beginnings of one in Birmingham. It was a pretty tough time to be a blues band in the UK. The blues boom had subsided, leaving in its wake hundreds of out of work, mostly boring bands who looked the same, wore the same battered jeans, smelt the same, stared at their boots in the same way, played the same repertoire and featured the same endless 200-mile-long guitar solos.

That description in no way fit Earth who ploughed a serious blues furrow, but unfortunately, although the band were many cuts above the competition, in the eyes of many a venue they were just another blues band. We tried, with some success, to put ink on the datesheet, but I had believed from the beginning that the band's name Earth was nondescript and tame and in no way reflected what the quartet did on stage. Believe me, even as a blues band, with Ozzy's dynamic vocals, Tony's powerhouse guitar riffs and the steaming rhythm team of Geezer and Bill, Earth made for a very special band. So I determined on a name-change as a launch-pad to move the band forward, even though, to a man, they were against it. I took to scouring the listings and small ads in the *Melody Maker*, the most important of our music weeklies, and very soon was rewarded for my efforts when I found not one band, but two, with the name Earth, both London-based and prominent enough to make it to the pages of *Melody Maker*.

So that was it – done and dusted! They reluctantly agreed to ditch Earth, but that led to another, even more difficult question: 'What are we going to call ourselves?'

Every name that any of us suggested was immediately crushed and ditched as rubbish by the other four. This process seemed to go on forever, in fact, certainly for so many weeks that by the end every suggestion was dismissed almost before it left someone's mouth. Fans who came to the band later on might be so obsessed with them biting the heads off everything from bats to bears that they find it ludicrous to think of them dutifully attending a weekly band meeting in my home in Edgbaston where we had a proper serious agenda and took and distributed meeting notes! I'm sorry if this disabuses anyone's preciously guarded impression of the band as drug-crazed hooligans who somehow found the time for the odd gig, but that's how it was: four young men utterly dedicated to improving their performance with regular rehearsals who demanded the same dedication to the cause from their manager, just as he demanded continual improvement from them.

So Geezer arrived late for a morning meeting, poked his nose round the door, somehow not as contrite as he should have been; in fact there was a positive glow about him.

'I've got it, chaps, I've got the name.'

There were random calls of, 'You're late! Where've you been?' and 'What is it this time?'

Still not deigning to enter the room, still poking his head cheekily round the door, he said, 'Black Sabbath.'

There was a collective intake of breath, followed by a deafening silence and an exchange of quizzical glances, before a unison yell of approval. It had taken the rest of us less than a minute to agree that Geezer's proposal of Black Sabbath was officially the new name for the band – and Earth was consigned to history.

From the moment we had a name that we could all subscribe to without reservation, a new musical direction began to emerge. The satanic overtones,

An early version of The Big Bear Ffolly, with Locomotive, Black Sabbath, Bakerloo, Roy Everett, JS.

rooted in neither knowledge of, nor conviction about, the occult, seemed a pretty beezer way to go. After all, you couldn't go on stage cheerily bouncing through *Got My Mojo Working* when your flag spelled out Black Sabbath. Musically, at that time, the material still had roots in the blues, but there developed a new intensity, a drive, a conviction that this is what we are, we're committed to a cause and, if you don't get it, then step aside because the Sabs are coming and we know exactly what we're doing. The print, posters, press releases and T-shirts took on a new meaning and there is no doubt that the band suddenly became prolific in their songwriting, more intense in their rehearsals and infinitely more self-critical of their performances. This was a period when I could not have been more proud to represent the band. We shared a self-belief and had no time for anyone who didn't get what Black Sabbath were about.

Inevitably, when the decision was made to move away from the blues, there was much discussion about repertoire – and some confusion. It should be remembered that most of the band had some interest in jazz before they met me, all but Ozzy in fact, so it's not surprising to find traces of jazz, soon abandoned, in their early repertoire. Their first recordings, unissued to this day, were *Evenin'*, inspired by the Jimmy Rushing recording with Count Basie, a Tony Iommi original, *A Song for Jim*, clearly influenced by Charlie Christian, Benny Goodman's ace guitarist, and an Ozzy-inspired excursion into rock and roll, Carl Perkins' *Blue Suede Shoes*. Clearly there was no definable direction, though the performances, instrumentally and vocally, were excellent.

This interim period was much tougher on Ozzy than it was on Tony, Geezer or Bill. They all had their instrumental technique to fall back on, but Ozzy, who had had no formal training – which was one reason why he became so phenomenally successful – found himself without direction and rapidly losing confidence in his ability to sing. We spent many hours at my record player going through my collection in search of inspiration. I'm still pleased that he enjoyed Jimmy Rushing so much, a particular favourite of mine, and it's interesting that, with both Ozzy and Rush, the vocals seem to emanate from somewhere deep down in the belly area.

I had to spend a lot of time trying to restore his confidence. He didn't seem to recognise the value of his contribution to the performance, and beat himself up because he couldn't actually play an instrument. In fairness to Ozzy, the other three were inclined to rib him over this, probably feeling it was unfair that they had had to learn to play their instruments properly while all Oz had to do was to turn up and sing. He was beginning to feel a bit of an outsider and at that time needed his confidence constantly boosting. Fortunately this phase was not to last for long.

My backyard: Black Sabbath look as if they just rolled up to lay the slabs!

4. From Earth To Black Sabbath

Black Sabbath and my garden fence.

One very interesting demo recorded by Black Sabbath is a fine example of how melodically Ozzy can sing when handling straightforward songs. The provenance of *The Rebel* remains a mystery, though the PRS catalogue may still have it listed as composed by the former Locomotive singer, Norman Haines. To be clear, Norman cheerfully admits that he didn't write the song and has no idea how it came to be accorded to him. I have no clear memory of how we came upon *The Rebel* except a feeling that we picked it up from a Canadian rock band whose name I don't know. We all felt that this had all the makings of a hit record, but on repeated playbacks agreed that, although the band's version was strong, it just didn't sound like we wanted Black Sabbath to sound. I remain amazed that *The Rebel* hasn't been a big hit for someone, it's such a strong song. It would have been a good fit for Levon Helm of The Band, for instance.

The pivotal event was when I arranged a month's residency at the Star Club in Hamburg, a name with an important place in Beatles folk-lore. Nobody believes it now, but this is the truth. Black Sabbath played six nights a week at the Star Club. Monday to Thursday they played six 45-minute sets: 8.00-8.45, 9.00-9.45, and so on. On Fridays and Saturdays the schedule was eight sets – 45 minutes on, 15 minutes off – from 8.00 pm to 4.00 am. This gruelling schedule was the same for every band that played the Star Club.

Sabbath came back exhausted, Ozzy's throat raw, barely able to speak, the others with blistered fingers and drained of energy. But, when they had recovered and went out to play a standard UK show of two one-hour sets, it was a stroll in the park for them. They didn't need to break sweat, but, being Black Sabbath, break sweat they surely did.

The sojourns at the Star Club – there were two of them – served to fine-tune the band's repertoire and had another effect, one that stood the band in good stead for many a year, certainly throughout my tenure. They had become what Count Basie referred to as a 'one-beat band'. He meant that the musicians no longer had to think about what the others were doing, or might do next, because their mutual understanding of what they were playing – the accents, the breaks, the diminuendos and crescendos – all happened naturally without any conscious thought. They were all so familiar with the repertoire and each other's performance that, when one hit, they all hit! As a result they were all free to project themselves in performance, they could showboat in the sure and certain knowledge that the other three would be there, a foundation as solid as a rock.

By this time we all knew we had something very special and needed to spread the message to the rest of the human race. I had negotiated serious recording contracts for the other bands I was handling at the time. Locomotive were on Parlophone and Bakerloo and Tea & Symphony on EMI Harvest, and Locomotive had enjoyed a hit single, so I didn't find it difficult to get meetings with London's A&R men. I took the band into Zella Studios at the back of Ladbrooke's Piano Store, which was a pretty basic four-track facility, but perfect for our needs, and recorded a demo version of precisely the same songs that would eventually appear on the first album. The production wasn't there – no rainstorms or thunderclaps – but the recording was clean, the repertoire strong and the performance right on the button, so with absolute confidence in what I had to offer I started my quest in search of the record deal that would take Black Sabbath to the top of the British rock tree – World Domination would come later. But not too much later!

I started off fairly picky, carefully selecting record companies I knew and A&R men who I believed would get what Black Sabbath were about, would understand the value of what was by then a very healthy datesheet, would see the significance of so many venues immediately re-booking the band at an increased fee and, most important of all, would appreciate the music and its, to me, terrific potential.

4. From Earth To Black Sabbath

David Platz, head of major publisher Essex Music, when confronted by a band on the hustle, seeking a deal and claiming, for instance, to be big in Japan, would say that Truth is a Royalty Statement – nobody pays out money on anything other than solid sales. The same applied here. If a promoter phones the manager to re-book the morning after a performance, then he's had a successful gig. If he then agrees to an increase in fee, then he's had an extremely good gig. It really isn't rocket science to work out that a band with a full datesheet is doing something right. Logically there must be a growing army of fans out there, waiting impatiently for the band's first record release.

I'm the first to admit that Sabbath was not your average rock band and there were no easy comparisons to be made, but it was there in the music for anyone who gave it serious attention to hear. I didn't expect everyone to enjoy the music, but the quality was undeniable, the presence and the power impossible to ignore.

I made the trip to London regularly over several weeks, sometimes seeing two or three companies in a day, and the response was uniform. Typically the A&R guys would play some of the first track, furrow their brows in a display of feigned interest, then jump to a couple of other tracks for a few moments before telling me what was already obvious, that they didn't have the first idea what was going on. They never actually put it that way; usually they told me that it was very nice – Sabbath, very nice! Were they crazy? – but it wasn't what they were looking for.

I would take the train back to Birmingham and sanity, not so much disappointed, more blazingly angry, and I have to admit the train's bar sometimes took a bit of a pounding.

This wasn't the last time I had a run-in with the folk who sat in those coveted chairs in A&R. Jumping ahead, when Sabbath charted, seemingly coming out of nowhere – actually Birmingham – I had phone calls from four of the cloth-eared clots who had rejected the band, not to congratulate me and admit they had been wrong, but to ask me what other bands there were around Birmingham that were like Sabbath and available to sign. Some years later, when I was publishing the monthly magazine *Brum Beat*, of course we championed our local bands. We were the first to give attention to UB40. Unsurprisingly, when *Food for Thought* hit, I received a procession of calls from A&R men asking what other Brum bands sounded like UB40 and it happened again with Duran Duran and with virtually every successful Birmingham group. I never did understand – and still don't – why most A&R men would shy away from a band that sounded different, yet stand in line to sign a band that sounded like one that was already successful.

I must have had more than a dozen rejections. Two of them turned me down twice after I persuaded them to give Sabbath another listen. It was clearly time for a change of tactic. I had been working with Tony Hall Enterprises in London on getting recording deals for Locomotive, Tea & Symphony and Bakerloo. Tony's production company was financed by David Platz's Essex Music to find new talent to sign up and record. Neither Tony nor David could see any value in Black Sabbath and they showed no interest. That was the standard London response so originally it didn't bother me. I could place Sabbath elsewhere and continue enjoying my good relationship with David and Tony regarding my other acts.

But now, after so many rejections, things were different. I went to see David and spelled out my frustrations. It took him less than an hour to come round to my way of thinking, telling me that he still didn't get the Sabbath thing, but that he would back my obvious commitment to the band. He agreed to book and pay for time at Regent Sound Studios in Denmark Street to record the Black Sabbath album. There were stipulations. He put in a new, as yet unproven Essex Music house producer, Rodger Bain, and set up the company Tuesday Productions, and I had to undertake to take on responsibility for trekking round London's record companies to get the release deal. I had already done that, so I knew the drill, but this time I would have the finished product. So that would give me the edge.

Or so I imagined.

Regent Sound wasn't one of the elite recording facilities, but it was a well maintained eight-track studio, unpretentious and comfortable to work in, with good separation, diligent engineers and a clean sound. The recording went smoothly, with no hitches; the levels were set and Black Sabbath did exactly what Black Sabbath did. Match-fit and at home with the repertoire that they were performing every night, it was just another gig to them. Never a band to hold back, they gave everything on every take. No overdubs, no drop-ins, no vocal or guitar solo re-takes, just Black Sabbath doing exactly what they did best.

On the way home, some of us wondered exactly what Rodger Bain had contributed to the recording. He had sat there at the desk, smiling benignly, offering quiet words of approval and accepting the takes. He didn't seem to be doing anything. It wasn't until some years and several productions later that I properly realised what a brilliant job he had done. Many producers seem to feel the need to get some of themselves onto a recording, maybe by creating a sound (think Phil Spector) or altering arrangements, adding instruments, overdubbing or whatever. The genius of Rodger Bain was to understand fully the quality of the music and the performances and to know that nothing more needed to be done. It takes self-control to refrain from adding to a recording, to realise it's perfect and shouldn't be messed with.

Having said all that, Rodger did actually mess with it at the mixing stage and the result was simply the icing on the cake. It was solely Rodger's idea to open side one of the album with the sound of a rainstorm and thunderclaps. Pure magic! The band and I had no idea what he was planning until we received the test pressing. I came back on the train, having arranged to meet the band at New Street Station and go to my house to hear the album for the very first time. Rodger Bain's introduction just floored us; it added a special something to a recording we already thought was perfect. That must be the very best introduction to a rock track recorded by anyone anywhere. I really believe that it's a unique and memorable moment when the band crash in on the opening track of that first album.

But then it was back to business. I had a record deal to land. The situation had become even more fraught because of the early successes of Led Zeppelin. We were all familiar with the Brummie half of the Zeps; the Band of Joy which featured Robert Plant and John Bonham had been one of the hottest bands in the region.

One of God's better human beings, Bonham was also a fully qualified and utterly committed hooligan whose onstage antics had Locomotive banned from two venues. He lived above his mother's general store in Astwood Bank, Redditch, and would always sense when I was about to bawl him out and would liberate a bottle of whisky or a carton of cigarettes from the store before we picked him up in the van. I had to sack him from Locomotive, three times in fact, but he was such a good bloke as well as being the finest of drummers, that he was always reinstated before sun-up. In the end he actually quit. He told me that he was going to join a band with a ridiculous name, Led Zeppelin. I told him that he was mad to leave Locomotive just when we were breaking through (though Locomotive had in fact been breaking through for a good number of years) and I offered him my considered advice that a band with such a name would sink without trace. I understood a little better when he said he was to be salaried, but still insisted it would end in tears.

Led Zeppelin brought together the remnants of the Yardbirds, who had just split, with Bonzo and Plant. Managed by Peter Grant, they walked into a recording deal, had an early release and charted in 1969.

Black Sabbath always regarded Zeppelin as competitors, even though half the band were southern softies. At that time bands aspired to be heavy. Of course none were anywhere near as heavy as Sabbath – that was an undisputed fact – but Zeppelin still made the spurious claim that they were the heaviest band around. We responded by using on our posters and leaflets the strapline, 'BLACK SABBATH: Makes Led Zeppelin sound like a kindergarten house band.' But with Led Zeppelin free-wheeling up the charts, it became imperative that I land that recording contract.

Don't Worry 'Bout The Bear

Amazingly, even though I was armed with exactly the same recording that would become known throughout the world as the first, eponymously titled Black Sabbath album, a worldwide hit, I met with precisely the same response as on my previous crusade. Not one A&R man at any of the 14 record companies I played it to wanted to release it. When I got back to Birmingham late at night after the final rejection, I met with the boys and gave them the bad news which I have to say was not totally unexpected by then. The question on everybody's lips was, 'What do we do now?' There was no question of us feeling beaten, we knew that Black Sabbath were an important band and that all these A&R men didn't understand what they were listening to.

I promised the band that I would find a way out of this and began to explore the pitfalls of manufacturing and releasing a 12-inch vinyl album – on Big Bear. My only foray into record releases up to that point had been a 7-inch single in a plain sleeve, so this would be very different. I still had my relationship with David Betteridge at Island Records although I was somewhat jaundiced by then as Island had been one of the 14 companies to turn us down.

I was starting to get to grips with the idea that the only way to get the Black Sabbath album released was to put it on Big Bear Records when I had a phone call from Olav Wyper whom I knew as Head of A&R at CBS Records and who had already turned down the Sabbath album for CBS. He told me that he had been headhunted by Phonogram to oversee the launch of their progressive label, Vertigo, that he had been thinking of that Birmingham band I had played him, whose name he couldn't recall, and that he wanted to do the deal. I replied that I would take the train down first thing the next morning so that we could go through the recording and discuss a deal, but he insisted he didn't need to hear it again and anyway there was nothing to discuss as the deal on the table was all he could offer. I pointed out that he had only heard most of track 1 and a bit of track 3 and he couldn't know enough about them as he didn't even remember the band's name. He was immovable. The deal offered a poor royalty rate and an advance of only £500, just enough to pay back the money owed to David Platz. The only attractive part of the offer, apart from the relief at actually getting a release on a major label and its European subsidiaries, was that he wanted a quick decision as he had a release slot only a few weeks away.

I met with the band and laid out the situation as it stood because I wasn't prepared to accept such a poor financial deal without the band's approval. As it turned out, none of them seemed at all perturbed by the paucity of the offer; the feeling I had was that they anticipated nothing better from the London suits. They felt that the important thing was to get the music out there so that the fans

4. From Earth To Black Sabbath

could buy it and we could all proceed to the next stage of the band's career. I felt similarly, even though I resented Olav's refusal to negotiate and his lack of any real interest in Black Sabbath. After all he hadn't even remembered the band's name, just that they came from Birmingham.

Once I gave Olav the go-ahead, things happened with such speed that he couldn't find time to produce photography for the album or to give us approval of the artwork. As it happened, he put the design work in the hands of Marcus Keef, the young designer whose work included all the early Vertigo albums, by such artists as Rod Stewart, Colosseum and Manfred Mann. Keef, whose real name was Keith Stuart MacMillan, changed his name to avoid confusion with an older photographer, also Keith MacMillan. By the mid-1970s he claimed to have designed 1,000 album sleeves at which point he decided to move into video production, starting at the top with Kate Bush's *Wuthering Heights*! Something of a man of mystery who is notoriously elusive when faced with someone else's camera, his eerie surrealist designs made him an iconic figure on the 1970s music scene.

Keef produced a killer of a gatefold sleeve design which we first had sight of when it was manufactured. It had our whole-hearted approval and, in fact, contributed considerably to the album's success. The spooky photograph of the ghostly girl by the mill in the pink-tinged woods was pure genius and still elicits

comments to this day, nearly five decades later. Sabbath fans still visit the scene of the watermill at Mapledurham, Oxfordshire, which, in a further brush with fame, later figured in a key scene in *The Eagle Has Landed*. Keef also created the symbol of the inverted crucifix which served Black Sabbath well.

Subsequently a Phonogram staffer explained to me why Olav called me so urgently and pushed the deal and put the album into production with such haste. The Vertigo policy was to release albums in threes. The first three albums, Jon Hiseman's Colosseum's *Valentyne Suite* (VO 1), *Juicy Lucy* (VO 2) and Manfred Mann's *Chapter III* (VO 3) had been released and Olav was readying up the second set with Rod Stewart's *An Old Raincoat Will Never Let You Down* (VO 4), Ancient Greece with *Woman and Children* (VO 5) and a third title which the producer had failed to deliver, leaving Olav working against the clock to find an album to carry the VO 6 catalogue number. This explained his lack of interest in the music, the band and creating any sort of a relationship with me. Since then I have often wondered what album it was that created the space for one of the most influential albums of all time to slide into. Could it be the self-titled *Cressida*, eventually issued on its own as VO 7 as Vertigo's release policy collapsed? Or could it be the work of some long-forgotten band who fell victim to a record company's aural myopia or a producer's procrastination?

The launch of the eponymously titled Black Sabbath album was textbook. The Phonogram sales and distribution teams did a great job, it was in virtually all UK stores on the day of release when the patient fans did exactly what we had told the A&R men they would do. They went out and bought the album.

The first week's sales topped 6,000 units and took the album into the mid-40s in the *Music Business Weekly* sales chart. Unsurprisingly Olav was delighted. 'You've done a brilliant job!', he shouted down the phone. 'How did you do it?'

I replied that I had told him about the band's burgeoning following and how hungry they were for the album, but he kept asking, over and again, how I did it. It became clear to me that he thought I had somehow bought the album onto the chart and wanted to know how I had gone about doing it. Even with the album firmly ascending the charts, he just couldn't accept that enough people out there wanted a piece of Black Sabbath for themselves.

Actually buying records into the charts was not at all an unfamiliar tactic in those days. Chart returns were by way of a diary kept at the tills of designated chart return shops, from major chains to small independents, giving a fair spread across the retail spectrum. The identity of the stores was supposed to be a secret, but there were ways to find out. One common way of buying onto the charts was to get the record salesmen to take a box of a current big-selling record into the store and tell the owner that he didn't have to pay for them – but would he mind giving a few ticks to an emerging band on the same label?

Tales abounded of a whole range of fantastic schemes to create hit records illegally. Some sounded feasible; most didn't. One major company was said to have an army of housewives strategically placed throughout the country who were paid to go into the chart return shops and buy whatever record the label was concentrating on that week. The nearest that most of us got to manipulating the charts was to go into the record store of whatever town we happened to be playing in and ensure that our album was placed at the front of the rack.

Supposedly, and I would like to believe it to be true, one enterprising chart hyper decided to cut out the middlemen and simply offer a sum of money in used five pound notes to the man whose job it was to input all the chart return results into the computer. It is said that his offer wasn't welcomed and he was taken out in the custody of the local bobby.

Once we had charted, things moved quickly on all fronts. With regard to live performances there was the situation where we were riding higher in the charts by the week, but still playing gigs contracted maybe six months earlier at a fee that matched the band's standing at the time of booking. Our way out was simple and provided an income that better reflected the band's current status while rewarding the belief in the band shown by the promoter. I talked to each venue, told them that I didn't want to pull the date, but we had to ensure that the fee reflected their success. We re-negotiated the fee to a guarantee of the original amount against a percentage of the door take, usually 70% or 75%, whichever was the greater. I would also ensure that the ticket price was increased so the band would receive a fair fee.

I have read much criticism of the way I handled this situation, by insisting the band honour their existing commitments, but the alternative would have been unthinkable. If I had cancelled all the agreed shows and booked new dates reflecting their status, they would have had no income for many weeks, the time it would take before a typical venue had an available slot. By honouring their contracted dates we avoided any possible legal action, kept a full datesheet at substantially improved fees, further promoted the album at every show they played and, importantly for me, retained good relationships with venues and kept our reputation intact within the music business. Naturally we were also booking ahead at fees that were rising in step with the chart position.

As the workload increased, I appointed a booking agent to enable me to concentrate on management. I already had a productive working relationship with Barry Dickens of the Harold Davison office as he represented Locomotive.

Barry was an extremely nice bloke and generally delivered a good service, but somehow it didn't work out with Sabbath, so I placed them with Marquee Martin, run by Scottish former journalist John Martin under the auspices of Harold Pendleton's redoubtable Marquee operation. My rewarding relationship with John lasts to this day in his role of reviewer for our *Jazz Rag* magazine. Barry Dickens went on to become a most influential figure at the highest level of the UK music business.

As Phonogram, encouraged by the domestic sales, began releasing through their European subsidiaries, this made for exciting times, with an improved level of venues and television shows to promote the album. It's always tough to market a record in a territory where the band is hardly known, but for the promotion team it makes a world of difference to be able to point to activity on the UK charts. American and UK charts command respect across the world, though it doesn't always work the other way round, with the UK and US taking little notice of activity in other countries.

We had a flurry of interest from American record companies, alerted by the UK success. I quickly plumped for Warner Brothers, impressed by the enthusiasm and energy of the President, Joe Smith. The company was based in Burbank, California, which I liked the sound of as a fan of the offbeat comedy show, *Rowan and Martin's Laugh-in*, which famously came from 'beautiful downtown Burbank'.

The resulting US release in May 1970 led to a year on *Billboard's* 200 chart, peaking at Number 23. How could the record-buying public resist this radio commercial with its dramatic voice-over? 'Times are usually tough in Aston, the funky section of tough Birmingham, England, and the music of the Aston group Black Sabbath reflects their harsh environment. Warner Brothers, aware as always, offer you music that is as gentle as an open wound, and, knowing you, I think that you will all identify marvellously with this group on Warner Brothers records and tape.' All this to a background of Aston's finest at their very gentlest!

At this point a Japanese release of the album on Philips meant that I was dealing with the band's affairs in countries in time zones 16 hours apart. I was still running the business mostly on my own from my office at home and frequently taking calls at midnight from either California (where it was 5 o'clock in the afternoon) or Japan (where it was 9 the next morning). Snatching a few hours sleep and then wakened in the early hours by a call from Tokyo, I was liable to find myself conducting phone business at midday, still in my pyjamas! In the days before mobile phones, going with the band to, say, Newcastle, meant that I would crucially be out of touch with the States for most of their working day.

It was a clear choice. I could accompany the band to every performance, fend off the circling wolves, and share in the nightly successes and the ever-wilder after-parties, spending most of my working week on the road. Alternatively I could do my job properly, in the office, as the band's anchor, exploiting business and media opportunities, enabling the operation to run smoothly rather than lurch from crisis to crisis. By this time I had a secretary, but I needed to be on the spot to make decisions without delay.

The logic of this didn't escape the band and, most importantly, we all understood that I had to trust them to be loyal, just as they had to trust me to look after their interests. This was agreed between the five of us, with hands solemnly shaken.

Black Sabbath.

Chapter 5

SABBATH BLOODY SABBATH

It started slowly, with only the occasional approach to the band, telling them that they were being cheated by their management – that was me – and that they would be much better off ducking out of their contract and committing themselves to whoever it was making the approach this time. In the beginning the approaches came from no-account chancers and the boys got rid of them without ado and kept me informed. Then the approaches got more serious and came from credible sources, so that, when I did go on gigs, I spent my time fending off would-be managers. At a show at the Adelphi in Liverpool one character sidled up, obviously figured I was the security man and offered me £50 (a considerable sum in those days) to arrange a meeting with the band in a discreet room as he had something to tell them which would be very much to their benefit. I wished afterwards that I had taken his £50, sat in on the meeting to hear his pitch, then introduced myself before having him seen off the premises. Sadly these cool ideas never come to mind at the time, only when it's too late to put them into practice.

An unusually significant approach came through Birmingham singer Charlie Wayne. I had known Charlie for years and had photographed him dozens of times, first as Carl Wayne and the Vikings, more recently as the singer with The Move, with Number 1 hits behind them as well as the accolade of making the first record heard on Radio 1, *Flowers in the Rain*. That Charlie should be part of a plan to poach an otherwise happy Black Sabbath from their rightful manager I thought was scandalous, but, as The Move were at that time signed to Don Arden for management and he approached Sabbath on behalf of Don, it's possible that a degree of coercion came into play.

Don was, I believe, a self-styled Godfather, a sort of UK music biz Mafioso. In a 1979 radio report investigative journalist Roger Cook did what was considered to be an in-depth exposé of Don Arden's supposed near-gangster tactics, but I felt then – and still do now – that Don encouraged him and fed him colourful information that may or may not have been based on fact, and that Don privately enjoyed being viewed as the hard man of rock and roll. Having said that,

5. Sabbath Bloody Sabbath

I would never have crossed the man. There was no way of ascertaining where the line lay between fact and fiction and I certainly did not want to be the mug who found out exactly where it was.

The band did meet with Charlie at the Wimpy Bar on Smallbrook Ringway in Birmingham. They told me about it and said they had sent Charlie back to Don with a clear thanks, but no thanks. Don was not a man to give up easily and he tried again, this time sending as his emissaries Wilf Pine and Patrick Meehan, who were an entirely different kettle of fish from Charlie Wayne. These were serious hard men who apparently enjoyed the full trust of Don Arden to whom they had to return with the news of another failed fishing expedition.

About this time an interesting diversion arose when a parallel bandwagon was created out of thin air. In 1970 the Leicester band Pesky Gee! reinvented themselves as Black Widow, doubtless figuring that the success of Black Sabbath was predicated on their supposed connections to black magic. They, and subsequently countless media people, clearly believed, incorrectly, that Black Sabbath were immersed in the occult. They carried it to its logical conclusion and adopted what they thought Sabbath were up to. Black Widow signed to CBS and recorded the inspiring-sounding album *Sacrifice*, but their success was short-lived and their place in this story is more to do with media than music. Their press agent must have been blessed with energy and imagination because soon they were all over newspapers such as the *Daily Mail* as a fascinating development on the pop scene – aided by interviews with 'the most famous white witch in England', Alex Sanders, also known as Verbius, the King of the Witches. Oddly, as Black Widow faded, many of these rather sinister stories were ascribed to Black Sabbath.

In the meantime we were contractually obliged to deliver a second album within six months, a tall order at any time, but a particularly tough ask with Sabbath's heavy gig schedule. Luckily they had unused material from the time of the first album, but most of the second was written and routined on the road and I have to admit being stunned at the time by the quality of their work – come to think of it, I still am. All of the eight tracks were originals written by, and credited to, Iommi, Osbourne, Butler and Ward and there isn't a makeweight among them and several absolute stunners, including the iconic *Paranoid*. Production was again in the extremely capable hands of Rodger Bain. Engineer Tony Allom was again on board, with Brian Humphries replacing Barry Sheffield as the other engineer and it was recorded at Regent Sound and the ritzier Island Studios.

The album was originally to be titled *War Pigs*, as evidenced by Keef's design which was clearly intended to reflect that title. The switch was made to *Paranoid*,

Black Sabbath on Belgian TV.

partly because its views on the Vietnam War were considered non-PC, though that dumb term was not in use in those particularly non-PC days, but also because it was felt that *Paranoid* had potential as a single – which it did, rising to the lofty heights of Number 2 in the singles chart. The lack of any connection between album title and sleeve image passed without comment at the time, though it was probably noticed by a lot of people who didn't want to be seen as uncool by not getting it – actually, there was nothing to get. All in all, not Keef's finest hour. That *Black Sabbath* gatefold sleeve design had proved to be an impossible act to follow.

None of this in any way hampered sales as *Paranoid* leapt to Number 1 on the album charts – the last Number 1 album for Black Sabbath until the 2013 release of *13*, forty-three years later. A lot of people believe they have a copy of that first pressing of *Paranoid*, but there's only one way to identify the genuine article. Just check the production credits and, if they carry the line 'Management/Jim Simpson, Big Bear, Birmingham', then you are holding the real thing. For reasons that will become obvious, if somewhat petty, that line is missing on subsequent pressings. Later versions even purported to be recordings by NEMS, Patrick Meehan's company, with the original packaging, but the addition of their logo.

In the week that the *Paranoid* album was Number 1 and the single Number 2, with the original *Black Sabbath* album re-entering the chart at Number 16, I had a visit from Black Sabbath roadie Geoff Lucas late one Friday night, telling me that the group had no money and couldn't afford to get to the gig at Liverpool University the following night. That they had no money was a most unlikely situation as they had been playing five or six gigs a week and picking up cash. I always arranged for payment by cash, primarily because I wanted the group to know exactly how much they were contracted for and that was the best way to do this. Also those people trying to turn them against me were already saying that Jim Simpson was taking their money and only giving them a fraction. The band knew that these stories were untrue, as they picked up the money themselves and paid my commission monthly. Years later Ozzy was to write in *I Am Ozzy*, '(Jim) is one of the most honest people I've ever met in the music business,' but that didn't mean that the band weren't affected by the malicious rumours.

On that Friday evening Geoff wanted £200 and told me the band knew of his mission and had actually instructed him, none of which I believed at the time any more than I would like to think it true today.

I scraped around and gave Geoff £200, intending to sort it out with the band at the next week's meeting at which the roadies would not be present.

It all became much clearer when I opened the Saturday morning post which contained a solicitor's letter telling me that Messrs. Osbourne, Iommi, Butler and Ward, trading as Black Sabbath, informed me that they no longer recognised the contract signed by them and their parents and instructed me that I could no longer act on their behalf as manager and that I was forbidden to contact them other than through these solicitors. The reason given was that they considered that I was not doing an effective job as manager. That, in a week when we had chart placings at numbers 1, 2 and 16, did seem a touch ironic. Upon reflection, I decided that Lucas, knowing what was in the post and confident there would be no next week's meeting and no reckoning, decided to use the situation to make a little money on the side.

I immediately consulted my lawyer, Andrew Mirams of Tyndallwoods, who had been responsible for drawing up the contracts in the first place. He went to court on the Monday and obtained an injunction restraining them from receiving money from recording or songwriting. Under UK law it is not possible to get an injunction against performance fees – something to do with interfering with earnings.

I learned the back story of this over a period of time from a variety of sources, one particularly close to a band member. Apparently Wilf Pine and Patrick Meehan had decided that they would make more money if they quit Don Arden and went to work on their own initiative. Their first project was to lure Black Sabbath away from their legitimate management contract and in this they were signally successful. They supplied 1st class rail tickets for the band to London, met them at Euston Station in a rented limousine, took them to a swish office suite that was rented by the day, and launched into their pitch. Patrick Meehan demonstrated how Jim Simpson was supposedly cheating them by phoning the Social Secretary at Bristol University and 'selling' the band for a future date at a price exceeding their current fees – not surprising as they had three records on the charts and the current dates had been negotiated some three months earlier.

I don't believe that the band found this ploy convincing: after all, it was them picking up the cash so they knew exactly what the fees were. With more than a touch of drama Patrick and Wilf had one of their tour managers, who had accompanied them to London, measured up by a fancy tailor for a chauffeur's uniform, averring that Jim Simpson was out of order to expect them to drive more than 100 miles to a gig when he should have been renting a helicopter. What was probably a lot more tempting to four straightforward decent boys from Aston who until recently had not enjoyed fame or a reasonable income, was the trip that evening to The Speakeasy in Margaret Street where they were introduced to the hedonistic delights of the metropolis.

To the world outside the Black Sabbath camp things must have seemed to be progressing as normal. There was a flurry of headlines in the music press about the split, but I heard nothing of dates booked by me being cancelled. Much of the music media still failed to give Sabbath their due and the records continued to sell by the truckload. Nowadays there is talk of the Ten Years War, referring to the consistently bad press coverage of Black Sabbath. I think that overstates it a little, but in the early years really enthusiastic media reviews were few and far between.

Tyndallwoods believed that I had a strong case against Sabbath, as they should – after all, it was they who had drawn up the contracts. I had wanted to do things properly and went round to discuss the contract, the position of the band and what I saw as their potential with each set of parents. The parents all duly signed, as did Ozzy, Tony, Geezer and Bill, so my lawyers had a strong hand. As the date for the court case neared, I started to receive phone calls from Patrick Meehan, at first explaining to me why I should desist as, in his opinion, I hadn't a case. The calls toughened until, in the two or so months before the date, he offered to pay me off. The figure started at £20,000, went up to £40,000 and crept up slowly over the weeks. At every stage I consulted Andrew Mirams who was being advised by our QC, James Leckie, and his response was always to tell me to say no as 'we will get a lot more than that.'

Around midnight just days before the case opened, Meehan phoned to say this was my very last opportunity to settle as he would be instructing his QC the next morning and would have to pay him, so it would be too late to settle. The figure he offered was £80,000 which Mirams and Leckie confidently told me to refuse as we would certainly get £200,000 in court.

The case in London's High Court was no laughing matter, although it was hard not to smile when I saw the Sabs across the court lobby, looking extremely uncomfortable in very smart suits with uniform Black Sabbath haircuts. At that moment the anger and disappointment at their betrayal fell away. I just wanted to walk over, tell them how nicely they had scrubbed up and ask them, 'Why are we doing this? We're the same five people as before. Just look at what we've achieved together!'

The court sessions plodded on interminably, with many of the exchanges not bearing much of a relationship to the facts. At one time James Leckie bounded over to me with a look of panic.

'Who's Norman Haines?', he asked. 'He says that he's been managed by you as the singer with Locomotive who had a hit single and that you're not a good manager. Why didn't you tell me this?'

'Because I don't believe it to be true,' I responded, and anyway I doubted that Norman would have the temerity to face questioning on oath in open court. How far was he motivated by his constant wish to be involved in Sabbath? Today myths about Norman's part in the rise of Black Sabbath still abound on websites and blogs: he arranged their music and played with them in their early days, he wrote the song *The Rebel*, he turned down a permanent place in the band (as if he would!), he was part of Sabbath's management team until he was ousted in the Meehan/Pine take-over. All pure fantasy!

As it happened, I never found out whether Norman intended to give evidence, though he subsequently denied it on various occasions, because James Leckie came over, as breezily as usual, to inform me that, as the result of a court conference, he now believed that Black Sabbath had no funds and advised me to accept their offer of settlement at £35,000. The man from Tyndallwoods was in agreement and both had the air of it having been a nice try, pity it failed and you can't win them all. Sabbath, Pine and Meehan came up with £8,000 on the day; James Leckie took £1,000; the repayment of Legal Aid, which had been financing Tyndallwoods, came to £6,000. Big Bear took £1,000; it took 14 years of action in various courts to secure the remaining £27,000.

Would I have been better to have taken one of Patrick Meehan's offers of a payoff? After all, his final bid was more than double the £35,000. However, I have often wondered whether he would have actually come up with the money.

I was never totally clear on the respective roles of Pine and Meehan, but certainly it was Patrick Meehan who assumed a management role for Black Sabbath while Wilf Pine went onwards and upwards to greater things. Facts gleaned from John Pearson's biography and fulsome obituary following his 2018 death and funeral attended by the great and good of show business suggest that he was an associate of the Kray twins, the adopted son of New York gang boss Joey Pagano and one of two Brits to have the honour of being received into the American Mafia!

When Sabbath embarked on their first American tour, I was interested to see that it was based on the dates that we had set up with Marquee Martin with the guidance of Warner Brothers US boss Joe Smith. Ironic really, as one of the reasons given for ditching me as manager was that they thought that I was unable to obtain appropriate bookings for the band.

In going through the courts to retrieve the remainder of my award, I received support from an unlikely source. In my experience Don Arden was a man who valued loyalty above most other qualities. When first Patrick Meehan, then Wilf Pine, left his employ, he must have had a glimmer of a suspicion that maybe they had a plan. When it became clear that they had planned to entice Black Sabbath away from Big Bear, he apparently developed a loathing for them that never went away. They employed all that they had learned from Don in their pursuit of the band, all the time fully aware that Don hadn't given up on the project and that he was controlling fellow-Brummie Carl Wayne in his attempts to win over Sabbath.

Such was Don's anger towards the pair that he immediately called me to see him, put a comforting arm around my shoulder and told me it was hard to believe they would do this to a nice guy like me! Wisely, in the interests of expediency, I refrained from making the obvious observation.

I really have to make it clear that the Don always, without exception, treated me fairly, even generously. I think he rather enjoyed the image as the Godfather of Rock, widely publicised during and after the Roger Cook radio investigation. The tale of how he negotiated the management of the Small Faces with their existing manager whilst having two of his henchmen dangle him by the ankles from a fifth floor window is now part of UK rock and roll legend. If Don didn't actually start the many stories of his reign of terror, then he certainly fanned the flames and did little in the way of issuing denials.

Although the court had made the award to Big Bear, actually getting the money from people as reluctant to pay as were Meehan, Pine and Sabbath was no easy process and the fact that it involved raising further cash to pay legal fees really did make it difficult for me. I had no financial reserves as such, was still owed a substantial amount in commissions by Black Sabbath, quite apart from the court award, and frankly was suffering generally in loss of earnings from having committed so much time and resources to developing Sabbath's career.

5. Sabbath Bloody Sabbath

Now I could expect to derive no benefit from that; instead I had had to devote yet more time and resources to prepare for, and play my part in, the pantomime known as a High Court Case.

This is where Don rode in on his white horse to save the day. He took advice from his lawyers which he passed on to me and they took on various tasks for which Don footed the bill. Later, when I started bringing in American bluesmen, he called me to his office and questioned me in some detail about my current activities and immediate plans before saying that he would like me to have the use of an office in his swish Portland Place establishment, adjacent to the BBC. He said it would be rent-free, no obligation either way, he just thought that what we were doing sounded interesting and he wanted me to keep him informed.

Don was as good as his word. There were no demands and no pressure. I must have been a good listener because he often asked me into his office for a chat. Back then I would take the train to London most days on record company business, and to have a base in Don Arden's office, with Chas Chandler, manager of Jimi Hendrix, upstairs, was neat.

One time I had an overnight break-in at my home, not a good experience. Among the things they took were my Revox stereo tape machine and my beloved big Tannoy speakers. Naturally I was late getting in to London. The girl on reception told me Don had been asking for me and wondering why I wasn't in. I gave her the full story and she listened patiently and said she would explain to Mr. Arden. As I went to leave the office that evening, the receptionist pointed to a line of cardboard boxes and told me that Don had said they were for me. There were a new Revox, an amplifier and a brand new pair of Tannoy speakers that I am still using today. No fuss, no asking for thanks, just the kindest of gestures. It was a bit of a struggle to get all the stuff into a cab and onto the train, but I will never forget Don Arden's kindness in understanding how important the equipment was to me.

By this time, Ozzy was no longer with Black Sabbath and, possibly to compensate for failing to land the band in the past, Don had signed him lock, stock and barrel. He told me many a tale about the exploits of Ozzy and how outrageous he was. He would say that musicians in general were 'fucking animals' and that the only person who could handle Ozzy was 'my little Sharon'. She had been given the task of managing Ozzy and Don was proud beyond belief at how well she was doing the job.

Don had recorded Ozzy and his first album was to spearhead the new Jet Records worldwide distribution deal with CBS who were based in Germany. Don told me that, at the media launch in some swanky Frankfurt hotel, in the presence of the President of CBS, someone made the mistake of inviting the Oz.

Don told me that after liquid refreshment Ozzy did just what you expect him to do: raising his arm in a Nazi salute and Sieg-heiling all over place. That might have been anticipated, but probably not what followed. Warming to his task of being outrageous, he took to dancing on the dining table, smashing and scattering glasses and plates of food, before pissing in the orange juice. The climax of his activity, as Don related it to me, was to dance, still on the table, into Herr CBS President, grab the bewildered record company boss by the ears and pull his face into Oz's crotch, writhing all the while.

Don did not relate this tale with glee. On the contrary he found it extremely distressing, though not as distressing as did the CBS President who, Don reported, was so disturbed by this unexpected activity that he had some kind of breakdown and had to take a few months off work to recover. Normal practice, I would have thought, when someone has been so resoundingly Ozzed.

'Fucking animals!' opined the Don.

There were other outbursts of Ozzy activity, none over-surprising to anyone who knows him, but there was one occasion, not in any way amusing, that is etched in my memory. As I walked into the office one morning, the clearly worried receptionist told me to go straight into Don's office – he was waiting for me. Don's face was resting on his arm on his desk as I entered. He didn't look up so I took a seat and after a while it appeared to me that he was weeping. This was unthinkable, so I just sat quietly for what seemed to be an age, but might have been as much as 20 minutes. Eventually he gathered himself together and sat up, the great man, Don Arden, who feared no one, sitting there with tears streaming down his face. He told me that his little girl was planning to marry Ozzy Osbourne.

To say that any of us actually saw it coming would be untrue, but it wasn't actually that much of a surprise. They had, of course, been thrown together in the most exciting and enthralling of settings and Ozzy, basically, is a most likeable man with an attractive personality.

But Don was distraught that his little Sharon was going to marry Ozzy, the wildest of all the wild men of rock and roll. It may seem ironic when we look back on that moment as a treat for gossip-mongers, but it resulted in irreparable damage to the Arden family as a whole and particularly that most family-oriented of men, Don Arden.

Reportedly Don cut himself off completely from Sharon and forbade his son David from even communicating with his sister. David was a charming man with none of his father's pugnacity or aggression, and I know that the situation affected him greatly. Sharon and David did keep in contact covertly, but the family was never again what it had been.

5. Sabbath Bloody Sabbath

I believe that Sharon (Osbourne by now) and her father made up shortly before his death in 2007, but his death was the occasion of a renewal of a previous feud between David and Sharon. David himself had had an earlier problem which, reportedly, was none of his making. It resulted in this kindly, mild-mannered man serving a few months in Ford Open Prison. It was reported that, when Don re-located to the Los Angeles office of Jet Records and David took over in London, a London-based company accountant was found to be embezzling company funds. Any employer would feel aggrieved, but for Don, with the importance he placed on loyalty, something, possibly outside the law, had to be done. Apparently the order came from Los Angeles for rigorous action to be taken and on his father's instructions David hired some appropriately experienced men to remonstrate energetically with the accountant. The police became involved and David Arden stood up and took the rap, presumably to protect his father, though an alternative version of events in Ozzy's autobiography has Don returning to the UK to avoid extradition and getting off scot-free by hiring the best lawyers in London.

Certainly the upshot was that David Arden was sentenced to two years at Her Majesty's Pleasure of which he served several months, mostly in Ford Open Prison.

If anyone was unsuited to prison, open or otherwise, it was David Arden. It was obvious to everyone, even the prison authorities, that he was not a habitual criminal who had to be incarcerated to protect society, so David was allowed some special privileges and, coming from a show biz family and feeling the need to entertain, he set up his own Punch and Judy Show. As far as I can ascertain, he entertained at schools, garden fetes and the like, but his luck failed him when he went into a bookmaker's shop, whether to entertain or to place a wager is not clear, and was spotted exiting said establishment. Ironically this was just before he was due for release, but entering a bookie's transgressed the terms of his day release and he had to continue his sentence. I'm sure he bore it with the usual Arden fortitude and I have to say I remember him with nothing but kindness.

Sadly that Arden fortitude has taken a battering over the years with the relations between Sharon and David. After a falling out followed by a reconciliation, things seem to have reached an irreconcilable breach over – of all things – whether their father should be buried in Manchester or London. A very public spat in the press in 2013 found Sharon hurling abuse at David and David pleading for a reconciliation, partly for the sake of his nephew Jack who, like David, had been diagnosed with multiple sclerosis. A sad series of events for a family who, in various different ways, were a constant in the story of Black Sabbath.

Chapter 6

SABBATH: THE AFTER-PARTY

I remember when banks used to employ real people. They called them Bank Managers. None of this memorising your first dog's date of birth or some instantly forgettable combination of numbers and letters – or any other system to keep you at a distance from actually speaking to a staff member.

When I first started working in the music business with any degree of seriousness, I was told that I had to have a Business Account; that's the same as a Personal Account except that the bank can charge you more. I remember my Dad's advice on this, 'Go and meet your bank manager and talk to him before you open your account. If you don't like him or if he doesn't get what you're on about, go to another bank. There's a lot of them about.' He always seemed very happy with his various managers at Lloyd's, so I took his advice. I went to National Westminster bank – they were called that in those days – and told the young chap staring out of the door that I wanted to open a Business Account – and could I see the manager?

'That's me,' he said. 'Reg Lewis. Let's sit down.'

My decision was made before my bottom hit the chair. He was really interested in what I wanted to do and always available, sometimes for a coffee at Andre Drucker's La Boheme where we would invariably talk about music. He would ask what was happening at Big Bear: was there anything interesting coming up? I would sometimes give him copies of my photo shoots: he was a committed Rolling Stones fan and kept my photo of Brian Jones on his desk. He was – shall we say? – flexible with regard to my account and in return I only abused his trust now and again and always apologised profusely.

One time, when I found a band that I would have to find some money to support in the early days, I figured that the best way to secure an overdraft was to invite Reg to see them gigging in a City Centre pub. He came along, listened to their first set with due concentration, then passed judgement:

'I really don't think you should get involved with this band,' he said. 'I don't understand their music and they're far too loud. If you really believe in them, I'll support you, but my advice is to stay away from them.'

6. Sabbath: The After-Party

Luckily I ignored his well-meant advice. The band was Earth, soon to namechange to Black Sabbath. Over the years Black Sabbath became a running joke between us – and, now that I had lost them, Reg could not have been more supportive. I miss Reg: he was a good man and an example, more relevant today than ever, of how a bank manager should behave.

If the court case with Black Sabbath was no fun, which it certainly was not, then the months that followed, punctuated by inter-lawyer correspondence and the occasional unpleasant phone call from the Pine/Meehan camp, were no picnic either.

One Tuesday night at Henry's Blueshouse it was business as usual with the support band in full flow and me standing at the back drinking it all in when I got the message that 'an old friend' wanted to see me, but wouldn't come upstairs into the gig room. It was, in fact, a real old friend, Mike Savage, who had, to the best of my knowledge, no connection with the music business. His wife, Angela, and mine, Kate, had been at school together and remained the closest of friends. I knew his younger brother, Rick, who night-timed as a DJ while Mike was a successful salesman at a reputable car dealer and had done me the deal of the century by finding me an MGB Tourer, only eight months old with 2,000 miles on the clock, at around half its price as new.

He and Angela also bred Old English Sheepdogs which had taken over their lives to such an extent that they had moved to the West Country to concentrate on dog-breeding. From seeing them regularly, I had been out of touch for a couple of years, so I was delighted to see him. I was immediately struck by his unfamiliar gloomy demeanour and surprised that he insisted on getting away from the live music to stay downstairs in the Crown's rough public bar. There was little of the anticipated friendly chat, he clearly didn't want to ask about Kate or tell me about Angela, and an increasingly stiff conversation ensued. After around half an hour he suddenly announced that he had to go – no explanations. As I walked him to the door, he said something totally bizarre, 'They won't kill you, you know. They may hurt you, but they won't kill you.' With that he turned on his heel and walked into the night. I never heard from him again.

I have no idea whether or not he had got to know anyone connected with Black Sabbath, but, if he had, it must have been a most unlikely liaison. But, other than believing Mike Savage to be a delivery boy of a serious threat against a man who had long regarded him as a close friend, I can think of no explanation for his visit.

Did I take the threat seriously? I'm not sure. For a while it interrupted my sleep and I did develop the habit of standing alongside my car when I started the engine in the morning. Probably stupidly, I imagined that the effect of a bomb blast would be that much more severe inside, rather than outside, the car.

If these were uncomfortable days for me, which they surely were, it wasn't long before the honeymoon period with Pine and Meehan was over for Black Sabbath.

It was disloyal, but understandable, that four kids barely out of their teens should be seduced by the glib promises of a couple of West End smartsuits in a luxurious office, not knowing, of course, that the office was rented by the day. In their view it must have been no contest when they compared this to me, their existing manager, working out of the living room of his modest Edgbaston home. The promise of chauffeur-driven limousines, helicopters to gigs and no-expense-spared nights at The Speakeasy must have been overwhelming. There would have been no thought that all the finery would have to be paid for by themselves.

Apparently they signed everything over to Meehan and Pine who in turn provided each of them with a house, a car of his choice and, reputedly, a fairly modest salary. Tony Iommi must have initially enjoyed the arrangement as I was told that he opted in turn for a Lamborghini, a Rolls Royce and a Ferrari. What the band didn't know was that the houses and the cars were owned by a company which the management subsequently put up as surety with a merchant bank. So, when the crunch came some four years later and they entered lengthy and expensive litigation to obtain release from their management contract, it's reported that they lost their homes and cars overnight.

The band remembers those times as extremely painful, coming to the surface in the final song of their 1975 album, *Sabotage*. *The Writ*, written by Ozzy, pours scorn on Patrick Meehan, with the lyric, 'You bought and sold me with your lying words.' Geezer recalls that the album title reflects their response to the situation around the recording sessions, with lawyers and affidavits seemingly ever-present in the studio.

They were so broke that they asked Warner Brothers in California to pay them an advance to extend their contract. The problem was that they hadn't the funds to enable them to travel to the United States, so they asked David Platz, their publisher, to advance their expenses. Subsequent to the court case, I had been given various injunctions against the band pending receipt of the funds awarded. Over time the injunctions had lapsed, with the exception of the one affecting their publishing which stopped them entering a new or extended deal. So David Platz came to me with the request that, as a favour to him, I release them from the injunction to enable him to extend the publishing agreement and advance the money needed for them to travel to America and re-sign with Warner Brothers. Platz and I had long enjoyed a firm friendship and I saw no point in clinging on to the injunction just to create more problems for the band, so I signed it off.

When that was done and dusted, Platz asked me, seemingly pointedly, whether I would consider taking on management again if the band approached

6. Sabbath: The After-Party

me. Without giving it much thought, I said that I would, although they would have to accept that there was no way I could pay them an advance and I would not relinquish my claim on moneys already owed to me. I had never had a disagreement or argument with any of the band, we had not parted on bad terms other than the statements through our respective lawyers and I believe that there was no animosity between us.

At first I rather liked the idea of a reunion, that the band would decide to work with someone they could trust, despite his lack of showbiz glitz. However, over the next couple of days, I began to realise the near-impossibility I would have in finding any available time in the middle, as I was, of a series of tours and recordings with a growing roster of American bluesmen.

In the event I needn't have worried as an approach from the band never materialised. I have to be honest: somewhere inside me, I did rather relish the idea of getting involved and bringing the band back to the basic tenets that we started out with and that I believed were missing from their post-*Paranoid* period.

Contact with Ozzy, Tony, Geezer and Bill was sporadic in the extreme after that. Bill and I, who always got on well together, never met after the court case. Geezer and I bumped into each other in a Birmingham department store, then Rackham's, now House of Fraser, and held an awkward conversation during which we were both, for some reason, clearly extremely embarrassed. He was probably just as relieved as I was when we found a way to end it.

The next time I met Geezer was at his beloved Aston Villa Football Club in 2018 when he came to town to collect his award on the Broad Street Walk of Stars. Geezer is still shy, doesn't court attention or overly flaunt his celebrity and apparently could not be persuaded to actually come to Broad Street to accept his star. Westside BID supremo Mike Olley neatly side-stepped the problem by rearranging the event for Villa Park, with Geezer unable to resist the opportunity to tread the hallowed turf while accepting his star from the Lord Mayor.

It was really good to be able to spend time with him after all these years. 'How long has it been?' he asked repeatedly, and all I could respond with was, 'Too bloody long.' From all that has appeared in the media about the excesses of Black Sabbath you would imagine it would have to radically change a man. In fact, talking to Geezer, the years fell away; the relationship, despite all that has happened to us both over the last more or less 50 years, seemed unchanged. He told me that he has now retired from playing. I looked him straight in the eye and asked, 'Are you certain about that?' He gave that trademark cheeky Geezer Butler grin and responded, 'Well, if you do find a nice little blues band…' I'm still waiting for his call.

Don't Worry 'Bout The Bear

JS with Tony Iommi on the occasion of Geezer Butler's Walk of Stars award.

Tony Iommi and I have met each other with increasing regularity over the years, mainly because he is the only one of the band to remain living close to the city. He has always been in demand for media occasions, a true rock and roll idol, living in our midst. The first time we met after the split was probably in the mid-1980s when a television crew was filming in the wreck of what used to be the gig room of Henry's Blueshouse, upstairs at the Crown in Hill Street. Around that time the room had been used for boxing events (almost certainly illegal, as no one I ever met had heard about them) and there was a full-size boxing ring dominating the room. Tony and I shared our frustration at the scandalous waste of what had been a first-class gig room. We met intermittently over the intervening years, but at the time of writing I'm pleased to say we seem to encounter each other rather more often – always a most pleasurable experience.

The most recent occasion was at the unveiling of The Black Sabbath bench, which is due to be sited, in perpetuity, on Black Sabbath Bridge on Broad Street. At the time, the bridge was being strengthened, I would like to say in preparation for the arrival of the bench commemorating the heaviest band ever, but actually the work was in readiness for the arrival of the new metro line.

6. Sabbath: The After-Party

It really does say something special about a band that launched some fifty years ago that more than 400 people, from far and wide and of all ages, paid £12 to go into a church to see a bench dedicated to their heroes. The fans started to gather as early as 7am for a midday start, Jasper Carrott held sway as brilliantly as ever, and Tony Iommi was there to bless the bench and to receive a Black Sabbath Star on the Walk of Stars. Up until then, Tony, Ozzy and Geezer had received individual stars, but Mike Olley wanted the group to be properly commemorated and to complete the set by awarding a star to Bill Ward. Unfortunately Bill wasn't feeling too good, back home in Los Angeles, and he asked me to accept his star on his behalf. A duty that I was pleased and unreasonably proud to perform.

That just leaves us to persuade Birmingham Airport to agree to be renamed The Ozzy Osbourne International Airport. Seriously. Think about it. Who do you consider to be the world's most famous Brummie? Please don't say William Shakespeare or Neville Chamberlain.

Ozzy and I have kept in irregular contact from the outset. Reportedly he was the one dissenting voice when the band decided to leave my management and there are many stories of pressure applied to him by Patrick Meehan and Wilf Pine at the time.

The first encounter with him after the split actually didn't quite happen. At that time, probably 1980, I had split from my wife Kate and was living with Marja, the mother of my son Merlin Daleman. Marja was very Dutch, with no discernible sense of humour and little tolerance of any form of music except classical, and extremely embarrassed that I had had anything whatever to do with Black Sabbath. She had studied classical piano at Tilburg Conservatoire and in Holland had taught Music in school.

Marja had always considered herself an Anglophile, in fact picking our son's name, Merlin, from the tales of King Arthur. But she actively disliked living in England. In truth she probably just disliked my England which has always been a bit too rock and roll for decent folk. Although qualified, she refused to teach Music in England on the basis that the pay was less than it would have been in Holland and she wouldn't sign on as unemployed as she didn't like mixing with the type of person who frequented Job Centres.

So, with Merlin to look after and – I have to say – a splendid golden retriever called Hamish, one of the nicest folk that I have ever known, times were tough and I found myself working all hours to make ends meet. I had been working on a concert in Middlesbrough one Sunday evening, eventually getting to bed in the not-so-early hours, and was catching up on sleep mid-morning when apparently Ozzy Osbourne knocked on the front door, telling Marja that he was a good friend of mine and asking to see me.

I heard two versions of what happened next. Marja told me that Ozzy said he was unable to wait till I woke, while Ozzy told me, with glee, that she had looked him frostily up and down and told him, 'I don't think that Jim has any friends who look like that.'

One time I saw Ozzy was when he invited me to the filming in London of the pilot for a television quiz show. I thought the show was great and Ozzy terrific, but it never got to air. At the green room post-show reception Ozzy was, unsurprisingly, surrounded by well-wishers so I lurked at the back of the room, unsure what my next move should be. I needn't have worried. Ozzy spotted me, broke away from his gladhanders, bounded over and clasped me in a bear hug, saying, 'I think of you every morning, man.' I don't care how much he meant it, it was just good to hear him say it.

An unusually nice occasion – though that might sound bizarre when referring to The Prince of Darkness – was when he came to Broad Street to accept his award on Westside BID's Walk of Stars. He invited me to tea with him and his aunts in a private room in the International Convention Centre far from the madding crowds of Ozzy fans chanting his name endlessly in Centenary Square.

His aunties were charming, well-presented, extremely friendly Birmingham ladies, rather of the old school. They asked me questions about my work that could not possibly have been of interest to them, though you would never have known from the apparent attention they displayed. Their relationship with Ozzy was fascinating. They called him 'John' in a faintly imperious manner, clearly unaffected by his celebrity. He in turn was polite, attentive and concerned that their teacups were full and that they had all the cakes they could wish for.

As the afternoon progressed, they all loosened up and started to reminisce, just the sort of things that any Brummie family of their era would talk about:

'Do you remember, John, when we hadn't got the rent and we all crouched down behind the kitchen sink so the landlord wouldn't see us through the window?'

The final two shows of The End tour, with Ozzy now reunited with Black Sabbath, were memorable for me as well as being in some ways a non-event. Over the years I have been regularly wheeled out as a talking head for most things Sabbath – and I've always welcomed and enjoyed the opportunity to put in my twopenn'orth. The official end of Black Sabbath's final tour, two concerts in three days, found me banging on about Sabbath being the most influential of all rock bands and an essential element in Birmingham's claim to be the Rock and Roll Capital of the UK on a couple of television programmes and half a dozen radio shows.

6. Sabbath: The After-Party

The first show saw me on camera outside the NEC as the audience excitedly poured into the arena, then making my way to the local station and slinking off into the night, as I hadn't been offered a ticket. The *Birmingham Mail* – and, subsequently, others – made a big thing of this and on the Saturday morning the *Mail's* Graham Young phoned to say he had been allocated two tickets – and would I like to join him for the final Black Sabbath concert? He was surprised when I turned him down, but understood that it wasn't so much that I wanted to be at the concert, just that I would like to have been invited.

In the event my good friend Dan Cole used the ticket and was delirious to discover that it included an invitation to Tony Iommi's after party. Dan had the temerity to approach Tony and tell him that he was there on my ticket. Apparently Tony looked around for me and told Dan, 'The silly bugger. He should have come.'

My Black Sabbath final performance saga didn't end there. The Black Sabbath Global Convention, organised by Ben Fahl out of California, was set to hold its annual event on the Saturday night between the two Sabbath shows and I was to be a guest speaker. It wasn't held in Miami, nor Paris, not even in London, but in a modest little rock and roll pub in Dudley, deep in the Black Country, called Ye Olde Foundry. Sabbath fans from all over the world were crammed into this small pub. I talked to folk from Japan, Argentina, Peru, the USA and Egypt. It was a splendid evening and I still get emails from some of the folk I met there.

And that for me was the final curtain for Black Sabbath, a band who not only single-handedly invented an entire style of music and remain the most copied band in that style, but are also directly responsible for spawning all the dozens of sub-metal genres that invariably still acknowledge Sabbath as the fountain-head.

Chapter 7

BLUES AND THE BEAR

With the loss of Black Sabbath, it seemed a bit dumb to search for another struggling band who I thought had potential, knock them into shape, do the hard yards to gain some sort of foothold, only to have them taken away by some glib smartsuit who could convince them I was simply a provincial loser with no top-level experience. I had become disillusioned with the efficacy of contracts, the seriousness of lawyers who draw them up and are then half-hearted in defending them, and the loyalty of musicians you have befriended, nurtured and developed.

I decided to step aside from the helter-skelter of trying to influence the destiny of rock and roll, though I have never lost the passion that informs that music. Living in Birmingham, the UK Capital of Rock and Roll, how could I?

I determined to go back to one of my first loves, mainstream, straightahead jazz, correctly played by the finest musicians. I wanted to go back to the fountainhead which to me meant Kansas City rather than New Orleans, Chicago, New York or Los Angeles, anything that bore the handprint of William James Basie, better known as the Count. I had been in touch for a long time with former Basie trombone genius, Dicky Wells, who had fallen on hard times and had been working in New York as a bank messenger. Thanks to Humphrey Lyttelton I had met that most cultured of mainstream trumpet players, Buck Clayton. Top tenor saxophonists Illinois Jacquet, Buddy Tate and Plas Johnson were all around, available and on top of their game.

This was where I wanted to be, bringing in the guys I considered the most important jazz players. I soon encountered what turned out to be an insurmountable barrier. It worked like this. I applied to the Home Office for a work permit for one of the jazz musicians. The plan was to bring them in one at a time to feature with a British rhythm section – and, believe me, we had as fine a selection of rhythm teams as anywhere in the world, including the U.S. The Home Office said that they could do nothing without the approval of the Musicians' Union who said fine, go ahead – all you have to do, as decreed by their stifling agreement with the AFM (the American Federation of Musicians), is to book the equivalent number of man days for British musicians in the States.

7. Blues And The Bear

This was the famous, but utterly unrealistic, Exchange System. Could anyone, while keeping a straight face, honestly believe that the Ted Heath Orchestra, fine band as it was, would be as attractive to American audiences as the Count Basie Orchestra was in Britain? As I had no reasonable way of booking British musicians into America, this put me on hold. The logic that booking one American frontman would provide gigs for three accompanying British players seemed to escape them.

I was going through this rant, albeit with a more than necessary number of expletives, at the 100 Club bar with blues guru Mike Leadbitter when he proposed an alternative tack. Go the Equity route, he advised, with VAEC contracts which applied to variety artists. 'Don't bring them in as bluesmen,' he advised, 'call them variety artists/entertainers.' I was interested. After all it had worked in 1948 when Duke Ellington had toured as a variety act with singer Kay Davis and trumpeter/violinist/singer Ray Nance who was admitted as a dancer – but then not many jazzmen had the range of talents of Nance, known as 'Floorshow'!

I put it to Equity – 'no problem', they said – then to the folks at the Home Office who thought this sounded nice – and suddenly I was back in business. This simple change of direction resulted in some 40 tours with a similar number of American blues musicians and singers who came to include Lightnin' Slim, Whispering Smith, Tommy Tucker, Mickey Baker, Willie Mabon, Doctor Ross – The Harmonica Boss, Homesick James, Billy Boy Arnold and a whole lot more. We managed to record pretty much all of the bluesmen, resulting in Chicago-based *Living Blues*, the world's leading blues publication, writing that 'the finest collection of American blues recordings of the 1970s probably belongs in the archives of the small recording company from Birmingham, England, Big Bear Records.'

My first venture was with Detroit-based Eddie Burns, singer, harmonica player and guitarist who had served both on the road and on record with John Lee Hooker. I was sidetracked somewhat during my preparations for Eddie's tour by the offer from Paramount to tour the Canadian King Biscuit Boy. But I was already having difficulty selling dates on Eddie Burns. I figured that the problems were two-fold. Firstly the standard response from university social secretaries and venue promoters to the name Eddie Burns was to ask if this was the guy from *77 Sunset Strip*. Edd 'Kookie' Byrnes was a big star at that time.

The other drawback seemed to be the ordinariness of the name. Eddie Burns, for Heaven's sake, could be the guy who fixes your exhaust at Halford's or – drawing himself up to his full height – Edward Burns sounds like your lawyer who is going to shaft you sooner or later – but don't worry, he won't forget to bill you. Eddie had sent me his publicity photographs, specially taken for this tour, his first outside of America. He was pictured looking extremely dapper, smiling, holding a nice Gretsch guitar. Unfortunately the photograph had been printed in reverse, making him appear to be a left hander playing a hcsterg guitar.

In those days bluesmen seemed to be considered more authentic if they worked under some romantic or earthy nickname, probably reflecting some physical defect or other. But Eddie appeared to be remarkably healthy, as, indeed, he turned out to be. So, displaying a singular lack of creative thinking, I re-christened him Eddie 'Guitar' Burns which luckily seemed to do the trick. I filled a seven-week datesheet with a total of 47 performances: colleges, clubs and broadcasts.

I was in my usual position at the bar of the 100 Club in London, ready to pick up Eddie on the Red Eye in from Detroit the next morning, with the usual 100 Club Blues Mafia, Mikes Leadbitter and Rowe and the rest. Everyone was quite excited that Eddie was on his way. Mike Leadbitter was recounting the recordings on which Eddie had featured, then paused to say he considered Eddie to be a fine singer and a top-notch harmonica player, but didn't know that he played guitar.

You can imagine my relief when Eddie came through Arrivals at Heathrow carrying his big old guitar case. Actually Mike Leadbitter did have it dead right, as usual. Eddie had one of the finest blues voices and his harmonica work was straight out of the top drawer. In truth he wasn't the greatest guitar player, though he derived a lot of pleasure from playing it.

At tour's end in February 1972 I took Eddie into Chalk Farm Recording Studios to cut his, and Big Bear Records', first ever album. Chalk Farm was known as the UK's home of reggae, the studio of choice for Trojan Records where they recorded the likes of Desmond Dekker, John Holt and Dandy Livingstone.

On Eddie's album *Bottle Up and Go* we used a band built around pianist Bob Hall, who served with such bands as Savoy Brown and The Groundhogs, and bass guitarist Bob Brunning who were both to become regular Big Bear session musicians over the new few years, plus drummer John Hunt. On this occasion we added as guests Chicago boogie piano player Erwin Helfer, who was in the UK for a few days before going out on the next Big Bear tour, and the fine tenor saxophone player and jazz author Dave Gelly.

This was only my second album as a producer and the surroundings could not have been more different from the first which was in the rarefied atmosphere of EMI's Abbey Road studios, with lab-coated tape operators, assistants in abundance and no less a person than George Harrison quietly listening at the back of the studio. That was The Dog that Bit People, a contender for the Rock Charts. This was The Blues and I couldn't have found a better home in which to record. Over the years I was to record some 15 albums in the rough and ready

7. Blues And The Bear

North London studios which I had chosen because I liked the way the studio captured those tough rhythm sounds of Trojan's reggae bands.

The Eddie Burns session was a bunch of fun. Everyone was relaxed, playing at the top of their game, and Eddie sang his tail off. Mike Leadbitter, ever the most discerning of reviewers, wrote, 'There is much criticism, usually of a scathing nature, for integrated blues recordings on British soil, usually rightly so, but this one, thanks to a sympathetic producer and well-rehearsed sidemen, is about near-perfect. This album will, in time, become a significant milestone for Anglo-American blues, establishing the name of Eddie "Guitar" Burns far outside the confines of Motown and greatly helping the new Blues Revival that is currently getting under way.'

The rest of the year was spent on the road through Britain and Europe with a series of tours, notably that of former Excello Records star, Lightnin' Slim. Over the next couple of years Slim became a Big Bear regular on this side of the Atlantic, his down-home guitar playing and laconic vocals winning him an army of fans.

We had found him through the efforts of the ever-helpful Detroit-based blues authority Fred Reif. Slim, whose real name was Otis Hicks, was born on a farm outside St. Louis, Missouri, moved to Baton Rouge, Louisiana, at the age of 13 to work as a farmhand and grew to be the undisputed King of the Louisiana Swamp Blues. His recordings for Excello, particularly *Rooster Blues* which reached Number 23 on the national R&B charts in 1959, best captured the raw, primitive swamp blues of his adopted state. In the 1960s, discovering that he was being cheated out of record royalties, Slim gave up performing and moved North. When we located him through Fred Reif, he was working in a foundry in Pontiac, Michigan, and didn't even own a guitar.

With a new guitar and a new cool wardrobe Lightnin' Slim went back on the road in 1972 in the first of his three Big Bear Eurotours, and in the short time left to him he never had to return to the factory, but remained a working musician.

Slim was a kind, gentle and humorous man. He didn't enjoy the best of health, but always went out of his way to help me whenever he could. He was blessed with an indomitable spirit. When we overnighted in the North Brabant town of Tilburg, some of us decided to walk over to a club to hear some local blues. It was a fair walk, maybe 30 minutes, but Slim insisted on coming along, despite me trying to persuade him to rest in the hotel. On the way back he dropped further and further behind. I joined him as he was clearly in some difficulty. I'll never forget him driving himself by constantly muttering, 'Feets, don't fail me now. Feets, don't fail me now.'

He was constantly concerned about my welfare, saying I worked too hard: 'Son, you're a young man, you s'posed to have some fun.' He would always bring in some beer and sandwiches when I was working and sometimes he would 'do some lawyering' for me. That entailed him approaching a girl and asking her to come over and talk to me, figuring I could use the female company after a day of driving and humping gear. Invariably the girl would find him interesting and spend the evening talking to him, not me.

So often, with Big Bear, a single chance opportunity has led on to much more significant outcomes that I could have foreseen. This time it happened when Rob Cowlyn, who worked part-time for Big Bear co-ordinating tours, decided to buy himself a bus and seek work roadying for local bands. Equipped with a spanking new Mercedes 10-seater splitter bus and finding no work was coming in, he started to fret over the repayments. Suddenly it all seemed to make sense. Rob had a van, it would be good to help him out, I was having fun touring American bluesmen, so why not use the bus to put together a travelling blues festival? So we set about booking the dates on a tour that would do justice to this brand new bus, a thing of beauty despite its revolting green paint job!

In January 1973 I checked six American bluesmen into an Edgbaston hotel and routined our programme for two days with Brummies Roger Hill and Tom Farnell who were to be, as bass guitarist and drummer respectively, part of the touring package. Then we set off, much in the spirit of the Duke of Medina Sidonia in 1588 when he sent the Spanish Armada to invade England 'in the confident hope of a miracle'.

From January 26th to March 1st 1973, American Blues Legends '73 toured the UK and Europe, appearing before 35,000 people in 33 concerts in 35 days. The show played ten countries, appeared on three television and seven radio shows and recorded an album for Big Bear. The musicians were Lightnin' Slim, Whispering Smith, Homesick James, Snooky Pryor, Boogie Woogie Red and Washboard Willie. Smith, Slim's erstwhile Excello Records harmonica player, the subject of Slim's often-recorded 'Play your harmonica, son' exhortation, was born in Brookhaven, Mississippi. Snooky, harmonica player from Lambert, Mississippi, and guitarist Homesick James from Somerville, Tennessee, were both hugely influential Chicago veterans with Snooky's *Telephone Blues* on Planet Records in 1948 the first recorded amplified blues harmonica. Homesick claimed to be the creator of *Dust My Broom* which later elevated his younger cousin Elmore James to the status of blues legend. Like so many things in blues history it's impossible to verify (Homesick's year of birth, for instance, was variously placed between 1905 and 1924 and he used at least three surnames), but Homesick seems to have been

American Blues Legends '73: returning to rehearsal after lunch, (l-r) Lightnin' Slim, Boogie Woogie Red, Snooky Prior, Whispering Smith, Washboard Willie, JS.

associated with Robert Johnson at the time he made the initial recording of (as it then was) *I Believe I'm Gonna Dust My Broom*, so who knows the truth of his claim? Piano player Boogie Woogie Red from Rayville, Louisiana, had relocated to Detroit, as had Washboard Willie from Phoenix City, Alabama.

If the recording at what had become our hometown Chalk Farm Studios went well, it must be admitted that the tour itself was not without incident. Early on Snooky and Slim had emerged as the elder statesmen. The ever-amiable Snooky adopted the title Little Bear and delighted in introducing himself as my brother, maybe because we looked so much alike! Slim assumed the responsibility of taking care of business, correcting other musicians whom he thought were stepping out of line. Mostly, that is!

There was an occasion, after an arduous drive from a performance in Liege in the extreme east of Belgium, with treacherous roads throughout, when I had to break up a fight between Slim and Boogie Woogie Red on the icy quayside at Zeebrugge while we were waiting for the Dover ferry. They had bought a bottle of cognac between them, polished it off on the journey and then started arguing about

Don't Worry 'Bout The Bear

Boss of the Louisiana swamp guitar, Lightnin' Slim, with his long-time cohort, Moses 'Whispering' Smith.

who had drunk the most, each accusing the other of having more than his fair share. And now there they were, in a bitter wind blowing off the sea, swinging punches that never quite landed and doing more harm to themselves than the other as they slipped over on the frozen quayside. Things didn't properly settle down until we had boarded and they were able to buy another bottle between them.

Moses Smith was the quiet one, smiling, taciturn, never giving away too much of himself. A serious, dignified man, he was a pleasure to be with. Killingly cool and hip on stage, he plied his trade building swimming pools in his hometown of Baton Rouge whenever no calls came to play the blues. Washboard Willie, back home in Detroit, drove a school bus for a living, unable even in a city of that size to get enough gigs to keep body and soul together. Boogie Woogie Red wasn't prepared to do anything else but play piano and sing, and why should he? He was a fine musician and a consummate entertainer who scuffled a living in the clubs, cabarets and dives of Detroit's underbelly. A most amiable man, I suspect he was never able to live with the dignity of a decent income, but I never heard him complain as long as there were a bed to sleep in, a piano to play and a bar not too far away. Food? That was probably a different matter.

7. Blues And The Bear

Homesick James Williamson, probably born William Henderson, was an enigma. He claimed to have fought in France during World War II in a black regiment which, he delighted to recount, put the fear of God into the German infantry when they descended on them, bayonets fixed, screaming wildly. Homesick said the Germans thought they were being attacked by apes. Given the Nazi propaganda about the sub-human status of blacks, this just might have been true, especially as the more level-headed Snooky Pryor backed up Homesick's story. As for the African-Americans themselves, Homesick claimed they screamed so loud because they were just so terrified.

Home would slap his leg and say that it was twisted because of a wound sustained in France. His leg certainly was dodgy and kinked as he walked or, more accurately, lurched. He did have something of a drink problem. When in his cups, which he usually was about the time the curtain rose, he became difficult, at first refusing to go onstage, then, later, refusing to come off. Slim would be very helpful on most occasions, but Home could very easily overstep the mark and I often had to read the Riot Act, though by the next morning it was always forgotten.

On one occasion in Stockholm I had to give him a real talking-to, of the 'You're on the first flight back to Chicago tomorrow morning' variety. Not unusually he tried to make up for his demeanour by playing a stormer. My telling off must have sounded as if I meant it because that night he pulled out all the stops, playing with guitar held behind his head, playing with his teeth, dropping to his knees with a drama that James Brown would have envied, all the time watching me, standing side-stage, to assess whether he had done enough for me to forgive him – which I actually had before he'd played a note. It has to be remembered that this was not a young man, all heart, it's true, but anything but fit, by no means sober and with a gammy leg. He suddenly realised that there he was, on his knees, onstage, in front of 800 people and unable to get to his feet. Responding to what had become an imploring gaze, two stagehands, despatched by the ever-attentive Lightnin' Slim, picked him up and put him back on his feet. Encouraged by the massive applause, the old rascal this time dropped down, rolled over onto his back and lay there, still playing guitar. The crowd went wild, unsurprisingly, and the look he gave me on the way back to the dressing-room, having been hoisted to his feet a second time, was one of pure triumph.

For someone like me who spent so much time with American blues musicians, the ban on the use of the n-word can be confusing. The word was in common use among the blues guys, even as a standard greeting. It was around the time of the Blues Legends tours that African-American Barbara Morrison cut *Nigger, Please* with the Johnny Otis Show.

Homesick James Williamson.

7. Blues And The Bear

Mickey Baker, a most cultured, well-read and educated musician, used it to describe less sophisticated African-Americans. Mickey was one of my favourite people. When American Blues Legends '73 played the Salle Pleyel in Paris, Mickey turned up, as he always did to our shows in the city. The group had been on the road together for five or six weeks, all pretence at polite behaviour had gone, so, when Mickey came into the dressing room, he was witness to all the squabbling that goes on between people who are over-familiar with each other. After listening to the unedifying level of conversation for a time, Mickey put on his stern face and said, 'Jim, I need to speak to you,' gesturing outside. Unsure as to why he seemed so upset, I followed and was relieved to see him visibly relax. 'How do you work with them niggers?' Mickey said. And I'm sure he wasn't just referring to the colour of their skin.

There were more Blues Legends tours over the subsequent years, the final one coming in 1979, but that first one was a real adventure. We really did feel, to steal a line from the wonderful *Blues Brothers* film, that we were 'on a mission from God'. Personally my eyes were opened: it was a real education travelling, living and working with those difficult, obstreperous, bickering, argumentative, wonderful, lovable bluesmen for some seven weeks.

Taking a break somewhere in North Germany, (l-r) Eddie 'Playboy' Taylor, Big John Wrencher, Cousin Joe, Doctor Ross, JS, George G.P. Jackson, flanked by the sound crew.

Don't Worry 'Bout The Bear

When I first watched *The Blues Brothers*, the favourite movie of most of the people I count as friends, I was particularly taken by the scene in Matt Murphy's eaterie where Belushi orders two chickens. Aretha Franklin asks if that will be chicken breasts or chicken legs, to which he replies, 'No, ma'am, that's two whole chickens.' This was something with which I'm familiar. On the road with Chicago-based bluesman Eddie Playboy Taylor on a subsequent blues tour I was witness to that conversation on an almost daily basis, and, yes, he did eat two whole chickens in one sitting. I'm convinced that Eddie was the inspiration for that part of the film's script.

Quite often we had blues tours scheduled almost back to back. One Spring I had seen Lightnin' Slim off to Detroit from Amsterdam Schiphol and was due to pick up Doctor Ross from Brussels Zaventem just three days later. There was no point in driving back to Birmingham, so I scuttled off to my usual bolt-hole, the small seaside town of Knokke on the Belgian coast, leaving Kate to run the office. I would take a hotel by the sea, catch up on the usual mountain of paperwork until maybe 8 o'clock, then go to a neighbouring bar for a bite to eat and a Belgian beer or two. One evening, the bar I chose was unlike any of the others I had been in. Every bit of wall-space was filled with Marvin Gaye ephemera: photographs, album sleeves, magazine covers. Obviously the bar owner was a fan of Marvin Gaye, but, when I commented approvingly on his taste and discernment, he grunted, 'Not really.' Questioned further, he explained without enthusiasm that this was Marvin's favourite bar, he came in most nights, was usually here by now and was certain to arrive soon. Naturally I didn't believe him, but a glass or two of Liefmans later I began to wonder. The barman assured me he was serious and I settled down to wait. Come 10 o'clock, with no Marvin in view, I decided it was simply a ploy to get customers to stay longer than they intended.

Some years later, after Marvin had been shot dead by his own father, I watched a documentary about him where it explained that, in order to escape the attentions of some hoodlums back home, he had taken refuge for some time in the Belgian resort of Knokke-le-Zoute. If only I had had the faith to believe what the barman had told me! I might have spent the evening getting gently drunk with Marvellous Marvin Gaye, become his lifelong pal and persuaded him to come out with us on tour with Doctor Ross – another, though less exalted, resident of Detroit!

Over the years Big Bear Records were lucky enough to record three million-selling blues-rooted musicians, but not lucky enough to have their hit records on the label. Even so I still don't get it that Tommy Tucker, Willie Mabon and Mickey Baker were ever in a position where I could approach them, let alone take them into the recording studio.

7. Blues And The Bear

The key things that they all had in common were their high levels of musical ability, their sophistication and their intelligence. Maybe anyone can get a hit record purely by chance, but it clearly enhances your prospects if you properly understand music and are smart enough to craft a good lyric.

That fine piano player, singer and songwriter Tommy Tucker's *Hi Heel Sneakers* on Chicago's Checker Records was one of the great rhythm and blues records of its time. I had always been amazed that they could capture so much drive with no bass player. When he was touring with Blues Legends '75, I told him how much I loved that recording and asked how he came up with the idea of using a chunky guitar, the heavy accent on the bass drum and the left hand of the piano part instead of a bass. Tommy gave me his quizzical look and growled, 'Motherfucker didn't show.'

How America's record companies didn't snap up such an obvious talent will always be a mystery. When we got together in 1975, he was at the top of his game, singing, playing and performing. He also had a bunch of strong songs, including *Alimony* which would have been a grand follow-up to *Sneakers*. I have the greatest respect for Leonard Chess, Sam Phillips and Ahmet Ertegun who operated

On the road again! This time with (l-r) Lonesome Jimmie Lee Robinson, Eddie 'Guitar' Burns, Billy Boy Arnold, Little Joe Blue and (front) Tommy Tucker, JS, Homesick James.

Chess, Sun and Atlantic respectively, along with Sue my favourite record labels, but not to sign Tommy Tucker? That is bordering on the criminal.

Tommy seemed to be a bit of a lost soul. When we finished the 1975 American Blues Legends tour with Eddie 'Guitar' Burns, Billy Boy Arnold, Homesick James, Little Joe Blue and Lonesome Jimmie Lee Robinson, he was at a loose end and came to stay with me for a few days, gathering his thoughts, I imagine, before going back to New York. I seem to recall him being preoccupied with some hassle about his copyrights. He seemed to want an uncomplicated non-litigious lifestyle, playing and singing.

Much of his adult life seemed to be anything but trouble-free. His hit, *Hi Heel Sneakers*, the last blues number 1 on Checker, was in 1964. By the end of the 1960s he had quit the music business and was working in real estate and as a journalist. When I contacted him for American Blues Legends he said that he hadn't been working in music – which to me is inexplicable. Apparently his ridiculously early death in 1982 at the age of 48 came about when the chemicals with which he was tending the floor gave off lethal toxic fumes – or, perhaps, according to another theory, it was food poisoning. Either way, I'm still angry at the neglect of such an immense talent.

There is a Big Bear album that captures Tommy and the guys in full flight. Attracted by the opportunity to view Tommy Tucker at close range, Jon Lord of Deep Purple, Martin Stone of Savoy Brown and Harvey Weston of the Alex Welsh Band all made appearances on the album, recorded live on Virgin mobile at the 100 Club in May, 1975.

Willie Mabon recorded the first Number One for Chess Records. In 1952 his *I Don't Know* smashed its way to the top of the *Billboard* charts where it remained for eight weeks and a quarter century later was featured in *The Blues Brothers* movie. In between is the story of a major, but neglected, talent, that of Memphis-born, Chicago-based pianist/singer Willie Mabon. A former US marine, by 1949 Willie was in Chicago, recording first for Apollo Records ('I didn't get paid nothing for that') and then for Chess.

After *I Don't Know* hit, Willie signed for a nationwide tour and then moved to New York to be managed by the legendary Joe Glaser, manager of Louis Armstrong. Willie had two more chart successes, the second of them the tongue-in-cheek *Poison Ivy*, later covered with huge success by The Coasters. His recording of the Willie Dixon classic, *Seventh Son*, was cited by Mose Allison as his major influence, but it didn't hit and Willie was dropped by Chess.

Chess Records, founded by Leonard Chess, born Lejzor Czyz in Poland, became a legendary force in the recording industry. Chicago's black blues musicians would refer to Chess as Cadillac Records in reference to Leonard's habit of rewarding a big hit with a Cadillac. Willie Mabon seems to have fallen victim to a policy of three hits, one flop and you're out – almost an unaccountable as dropping Tommy Tucker, a singer who had shared top billing with Ray Charles on a coast to coast tour.

I first heard Willie Mabon in Paris playing in a small restaurant. I was staying with Mickey Baker in his swish Place de Bastille apartment when Peter Chatman – aka Memphis Slim – called to ask us to go over and listen to Mabon. He wasn't singing, just playing background blues piano to an audience of maybe 20 people who neither knew nor cared about who they were listening to. The piano was pushed against the wall, with Willie playing with his back to the audience.

Willie Mabon looked great, as he always did, and, most importantly, he was playing well. Before we left the restaurant that night, we had put together the recording schedule and spent the next day working on the repertoire, agreeing keys, tempos and arrangements, and deciding on the other musicians.

Willie told me, 'I just quit music completely for four years. I got disgusted, too many disappointments, so I went to truck driving. In '69 I went back to playing and decided that later on I would get the chance to record more things.' Things didn't improve a lot, although he did record a single for Checker in 1969 and an album for Al Smith's Blues on Blues label in 1972, but it wasn't enough to sustain him and he kept on with the day job.

On September 24th 1972 Willie Mabon finally quit trucking and flew to Paris on a ticket bought for him by Memphis Slim. He arrived with little money and a lot of hope, and, of course, the invaluable support of Memphis Slim who knew just about everything and everyone to do with the blues on this side of the Atlantic.

We recorded Willie's Big Bear album, *The Comeback*, over several sessions in January, February and March the next year. Eleven of the songs were Mabon's, the twelfth, the title song of the album, by Memphis Slim. We had to fit the recording around Mabon's burgeoning datesheet – Mickey had fixed a residency at Les Trois Mailletz – and we quickly put together a series of UK dates.

The studio sessions rocked. Mickey featured on guitar and the bass player was American Dan Armstrong, famed as an innovative guitar maker and as a possible subject for the song *You're So Vain* by his former lover Carly Simon. We added the charting group Arrival for the backing vocals and at the end of a take when one of them hit a particularly high note, I bounded out of the control room to congratulate the girl singer, Dyan Birch. 'It wasn't me,' she replied, 'it was Frank (Collins)!'

Willie Mabon was undoubtedly a class act. He wrote great songs, was a masterful piano player, inspired by his mentor Sunnyland Slim, and his laid back, cooler than cool vocal style has been much imitated, notably by Mose Allison who in turn passed the baton to Georgie Fame. Willie remained in Paris, featuring at clubs and festivals, playing concerts and occasionally recording, until his death in 1985 following a long illness. He was 59 years old.

McHouston Baker, born in Louisville, Kentucky, in 1925, was no stranger to hard times. Known wherever Rhythm and Blues is spoken as Mickey Baker, he became one of the most influential of guitarists in the popular music of the 1950s before reinventing himself as a bluesman in the 1970s.

His mother was 12 when he was born; his father, an itinerant white pianist, was long gone. As a kid he was the wild one, stealing, hustling and regularly in fights over the taunts his yellowish complexion brought. His aunt was turning tricks, but, Mickey said, couldn't stand close contact with men she didn't know. So, between them, they came up with a plan whereby she would lure a potential John into an alleyway where the 12-year-old Mickey was lurking. Mickey would whack the victim over the head with a baseball bat and they would both scarper after rifling the victim's pockets.

Finding that the career prospects for such a profession were not good, Mickey, who by the age of five had already determined to be a jazz trumpet player, made his way to New York. He remembered, 'I stayed in a detention centre for three months when I was 11 for stealing. Then they sent me to an orphan home, but I kept running away and they kept sending me back. But, when I got to New York, the war had started so the authorities let me alone.'

In New York Mickey found work washing dishes and his first objective was to raise 200 dollars he needed for a rather grisly purpose. Mickey was embarrassed by a lazy eye which could have been corrected with therapy. He worked and saved hard to get 200 dollars to pay the hospital to remove his right eye. Which they did without question. He was 15 years old.

Still working washing dishes, Mickey had been talked into buying a guitar by some smooth-talking salesman when he had gone into the shop to buy a trumpet. Indefatigable as always, he set about learning to play guitar properly, taking lessons with a local guitar teacher, though he was hindered somewhat as his new acquisition had a twisted neck, making tuning difficult. After each lesson he made and kept copious notes which became very useful when, in a later life, he began writing his series of guitar tutor books, *The Complete Course in Jazz Guitar*, still in print after more than 50 years, having inspired tens of thousands of young musicians worldwide.

Still determined to make it as a jazz musician, Mickey got the guitar chair in a combo setting off from New York on a coast-to-coast tour. They didn't make it,

7. Blues And The Bear

McHouston (Mickey) Baker from Birmingham, Alabama, taking care of business in Coventry, Warwickshire.

running out of gigs, food and determination before reaching California. When Mickey hitched to Oakland, California, and tried to hustle up a gig, someone advised him to go see Pee Wee Crayton and his band – his first encounter with the blues. Mickey was more impressed with the bandleader's white Cadillac Eldorado than he was with the music, reportedly going up to Crayton and demanding, 'How come a chickenshit guitarist like you gets to drive a short (car) like that?'

From that moment Mickey Baker's guitar style broadened to take in the blues and rhythm and blues for which he became known. Back in New York, he was heard by Jerry Wexler who offered him the job of house guitarist for Atlantic Records. Fame came quickly. Mickey's skilful guitar playing was enhancing the recordings that established Atlantic as just about the coolest record company in town, as well as being widely featured on recordings by Savoy and King. On tracks such as Ruth Brown's *Mama, He Treats Your Daughter Mean* and numerous recordings by Nappy Brown, The Coasters, The Drifters, Little Willie John, Ray Charles, Big Joe Turner, The Platters and LaVern Baker, Mickey's fluid guitar was always to the fore.

Mickey was giving guitar lessons to the voluptuous and extremely determined Sylvia Vanderpool when he wrote the extraordinary *Love is Strange*. Released by RCA Groove in 1957 as by Mickey and Sylvia, it became a multi-million seller and topped the Rhythm and Blues charts, catapulting Mickey and Sylvia into a major attraction. *Love is Strange* has had a very full after-life, appearing on a UK Top 3 album by Lonnie Donegan and also charting for the Everly Brothers, Peaches and Herb, Kenny Rogers and Dolly Parton, and Everything but the Girl. I was in the office of Essex Music's publishing boss David Platz when he was allocating copyrights for the first Wings album, *Wild Life*. *Love is Strange* was on the album and he noted with some amusement that someone in the McCartney office had named Stella McCartney as composer. David corrected that on the proposed single release by Wings which never materialised for some reason.

Mickey and Sylvia became a top onstage draw and Mickey also was occupied with his never-ending recording session work when he made a discovery that was to initiate a major change in his life. Sylvia, who married Platinum Records boss Joe Robinson and later, as Sylvia Robinson, hit with *Pillow Talk*, had a more sophisticated business head than Mickey which came home to him with considerable impact when he discovered royalty statements for *Love is Strange* sales that had been hidden from him. He was already only too aware that he was being exploited, angry at the treatment of blacks in general in the USA, and this was the final straw.

Mickey told me that he had long been intrigued by the reports of the success of Josephine Baker in Europe and how Paris had taken her to its heart – and, after all,

7. Blues And The Bear

she was black *and* a Baker like himself. Almost overnight, he gathered together all the money he could and, with his suitcase in one hand, guitar in the other, he boarded the S.S. *France* for Le Havre, knowing little of the country, to start a new life.

Taking the train to Paris, Mickey made his way to the offices of Barclay Records, having enquired which was the most important French record company – he wasn't interested in doing business with anyone who had links to American labels. Mickey told me that he marched up to reception and asked to speak to Eddie Barclay. He was asked to wait and offered a cup of coffee which mightily impressed him. He said that that was the moment that he became certain that he had made the right decision.

Many years later Barclay told me that his secretary came in and told him that there was an American to see him: his name was Mickey Baker and he said that he played guitar. Eddie said that he bounded out of his office, clasped Mickey with both arms, welcomed him to Paris and assured him that Disques Barclay was now his home. Mickey was immediately put on a retainer, Eddie found him an apartment and the next phase of his career opened before him. He was to appear on French hit recordings by Johnny Hallyday and many others.

Mickey once told me that, whenever things were a little quiet on the gigging and recording front, he would rent a cottage on top of some French mountain and take off for a month, write another guitar tutor book and pick up a thousand dollar advance.

In 1972 I was at the Nancy Jazz Festival with Doctor Ross, the Harmonica Boss, and more than a little excited to see that the venerated Mickey Baker was also to star at the festival. At that time I knew about the Mickey and Sylvia hit, the first time, I think, that anyone had ever recorded a distorted guitar sound, and, of course, I knew of his essential contribution to a string of Atlantic, Savoy and King records, and I couldn't but wonder what sort of band Mickey Baker would be fronting.

The Doc and I arrived at the musicians' hotel at around the time Mickey was due to start his set at an address on the edge of town. I saw the Doc to his room, dumped my luggage and grabbed a cab. I had written down the name of the venue – Carrefour which at the time meant nothing to me – and handed it to the cabbie. A 20-minute ride later, I was staring at a supermarket and insisting to the cabbie that this was not the right place.

However, it was.

Mickey was playing a solo blues spot in the supermarket's café, albeit to an audience of maybe 150 people. He was, by the way, absolutely stunning and I soon forgot about the unusual location. Over the following days Mickey must have thought I was stalking him, popping up at breakfast, dinner and every gig he played. From the moment I heard him play the not-so-primitive (in Mickey's hands) *Make Your Bed Up, Mama,* and *Blues Fell this Morning,* I knew that I had to record Mickey Baker for Big Bear Records. Luckily he saw this as no bad thing. At the end of the Doctor Ross tour I visited Mickey in Paris and found him one of the most interesting people I ever met. He was wildly amusing, musically fascinating, easily enraged at anything he saw as improper, particularly the exploitation of the poor and weak. His French wife, Monique, with whom he had a daughter, was the perfect partner for this at times explosive, at others hilarious, man. Time spent with Mickey was never boring.

In those days, as I recall, a French rule of the road required that main road traffic had to give way to that joining from the right. Driving us both to a gig in his peppy Renault 16, Mickey seemed to disregard this a couple of times when he cut up cars joining from the right until finally a car appeared directly in front of him, making him take sudden evasive action.

'Where did he come from? Goddam French drivers!' cursed Mickey. When I remarked that actually the offending car's intentions had been clear from a distance away, he growled, 'My goddam nose!' It took a few seconds for me to realise what he meant and then I collapsed in laughter. It was his right eye that had been surgically removed and the remaining eye couldn't see over what, one had to admit, was an unusually protruding nose! From that moment I took on the role of passenger seat driver.

I've always been amazed that Mickey Baker is not a household name when you consider his immense contribution to popular music guitar styles. In the 1950s his was the archetypal electric guitar, heard on hundreds of New York rhythm and blues records which were to help to turn a ghetto culture into the root of a youth-based popular music.

When I first knew him in France, he was really enjoying a journey of discovery, delving backwards into the blues. 'Not just the B.B. King kinda thing, but Robert Johnson, Son House, the heavy things, these are the deep roots,' said Mickey. I hope that, on his Big Bear album, *Take a Look Inside*, we properly captured Mickey's extremely musical take on what is, essentially, a fairly primitive music. Tony Cummings, feature writer with *Black Music* magazine, wrote, 'In this quite extraordinary album, Baker plays acoustic bottleneck in the same expert manner as his elegant electric. Here is a man who has fully absorbed the country blues; listen to his stunning intro to *Make Your Bed Up, Mama*, the pure sound of the Delta. Doesn't *New York, New York* perfectly personify the backstreet life of the performers and isn't *Take a Look Inside* with its charging gospelesque choir the very embodiment of joyous fervour? It is fitting that

7. Blues And The Bear

Mickey Baker, the legendary father of the modern Rhythm & Blues guitar, should lead the journey back to an earlier kind of musical truth.'

The year before we recorded the album I had Mickey with Lightnin' Slim and Eddie 'Guitar' Burns booked into the 1972 Lanchester Arts Festival in Coventry as a support act for Chuck Berry. We had spent the day at my house talking about the upcoming show until the three of them got into singing dubious lyrics from their youth, taking it in turns to play Mickey's acoustic. The song that caused most hilarity was *My Ding-a-Ling* which had a particularly spicy lyric. That night, in the dressing room with Chuck, they were all fooling around with him, exchanging reminiscences, and again that song amused all four of them. It would be good to see Chuck's original set-list because my guess is he included it in his set as a direct result of these off-stage shenanigans. Whatever, a cleaned up version of *My Ding-a-Ling*, recorded live that night, became Chuck Berry's only Number 1 on the *Billboard* Hot 100.

Mickey continued to work with Big Bear, playing concerts and festivals. He wrote some terrific arrangements for Eddie 'Guitar' Burns' second album, *Detroit Blackbottom*, and led the band for *Let the Good Times Roll* by The Mighty Flea.

I always got a lift from putting together singers and musicians who had not previously worked together and, in most cases, had never even heard of each other. On *Detroit Blackbottom* I felt something different was needed to add colour to the wonderfully primitive guitar and vocal country blues performance of *Mississippi County Farm*. After much thought I asked Mickey if he would come up with a Salvation Army brass band arrangement, to which he replied, 'Salvation What!'. I explained, he got the drift and wrote some classy parts, and we overdubbed an eight-piece brass band consisting of jazzers such as George Chisholm and Colin Smith in my total ignorance of straight brass players. It was neither authentic nor completely free from jazz inflection, but it sounded wonderful to me.

Mickey, living in Paris, was never far away when I needed unusual arrangements. We took advantage of any opportunity for me to visit him in Paris or him to come to Birmingham, though with all respect to my home city I always thought Mickey got the fuzzy end of the lollypop.

In his later years Mickey, placed at Number 53 in the *Rolling Stone's* list of the 100 Greatest Guitarists, left Paris for Montastruc-la-Conseillere near Toulouse where he lived until his death in 2012 at the age of 87.

Chapter 8

NOT SO FOOLISH AS I'M BADLY DRESSED

The arrival of Cousin Joe was a moment that had been a long time coming. Endless letters across the Atlantic, near-weekly phone calls to and from a payphone in a drugstore in the Vieux Carre district of New Orleans, confusion over the real name on the work permit application – but now he was here, and I wasn't disappointed! Bursting through the Arrivals gate at Heathrow, suited, hatted and booted in bright red, radiating an almost visible energy, came the object of my attention, Cousin Joe on the Red Eye from New Orleans.

Unfortunately the joy of actually meeting each other after six months of communicating was not mutual. Figuring from my silly grin that I must be the guy he was looking for, he strutted over and, pointing his finger at my chest, questioned, 'You Jim Simpson?... I travel 3000 miles, get no sleep, get off the plane, and what do I find? My manager's a goddam hippie!'

As I was to find out over 14 tours, innumerable radio and television broadcasts and recordings, nothing fazed Cousin Joe for long. At heart he was a most kindly and courteous man, always making fun, often of himself, and loyal beyond reason.

Cousin Joe, Joseph Pleasant, Pleasant Joe, Brother Joshua, Smiling Joe and Pleasant Joseph – he responded to all these names, though he was properly known to his huge European following as Cousin Joe from New Orleans. He was born in Wallace, Louisiana, in December 1907, moving with his family to New Orleans at around two years of age. He sang in church, taught himself ukulele, then guitar, and found himself working in the fields cutting sugar cane. 'That's not for me,' he told me, 'those fields ain't even air-conditioned.' He grew up playing rough two-fisted barrelhouse piano which contrasted nicely with his cool, sophisticated, usually hilarious blues-rooted vocals, in the gambling houses of New Orleans, as well as a spell on the riverboat S.S. *Dixie* out of New Orleans. In 1942 he moved to New York and began his recording career with the Mezzrow/Bechet Septet, handling the

Gospel-Wailing, Jazz-Playing, Rock'n'Rolling, Soul-Shouting, Tap-Dancing Bluesman from New Orleans… Cousin Joe!

vocals on an Earl Bostic session and with the Tiny Grimes Band. With the Mezzrow/Bechet group he recorded *Saw Mill Man Blues* for King Jazz and, as Brother Joshua, cut *Lightning Struck the Poorhouse.*

I first met Joe briefly in 1964 when he toured Europe with Lipmann and Rau's Blues and Gospel Train which was headlined by Muddy Waters, Joe's card-playing partner, and featured Otis Spann, Sister Rosetta Tharpe and Rev. Gary Davis. I photographed the show in Birmingham for *Melody Maker* and local music magazine *Midland Beat.* Joe and I kept loosely in contact and eventually I was able to bring him into the UK as a solo. In the decade or so since our last meeting, the fairly clean-cut 1960s version of me had gone through the change of image caused by prolonged exposure to Black Sabbath – hence Joe's 'goddam hippie' comment.

Seeing my car for the first time did little for Joe's confidence in me. I had an admittedly fairly cramped Jensen Healey sports car which, with careful packing, could take a vocal PA and some luggage in the boot. The rest was packed into the space behind the two seats. What it lacked in comfort it made up for in speed and

Cousin Joe sold out the then-prestigious Venue in Victoria, London, with a band including Jack Bruce, Dick Morrissey, Charlie Watts, Alexis Korner, Colin Smith and Bob Hall.

8. Not So Foolish As I'm Badly Dressed

it was a pretty neat way to tour. Joe initially hated it with a passion, telling me when to slow down, when not to overtake, monitoring every move. About four days into the tour, after a refreshment break in Aalter in Belgium, Joe had a significant change of heart. As we got back into what he referred to as a 'short', he said, 'Wait a minute. I got my London fog (a leather overcoat), a pack of cigarettes and a flask of coffee – let's go!' From that time on he encouraged me to overtake and drive faster, introducing me to bewildered folk as Willie Mosconi, the famous American race driver.

Cousin Joe might just have been the coolest, hippest character I ever worked with – or was that Clark Terry? Whatever, Joe was certainly the most colourful when it came to clothes, his songs and, particularly, his language. Probably the hippest phrase I ever heard – and even now I still don't really get its meaning – was Joe's response when offered a compliment. He would chuckle before saying, 'That's right. I ain't so foolish as I'm badly dressed.' Another phrase we all loved to hear was his braggadocio introduction, 'I'm a Gospel-wailing, Jazz-playing, Rock'n'Rolling, Soul-shouting, Tap-dancing Bluesman from New Orleans.' It's a great line, but, truth to tell, it didn't originate from Joe, but from pianist/singer/songwriter Geoff Brown. The mainstay of Big Bear recording artists, the soul band Muscles, Geoff coined it as the opening line of his song, *Cousin Joe from New Orleans* which Joe recorded with Muscles. Joe didn't care about its provenance and instantly adopted it as his. I know that Geoff didn't mind and was secretly delighted.

From where we stand now, it's difficult to remember what drove me to believe that, in an era when great singles were commonplace, we could somehow carve out hit singles from recording fairly obscure, somewhat elderly, but totally captivating, blues singers. Maybe I was arrogant or misguided enough to believe that, if it touched me, it would touch other people. Whatever the reason, we had a tilt at the pop charts with the then 67-year-old Cousin Joe, Geoff Brown's songs and Muscles' backings. What chemistry and what fun! We didn't do too badly, either, reaching BBC playlists and even registering a small hit on the French charts with *Cousin Joe from New Orleans* – the French always have superior taste when it comes to jazz and blues. Another of Geoff's songs to do well for Joe was *Never Too Old to Boogie*. We recorded four singles in all with Joe, then there were three releases from ex-Johnny Otis trombonist Gene 'The Mighty Flea' Connors, a superb single by Mickey Baker entitled *I'll Always Be in Love with You* and a surprising Top Twenty hit in France for Big John Wrencher from Sunflower, Missouri, with a release sponsored by Coca Cola.

Any recording with Cousin Joe was guaranteed to be a bundle of fun, even more so when Mickey was involved. The session when we cut our version of the

Cousin Joe in Chalk Farm Studios.

8. Not So Foolish As I'm Badly Dressed

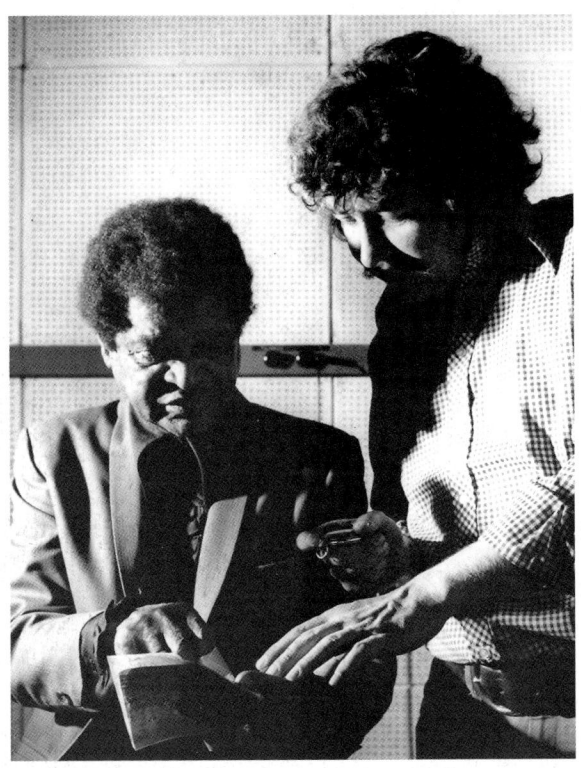

Left: Cousin Joe and JS in our favourite place, the recording studio.

Below: Sound-checking at the Venue – spot the stars!

Benny Spelman classic, *Lipstick Traces*, cried out for a backing vocal and at that time the Liverpool vocal group, Arrival, was enjoying a hit record, *Friends*, on Decca. They were signed to Tony Hall Enterprises and Tony owed me a favour for delivering Black Sabbath to him gift-wrapped, so I leaned on him and got Arrival, who had never heard of Cousin Joe, to back Cousin Joe who was totally unaware of Arrival. It was a wonderful session that also featured Ken Elliott who had recently had a hit with Seventh Wave – and we always had Mickey on hand to take care of business when it came to arrangements.

Cousin Joe was indefatigable and an absolute joy to be with. He prided himself on being what he termed 'The Big Bear Office on the Road'. Because we toured him so often, I couldn't possibly absent myself from the office for weeks at a time, much as I would have loved to, so we set up a system by which we arranged and prepaid his travel and he would go off on his own for 10 or 12 days and take care of all business himself: paying expenses, getting receipts, picking up cash, the whole tour manager schtick. Hand on heart, I can say that he never failed to balance the books; I believe I could trust that man more than I could myself.

He was also very frugal. He enjoyed a drink, only slightly to excess, but was careful to ensure that it was on someone else's tab. If an audience member got up to go to the bar during his performance, he would polish off whatever was left in his glass, upend it on his head to show it was empty and, with a 'best hair tonic in the world', proffer the glass to the guy. It worked most every time, but he never allowed his liking for a taste to affect his performance.

He would jealously guard his tour earnings, taking most of them back home, intact, and would invariably use the money to buy something tangible. That way he felt he really got a benefit out of every tour. One time, for instance, he bought a new outboard motor for his boat; another he was able to pay for some element of his much loved son Michael's education. Whenever he mentioned Michael, which was often, he would say, 'Man, I love that boy's last week's dirty drawers.'

One time, after a tour, he called me from a payphone in some Bourbon Street bar, and asked, 'What do you think I'm doing, man? I'm standing here by my brand new lemon yellow Mustang. I'm wearing my brand new lemon yellow suit, my brand new lemon yellow hat, my brand new lemon yellow shoes – and guess what! I'm wearing my brand new lemon yellow underplunders!' I cried with laughter for days.

Joe was the most immaculately turned out man I ever met. On the road his 'London fog' was standard attire, but on stage it was a different matter altogether: suit, hat, shirt and shoes had to be co-ordinated, be it light blue, dark blue, red, green, whatever. He would always go on stage looking pristine: 'They come to see a show, man, it's my job to look cool.' You can't argue with that.

8. Not So Foolish As I'm Badly Dressed

One summer's day in 1975 we were sitting in a field, in a bus that had been put in use as a dressing room at the Aalter Jazz Festival in Belgium – and it was pouring down. All of the artists and crew were hunkered down in this none too comfortable bus, waiting for the rain to subside so we could get on with the show. Cousin Joe and I were stretching out on the back seat when suddenly there was a commotion at the front of the bus. Uber-cool bebop vocalist and man about New York jazz Babs Gonzales had boarded – unexpectedly, as he wasn't booked to appear at the festival, but was freejacking around Europe trying to sell his book, *Movin' on Down De Line*. I knew that he had roomed with Cousin Joe in New York in the early 1940s and that Joe had very little time for him. I soon found out why. As Babs worked his way down the bus, he spotted Joe and hollered, 'Hey, babe, how you doin'? It's been too long!' Joe opened one eye, managed to look disgusted and growled, 'Where's my fucking suit?' Gonzales retreated, well and truly put in his place, for apparently he had stolen one of Joe's fine suits on the pretext of taking it to the dry-cleaner's. Joe, shrewd as always, had skipped back mentally some 30 years without a blink. Babs slunk off the bus, without further comment, and disappeared into the rain.

That turned out to be a memorable day for Big Bear as another passenger going nowhere on that mud-bound bus was bill-topper and one of the half dozen finest trumpet players in the history of jazz, Clark Terry. I had met Clark previously at European festivals, but this time we really got to talking – there was little else to do on a bus, in a field in Belgium, with no sign of any let-up in the rain. I told him about what we got up to at Big Bear and he seemed quite interested in how we could survive as an independent with no financial backing, yet somehow co-ordinate releases with licence deals with a dozen European countries.

Clark had just released his first album on his own label, Etoile Records, *The Clark Terry Big Bad Band*. I was encouraging him to licence it throughout Europe as I knew a live album by this stunning band would be of wide interest, when he came up with a proposal which floored me. My hero, Clark Terry, would licence his big band album to Big Bear Records for the princely sum of 500 dollars.

On Clark's US release he simply called it by the name of the band, but I considered that it would attract more attention if it was advertised as being recorded in some notable place. Clark had told me that the recording had taken place in 'that Big Old Barn on 57th Street'. I didn't much like the barn bit, but 57th Street sounded pretty cool to me, so in 1976 Big Bear 13 was released to rave reviews as *Clark Terry's Big Bad Band: Live on 57th Street*. It was much later that Clark asked me why I hadn't used the venue name, it would have carried weight. I fully agreed, but it just hadn't clicked that the Big Old Barn was, in fact,

Carnegie Hall! And yes, *Clark Terry Live at Carnegie Hall* would have had a resonance throughout the jazz world.

Clark would always sign off his letters with 'Hope You Can Dig It'. Well, Clark, we all did dig it and we dug pretty much every darn thing you did – and that was plenty. There's a beautiful and touching little film out, with Clark in the great man's last years, moving into his 90s and losing his sight, but still mentoring a young blind piano prodigy. It's called *Keep on Keepin' On* – and You Will Dig It.

I first toured Cousin Joe on the American Blues Legends '74. Also on that tour was Doctor Ross The Harmonica Boss. I had first brought Doctor Ross over as a single act in 1972 and in the end must have toured him something like a dozen times. Life on the road with him was never dull – of course the same can be said about many of the American bluesmen we toured and recorded, but Doctor Ross really was a special case. He was nuts, that's true, but he was predictably nuts which, for reasons I can't explain, I found endearing. Boogie Woogie Red once confided in me in a whispered aside, 'The Doc's crazy, man, everyone knows that, but he can't help it, he's half-Apache.' Probably not very accurate: I did recall Washboard Willie telling me almost the same thing, but this time about Boogie

(l-r) George G. P. Jackson, Cousin Joe, Doctor Ross in mob boss pose, Eddie 'Playboy' Taylor, Big John Wrencher.

Woogie Red! Bluesmen with some Native American blood were not a rarity: the high cheek-bones were said to be a giveaway, certainly in the cases of Lightnin' Slim and the good Doctor.

Born in Tunica, Mississippi, in 1925, Isaiah Ross settled in Memphis after military service. His big break came when he was discovered in 1951 by Sam Phillips who took him into what was to become the legendary Sun Recording Studio, but at that time was known as Memphis Recording Service. The way Sam worked initially was to record interesting bluesmen, including Junior Parker, Howlin' Wolf and BB King, and lease the masters to a record company. Thus early Ross recordings found their way onto Chess.

When Sam got his Sun record label off the ground, Ross was an important part of his roster recording what were then known as race records, essentially black musicians recording for the black audience that was emerging through the juke joints across the Southern states. Subsequently Sam Phillips famously began recording white musicians, at one time able to boast Carl Perkins, Elvis Presley, Jerry Lee Lewis and Johnny Cash on the label, probably the greatest gathering of American rock and roll talent ever seen on one label at the same time – in fact, known as The Million Dollar Quartet.

Doctor Ross – named the Doctor as the small case he used to carry his harmonicas resembled a medic's – told me he remembered Elvis well:

'Nice boy, real polite, drove a truck out of West Memphis. Used to fetch in beers for us when we recorded. Elvis Preston, yes, yes.'

Moving to where the work was, Doc made his way to Flint, Michigan, to work in a factory serving the automobile industry. It was there that he refined his famous one-man band. Seated, he played pedal bass drum with one foot, hi-hat cymbal with the other, and guitar left-handed without re-stringing the instrument: 'It was that way round when I picked it up.' On a chest rack he had a Marine Band harmonica and a kazoo – and, of course, he also sang. Some years later, maybe on his fourth Big Bear tour, he proudly told me that he had learnt to dance, in case the audience didn't think he was doing enough. He would laboriously disentangle himself from his chest rack and guitar and launch into a totally manic, seemingly out of control buck and wing which inevitably brought the house down.

From about 1960 he recorded several sides for Fortune Records of Detroit, including the legendary *Cat Squirrel*, subsequently recorded by Cream, Jethro Tull and others. The good Doctor made an impact when he first toured the UK and Europe in 1965 and, by the time he embarked on his first Big Bear tour in 1972, the audiences knew what to expect – and he didn't disappoint. One thing about the

Doctor was that he never let an audience go until he had them in the palm of his hand which he always did, no matter how long a set he had to play to win them over. Most blues venues asked for two sets, each of 50 minutes or an hour, but I've seen Ross play a straight 90 minutes, no mean feat for a one-man band, not stopping until they went wild. The audiences loved his innocently self-congratulatory remarks, 'Yeh, yeh, yeh, Doctor Ross the Harmonica Boss. I can't lose with the stuff I use.'

Offstage the eccentric, egocentric Doctor Ross never stopped chattering. So much of it seemed meaningless that it was very easy to dismiss everything he said as nonsense. That would have been a mistake, although it was a different matter when he had been drinking whisky. One time we were in a cab stuck in traffic on Oxford Street and I realised that he was looking at me curiously. 'You face me, man,' he said which meant that I looked like somebody else. 'Yes, yes, yes, you do, man. Eric, that's who you face.' It should be remembered that in the early 70s we all wore the same denim shirts, jackets and jeans and had the same regulation shoulder-length hair. Remembering that Eric Clapton had recorded the Doctor's *Cat Squirrel*, it dawned on me that he might just be likening me to him. When I suggested this to the Doctor, he responded, 'That's it, man, they came to see me at my house in Flint.'

Pretty much overwhelmed that he had not only met, but had welcomed, Clapton, Jack Bruce and Ginger Baker into his house, I pressed him for details. Apparently, en route to the Ann Arbor Blues Festival, Cream had dropped in to see the Doc and present him with some money for having covered *Cat Squirrel*. I asked him how much they paid him and he told me with pride, 'Two hundred dollars, man. Cash.' Unsurprisingly I was, and still am, unimpressed that musicians of their status would consider that to be anything approaching a fair payment.

Doc went on to tell me that they had taken him with them to the Blues Festival and I was struck by the fact that Cream brought him on stage to play with them. With Cream! I asked them what they were like. He gave the question careful thought before replying, 'Well, they was nice boys – but awful loud.'

As part of his first Big Bear tour, Doctor Ross was due to feature at the 1972 Montreux Jazz Festival in Switzerland as support to the Muddy Waters Chicago Blues Band which, as far as I was concerned, was as close as anyone could get to blues royalty. We had arranged for the Doc to play two sets, the first solo, the second with a band. Not just any band, but Lafayette Leake, Louis and David Myers and Freddy Below, the Chicago Aces, the famed rhythm section of McKinley Morganfield, aka Muddy Waters. It was all arranged quite casually with Muddy who was charm and generosity personified:

'You just go ahead, boy, but give the guys a hundred bucks each.'

8. Not So Foolish As I'm Badly Dressed

Of course I told him I must pay a fee for using his musicians.

'No need, boy,' he said. 'You don't need to be paying me, I ain't going to be playing nohow.'

That was my first encounter with one of the greatest of all bluesmen, and he never forgot my name and was never less than courteous and disarmingly friendly.

That Montreux weekend did not pass without incident. By that time I had only been on the road with Doctor Ross for around ten days and he and I were still feeling each other out, he probably wondering if I could be trusted. As we checked into the Montreux Jazz Festival hotel, the man in front turned away from the reception desk to leave, sort of confronting me. I immediately realised that his face was familiar, so gave him a big grin and an enthusiastic 'Hi, man.' 'Good to see you,' he replied. 'Let's get a beer after the show.' I noticed Doctor Ross was agape. 'What's the matter, Doc?', I asked. 'You know T-Bone Walker?', he asked. It was my turn to gape, but I didn't let on that I had never before met T-Bone and that he had responded to me only out of politeness. Funnily enough Doc and I were noticeably closer from then on and for years he would introduce me as 'my record producer – he knows T-Bone.'

It's good that the passage of time enables me to look back and find humour in things that, at the time, were annoying in the extreme. One – no, several such moments occurred at Montreux that year. There's no denying that Doctor Ross had a drink problem – or, to be properly accurate, everybody else had a problem with Doctor Ross when he was drinking which was pretty much every waking hour. We had a clear day before we were due to record the evening show, opening for Muddy's band. So I figured the way forward might just be to persuade him to drink in moderation as, left to his own devices, he would drink himself unconscious by tea-time. I explained in detail how important it was for him to be more or less sober when he hit that stage, not only because it was being recorded and folk would listen to how he played for generations to come, but also the recording was costing me dear and the audience would have travelled a long way and deserved to hear the Doc at this best. Finally I pointed out – and this clearly resonated with him – that Muddy Waters would see him at work and we surely didn't want any embarrassment in front of the Great Man himself.

So we made an agreement and formally shook hands. I was to supply a bottle of whisky for the Doc to sip at gently throughout the day, he would be bright-eyed and on the ball for the show, then we would hang out with Muddy and the guys and he could drink as much as he wanted. The day seemed to start well enough, with me putting chinagraph marks on the bottle to monitor his consumption, but

Doctor Ross in a familiar pose.

8. Not So Foolish As I'm Badly Dressed

by mid-afternoon he was getting wild, playing harmonica on our room's balcony to passers-by who were gathering four floors down to enjoy the show. However, the bottle was still 80 per cent full, so probably it was my paranoia.

By tea-time he was clearly in his cups, manic and shouting. I was annoyed and confused: clearly something had gone wrong, so I pulled him in from the balcony, ordered black coffee from room service and told him to get into the shower and not leave until he was sober. With that, I threw myself down on his bed to wait and felt a lump under his pillow. It was a near-empty litre bottle of whisky, the obvious source of Doc's increasing good humour.

He didn't seem bad when we got to the Casino, although he did insist on cheerily introducing himself to all he encountered. I explained to him how important it was to keep speech to a minimum and to concentrate on giving a great performance. I left him, with just one tot of whisky at hand, ready to go on stage, while I dashed up to the recording control room, situated high at the back of the theatre. When Festival Director Claude Nobs finished his introduction with, 'And now, Monsieur le Docteur, Doctor Ross,' and the place erupted in greeting Doc, I was ready to press Record and get under way. However, Doctor Ross was not. Clearly moved by his reception, he started at one side of the stage and worked his way round, shaking the hand of everyone in the front row of the massive theatre, all the time calling, 'Yes, yes, yes, here's the Doctor come to heal all your sickness!' and 'I can't lose with the stuff I use!'.

Now the tape was 2-inch Ampex and I was running it at 15 inches per second to get the highest quality recording, and that tape was not cheap! 'Record,' I would call to the engineer, then a few minutes later, 'Stop. Rewind', every time the Doc looked as if he was going to start the set. I don't know how many times we went back over the tape, but, from the safety back-up tape, I know that it was 22 minutes from Claude's introduction to the start of the Doctor Ross performance. The second set, with Muddy Waters' rhythm section, looked destined to descend into chaos, with the Doc now at his wildest, until guitarist Louis Myers took charge and ensured that we had a memorable set to record.

The eccentricities of Doctor Ross were not confined to the stage. One night after a show in Brussels, he refused to go to bed, insisting I drove him to where he could encounter some ladies of the night. The hotel porter, though clearly disapproving, told us exactly where we could find such action. Following his directions, I stopped the car short of where several women were gathered by a large wrought iron gate under a street-light and watched the diminutive, shabbily dressed, wild-eyed Doctor shamble up to the group, no doubt hollering, 'Yes, yes, I'm the Doctor!' or something similarly immodest. The group scattered. Doctor

Ross, looking very angry, came back to the car, telling me, 'You messed up there, boy. Them's respectable married ladies waiting to go into church!' By then it was well after midnight.

Once that man was on stage, it was impossible not to forgive him any problems he might have created during the day. He was so committed to his music and so determined to share his enjoyment in full with every member of the audience that it could sometimes be almost a religious experience. For all his wacky behaviour he knew how important his message was. It came from the very roots of the music, pure, unadulterated and direct from a different age.

There have been other fine one-man blues bands. Jesse Fuller, the Lone Cat, was a particular favourite of mine. There were Juke Box Bonner from Texas and our own Duster Bennett who died one February night driving home after a gig with Memphis Slim. But I am convinced that Doctor Isaiah Ross, for all his foibles, eccentricities and those liberties with time that pervade his music, was somehow the real thing, unschooled, absolutely unself-conscious, but direct from the fountainhead. It was much easier to get Doctor Ross when seeing him live, high on enthusiasm, sweeping all before him, but it is still worth anyone's effort to listen seriously to his recorded work.

Having recorded him in concert, I wanted to record him in a controlled environment, but didn't feel that the atmosphere of a recording studio was quite right for such live music. So I compromised and booked him into Chalk Farm Studio, but also brought in an invited audience whom I credited in the sleeve notes as the Soho Deadbeats. Actually the dozen or so blues fans were pretty much selected from my chums who populated the bar at the 100 Club and who had all been helpful in getting Big Bear Music off the ground. The mighty Mike Leadbitter was there, with Mike Rowe and his *Blues Unlimited* cohorts, blues journalists Cilla Huggins, Jerry Gilbert and Tony Cummings as well as pianist Bob Hall and assorted Blues Mafia. It was a somewhat unruly affair for a studio recording, with me having encouraged the assembled mob to immerse themselves in a small-town Mississippi juke joint in 1950, but by good fortune it worked, was distributed throughout Europe and became a Big Bear best-seller. Doctor Ross was superb, absolutely in his element among folk who understood exactly what he was about, and he had a surprise for me.

'I've got a new song,' he told me. 'Listen to the words.' The song, which we recorded, was *Don't Worry 'Bout the Bear* which I found touching – and, truth to tell, still do.

Doctor Ross and I toured together through much of the 1970s, and some years before his death in 1993 he once again toured the UK and I booked him for a night at my Blues at the Bear at Bearwood. To my utter amazement he was drinking orange juice – no alcohol – talking coherently and intelligently and lecturing me on my foolishness in taking the occasional glass of wine. We talked about old times with affection, but somehow the spark was gone and he was, frankly, a little dull. That was until he got on stage – then once again Doctor Ross was most certainly rocking!

The tried and trusted formula for our American Blues Legends tours worked well. I would mobilise the US branch of our Blues Mafia to locate the musicians on my ever-increasing wish-list, put together a notional programme, make the offers, note the pull-outs and revise the programme. Typically we would recruit six blues musicians/singers, often with a UK bassist and drummer, planning to pair them off in a series of smaller bands and building to a climax with everyone on stage.

I would locate then and now photographs, write the biographies and persuade promoters across Europe to take the show. An American Blues Legends tour would typically last six or seven weeks, with a performance or recording every day. We would rent a bus or splitter van and a PA, hire a sound engineer and set off on our mission to carry the blues message far and wide. At tour's end we would take the band into the studio or record a live show on the Virgin mobile and release an album. And therein lay the problem: how could we make contact with our prime audience of 30-40 thousand fans who had seen the show throughout Europe? For American Blues Legends '79 we did the obvious and recorded the album in advance in order to sell it to fans during the actual tour.

Chicago was the obvious place to record as that city can rightly claim to have more bluesmen per square mile than any other place on earth! As ever, Jim and Amy O'Neal, whose monthly magazine, *Living Blues*, was the most important of all blues publications, were generous with their time and helped me make contact with probably as many as 15 musicians. I was able to locate my old pal, Jimmy 'Fastfingers' Dawkins – how he hated that 'Fastfingers' tag! – to effect the introductions.

It was amazing the difference it made having Jimmy, one of the really great Chicago bluesmen, respected by all, making the introductions. Almost all of these guys had some sort of day job; even in a city with as huge a blues heritage as Chicago it was extremely difficult even for established blues musicians to scrape a living from their music.

So here comes this Englishman – and what does he know about the blues? Where is England anyway? – wanting to record you, pay you a recording fee, and then what? Take you across the Atlantic to a bunch of damn fool countries you've never heard of to play different cities every night, stay in nice hotels and get paid a salary? Fat chance! Unless he's a crazy sonofabitch millionaire and he sure don't

In front of the Wrigley Building, Chicago, JS photographed by Jim O'Neal, founder and editor of Living Blues.

8. Not So Foolish As I'm Badly Dressed

look as if he's rich or something. But, if Dawkins says he's OK, that'll do for me – Dawkins is no fool.

I arrived in Chicago in early August 1979. This was my first – and, as it turned out, my last – visit to this legendary Home of the Blues and I was determined to make the most of it. Arriving at O'Hare Airport, I carefully selected the hippest-looking of the black cabbies and asked him to take me to a cool, but not expensive, hotel close to the South Side and the Chess Recording Studio.

He gave me a funny look and muttered, 'You mean Cody's. Ed Cody's got it now.' At that moment I began to believe that just about everyone in Chi Town was hip to the blues narrative of this great city.

We spent the next two days meeting the guys, often in their homes, always in their neighbourhoods, discussing the music and the touring plans. Slowly it all began to take shape. The cabbie at O'Hare was right on the button, if only he had known. As far as I was concerned, there was only one studio in Chicago where I wanted to record, the legendary Chess Studios at 2120 South Michigan. Chess Records had re-located to larger premises in 1965, but 2120 was where all the

Taking a break from recording American Blues Legends 1979 at 2120 South Michigan, Chicago. (l-r) Billy 'The Kid' Emerson, Jimmy 'Fastfingers' Dawkins, JS, Lester Davenport, Little Smokey Smothers, Eddie C. Campbell, Good Rockin' Charles, Chico Chism.

early Muddy, Wolf, Willie Dixon and Little Walter classics had been cut and where The Rolling Stones had recorded their album, *2120 South Michigan Avenue.* When Chess moved out, former Chess engineer Ed Cody took over the building, renaming it Odyssey Sound Studio, but to me and millions of blues fans it will always be 2120.

Eddie C. Campbell, Good Rockin' Charles, Billy the Kid Emerson, Lester Davenport, Chico Chism and Little Smokey Smothers were the six who made the final cut and, although Smothers would play bass on the ensuing tour, I brought in Willie Black as back-up and also made full use of Jimmy Dawkins' fine guitar work. It was a wonderful session, we cut around 20 songs in two days, 12 of which made it onto the final album – in those days, with vinyl LPs, there was a maximum playing time of around 19 minutes a side, so a lot of perfectly good recordings were left on the editing room floor.

I finished mixing at around 3 in the morning, cleaned up and picked up my things from the hotel, and checked in at O'Hare at 9.00 am for a flight to Kansas City, Missouri, to record jazz veteran Claude Williams – but that's another story.

Despite what I had fondly imagined were fool-proof plans, things didn't quite work out as expected. Back in England, with the American Blues Legends '79 tour only six weeks later, I had only just given the OK to print the sleeve when I had an emotional phone call from harmonica player Little Smokey Smothers. He hated doing this, he said, but the boss at his day job, despite agreeing earlier, had told him that he could not guarantee that his job in the construction industry would be there for him when he returned from the tour. Smokey was really upset; he said that a tour of Europe, playing his blues, would have been his dream. He even offered to pay back his recording fee, which of course I didn't accept, and we promised each other that one day I would bring him to Europe. Sadly, this never happened. He persevered with his day job to look after his family, but increasingly had serious health problems. He had open heart surgery in 1995 and subsequently had both legs amputated through diabetes. He died in Chicago in 2010. It would have been good, just once, to give the man a proper platform to sing and play the blues. Smokey's place on the tour was taken by the impressive singer and bass player Nolan Struck who did a fine job, but I still feel bad about Smokey.

There is a footnote concerning Billy the Kid Emerson to what was a successful American Blues Legends tour. On stage Billy was dynamite, a hard-swinging piano player, an understated singer of unusually cool and hip lyrics who put me very much in mind of Tommy Tucker. His lyrics were classic, for instance:

'Ain't nuthin' in my pockets but the bottom,
And that's more than you can say for my shoes.'

8. Not So Foolish As I'm Badly Dressed

Off stage he could not have been more different, sitting isolated at the front of the bus, making regular trips to the back to deliver a lecture about the evils of having too much fun and drinking, shouting and cursing while God-fearing folk (meaning him) were trying to sleep. This grew steadily worse over the last couple of weeks, especially when the tour was nearing its end and everyone was getting demob-happy. After our last show we stopped off for a bite to eat at a remote transport café somewhere in the Pennines. Billy the Kid stayed in the bus while the rest of us trooped into the café. Maybe an hour later we returned to the bus to find that Billy and his luggage were gone. Vanished. He had money – they had been paid off for the tour – but his flight ticket was still in my briefcase. We searched, called the Police from the café and eventually carried on back to Birmingham confident that he would show up at the hotel. Which he didn't. At all.

I never found out what Billy got up to that night or how he got back to the States, but it seems very appropriate that by 2005, as the Rev. William R. Emerson, he had his own church in Oak Park, Illinois.

Chapter 9

GOIN' TO KANSAS CITY

New Orleans, as the birthplace of jazz, has a special place in the heart of every fan of that wonderful music, although I have to admit that my loyalty is divided. I spent my early years firmly in the belief that I would visit and get to know the Crescent City, but I never did. Not yet, anyway.

For me, since I discovered the music of the Count Basie Band with Buck Clayton, Lester Young and the All-American rhythm section of Basie with Freddy Green, Walter Page and Jo Jones, I had Kansas City on my mind. That doyen of swing drummers, Kansas City Jo Jones, was always a particular favourite of mine. I got to know him a little and, when he went into a season at Ronnie Scott's in London with organ maestro Milt Buckner, I didn't miss a show. They were tremendous, just the two of them – nightly, they would swing the room into bad health. (That's a line I borrowed from Cousin Joe, along with a bunch of other stuff.) Onstage Milt and Jo had a perfect understanding; offstage things were a little less friendly. Now it has to be understood that Jo was a little unusual, wild, you might say. To a fan like me, it didn't matter, I loved every nutty thing he said and did. But Milt was a serious guy and thought all musicians should deport themselves with a degree of dignity. The upshot was that Milt wouldn't speak to Jo and every night after intermission Milt would come to me and say, 'Tell your crazy friend to get on stage.'

Everything to do with Kansas City – Piney Brown, Mr. Five by Five, 12th Street and Vine, the Reno Club, all-night jam sessions, Yardbird with Jay McShann – these were the things of my dreams. There were the years of Prohibition when Tom Pendergast's Democratic Party machine and a bribed police force allowed alcohol and gambling to be freely available. Club operators and dancers, barmen and gunmen, not to mention jazz musicians, came to KC for work, creating the ideal atmosphere for the right kind of music to flourish.

Who could resist the tale of pianist Mary Lou Williams, walking past the Cherry Blossom Club on her way home from her regular gig with Andy Kirk's Twelve Clouds of Joy and dropping in for a while? Local tenor saxophone stars, Ben

Wilbur 'Buck' Clayton from Parsons, Kansas. The Best.

Webster, Herschel Evans and Lester Young, were there awaiting the arrival of Coleman Hawkins, in KC for a one-nighter with the Fletcher Henderson Orchestra. The great man arrived and the jamming led to a regular KC cutting contest, a battle of the tenors, each determined to blow the others off the stand. Sensibly Mary Lou left for home before things got too intense, as the ensemble went into *Honeysuckle Rose*. She passed by the club shortly after 10 the next morning and found that Hawk and Lester were still playing *Honeysuckle Rose* and still battling each other. Coleman Hawkins, boss of the tenor saxophone, bested that night by Lester Young, refused to give up the struggle until so late in the day that he blew the engine on his new Cadillac racing to the Henderson band's next gig in St. Louis.

In 1979 I was at the North Sea Jazz Festival with Cousin Joe from New Orleans and was delighted to see that Kansas City veteran Jay McShann was there with his Quartet – but on stage there were five of them! The programme listed former Basie-ites Buddy Tate on tenor saxophone, Gene Ramey on double bass and Gus Johnson on drums. The unlisted member was a violinist – and he was dynamite! I mentally went through all the possibilities and there weren't many: black, middle-aged and absolutely phenomenal. I went backstage to say hello to McShann and asked him who the fiddle player was. Claude Williams, I was told, and, to be honest, no bells rang.

Don't Worry 'Bout The Bear

I talked briefly to Claude and went to set up the Cousin Joe show, but afterwards phoned my brother, Ron, in what were by then the early hours. Usually the fount of all knowledge, this time he declared himself floored, but determined to get on the case immediately and phone me back. Back then there was no internet, so it was all book research, but eventually Ron came back asking me if I was a little dazed and confused – or even tired and emotional as Humph would say, meaning drunk – as there was indeed a Kansas City musician by the name of Claude Williams, but he was a guitarist. Not just any guitarist, but the winner of the 1936 *Downbeat* poll when he was playing with the Count Basie Band. By then I was indeed dazed and confused and went to bed.

After breakfast I went for a swim in the near-deserted hotel pool – I say, near deserted, because there was one other person there, none other than Claude. I joined him, tried without much success to match him stroke for stroke while pestering him for his life-story. It turned out that he was 71, born in Muskogee, Oklahoma, came to KC in 1927 to join the Twelve Clouds of Joy, played guitar, but regarded the violin as his favoured instrument. He joined Basie in time to take part in the legendary Reno Club broadcasts in 1936 that brought the Basie Band to a wide public and gave them the first step on the ladder to World Domination – at least, as far as big swing bands were concerned! However, Claude missed playing the violin and, after a failed attempt to persuade Basie to adapt his arrangements, he quit. As usual, there is an alternative version of the reasons for Claude leaving Basie: did he miss the violin or did the all-powerful John Hammond decide that he was too much of a soloist and get Basie to sack him? Certainly his successor, the great rhythm guitarist, Freddie Green, never gave any worries on that score in his 50 years with Basie!

After leaving Basie, Claude continued to play violin, mostly in and around Kansas City, seldom moving far afield until his long-time friend and fellow-Muskogee native Jay McShann made him a late addition to the Europe-bound band that I heard in Holland. As it turned out, this proved something of a watershed in Claude's career – or, at least, his fame outside Kansas City. European jazz critics responded with such comments as 'the most immaculate swing fiddle I've ever heard' from Dave Gelly in *The Observer*. Though celebrated in later years as the longest lived musician to have recorded before 1930, by 1979 he had cut only one album under his own name. From this time that all changed and the last quarter century of Claude's long life was filled with recordings and such honours as playing at Bill Clinton's first inauguration and being the first inductee of the Oklahoma Jazz Hall of Fame.

Having sort of discovered Claude Williams and finding him to be one of the really good guys as well as a superb jazz violinist, I wasn't about to let him go

Claude Williams in Kansas City, Missouri.

easily. As the McShann tour ended, Claude jumped ship and came to Birmingham to stay with me for a few weeks. It was then that we hatched our plan for the first move in developing a wider audience for Claude. I was due to fly to Chicago to audition, rehearse and record the musicians who were to tour Europe as American Blues Legends '79. I shifted my travel plans so that, when I finished mixing the blues album, I would fly from Chicago to Kansas City coach class, the cheapest available – which involved checking in for the first flight of the day, then waiting for a seat on all subsequent flights. As it was, I finished mixing around 3.00 am, snatched some sleep for an hour or so and arrived at O'Hare Airport around 9, eventually getting a flight at something like 1.00 pm.

So by the time I reached KC I was ready for bed, happy to leave the exploration of the joys of Kansas City until the next day, but that was reckoning without Claude. I still believe that, if he had stood for Mayor of Kansas City, it would have been a shoo-in. Nobody could have been more loved in that city than he was. From the moment he met me at Arrivals and briskly marched me to his parked car, the 'Hi, Claudes' just didn't stop. Check-in girls, porters, cleaners, baggage handlers and cab drivers, it seemed that everyone knew and loved him – and Claude never failed to acknowledge them.

His wife Maybelle was ready for us and armed with a mountain of food. Claude put my week's worth of clothes into the washing machine and so hot was Kansas City that they were ready to wear by the time we finished eating. I was so tired that I couldn't help nodding off a few times during the meal and then Claude started telling me we had to go out that night to meet the band before the next day's recording session. I told Claude that there was no way I could do anything but go to bed, but he dug in his heels and told me straight that, if I didn't meet the guys, he could not guarantee any of them would be there for the recording. So I agreed, but, as soon as we got into his car, he told me, 'I'm really sorry about that, man, I didn't want to do it, but you're the only excuse I have to meet my girlfriend.'

We drove across town, then he left me in the car to sleep while he made his visit. By the time Claude returned, maybe two or three hours later, I had recovered enough to be keen to meet the group at their resident gig at the Papillon, an extremely cool night club where Claude was treated like royalty – so no surprise there! Naturally Claude had brought his fiddle and, as expected, the session didn't finish until very late by which time I was so elated by the wonderful playing that I found it difficult to sleep.

That Kansas City is a pretty special place is evidenced by the fact that so many fine musicians choose to live there in relative obscurity, playing the small clubs for a fraction of what they could pull down in Los Angeles, Chicago or New York. Take

Claude's band. KC-born pianist Frank Smith had worked with Miles Davis, Coleman Hawkins, Johnny Hodges and Anita O'Day. Bassist Gerry Leonard had enjoyed pop music success with rock act Union Gap, but had made Kansas City his home. Richard Ross was from Leavenworth, Kansas, had turned professional as a singer in 1948 and worked as a drummer with Clark Terry, Ray Brown and Ben Webster.

We didn't want to rush the recording. I suppose I could have finished it in a couple of days, but we all wanted it to be perfect and restricted recording and mixing to around five hours a day over a week. It was an extraordinarily happy series of sessions. I managed to bully Richard into giving up memorable vocals, particularly on *Teach Me Tonight*, but only after some concessions on both sides. All his career, on gigs, Richard had delivered his vocals from behind the drum kit while playing. Over the years this had become second nature to him and he found he couldn't sing comfortably and with feeling while not playing drums. On the other hand I wanted to ensure that we got a clean vocal track, without picking up any sounds from the drumkit, so, as is normal, I wanted to record the instrumental track without his singing, then overdub the vocal track separately. This proved impossible for Richard, so we rigged up a series of sound shields between Richard's mouth and his drumkit, only 12 inches away. After several attempts, we somehow got away with it, but I still wince when I listen to the album, imagining what might have been, had it not gone so smoothly.

After much persuasion and an eerie coincidence I got Claude's only recorded vocal. It was while driving to the studio on the second day of recording that I told Claude I had had a dream of him singing.

'What song was that?', he asked and suddenly went very quiet when I told him *One Hundred Years From Today.* Clearly surprised, maybe even spooked a little, he told me this was the only song he had ever sung in public; it had been his feature with the Alphonso Trent Band. Thereafter Claude folded and agreed to everything, even the multi-tracking of that song with Claude singing and playing violin and two guitar parts, as well as bass. He was unfamiliar with the process, but allowed himself to be led and thereafter introduced me to everyone as 'The Magician' – which was not really warranted.

One afternoon, we heard a recording on Claude's car radio by a group I had never heard of, the Charlie Daniels Band. It was *Jitterbug* and it sounded sensational. Claude said that he knew the folk at the radio station – of course! – so we drove over. The on-air presenter took us into the studio while he finished his shift, telling me that by luck Charlie Daniels was playing a club just up the road that evening and he was going along – so would I like to accompany him? Obviously the answer was yes, even before he finished asking the question.

The club was some 35 miles away in Leavenworth, Kansas, and the six-piece band was stunning. It was shortly afterwards that the Charlie Daniels Band hit with *The Devil Went Down to Georgia* and, though I was delighted with their success, I felt that the song didn't feature the band at their best and wished it could have been *Jitterbug* on the charts. I'd always had a bit of a sneer at country music, a bit like Buddy Rich, looking anxious on a hospital trolley, waiting to go in for an operation. Reportedly a nurse asked him, 'Does something trouble you, Mr. Rich?' and got the reply, 'Yes, country music!' This Charlie Daniels performance blew away all my prejudices; well-played country rock is now firmly on my agenda. When you think about it, any musical form, when played by good musicians, is probably worthy of attention.

There were many memorable moments in my brief stay in Kansas City, Missouri, not all of them connected with music. Claude took me along to an extremely posh garden party. I had never mixed with such high-stepping professional folk before, and very rarely since. I met the US Ambassador to Egypt, no less, with whom I had an hour's deep conversation about a shared interest, the Spanish Civil War. What I found fascinating about this event was that all of the attendees, other than me, were black.

Most of our evenings were spent at The Foundation, one of the two buildings the American Federation of Musicians (their Musicians' Union) has in KC. The other one was for white musicians, this one for black. Scandalous that, in 1979, in a place known worldwide as a wide-open city and home to some of the finest jazz ever heard, there should still be an attempt to segregate musicians, of all people. It didn't actually work: a group of white musicians was always jamming at The Foundation and the black musicians didn't seem to care. They knew they were having far more fun than the folk over at the other place.

It became increasingly obvious to me that there were two distinctly separate Kansas Cities. Not just the river/political divide between Kansas City, Missouri, and Kansas City, Kansas, but the racial split into black and white. In my time there I hardly had any contact with white folk unless they were musicians or worked in the night-time economy. This was fine by me because everything in Claude's world was just swinging. They were not nearly as bothered as I was about the unfairness of society. The AFM building was a case in point. The fact that there were segregated union branches – and, thus, clubs – was appalling enough, but the white club had long been granted a liquor licence and the black one still didn't have one. The Federation overcame that in a simple and practical way by installing lockers for which the members paid rent. The bar sold over-priced mixers and the guys brought in their own hard liquor and kept it in their locker.

9. Goin' To Kansas City

The American Federation of Musicians building (black section) in Kansas City, Missouri.

Claude was a regular at the jam sessions at the Foundation which often continued until daybreak. He was rightly regarded as the number one; he was also rated pretty highly in the pool rooms and card schools! The Foundation Building was the setting for *The Last of the Blue Devils*, a wonderful film recorded in 1974 about these legendary jam sessions, and featuring Count Basie and Jay McShann among many others.

I quickly became extremely comfortable in Kansas City and was intrigued to discover that it was a sister city to Sevilla in Spain, with an Avenida de Kansas City in the Andalucian capital and a half-size replica of Sevilla's landmark, the Moorish Giralda Tower, re-created in KC. Sevilla had been a favourite place of mine since I first went there as an unworldly 18-year-old, so I guess that made KC even more special. That and the ease with which folks made friends – well, some folk, that is.

I almost didn't notice that all the people I associated with were black until a chance encounter dispelled my sense of security. I decided to stay for a while in KC after the recording and moved into an address at 51st and Swope (Avenue) which inspired the title of the Claude Williams composition on our album. I was keen to visit the Spanish quarter and see the Giralda and was on my way there with two young women, one the girlfriend of Richard Ross, the other a new-found friend, each hanging on to an arm, when we became the target for abuse from a group of unpleasant white people.

We abandoned our tilt at tourism after realising that the area around the Giralda was a whites-only prestige development, originally subject to covenants barring African Americans. Claude gave the girls a bit of a telling off for not knowing better, but they replied that they had felt good holding on to a white boy and venturing into that vicinity. For my part, I was shocked, angry and powerless, but I knew which section of the community I felt most comfortable in.

The following year I brought Claude over to Europe to feature at the Birmingham Jazz Festival and then go on the road. He tore up the place in Birmingham and people still tell me they remember how great he was. Along with fiddle players Joe Kennedy Jr. from Pittsburgh (who was also Director of Jazz Studies at the prestigious Virginia Tech.) and Birmingham's Pete Hartley, Claude featured in a cracking short film called *Fiddlers Three*. It was made by John Jeremy who has films about Ben Webster and Billie Holiday on his CV and it's well worth while trying to find a copy.

On the road, Claude was set to play at the Salle Pleyel in Paris, supporting the star French violinist Stephane Grappelli, former member of the Quintet of the Hot Club de France with Django Reinhardt. Not a great idea, I felt, but I kept my thoughts to myself partly because I didn't want to lose the gig, but mostly to satisfy my sense of mischief.

I have to admit that I've never been a Grappelli devotee. He was charming, of course, far too much so for my liking, but I always found his playing superficial and flashy, with not a lot of real jazz content. Claude, on the other hand, had been brought up during the Kansas City jam session era where he learned to play 'rough, tough and loud' (his words) in order to compete with the robust horn players who inhabited KC at the time.

Claude and I were ushered into the dressing room and introduced to Stephane. Wearing his trademark flowered shirt, he flounced over to Claude, clasped him close with both arms, much to Claude's obvious embarrassment and my barely concealed amusement, telling him, 'Claude, tonight we will make the most beautiful music together.'

When the initial kerfuffle had died down, Claude took out his violin, ran his scales and ripped off a few arpeggios, sounding great, just as he always did. Stephane paled, visibly shaken by what he was listening to, his face a perfect image of panic. Unsurprisingly Stephane did not invite Claude to join him on stage, as he had promised, and equally unsurprisingly Claude did the business so

Claude Williams with Humphrey Lyttelton at the Birmingham Jazz Festival.

effectively in his opening set that it was well into Stephane's performance before the excitement began to subside.

Claude and I kept well in touch over the years, but I never did get around to returning to KC. His wife Maybelle died early and, after a decent interval, he married the patient, loyal and ever-loving Blanche Fousse outside whose apartment I had slept so peacefully on my first evening in Kansas City. They spent many happy years together, with the resourceful Blanche acting as his business manager, until his death in 2004 at the grand old age of 96. He always told me, 'You had such fun in Kansas City, man, I'm just surprised you ain't been back.' He was right, of course, and to this day I regret not taking up his many invitations.

Chapter 10

MAKING TRACKS

The early 1970s witnessed the emergence of a new wave of American soul bands, heavily influenced by James Brown, but more street. Their recordings dominated the airwaves, they were omnipresent on TV and, when they came to the UK, they filled nightclubs and theatres. Suddenly everyone knew about the Commodores, the Fatback Band, the Ohio Players, Gloria Gaynor, KC and the Sunshine Band, Tower of Power and Kool and the Gang.

Britain produced its own funk bands, but one band, from Birmingham, stood head and shoulders above the rest because they were the real thing. Anyone questioning that should look at the above list of American giants of funk and realise that the band, Muscles, toured the UK and Europe as the opening band for each and every one of them – they were even the UK and European rhythm section for the totally outrageous, but sensational, Disco Tex and the Sexolettes.

I first heard Muscles playing Eddie Fewtrell's Rebecca's niterie in Brum. Eddie was blessed with a bevy of daughters and named his night clubs after them: Barbarella's, Rebecca's and Abigail's. The dance floor was full and the kids were going wild for Muscles who sounded for all the world like they had just emerged from the Southside of Chicago. Apart from their musicianship and irresistible drive I was impressed by their repertoire, which was a mix of their own songs with reworkings of funk standards, done with originality and in no way resembling cover versions.

By midnight I'd struck a deal with mastermind and bandleader, Geoff Brown. I had met Geoff in an earlier life when he sang and played guitar with one of the best local blues combos of the 1960s, The King Bees, but with Muscles he played electronic keyboard, sang and, most importantly, wrote the songs.

That early Muscles line-up, alongside Geoff, consisted of guitarist John Lynam, bass guitarist Andy Abbott and Steve James on drums – all star players locally. We got into the recording studio without delay and cut a single, *Space Party* and *Scuttlin'*. It was immediately picked up by national radio and enjoyed enough sales to get us back in the studio the same year, 1975, to record the follow-up, *Make Me Happy* and *Funky Music*.

10. Making Tracks

Muscles signing their recording deal with Big Bear Records: (l-r) Steve James (later replaced by Mel Gaynor), Richard Ford, Stuart Scott, Geoff Brown.

By now the date-sheet was filling, a neat mix of club dates across the UK and Europe and major halls such as Hammersmith Odeon in support of visiting American name bands. We were getting a bunch of radio plays and TV appearances, press reviews were plentiful and pleasing and sell-out signs were going up in clubs and colleges. We were recording two, even three, singles a year, using first-class studios such as Chipping Norton and Essex Music.

But we weren't selling records – at least, not in the numbers we had come to expect. Who knows why? Perhaps our audiences were dancers who just didn't buy records. I wasn't overly concerned, so long as we produced records I could be proud of, but Geoff Brown took it personally and that's where the problems began.

First of all, it's important to know that Muscles was Geoff's brainchild. He came up with the name, recruited the musicians, wrote and arranged the repertoire and invariably handled the vocals. All of this left very little room for any other influence which, if offered, would be immediately rejected by Geoff.

The great blue-eyed funksters, Muscles, opening for the Fatback Band at Hammersmith Odeon.

Signing Big Bear Records to EMI's Licensed Repertoire Division. Our label manager Hugh Rees-Parnell and music industry legend Colin Burns are on the right.

10. Making Tracks

I've always been very hands-on musically, producing records, developing repertoire and having my voice heard. What I crave, rather than making money, are enthusiastic media reviews, proper appreciation by the industry and playing my part in creating and recording great music.

So, looking back, was a combination of Brown and Simpson, working together, but each seeking to control matters, a disaster waiting to happen? I don't think so, but, if we could both have been more patient with each other, then perhaps today Muscles might still be a name to be reckoned with. Now Geoff wanted action. Chart action! After three singles had failed to dent the charts, the Big Bear distribution deal was up for renewal and I allowed Geoff to convince me that it was the distribution that was letting us down and we needed to enlist the services of a big hitter.

I had been comfortable with Transatlantic: they were like family and it was always a pleasure to work with Ray Cooper, Martin Lewis, Mike Watts and Roger Upright. They knew and understood Big Bear and I believe that we achieved a lot together. Good days! In hindsight I should have left Big Bear Records where it was and fought it out with Geoff and Muscles. As it was, EMI had been keeping a watchful eye on Big Bear and came in with an invitation to place the label in its newly formed Licensed Repertoire Division along with their two existing labels, Mickie Most's RAK Records and the burgeoning Tamla Motown. I had my own office and secretary and it meant that all our UK releases were to be released Europe-wide on EMI's wholly owned international labels. EMI and most of their European licensees were enthusiastic about the recordings, resulting in releases through 6 or 7 territories, but it was probably inevitable that our series of Muscles singles met with a similar fate to the first three: a bunch of positive media attention, decent, but not sensational, sales.

By now the band had become a powerhouse. Alongside Geoff we had Stuart Scott on guitar, bass guitarist (and great singer) Richard Ford and Mel Gaynor who was later to make a name for himself with Simple Minds and become regarded, rightly, as one of the country's finest funk and rock drummers.

It was then that I made the fatal mistake of insisting that we release *Love is All I've Got* as a single: it featured the voice of Richard Ford and was pure Philadelphia Stylistics. It was Tony Blackburn's record of the week, had saturation air play and became a small hit. But the vocal was by Richard Ford. Not Geoff Brown.

At this point we had an unwelcome reassurance, if we needed it, of the potential of this fine band. Jack Stewart-Grayson, our label manager at EMI, came to Birmingham to visit Geoff Brown at his home and ask him to walk out on his Big Bear contract and sign directly to EMI. To his credit, Geoff gave him a

Muscles with (l-r) Mel Gaynor, Stuart Scott, Geoff Brown, Richard Ford.

categorical no and sent him packing with his tail between his legs. Whether Jack was sent on the mission by EMI or had decided to do a bit of freelancing on his own account I'll never know, but I strongly suspect it was the latter. What else do you expect from an Arsenal fan?

The situation between Geoff and me worsened. Ultimately we had a bit of a shout-up. I suggested we needed a new producer, not me, a song not written by Geoff, another vocal by Richard, not Geoff. Unsurprisingly Geoff walked out of the meeting. The band and I staggered on, but the writing was on the wall.

Geoff was certainly a control freak, but he was also extremely talented, as evidenced by his post-music career. He set up a video games company which undoubtedly gained a lot from his emergent computer skills which had begun to surface even in the Muscles era. *Sounds* magazine noted that Muscles was the first band ever to use a synthesiser to play a bass line on record. Today, over 40 years later, it's become commonplace.

Geoff's computer business became a world leader. He became a multi-millionaire, re-located to Santa Monica, California, and employed an army of people. Control freak? Undoubtedly. Perhaps I should have listened and backed off a little. On the other hand I might have denied myself the opportunity of producing a fine series of recordings.

10. Making Tracks

Geoff has since moved on to Mexico and retired from active service, but he still leads a trio in which he plays banjo. I'm delighted that he still plays music and hope he gets the pleasure from it that he deserves.

I also believe, looking back, that we didn't do too shabbily together.

Whilst touring American blues singers through Europe, I managed to find time to work with, and record, plenty more British bands and singers with varying degrees of commercial success.

Chris Evans, singer and guitarist, had featured with the group The Casuals, who enjoyed a Number 2 hit with their fine single, *Jesamine*. Back home in Daventry, he was keeping body and soul together truck-driving when he sent me a demo recording of some of his songs. It probably took me all of a minute to decide that I wanted to work with him. His lyrics were profound, but accessible, and his melodies of the type that, once heard, refuse to leave your mind. The favourable comparisons to David Bowie in many articles and reviews were perfectly understandable. I like to think that we had a mutual understanding from the outset, as we got to work on an unusual project. Onstage he preferred to perform solo and he was mesmerising, delivering every word with thought and intensity. However, for recording, his songs demanded more lavish treatment, not just a top-class band, but the full schtick, strings and all.

Luckily, from the years of touring American bluesmen, often solos such as Doctor Ross and Cousin Joe, I had built a network of contacts for appropriate venues throughout the UK and Europe, that entirely suited Evans' performance. So we hit the road in my Jensen Healey rag top roadster, just him, me, his guitar and a PA. But first he needed a new name. He quickly came up with the name Garbo which I thought not at all appropriate for a rough and rocking off-stage girl-chaser, but he was unshiftable.

When it came to recording, I knew we had to push the boat out. It would have been criminal to produce those fine songs in any but the correct manner. It was clearly going to be expensive, but to this day I know it was the right decision and I can still listen to those recordings with pride.

We took Garbo into Essex Music Studio in Poland Street. We booked the cream of the day's session players including Herbie Flowers, Clem Cattini and Chris Spedding, laid down the rhythm tracks, over-dubbed the wonderful Jack Emblow on piano accordion, commissioned arrangements and booked in a 20-piece string section drawn from The Royal Philharmonic.

This was the first time I had enjoyed such luxury in a recording studio and it was an exhilarating experience. I was initially thrown a little off-centre by the apparent lack of interest of the gypsies of the string section – horse racing and

Christopher Evans, aka Garbo of Celluloid Heroes fame.

10. Making Tracks

football dominated their conversation – but the moment the conductor tapped his baton on the lectern they just took care of business. As soon as the take was over, they went back to their non-musical conversations until called on again. They played impeccably and, at the end of the session, when they were packing away their instruments, I thanked them and remarked how impressive it was that they had nailed each song first time, with no need for second takes. In reply I got strange looks and the question, 'What's a second take?'.

EMI, our distributor, was as excited as we were at the results and turned over the full force of their mighty marketing machine to support the first release, *It's Over*. They organised an impressive photo shoot that captured the image of a Garbo we could not have imagined as well as producing imaginative videos. The euphoric mood was fuelled by the responses of all our European and Australian distributors who all clamoured to release the single. Everyone's conviction that we had a hit on our hands was confirmed when Tony Blackburn made it his Record of the Week on the BBC Breakfast Show. Nobody could fault the power of EMI's distribution or its marketing muscle which delivered significant radio plays. Everyone on board believed we had a sure-fire hit.

There were sales, but sadly not enough to threaten the Top 100. However, we all still believed in Garbo, so we quickly put Plan B into operation and followed up with *I Live for your Love*, a beautiful ballad delivered with a virtuoso vocal and a spine-tingler of a Jack Emblow accordion solo – again, a turntable hit. Across all territories we probably clocked up a total of something approaching 25,000 units which really didn't justify proceeding with the planned album.

Chris, unabashed by what we all perceived as unaccountable failures, was philosophical with a, 'Never mind, mate, we made some bloody good recordings and that's the most important thing.' He then cheerfully proceeded to persuade me to support the other side of his musical persona – which he did with ease. Chris was enthralled by the freedom of spirit enjoyed by the punk movement, but, with a few exceptions, dismayed by the poor musicianship and lack of good songs.

So we recruited a tough little band, took it on the road to work on repertoire and in 1978 went into the recording studio and cut six titles. The resultant single was angry, played far too fast, irreverent and my favourite punk record ever: *Only Death is Fatal* c/w *Won't You Come to My Funeral?* by Garbo's Celluloid Heroes. The live performance was riveting, but – in retrospect unsurprisingly – the band was largely ignored by the mainstream punk audience. Early on, when Garbo's Celluloid Heroes played the John Peel BBC radio show, John had taken me aside and advised me that the band would never make it as they played too well. I laughed it off at the time, but came to realise just how right he was.

We carried on working with Chris, recording a song he had written for a jeans commercial and trying to place his songs with name artists, but too much failed expectation pretty much floored our conviction, and Chris drifted away, another sad loss to music. I have tried to find his whereabouts several times, but can find no trace of him. Perhaps he is as monumentally successful as he deserves in another place, under a different name. I really hope so.

The excitement of taking a tilt at the singles charts didn't go away easily. I find it remarkable, looking back, that I could so often convince myself and those around me that we had a hot 45 on our hands, but that's the way it was in the mid to late 1970s. We had the enthusiastic support of overseas distributors, all recruited personally from encounters at the Midem music trade fair, and almost every Big Bear UK single release also saw the light of day across Europe, some even further afield. It should be noted that, just because a single didn't chart, it didn't mean it was a financial disaster. On the contrary, most of our singles racked up enough sales to make them a worthwhile proposition, the main exception being the uber-expensive Garbo productions. While the modest advances of a few hundred dollars from each of our licensees didn't effect a lifestyle change, at least they shared the investment.

Birmingham was bristling with interesting bands at the time – nothing unusual there – so it wasn't hard to find music that tickled my fancy. Harry Lang was a cynical sod with an abrasive sense of irony and matinee idol looks. He wrote good copy for our *Brum Beat* publication, was very much a man about local music and, most importantly, he played guitar, sang and fronted Bullets, an uninhibited, blues-rooted Birmingham band. He's been a pal for something like 40 years, now divides his time between homes in Brighton and Nice, and leads the rhythm and blues band, The Catfish Kings. I book them every year for the Birmingham Jazz Festival and have yet to be disappointed at any of their performances.

In 1978 we released the Bullets single, *Girl on Page 3* c/w *Grammar School Girls*. As the A side dealt with the fleeting fame of a page 3 pin-up, pride of place on the news-stands today, fish and chips wrapper tomorrow (or worse, as Harry was to demonstrate), it was possibly unwise of us to approach *The Sun* newspaper for sponsorship. They threatened Big Bear with a good drubbing in court as we were infringing their copyright on the words 'Page 3 Girl'. We felt bullish about this, as our words were slightly different – 'Girl on Page 3' – and anyway we didn't feel that they could hijack whole slabs of the language and claim ownership – and told them so.

They blustered a little, then we heard no more, even when the 7-inch 45 was released with a photograph of an extremely scruffy outdoor lavatory, with a cut up newspaper containing a clearly recognisable Girl on Page 3 instead of a toilet roll.

10. Making Tracks

We must have been having fun back then as the flood of singles showed no sign of abating. It must be admitted that some of them could have been considered downright silly. Silly they may have been, but the music was always properly played. We had an extended period on the regional dance charts with *The Longest Running Disco in the World* which we billed as by Ike and Turner Korner. Popular Coventry outfit the Ray King Band dented the national reggae charts with two delightful singles, *What You Gonna Do* and *A Woman that Understands* and later Ray featured as singer with the Gangsters on a couple of singles. However, as a Coventry City fan, he may well regret agreeing to put the vocal on a particularly nice football anthem that I produced, as Phil Spectator, extolling the virtues of West Bromwich Albion's Laurie Cunningham, Brendan Batson and the magnificent Cyrille Regis. It's certainly not as crass as it sounds: how many football records feature authentic West Indian steel drums over a ska/rock steady rhythm? At the time of release, 1979, the club would play the record loudly as the teams took to the pitch at the start and after half-time, and 40 years later they still play it at every home game! It must be the pure poetry of the line:

'West Bromwich Albion, you gotta go, man, go for Ron Atkinson.'

Roy G. Hemmings was, and still is, something of a legend in these parts. He first surfaced in the leading Birmingham soul band, The Stringbeats, but really came to fame as the featured singer in the gloriously chaotic and totally irreverent J.A.L.N. Band, led by the much loved guitarist and singer, the late Charlie Sylvester. J.A.L.N. – an abbreviation for Just Another Lonely Night – was a discotheque phenomenon, the most successful of their three hits, *Disco Music (I Like It)*, peaking at Number 21 in 1976. When the disco bubble burst, Roy, always serious when it came to the music, formed his Roy Gee and Energee, delivering the funkiest soul music that Birmingham has ever heard.

He and I are pretty much besotted with the recording process and, in a restaurant one night, we were talking about studio rates, how some studios quoted a daily rate and, when asked how long they meant by a day, would glibly respond, '24 hours', knowing that no band could perform at any meaningful level for that length of time. So we drafted a cunning plan to record sensibly for a non-stop 24 hour session. The songs we chose were both Roy's compositions, no lengthy arrangements, and the plan was to produce a 12-inch 45 rpm single, an unusual configuration.

I approached Richard Vernon at my then favourite studio, Chipping Norton Recording Studio, and explained our plan which he found very amusing and extremely silly, in about equal parts. He volunteered to provide an additional engineer, which was very sporting of him, and we were ready to go. Chipping

Norton was a residential studio, with half a dozen bedrooms and a refectory where Richard's wife, Shirley, gained fame throughout the music world for her ability to magic up splendid grub at no notice at all. She did make the point that there was no way she was going to lose any beauty sleep over this nutty project, but, nice lady as she was, she said that she would prepare meals and leave them in the fridge for us to heat up when hunger struck in the small hours.

Come the day and we – that is, Roy, his band and me – left Birmingham at 7.00 am and set up the gear by 10.00 am, our starting time. By the time we had sound-balanced and done the run-throughs, we were ready to lay down the backing tracks which we did by mid-afternoon. Just time for Shirley to come to the rescue with a late lunch before the backing singers arrived. We ran the track past them a dozen times and went for takes. We completed all the backing vocals by early evening, just as the horns, from the London-based funksters Gonzales, arrived to record their parts.

The rhythm team had gone home by this time, Roy was feeling bushed, so I packed him off to get some sleep while I recorded the horns which must have taken until around 11.00 pm. Gonzales disappeared into the night, wishing us luck and clearly wanting to hang around and enjoy the process. I woke Roy up and, as he set about recording his lead vocals with the newly arrived second engineer at the desk, I went to bed for some much needed shuteye. Roy woke me around 3.00 am to say he was happy with the vocals he had laid down. I listened through with him and agreed that he had really nailed it.

It was Roy's turn to go back to bed, leaving me to do the mix, but not before we had raided Shirley's refrigerator. We must have started to mix sometime after 4.00 am and were soon joined by Roy who said that he was too excited to sleep and didn't want to miss any of the action. It went smoothly. Richard came in around 8.00 am with coffee and bacon sandwiches and at about 9.30, just inside the 24 hour limit, we were able to agree that we were delighted with the result. Richard complained that he had been hoping to charge us for over-run time, but actually he was just as pleased as Roy and I.

I'm For Real c/w *Jump Up* was a dance-floor hit, figuring on several regional dance charts and, much to our delight, becoming a small hit in Brazil!

Roy's quality as a top-level soul singer was confirmed when he was offered the irresistible, a place in one of the finest of all the New York vocal groups, the Drifters. He remained a Drifter for nearly 16 years, making him the longest serving singer in that famous group. He now lives in the Birmingham suburb of Harborne, occasionally going out with his extravagant all-action soul show, Roy Gee and the Dictionary of Soul.

10. Making Tracks

As a result of our regular tour dates in Holland and Belgium, I found myself releasing *Milk Cow*, a single by Belgian punk outfit Tjens Couter, pressed in Brussels sprout green vinyl, of course, which hit throughout the Benelux countries and did decently in the UK. The same year I was with Cousin Joe in Liege, East Belgium, where we heard balladeer Alain Braine in an after-hours club. Joe was totally taken with him, and I found his enthusiasm so contagious, that, the wrong side of a few Westmalle Trappist beers, we found ourselves drafting and signing a recording contract on the club's paper table cloth. I am actually rather proud of that recording, though it has no connection with the jazz, rock and blues for which Big Bear is known. Alain was a splendid singer and a year or two later took first prize in what was known as the Promotion Artistique Belge before emigrating to Quebec.

In Holland I several times ran into Hans Dulfer, a jazz saxophonist who had a catchy little song about the pleasures of ingesting certain dubious substances. Muscles liked the song, but quite rightly figured it might not enhance their funky reputation. So we recorded it with Muscles operating under the alias of Zulu, a most enjoyable session with drummer Mel Gaynor doing a grand job on the not exactly poetic lyrics. The song was *Red Red Libanon* which is a bit of a giveaway to people who study these things, while the B side is a splendid jam, *Okavanga Swamp*.

Among so many single releases the story of Bob Catley and *Lights Went Out* stands out. Bob is now known worldwide as the singer with one of Birmingham's finest ever rock bands – and one of the heaviest, to boot – the mighty Magnum. But back then, shrouded in the mists of time, he recorded a fine rock ballad for Big Bear. I had received a tape with two songs written by an unpublished songwriter, Joe Monkton, of Blackheath, and they were rather good. We exchanged letters and tapes over a period of a few months and met a couple of times when I told him that, in my opinion, there wasn't a dud among his songs, but probably not a hit either. He was totally non-music biz, held down a proper job and was a really nice regular bloke who must have spent all his available time writing songs. Then he sent me a ballad, *Lights Went Out*, which I found irresistible and decided to record.

Bob Catley was my first port of call and he loved the song. I assembled a band of hotshot Birmingham musicians and recorded *Lights Went Out* in the excellent recording studio at the bottom of the garden at Ron Lee's Pelsall home. I had such confidence in the song that I brought in a string section to add the final touches.

In the afterglow I stepped back and made the decision, unfathomable from where I stand now, not to release it as it was too commercial! It's hard to imagine why I would be so precious about Big Bear that I would refuse to release my own production on the basis that it might sell too well and cause confusion over the company image! Actually and surprisingly, dear old Joe Monkton didn't seem at all disappointed at my stupid decision; he was just delighted that one of his songs had been properly recorded. As a footnote, Bob Catley's tremendous version of the hitherto unreleased *Lights Went Out* is due eventually to see the light of day on a compilation CD to help mark 50 years of Big Bear.

Towards the end of the 1970s, along came The Quads. Arriving at the office one morning in the Spring of 1979, I found that someone had pushed a cassette through the letterbox, bearing the word Jones and a phone number. As is my habit – I listen to every demo I'm sent, even if often only briefly – I played it straightaway and was impressed. I phoned the number and arranged to have a beer that evening with Josh, Jack and Johnny Jones, along with their friend from their schooldays, James Doherty – The Quads. I asked to listen to the master, but all they had was this well played, but rickety, cassette. Although the recording perfectly captured the song, *There Must be Thousands*, from a quality viewpoint we really needed the master.

The Quads told me they had already sent the recording to all the major, and some not so major, recording companies and nobody had responded, not even to say no, thank you. At that time I was working on a live Fairport Convention album which luckily had tremendous audience reaction, so the way forward was obvious. I took the cassette into Zella Recording Studios, transferred the stereo tracks onto an eight-track tape, added a selection of the Fairport applause onto two of the remaining six tracks, and mixed it, disguising the scratchy sound and poor quality lead in with enthusiastic applause. That actual recording, rejected by a long list of major companies, became a hit in several countries and propelled the band onto John Peel's *Top Gear* BBC show. John Peel's love of the record is well documented: he declared it to be his favourite single of the decade and in 2005 it was revealed to be among the chosen singles in John Peel's Record Box.

Some music papers wrongly lumped The Quads in with the mod movement, which was then in fashion. In fact they were a fine example of a straightahead Birmingham rock band with fearsome guitar riffs and tough three-part vocal harmonies. Their initial image was something of a shock, dressed identically as vicars, but, once that riff machine swung into action, all was well.

The Quads were always a pleasure to be with, working hard at writing and rehearsing their material and equally serious about their political views, as can be deduced from their lyrics. Their follow-up single later the same year, *There's Never Been a Night*, fared well on radio and in sales and was released throughout Europe, as was their 1980 release, *Astronaut's Journey*, a double A side with *UFO*.

10. Making Tracks

I'm never sure if it's very clever to release a double A side single: you automatically reduce the airplays and, thus, the impact, as no DJ is going to play both sides. That's what happened here, but the boys stepped back into the spotlight with their May 1981 release.

They supported the People's March for Jobs in which 500 unemployed marched the 280 miles from Liverpool to London and delivered a 250,000-signature petition to Parliament. The Quads joined the trek at Stoke-on-Trent and marched shoulder to shoulder with the demonstrators all the way to London. The marchers were accommodated on their epic journey in town halls, civic centres and church halls, and every night The Quads performed for their fellow-marchers. It was a special thrill to hear the song we had recorded to coincide with the march, *Gotta Get a Job*, sung by the marchers.

The Quads are fondly remembered – and not just in Birmingham. As recently as 2013 a skin care company, JooMo, used *There Must Be Thousands*, in a commercial, 34 years after release. Despite efforts I have lost touch with Johnny,

The first photograph of The Quads, dog-collared and outside a church: brothers Josh, Johnny and Jack Jones and their friend from childhood, James Doherty.

Jack and James, though eventually I found that Josh is currently a vicar somewhere in New Zealand, so those early photographs of them in priestly gear complete with dog collars proved to be a portent.

With the benefit of hindsight it would appear to be an unusual sort of madness for a small independent provincial record label to release some 43 singles over something like four years. If that's not strange enough in itself, the music styles were so diverse: funk, rock, reggae, disco, jazz, blues, soul – even a couple of ballads. I guess it happened quite naturally because the vinyl 45 format and the arena into which it was released were so exciting and so much out-and-out fun. As long as the music was good – and there was so much good music around in those days – and you liked the band, then that was enough.

The International Debt Crisis of 1982 took its toll on the recording industry as it did on most other things and the effect on Big Bear Records, though not catastrophic, was bad enough. Three of the European record companies that licensed our product went bankrupt and were unable to pay moneys due; worse than that, we lost good friends. It was to be seven years before we released another single, a three-tracker by King Pleasure and the Biscuit Boys which included their version of Slim Gaillard's *Chicken Rhythm*, complete with the rather dubious lyrics. Naturally.

Black Sabbath. The classic early photograph of the band on a grassy bank opposite my house – just after the name change from Earth.

From Monroe County, Georgia, the Stoop Down Man, Chick Willis.

Birmingham Jazz Festival favourite Marty Grosz, guitarist, singer, raconteur and all-round good bloke.

Authors Jim and Ron Simpson on the outside looking in. So nothing new there!

Roy Williams and Digby Fairweather, two of an exceptional generation of world class British jazz musicians.

England's finest jazz swing singer Val Wiseman.

An everyday sight in Birmingham during the Jazz Festival. Swedish sousaphone player Jonas Molbeck from the New Orleans Jump Band from Sotogrande in Spain takes a stroll.

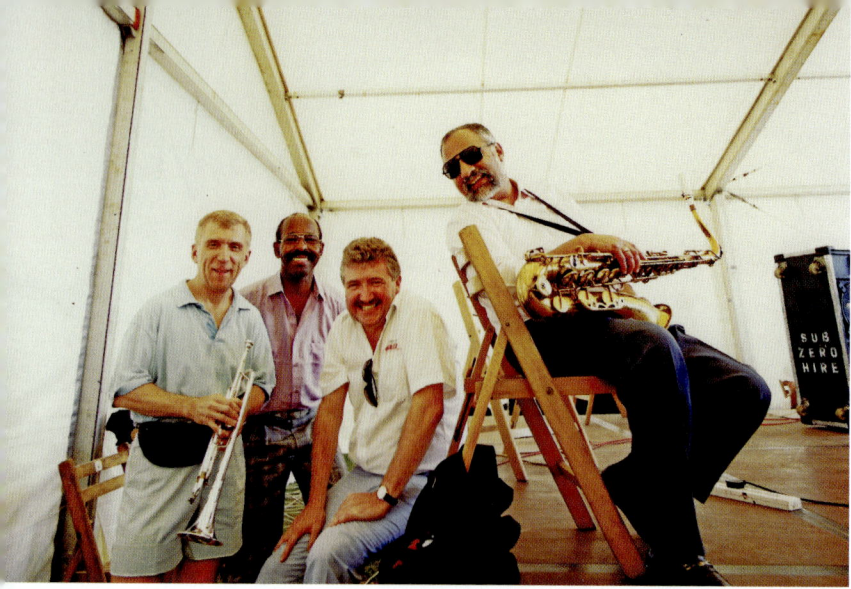

An international gathering backstage at a Cannon Hill Park Jam Session. Russian trumpeter Valery Ponomarev, Gene Connors from Alabama, JS, Nairobi-born saxophonist Olaf Vas.

Kenny Baker leading his Dozen in a six-day romp at Birmingham's Ronnie Scott's.

Rehearsing The Marbella Jazz Suite for its debut at the Palacio de Congresos in Marbella: (l-r) Alex Garnett, Alan Barnes, Bruce Adams, Simon Gardner, Mark Nightingale.

Studio shot of King Pleasure and the Biscuit Boys.

Members of King Pleasure and the Biscuit Boys with JS outside Phoenix, Arizona.

Annie Ross.

Annie Ross sound-checking at the Palacio de Congresos.

Val Wiseman spots her hero, Annie Ross, backstage at Marbella.

A day off in Marbella and Bruce Adams over-celebrates!

Leader of the Count Basie Orchestra and good friend to Big Bear, Bill Hughes.

Big Bear's Sarah Yang at the British Midlands Music stand at Midem.

The Duke of Edinburgh questioning Sarah Yang's Chinese Jitterbug Squad.

Recording Tipitina's second album, Takin' Care of Business, at Birmingham's Hotel du Vin: Justin Randall, JS, Debbie Jones.

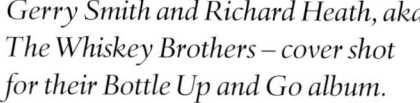
Justin Randall and Debbie Jones of Leyland-based Tipitina.

Gerry Smith and Richard Heath, aka The Whiskey Brothers – cover shot for their Bottle Up and Go album.

Chapter 11

JAZZ CITY UK

Through the 1970s I was more preoccupied in career terms with rock and blues than with jazz, but in the 1980s I became closely involved with jazz again. At the time I was becoming increasingly disturbed by the goings-on in what then passed for jazz. It came to a head when I went to a gig at the splendidly named, but ineffectually run, Cannonball pub in – where else? – Adderley Street. If the first set was drab, dull, unswinging and musically inept, the second set failed to live up to that standard. At the outset the trombone player took off his left shoe and sock, rolled up his trouser leg and played the entire set with his foot in a bucket of water. For the finale he attached a plastic hose and plunger to his horn, waving it around with abandon. The tour was sponsored by the Arts Council. There were maybe 20 people in the audience and, if this was the first time at a jazz performance for any of them, the odds were very much in favour of its also being the last.

Maybe I had become isolated in those years in the worlds of blues and rock and hadn't noticed jazz slipping into the hands of intellectuals and non-jazzers. It was the time when everything had to be fusion. Now any clear thinker would agree that experimentation is a good thing, well worth trying, but needing to be worked through in the rehearsal room rather than in public on an Arts Council-sponsored tour. The very last straw was a performance which purported to be a fusion of Norwegian folk music and jazz and was unrecognisable as anything but a weakly conceived and poorly performed mess.

What finally made me snap was a concert I attended at Birmingham Town Hall where the entire programme lacked any attempt to swing, endless meaningless improvisation climaxing with a pompous Italian pianist – I use the word extremely loosely – studiously dragging a chain backwards and forwards across the strings of the grand piano. The tiny audience, wisebeards to a man, were delirious with excitement while I scuttled off as quickly as I could to put *The Atomic Mr Basie* on the turntable.

I took my indignation to the office of my pal, the jazz-loving Malcolm Powell, Special Projects Manager at Mitchells and Butlers, the nationally distributed Birmingham brewery. They were a major player in the licensed trade until the

Every jazz festival should have a friend like Malcolm Powell. To him, nothing was impossible.

Monopolies and Mergers Commission waded in with an edict that pubs owned by breweries were no longer allowed to sell exclusively their own beers. The resultant loss of profits took away much of the financial incentive for pubs to present live music and meant that music across all styles lost out on sponsorship.

Malcolm was a maverick within M&B. Personally appointed by Chairman Sir Charles Darby, he was given a free hand with the Special Projects budget as long as he delivered – which was pretty much always. I was always amused by the stories Malcolm told about the Ivy Bush pub on the Hagley Road, adjacent to the Big Bear office. Sir Charles lived on the other, posh side of the Hagley Road and apparently, whenever their window cleaner, an Ivy Bush regular, complained to Lady Darby about the toilets or anything else, she had a word with Sir Charles and the problem was always swiftly put to rights.

I complained about the state of jazz in this country to Malcolm who asked what I would like to do about it. I told him I would like to put on a major concert

11. Jazz City UK

in Birmingham, borrowing an idea from Eddie Condon's New York Town Hall show of two all-star front lines alternating over the same rhythm section in an organised jam session. I wanted to use Cannon Hill Park's open-air Arena Theatre and record the whole thing for posterity. Without hesitation Malcolm gave me the go-ahead and I set to work.

Humphrey Lyttelton, my Number 1 choice to lead the operation, bought into it immediately, even before I had finished laying out the plan. Trumpet/cornet ace Digby Fairweather was the obvious choice as leader of the opposing front line and the resultant line-up was just about as all-star as you could get in this country at that time. Humph was to front Roy Crimmins, Dave Shepherd and Dick Morrissey, while Digby led Roy Williams, Randy Colville and Bruce Turner. The rhythm team was Mick Pyne, Jim Douglas, Harvey Weston and Johnny Richardson. There was a strong representation from the legendary Alex Welsh Band here – no bad thing – as well as present and former members of Humph's own band and Average White Band tenor man Morrissey who was to turn in a stunning performance, so no surprise there.

The concert on August 12th, 1984, was a sell-out, with 860 people enjoying a perfect summer's evening. Malcolm had agreed I could rent Richard Branson's Manor Mobile: no point in bringing in anything but the best for such an illustrious gathering of musicians. When we released *The M&B Jam Session Volume One* on Big Bear, the reviews were uniformly enthusiastic – why wouldn't they be with such a line-up? – and the album picked up the award of Jazz Album of the Year.

Laying down the principles behind the session, the sleeve notes read, 'The M&B Jam Session was conceived as a positive gesture against the introspective, self-indulgent, over-intricate music that, masquerading as jazz, often threatens to obscure the true spirit of the music. To this end, a galaxy of the most exciting and consummate musicians gathered together in a Birmingham park to demonstrate that masters of their craft are still prepared to take risks, compete with their peers and produce red-blooded swinging jazz that really does move the spirit.'

It was a memorable, exhilarating and inspiring session: the album attests to that. However, it didn't finish at sundown and, in a way, it's not over yet. At the after-party I was approached by Humph and Malcolm with Stephen Carter, manager of the then-new and very swish Holiday Inn off Broad Street. They all thought it would be profligate to let it end there, so why not do a multi-day version the next year, a jazz festival in fact? Stephen opined that July was a poor month for hotel occupancy in Birmingham, Malcolm could commit a portfolio of appropriate venues and Humph asked me to think what fun I could have, coming up with ideas and booking the best of musicians. There was really not much I could say other than yes, but at least I did have the presence of mind to ask Humphrey Lyttelton to become Festival Patron. 'Of course I will,' he said. 'I see it as a role not unlike that of the Queen Mother.'

The next year I was planning the first Birmingham Jazz Festival, thinking of it as a one-off, a nice follow-up to the Cannon Hill Jam Session, presenting good music in Birmingham with no thought of doing it again. Mitchells and Butlers gave us financial support; after all their man Malcolm Powell had helped persuade me to do it. Then out of the blue came a phone call from Brian Martin of the City Council's Leisure Department inviting me to have a coffee in his Auchinleck House office.

'I hear that you are planning a jazz festival,' he said. 'The city would like to support you. How much do you need?'. This was not a conversation I had often had, so I mentally groped for a figure and suggested £5,000. He said he would let me know and a couple of weeks later I received a letter from him telling me that the City had allocated £6,500. No form filling, no questionnaires about the racial profile and sexual preferences of our anticipated audience, just a note telling me that his door was always open.

Trombonist Gene 'The Mighty Flea' Connors with Roy Williams, Jack Parnell and Len Skeat in an early Jazz Festival Jam Session.

11. Jazz City UK

The 1985 inaugural festival opened with a Champagne Breakfast Launch, typical Malcolm Powell. Lord Mayor Frank Carter welcomed hot jazz back to Birmingham and spoke of 'More Jazz Than You Can Shake a Stick At'. We presented just 40 performances in eight days, with 150 musicians in 21 venues, a modest beginning, but then administratively the festival was just a one-man show.

Musically I had a great few days with the always splendid Humphrey Lyttelton Band, Morrissey-Mullen and veteran American guitarist Al Casey who first played with Fats Waller as a teenager and joined his band permanently on graduating from high school. Other personal favourites included Ronnie Verrell, who played Animal's drum part in *The Muppets Show*, and world-class British trombonist Roy Williams.

I am the first to admit that our festival has, over the years, enjoyed much more than its fair share of silliness and will continue to do so and in that first year there were signs of what was to come. There was Mr. R. White's Secret Lemonade Drinkers' Jazz Party, featuring some wacky jazz and pitched at youngsters, and, more bizarrely, an attempt at a world record, if indeed there was one, a Jazz Marathon of playing *Honeysuckle Rose* non-stop for 24 hours with relays of musicians taking part. It was extremely untidy, some excellent and some not so excellent music played by a total of 61 jazz musicians of all standards. It was an unforgettable exercise in creating camaraderie among musicians, but a dead loss when it came to breaking records – as if we really cared.

Come the Autumn, we were encouraged by a feature in the trade paper, *Music Week*, which described Birmingham as 'an exhilarating, freewheeling festival, a breath of fresh invigorating air among the turgid, tepid morass so frequently passed off as jazz these days.' With Humphrey Lyttelton volunteering himself to continue as Festival Patron, a position which he retained for the rest of his life, it became obvious that we had inadvertently taken on an annual festival.

The second year was a significant step forward with the beginning of what became a regular feature, the American invasion. The Buddy Rich Orchestra, Art Blakey's Jazz Messengers, Harry 'Sweets' Edison and Gene 'The Mighty Flea' Connors headed the bill of 140 performances, with the British contingent including the Humphrey Lyttelton Band, Georgie Fame and the Blue Flames and two significant firsts of artists who would play an important part in the future of Big Bear and the festival: singer Val Wiseman who featured with Eggy Ley's Hotshots and a young, raw, exhilarating band from Walsall called Some Like it Hot, destined to namechange to King Pleasure and the Biscuit Boys.

My salient memory of that year was sitting with legendary New Orleans blues piano player and singer Champion Jack Dupree sharing a beer with hard bop

The Count Basie Orchestra backstage at Birmingham Odeon – JS is in there somewhere.

Frank Foster, leader of the Count Basie Orchestra, on the sad night Birmingham Odeon closed as a live music venue.

Legendary bebopper Art Blakey and New Orleans piano professor Champion Jack Dupree, flanked by members of the New Orleans Mardi Gras Marching Band – from Lincoln.

pioneer Art Blakey, listening to them discussing Louis Armstrong! 'Now this is what should happen at a jazz festival,' I thought, and in many ways it was that moment that drove me to decide to give the festival the dedication it deserved.

The next few years saw Birmingham welcome such great names as the Count Basie Orchestra, the Modern Jazz Quartet, Claude Williams, Cab Calloway and the Cotton Club Orchestra, and Miles Davis. The Blues Brothers Band played six shows in three years at Birmingham, fronted by Eddie 'Knock on Wood' Floyd with Mr. Fabulous Alan Rubin, Tom Bones Malone, Matt 'Guitar' Murphy and all the original band from the movie. The blues began to take its rightful place at the festival, with appearances by the Buddy Guy & Junior Wells Band, Shuggie Otis, B.B. King, Albert King and Magic Slim who shared a bill with Birmingham's own Spencer Davis Group.

The Grand Hotel became the hub of the Festival. We had some terrific concerts there, including such oddities as The Tokyo Hot Club, a Japanese five-piece playing the gypsy jazz of Django Reinhardt. In its only UK appearance, the legendary Illinois Jacquet Big Band played a live BBC2 broadcast from The Grand, we held memorial jam sessions there to give a proper Jazz Festival farewell to Humph and to Malcolm Powell, and it was at the Grand that I had the unforgettable experience of seeing Van Morrison in the audience, alongside Georgie Fame, for a Mose Allison concert.

The Festival's 1990 Miles Davis concert at the NEC became a turning point as far as future policy was concerned. Our sponsors, Mitchells and Butlers, were insistent that we present the biggest name in jazz at the time, so booking Miles was a no-brainer, despite the $45,000 fee plus a truckload of additions. They required travel and hotel costs for a travelling party of ten, although there were only five musicians on stage – three of the additions were lawyers! The sponsors' guarantee looked fine, they supported the performance with huge billboards throughout the city, but, despite the best marketing campaign for a jazz event that Birmingham has ever seen and resulting sales of 2,700, this fell well short of break-even.

It took a while to pay back the loss, but it made us look carefully at the Festival itself. As the event's reputation grew among musicians, we were able to increase the status of bands appearing on the Free Jazz Trail until it featured attractions that would command a £10 or £12 ticket price at any other festival. So, in effect, we were competing with ourselves and decided to drastically reduce the ticketed events until we reached the point where almost all the events were free admission. This is now one of the main characteristics of the Festival.

We started what became an annual occurrence, collecting money to buy a Guide Dog for the Blind which every year was named after a different musician and presented to the Guide Dogs Association by the musician in question. Thus a series of extremely handsome dogs carried such names as Humph, Melly, Digby, Marty, Dusko and – in a departure from normal practice – Barnett, named for Dave Barnett, for many years the festival's champion collector of money for Guide Dogs, earning himself the soubriquet Dave The Dog.

Within a few years we had on board my invaluable wing man for (to date) 31 festivals. Tim Jennings came to Big Bear in 1988. He had previously worked for the Prince's Trust before a sojourn in France with his band, busking to raise funds for food and lodging. He played tenor saxophone, was a jazz lover, and was clearly fascinated by what Big Bear got up to. He was intelligent, enthusiastic and seemingly desperate to find a regular job in the music industry. He turned up for interview wearing a crumpled cream-coloured linen suit. I was rather taken with the suit, but he has never again worn it to work – I must have a word with him! Besides the 31 Birmingham festivals Tim and I have managed musical events without number and looked after the careers of too many bands and musicians to even think about, his skills as Business Manager essential to Big Bear.

As we entered the 1990s we found our work-load significantly increased with a burgeoning portfolio of festivals of one sort or another – and the work-force grew accordingly. At one time Big Bear employed twelve full-time staff, but, looking back, that was something of a luxury with, for instance, our own in-house design team. Long-server Juliet Kenny took care of our accounts for almost 25 years and attained legendary status as the instigator of much of the office parties' bad behaviour.

However, many of the folk were sensible enough to get out while the going was good, with Sue Elwell taking a responsible post at the Arts Council, Matthew Robinson going to Channel 4, Clare Jepson-Homer becoming Marketing guru at Birmingham Rep, Esther Blaine moving on to Huntingdon Hall, Worcester, and our star graduate, Pete Winkelman, making his name at CBS Records before taking up the reins as Chairman of Milton Keynes Dons.

The Festival generated an increasing number of what we might call 'special projects'. *Lady Sings the Blues* came early in the Festival's history and many others followed. *Swinging Down Broad Street* was a musical stroll through a random series of events that contributed, more or less, to Birmingham's musical heritage. The Broad Street area has long been the busiest area of the festival, which in recent years has been recognised by the Westside BID who have strengthened ties by providing financial support.

I came up with a series of short stories, binned many of them and then invited various musicians to write a piece to illustrate one or more of the tales. We recruited

11. Jazz City UK

Bruce Adams and Alan Barnes, the pack shot for their Let's Face the Music album.

and rehearsed an eight-piece band of what Tim referred to as The Usual Suspects, meaning my favourite British jazz musicians, in this case including Bruce Adams, Alan Barnes, Mark Nightingale, Dave Green and Ralph Salmins. The suite was premiered at the Moulin Rouge Spiegeltent as part of the 2005 Festival and, sadly, has never been performed again – yet. The contributing composers were Humphrey Lyttelton, Alan Barnes, Jack Parnell and Mark Skirving and Danny McCormack of King Pleasure and the Biscuit Boys.

The titles included *Lily's Dancing Feat*, the story of a 16-year-old Birmingham girl who in 1923 won the national dance marathon, wearing out three male partners in the process. *This One's for the Boss* was dedicated to the memory of Kenny Baker and *Pops and the Peg Leg* recalled the time that Peg Leg Bates opened for Louis Armstrong in Sparkbrook. *The Night the Pres Went Down* was about the memorable Stan Kenton concert at Birmingham Odeon on the day of Kennedy's assassination when Kenton made his famous 'We're gonna keep shop' speech.

In all the first 34 years of the Festival the only time the police were involved was in that same Spiegeltent on what is now Centenary Square. A wonderful construction dating back to 1910, owned and operated by the Klessens family in Rijkevorsel in Belgium, the tent was in place for the full ten days of the Festival with workshops by day and concerts every night with the likes of Chicago's Red Holloway, Joey DeFrancesco and George Melly with John Chilton's Feetwarmers, plus the latest staging of the British Jazz Awards.

It was on the Melly night that the police were summoned by the girlfriend of a young man who had approached Gorgeous George to ask for his autograph. George had asked if he had something to rest on while he signed, so the chap handed over his wallet which George promptly trousered. No amount of persuasion, reasoning or threats could persuade Melly to release the wallet. The young man was getting more frantic by the minute and his girlfriend made the call. The law arrived in the impressively large shape of a seasoned bobby who asked George to be reasonable and hand over the wallet. To the surprise of everyone in the rapidly growing crowd George began to attack the constable. Perhaps 'attack' conveys a misleading impression. George reached up as high as he could and struck the officer, ineffectually, half a dozen times on the chest. Clearly not injured in the slightest, the officer drew himself to his full height, towering over George, and simply bellowed, 'How dare you?' which had the desired effect. George apologised, we invited the young couple into the concert as our guests and the constable disappeared into the night, chortling.

This was a one-off blip in George Melly's behaviour in our experience. We booked his band for the Festival many times, usually in the splendid Grosvenor Suite of the Grand Hotel, our favourite festival venue. His shows were invariably sell-outs and he always delivered a fine performance. It has to be said that George was not a particularly good singer – actually, that is being kind. He was, however, extremely knowledgeable about the music, compiled an interesting repertoire, surrounded himself with capable musicians and, above all, had unquenchable enthusiasm and irresistible charm. Jazz was not his only specialised subject: a noted cultural commentator, a respected film and television critic and author, he was particularly distinguished as an expert on surrealism.

11. Jazz City UK

When he was invited, as the guest of honour, to open a very serious exhibition on the Harlem Renaissance at the University of Warwick, he asked me to drive him there. It was a most satisfying day. My knowledge of Harlem before that was probably limited to Harlem's Harmful Little Armful, Fats Waller, fellow stride pianists Willie 'The Lion' Smith and James P. Johnson, rent parties, the Cotton Club and the Apollo Theatre. On the journey there George talked non-stop about the literature and art of the 1920s. It was just like watching a television programme, except that at exactly midday he insisted I find him a hostelry where he could have 'a glass of the black stuff' – which turned out to be three glasses! His opening of the exhibition was captivating, though it must be admitted that the return journey became increasingly chaotic, punctuated by regular pauses at a variety of watering holes.

In truth Melly was one of the great English eccentrics and the worlds of music and art are a lot less colourful now that he has gone.

There was one other occasion during the festival when police activity was greater than normal, but the cause was nothing of the festival's doing. Philadelphian Hammond organ maestro Joey deFrancesco was holding sway in the Spiegeltent, just settling into his second set in front of a sell-out audience, when a police constable skidded to a halt, on his bicycle, at the entrance and yelled to me, 'Bomb scare, get everyone out!'

I asked him to hang on for a minute and to give me a little more detail, such as where we should send the 350 people. Clearly in no mood for a cosy chat, he yelled, 'Use your initiative', and whizzed off into the night. I can say, with a degree of confidence, that I did not become the most popular man in that room when I went onstage, hijacked the microphone and tried to calmly explain the situation to the seriously annoyed jazz fans. Our festival volunteers were heroic that night, and, although it was eventually exposed as a bomb hoax, there was no way they could have believed that it was other than the real thing. We emptied the theatre from the back in something resembling an orderly fashion and guided what has to be said was an increasingly unruly mob, to what we had designated as a collection point as far away as possible from The Spiegeltent within the confines of Centenary Square.

In fairly short order a police sergeant arrived, expressed some satisfaction in the by then orderly behaviour of our audience, and told me to usher them across the road, march them south towards Chinatown, and disperse them with the order not to return to anywhere near Broad Street for any reason whatever – including picking up their cars. We followed his instructions, two of us went back to the Spiegeltent, turned off the electrics, locked the doors and set off to our respective homes.

I got to bed for an hour or so at around 4 am, but needed to know what was happening on Broad Street so I returned there at around 7 in the morning. Hotel, restaurant and bar furniture was scattered the length of the street, left by revellers who had been told to evacuate and had taken their chairs and their drinks out onto the street to continue their party. When I got to the City Inn I found a scene worthy of a disaster movie. There were unfinished meals, half empty wine bottles and chairs in a chaotic state – all evidence of an extremely quick evacuation. As I was taking in the situation, Stephen Cresswell, the hotel manager, appeared, greeted me cheerfully and invited me to join him for breakfast. He hadn't been to bed, but like me felt somehow invigorated by the whole experience. Big Bear staffer Sarah Yang always tells me that I seem to enjoy problems and crises, and maybe there is a germ of truth in there.

It was always a very special time when trumpet player Dusko Goykovich played our festival. Born in Bosnia Herzogovina in 1931, Dusko began attracting attention in the States and, after studying at Berklee College from 1961 to 1963,

A clearly ill-at-ease Dusko Goykovich poses for a publicity shot in Birmingham's Botanical Gardens.

he featured in the acclaimed big bands of Maynard Ferguson and Woody Herman before returning to Europe and leading his own bands as well as featuring with the Clarke-Boland Big Band for some years.

Dusko was a fearsome bebop trumpet man, sure-footed at any tempo, with perfect intonation and the ability to swing anyone into bad health. When it came to playing ballads, Dusko was almost without equal. He didn't play a note that wasn't necessary and he placed them exactly where they should go with elegance. Benny Green described Dusko's playing as 'like Miles Davis on a good day', but, much as I respected Benny's opinions on all matters to do with jazz, on this occasion I have to disagree. Dusko was far better than Miles and probably still is, well into his 80s leading his own big band in Munich.

But it didn't always go Dusko's way. We had a festival gig at Birmingham's historic Barton's Arms pub where Laurel and Hardy are supposed to have taken a taste in the intermission of their appearance at the Aston Hippodrome, just across the street. A smartly dressed young couple came to the door, paid their admission and went into Dusko's gig, only to emerge 15 minutes later and politely take their leave. They were very nice about it, wouldn't accept a refund and explained that it was fine, but not what they expected. They had come for Disco Goykovich!

Most times we were able to ensure that pianist Nat Pierce, a fellow-Herman alumnus, was in town at the same time as Dusko. Nat, a dear friend of the festival, died three weeks before the 1992 festival started, so naturally it was dedicated to that tremendous pianist and arranger, a man with a huge appetite for life – and for food. Whenever he had time off during the festival, he would go out looking for opportunities to jam with other festival artists, often in small local pubs as long as the guys in the band were proper players. As for food, the first time we ate together he ordered two main courses for himself. That was a bit of a shock, as it would continue to be at all those other convivial meals we not quite shared.

Born in Somerville, Massachusetts, in 1925, Nat had a formidable and huge CV which included regularly depping for Count Basie; he played all the piano parts alongside Basie legends Freddy Green, Eddie Jones and Sonny Payne on the magnificent Lambert, Hendricks and Ross album, *Sing A Song of Basie*. He also wrote arrangements for the Basie Band and many other household jazz names, as well as holding the piano chair with Woody Herman's Third Herd in the 1950s, recording his own compositions in impeccable small group arrangements and co-leading the formidable Capp-Pierce Juggernaut.

Nat became a regular visitor to Birmingham festivals, sometimes with his wife Cathy Sweeney, herself a fine working singer, and I like to think that he

Nat Pierce, Teddy Edwards, Jeff Clyne, Pete Strange and Dusko Goykovich in one of the now-legendary Jazz Festival Jam Sessions.

became a real pal. He was the most knowledgeable and entertaining companion – and generous, too. He just loved music and he often wrote arrangements for our jam sessions without being asked and always refused payment.

Another jazz great whom it was always a pleasure to welcome to Birmingham was tenor saxophonist Teddy Edwards, one of the most cultured and innovative players to emerge in the bebop era. At that time he worked with such giants as his good friend Charlie Parker and in 1947 famously recorded *The Duel* (title self-explanatory) with Dexter Gordon.

Teddy also featured on the brilliant soundtrack of one of my favourite films, *One from the Heart*, where Tom Waits' songs, sung by him and Crystal Gayle, replaced large chunks of the dialogue, a stunningly effective ploy of director Francis Ford Coppola. Teddy was a main feature in Tom Waits' touring band, most notably on the 1980 *Heart Attack and Vine* tour which opened in London. Tom was so impressed with Teddy's playing that he sent the other band members back to the States and completed the tour as a duo with Teddy.

11. Jazz City UK

My most embarrassing moment with Teddy was not in Birmingham, but at the Cork Jazz Festival where I'd booked him in for the duration of the festival. The airline bringing him in from Los Angeles managed to mislay all his luggage. Now Teddy was a very smart dresser, nothing fancy, but never anything but immaculate. By the second day of wearing the same clothes Teddy was getting fractious, but he continued to ignore my suggestion that we walk into town, re-equip him with the necessities and claim the money back from the airline which was constantly promising to re-unite him with his baggage. Come the third day, Teddy gave way and let me take him to Marks and Spencer where he went rather over the top in the shirts department. On our return journey, weighed down with M&S bags, I was embarrassed to see a Pan Am van sitting outside the hotel while Teddy's luggage was offloaded! He said he forgave me and I made a contribution to his purchases, but I couldn't help wondering how he managed for the rest of the tour, carting around all that additional luggage.

Top tenormen Teddy Edwards and Dick Morrissey taking care of business at the Adolphe Sax Birthday Celebration.

Early in 2003 I received a touching handwritten letter from Teddy, telling of the good times and how much he valued our friendship. At the time I wondered what had inspired such a letter. We both knew we were chums, there was no need to spell it out. The reason became clear a month or two later when I learned that he had died on April 20th, six days short of his 79th birthday.

Guitarist and singer Marty Grosz was born in Berlin, son of the highly successful artist and political caricaturist George Grosz who emigrated to New York in 1933 in order to escape arrest for his savagely satirical depictions of Nazism.

Marty grew up to be the archetypal English-gentrified New Yorker, accent, tweeds and all, which he referred to as his schtick. Announcing himself as 'playing guitar like George Burns, telling jokes like Django Reinhardt', Marty's performance was witty and clever, displayed absolute knowledge of, and affection for, the American Songbook – and he could swing you into the next room! His vocals and humour were very Fats Waller – and that's no bad thing! He was also a fine guitar player – one of the best rhythm guitarists – and delighted in putting together jumping little combos rejoicing in such names as the Orphan Newsboys, Destiny's Tots and Keepers of the Flame.

He was so popular on his first appearance at the Festival that we immediately booked him for the full ten days the following year – a rare accolade, only ever equalled by the virtuoso Harlem stride-style pianist Duncan Swift. On this second visit Marty was chosen as the name for that year's guide dog. He made the presentation of the pup to the Association with great solemnity, declaring himself much moved by the fact that this handsome young hound would carry his name through life and announcing that, in return, he would in future be going out under the name of Spot.

One of the best of the festival bands we organised for Marty included the then impossibly young Ralph Salmins on drums. Ralph at that time sported an impressive pigtail, so Marty immediately re-christened him Sabu after the Indian-born Hollywood actor who starred in a string of 1930s and 1940s movies, including *The Jungle Book*. It took many years for Ralph to totally shake off the nickname, if indeed he has! Interestingly Mysore-born Sabu, whose public image found him mostly at home on an elephant, served in the American Air Force in the Second World War as a turret gunner in Liberators and won the Distinguished Flying Cross.

Back home Marty, unsurprisingly, played and recorded with New York's finest, in his own combos and, notably, in Soprano Summit with Bob Wilber and Kenny Davern and the Classic Jazz Quartet with Dick Wellstood, Joe Muranyi and Dick Sudhalter. In Birmingham we had a bunch of fun putting together the Orphan Newsboys, the classic line-up being Digby Fairweather, Alan Barnes and Len Skeat.

11. Jazz City UK

At the time of writing Marty is still an attraction in New York clubs at the age of 89.

I first encountered the work of Gene 'The Mighty Flea' Connors, trombonist extraordinaire and an extremely good vocalist, on a bunch of Johnny Otis records, particularly his stunning feature *Preacher's Blues* on the indispensable *Live at Monterey* double album. The filmed version appeared in the Monterey Fairground sequence of the Clint Eastwood movie, *Play Misty for Me*, where Otis back-announced *Preacher's Blues* with a disbelieving, 'That's triple tonguing, man.'

If the Johnny Otis Show on record was something, on the road it was quite something else! The sheer quantity of folk in the band compared favourably with that in Joe Cocker and Leon Russell's *Mad Dogs and Englishmen* tour, except that this was Otis' regular aggregation. He featured two vocal groups: The Three Tons of Joy, who had enjoyed their own hit single, *Ma, He's Making Eyes at Me*, with Otis back in 1958, and the Otisettes, hired not only for their singing, but also their looks and admittedly impressive terpsichorean skills. Johnny's impossibly young son, Shuggie – short for Sugarland, Otis assured me – was 16 at the time of Monterey, a main feature on the show, delivering his own take on the Otis hit, *Willie and the Hand Jive*. In truth he could have headlined on his own. Shuggie somehow never capitalised on his early success, though he remains an exceptional guitar player to this day. I had the pleasure of producing his album for Big Bear and he didn't put a foot wrong in the studio. Gene Connors, nicknamed 'The Mighty Flea' by Otis, was the star of a horn section which included trumpeter Melvin Moore and saxophonists Preston Love, Richard Aplanalp, Clifford Solomon and Big Jim Wynn.

I had known Flea from various encounters in European jazz and blues festivals, so, when the Johnny Otis Show came to play Oxford Street's 100 Club, we spent a little time together. The band was rehearsing in the club on the afternoon of the opening when Flea and I were a little late returning from a break at The Blue Post. Otis flew off the handle, so much so that I am convinced there must have been some history of a bad relationship there. Flea was a cool-looking, snappily dressed man, diminutive in stature and accustomed to being liked by the girls. What you don't do to a not very tall, but very proud, man is bawl him out in front of a group of foxy young women like the Otisettes, but Otis was a bully; maybe he had to be to keep a show of that size on the road. He clearly thought he was on safe ground humiliating Flea, thousands of miles from home, dependent on Otis for travel, hotel, food, money, but he couldn't have been more wrong.

'Otis!', hollered Flea. 'I quit. Now come on, Jim.' I followed meekly as he strode towards the door, trombone in hand, only to shout back, 'Otis! Why don't you go keep a restaurant, like all them other Greeks?'

Johnny wasn't the world's greatest drummer by any means, his talent lay in organising a fine band and keeping it on the road. He also tried to pass himself off as black in order to appear cool. He had a glamorous black wife – half African-American, half Filipino – and cussed in the coolest urban style, but was actually born Ioannis Alexandros Veliotes, the son of Greek immigrants. So Flea knew exactly how to hit home.

Outside I asked Flea, 'What now?'. 'You live here,' he said. 'Let's take a cab.' Americans do seem to have a problem in understanding that Birmingham – or Manchester or anywhere else for that matter – is not exactly in London. So we came back to Brum to deliberate which took maybe three days before he came to an arrangement with a no doubt delectable fan in Denmark and promptly decamped there.

We took full advantage of having such a fine musician virtually on our doorstep, so his fiery trombone and throwaway vocals became an integral part of the Birmingham Jazz Festival for many years. Naturally he recorded for Big Bear. In 1972 we cut the album, *Let the Good Times Roll*, with Flea in the company of Mickey Baker on guitar, pianist Bob Hall and three Birmingham musicians who could acquit themselves as well as anyone and better than most: Mike Burney on tenor saxophone, Roger Hill on bass guitar and drummer Pete York – raucous, romping, good time rhythm and blues was the order of the day! At the time Mickey Baker declared it the most enjoyable session he had played on in 15 years. Flea later recorded funk 45s for Big Bear in cahoots with Muscles whose leader, Geoff Brown, penned *Boogie Down wit' the Boogie Man* and *Night Flight* for him. He also featured on the seminal King Pleasure and the Biscuit Boys' album, *Blues and Rhythm Revue Volume 1*, alongside Charles Brown, Howard McCrary and Val Wiseman.

Occasionally, very occasionally, a recording session almost seems to produce itself, with everything planned just falling into place naturally. This was such a session. Flea was to record *So Tired*, a song he was not totally comfortable with, but one that we thought was a good fit for his vocals. On the third take, he delivered with perfection. On playback, visibly moved, he declared, 'That's the best damn vocal I ever did.'

Eventually Flea got married and settled in Germany, invested in a luxury car rental business while sending money back to the States to increase his investment in his brother's chicken farming business. Late in life he returned to the States and died in Arizona in 2010 at the age of 79. There are many Birmingham Jazz Festival fans who still miss a good friend to our city, Gene 'The Mighty Flea' Connors.

The genial tenor saxophonist Gianni Basso has graced our festival several times and is always welcome. A tough, no nonsense full-toned player, he has long been among the leading Italian jazz musicians. When American trumpet star Chet Baker decided it would be unwise to return home, he gypsied around Europe and enjoyed a 6 year sojourn in Italy, immediately buddying up with Gianni, who played regular gigs with him.

Gianni, or Johnny as he often called himself, told me of the time they played together in a jazz club in Rome where the pianist was Romano Mussolini, son of Il Duce. Romano had long been a deservedly well-respected jazzman, and not only in Italy, but Chet was unaware of his family connection. During the intermission Gianni told Chet about the dictator and Chet was visibly upset at the manner in which Mussolini was executed. Back on stage, Chet put his arm comfortingly around Romano's shoulders and told him, 'I'm sorry about your dad, man.'

A Jazz Festival stalwart for many years, Digby Fairweather and I knew each other a little before I invited him to lead the front line opposite to Humphrey Lyttelton in the 1984 Jam Session. Digby told me he felt he should buy a new shirt in honour of the occasion. To his delight he found that the shop he went into was playing the Locomotive single, *Rudy's in Love.* He became increasingly frustrated trying to explain the relevance of the shirt he was buying to the record they were playing to a shop assistant who barely spoke English. How do you make it clear that you're buying a shirt to play a gig the next day for the chap who made the record that's playing?

Digby quickly became an ever-present at the Festival as a musician and adviser. When I need to talk about musicians I am considering, it's always Digby that I turn to. With Humph's passing the question of his successor as Jazz Festival Patron was never in doubt: Digby was a natural fit. Both were trumpeters and bandleaders, both were broadcasters and writers, both even ran their own record labels, Calligraph and Rose Cottage respectively. Most importantly both enjoyed the respect of the UK jazz fraternity and both were amazingly supportive of our festival. Digby and I still retain the firmest of friendships, though I fear he is able to give me far more support than I can offer him.

Every year an army of good folk help man the barricades for the festival, essential with the decreasing numbers of full-time staff at Big Bear. Nowadays a team of four seem to handle a similar amount of work to three times as many people in the 1990s.

In 2005 one of the volunteers was a delightful young woman from Shen Yang in the North East of China. She was at Birmingham University doing her Master's degree, had encountered the jazz festival the previous year, thought it interesting and wanted to be involved. We got on well and after the festival she

Don't Worry 'Bout The Bear

asked to join Big Bear as an intern. We were impressed by her work ethic and successfully applied for a work permit for her to join the full-time staff. Her name is Yue Yang, better known as Sarah, and, as I write, she has been at Big Bear for more than 13 years and is now an indispensable member of the team.

Three years ago we struck gold when we recruited Nick Hart as the fourth member of the team, alongside Tim, Sarah and me. Nick is a splendid young fellow whose comprehensive practical knowledge of all things computer-age has bridged the chasm that was beginning to appear between Big Bear and the modern world. What makes Nick special is his overwhelming knowledge and insatiable appetite for work – and, of course, he is a musician, with mandolin his weapon of choice.

At the time of writing we are busy preparing for the 35th year of the festival. Our area of operation has spread – it is now known as the Birmingham, Sandwell and Westside Jazz Festival in recognition of the financial support and increased involvement of Westside BID and Sandwell Council – but the contents of the event remain as eccentrically diverse as before. The quality of the music is – and

You're never too young to get down to some good rocking rhythm & blues – dispensed by Ricky Cool and The In Crowd.

always was – paramount, but we pay little attention to drawing lines between the many styles of jazz and blues.

There's little point in denying that our festival does zig off at some unusual, and often quite silly, tangents. Musically there are few no-go areas, with reggae, ska, and various forms of rock often on the programme as well as most known forms of jazz and blues. We delight in presenting great soul music, and have included such as Earth, Wind and Fire, Tower of Power and The Commodores in the programme. Then of course there has been Cajun with Rockin' Dopsie and The Twisters. Ukulele and jitterbug lessons are open to allcomers regardless of ability, and we have a Sketch Crawl which is like a pub crawl but with sketch pads and not quite so much beer. It gets still quirkier with performances on canal boats, trains and the number 9 bus, barbershop quartets in barbershops and a poetry programme in conjunction with our pal Phil Thomson called *Hit The Ode Jack*.

For many years my son Merlin Daleman has been our photographer-at-large. His photographs are the centre-piece of an annual exhibition at New Street Station and he conducts masterclasses and photographic clinics during the festival.

When Sarah came on board, it didn't take her long to make her mark. Pretty soon she recruited other Chinese girls, worked up the dance routines and formed her own Chinese Jitterbug Squad. Originally this was intended as a one-off, but audiences were so enthusiastic that it has become an attraction in its own right. When the Queen made her Royal visit to Birmingham, the Chinese Jitterbug Squad was engaged as part of the entertainment. As the Queen floated regally through the crowds, Prince Philip made a beeline for the Chinese girls. Looking them up and down, he demanded, 'What are you doing here?'. I collapsed in laughter – it was just what he was supposed to say. Perfect! Sarah, however, took him at face value and politely and patiently explained at some length the reasons why each of the four girls was here in Birmingham.

So, from Jam Session to jitterbugging Chinese girls, via the likes of Count Basie and Miles Davis, Birmingham can make a good case for being 'Jazz City UK', as claimed by the series of Big Bear compilations brought out in the last two years.

Chapter 12

LADY SINGS THE BLUES

The most prominent jazz venue in Birmingham during the 1960s was the Midland Jazz Club, housed twice a week in Digbeth Civic Hall, now known as the Digbeth Institute and home to touring rock bands. The resident band was the vaunted Second City Jazzmen who might just have been the country's most respected provincial band. Led by Stan Keeley, unusually featuring two clarinets, they were, to a man, fine musicians. Maybe a little formal with not much of a sense of enjoyment, but they did perform some very intricate arrangements with precision.

The most striking feature of the band was their singer, a young, slight girl named Val Wiseman. Even at an early age, she already had lift, a sense of swing that ignited the performance of the rest of the band. Much of the band's repertoire was in the Trad vein, though Val remembers, 'The band played lots of Ellington and taught me much, lending me records of singers I hadn't heard of, such as Julia Lee and Helen Humes', but, whatever she sang, in her hands it always sounded like the real thing. I gave her the big hello on several occasions to absolutely no effect, though many years later she told me it was due to her short-sightedness and her vanity in not wearing her glasses. Neat get-out!

Val was born in West Bromwich, not an area normally associated with producing international jazz talent, although her brother Pete was an accomplished and locally well-respected clarinet and saxophone player. Pete could never quite hold it together long enough to step up to a professional career, but he did keep a place in many of the best bands from this region. At one time he was the UK representative for the mighty Mellotron, a Birmingham-made polyphonic tape replay keyboard that was a great favourite of television personalities (and reputedly Princess Margaret) in the 1960s and later became a more respectable footnote in music history when taken up by the Moody Blues, King Crimson, Genesis and other groups.

It never occurred to Val to seek any musical training – just as well as things transpired: it would have been counter-productive to burden that natural ability and lack of fear with formal disciplines and exercises – so she just sang along to her

12. Lady Sings The Blues

brother's jazz records at home. As her confidence grew, she began getting herself around the clubs as well as doing gigs with the West Side Jazz Band who invited her to sing as their regular vocalist. Later her brother Pete also joined the band.

As a teenage art student in those heady 1960s beatnik days, when her fellow students realised they had a talented jazz singer in their midst, they would always encourage her to approach the bandleader at any dance and ask if she could sing a few songs with the band. She was young, enthusiastic and pretty, seemed to know about keys and tempos, so why would they refuse? It was getting up to sing in front of 1,500 people at one of the Sunday jazz nights at the West End Ballroom that caught the attention of a committee member of the Midland Jazz Club who recommended her to the Second City Jazzmen. It wasn't long before the invitation came from Stan Keeley to join the band and that's where, with regular appearances with a first-class band, Val developed her style as well as a significant following.

The Midland Jazz Club, probably the most important provincial jazz club in the country, would regularly present name bands, with the Second City playing support. The Monty Sunshine Jazz Band, a leading attraction of the day, was one such guest. Monty's clarinet had been featured on Chris Barber's recording of *Petite Fleur*, a Number 4 hit in 1959. The band's appearance in Digbeth was a sell-out, but more significantly Monty got to hear Val Wiseman sing. That was enough for him, there and then, to invite the 20-year-old to turn professional and join his band. This was the break she had been waiting for and she instantly accepted, although it must be said that, good musicians as the band members were, they were very much a product of the all-enveloping Trad Boom and musically Val Wiseman was streets ahead of the rest of the band.

There had been one particularly memorable night at the Midland Jazz Club when the Count Basie Orchestra, after playing two concerts at the Birmingham Odeon, allowed me to drag them along to the Digbeth Civic Hall for a jam session. To their credit, having already played for nigh on four hours, most of the band came along as did the extremely affable Count Basie himself, piano star Erroll Garner and that classiest of jazz singers, Sarah Vaughan. Maybe the temptation of an after-hours drink or a fraternise with female clubgoers or, most likely, the opportunity to get a blow in a jam session was enough for the boys in the band.

I drove two of the guys – unsurprisingly, both trumpet players – down in my tiny, but very cute, MGTF two-seater sports car and, as we entered the club, Al Aarons was already opening his trumpet case, balancing it on his thigh as he scuttled across the room, mouthpiece in place and trumpet in hand, so that, as he hit the stage, he was already playing. Don't tell me that these guys do it for the money. The band had travelled by road from Manchester on a miserably wet day, checked into the hotel, arrived at the Odeon at 4 to sound-check, hit for the first show at 6.15 and finished the second around 11 – and the guys still couldn't wait to get on stage and jam. Val remembers calling *Am I Blue?* which she sang in her best Billie Holiday voice with the Second City and we all noticed members of the Basie Band dashing out of the bar to see who was singing.

Before long the stage was full of Basieites who looked set to play through the night until the hall's caretaker, who didn't share the audience's enthusiasm for the occasion, called a curfew. I bought him off the first time with some folding money, but was unable to convince him at the second time of asking, and he pulled the power, leaving the Basie musicians, a room full of jazz fans and Sarah Vaughan and Erroll Garner, who were both enjoying the jam, but had politely declined to take part, blinking in the light.

In those days you had to audition to get a gig on the BBC which Val did with the Second City. Her very first BBC broadcast was on *Jazz Club* from London as a guest with the Alex Welsh Band who had heard her when they played the Midland Jazz Club. While Val was living in London after joining Monty she was also invited to guest with Sandy Brown's Jazzmen, the Humphrey Lyttelton Band and Alan Elsdon's Jazz Band on BBC broadcasts.

Val sang at concert halls and jazz clubs, on radio and television, with Monty's band, spending three years constantly on the road, before marrying the double bass player Tony Bagot and taking time out to raise a family. However, in the late 1970s, Val did feature on a Midland Youth Jazz Orchestra album as a guest – alongside Kenny Baker.

In 1986 I booked Eggy Ley's Hotshots to play in the Birmingham Jazz Festival. Eggy had a fine swinging little combo with excellent musicians – Eggy himself and guitarist Paul Sealey included – and their singer was Val Wiseman, now based near London and in the process of making a comeback. Naturally I was more than intrigued and checked out their first gig, at the White Swan in Harborne.

It took me about 20 minutes to realise that here, in a small pub in a neat Birmingham suburb, I was listening to Britain's finest female jazz singer, with the possible exception of Scot Annie Ross. Her intonation, sense of time and diction were impeccable, but that was only the beginning. The way she got hold of a song and made it completely her own with such absolute conviction was a very rare quality. There were influences of Peggy Lee, Anita O'Day and, particularly, Billie Holiday, but through it all you could clearly hear the voice of Val Wiseman. She was drinking lager at a fairly decent rate and I realised it wouldn't be too long before she

12. Lady Sings The Blues

Left: An uber-glamorous Val Wiseman publicity shot from the late 1980s.
Right: A somewhat raffish Digby Fairweather featuring with Lady Sings the Blues.

went to the toilet. I positioned myself accordingly. When she emerged, again she didn't notice me until I told her I had only three words to say to her, 'Billie, Anita and Peggy.' That seemed to capture her attention. 'My favourite singers!', she replied.

Eggy Ley's Hotshots were to play several shows over three days of the festival, so Val and I, who clearly had a lot to talk about, hung out whenever we could. Before the end of the festival I had convinced her – well, almost – that we should work together and form a band of the best available players to properly present the wonderful, but neglected, repertoire of Billie Holiday. My first port of call, as so often during our long and utterly fruitful relationship, was Digby Fairweather. He got it immediately and took about two seconds flat to agree to be the bandleader. We recruited Humphrey Lyttelton's trombone player Pete Strange, an inspirational arranger and one of the nicest of God's creatures, to write the arrangements for 35 songs, conscientiously selected from the vast Billie Holiday repertoire. The material was fairly evenly distributed between the 1930s, 1940s and 1950s, though we decided to avoid the hackneyed over-dramatic songs that formed many people's total experience of Billie Holiday. Hugely respected as trumpet player, journalist, author and arranger, Ken Rattenbury was invited to supply additional arrangements which he did with alacrity, expressing his delight at the prospect of hearing his arrangements played by these top musicians.

The next step was to kidnap the great Midlands jazz pianist Roy Fisher whose other life focussed on poetry at which, I was told, he was something of a dab hand. A week's woodshedding and we had identified the keys and tempos, added a few more titles and dropped a couple – and then the package, and the responsibility, was handed over to Pete Strange and Ken Rattenbury.

It is always a particular pleasure to be able to build a band from scratch, inviting not only the best and most appropriate musicians around, but also a bunch of my favourite people. But there was more. I spent many a happy evening balancing the choices and considering the individual musical preferences of the guys and how comfortable they might be playing together. Hence a certain similarity to the earlier, remarkable Alex Welsh Band might be noted in the final line-up: Digby with Roy Williams (trombone), Al Gay (tenor saxophone and clarinet), Brian Lemon (piano), Jim Douglas (guitar), Len Skeat (double bass) and Eddie Taylor (drums). This was the stellar line-up fronted by the self-taught West Bromwich girl, Val Wiseman – some responsibility then, but to this day I am convinced that no other singer I know, or have heard of, could have handled this difficult repertoire with such style, accuracy and aplomb.

Val Wiseman featuring with Lady Sings the Blues.

12. Lady Sings The Blues

Lady Sings the Blues: A Celebration of the Music of Billie Holiday, gave its first performance in the 500-capacity Adrian Boult Hall in Birmingham Conservatoire as a main feature of the next year's festival. It was a complete sell-out, attracted a bunch of media attention and was immediately re-booked for the following year. Then the offers of gigs started to come in, firstly a four-day tour in Scotland, including a performance in Carnegie Hall – the one in Dunfermline, Andrew Carnegie's birthplace. Overnight we had a working band on our hands, without doubt one of the UK's finest regular jazz swing bands of our time.

We went into the residential Black Barn Studios in Ripley, Surrey, to cut the first album. We took our time and did it properly, and subsequently we got Europe-wide distribution on Big Bear Records, resulting in picking up dates in Holland, Germany, Belgium and France along with television and radio appearances. A few months later Eddie Taylor was headhunted by George Melly for John Chilton's Feetwarmers, to be replaced by the effervescent Bobby Worth, formerly a star of the National Youth Jazz Orchestra, and this line-up remained pretty much constant for many years.

Val and I had so much in common that very soon she moved in and we set up home. At the same time she came to work at Big Bear where her knowledge of music and musicians proved invaluable. Being based in Birmingham provided the opportunity to develop relationships with local bands which enhanced everyone's prospects of getting more gigs.

On the Dixieland front, where Val was still a big name, she teamed up with Burnett's Jazz Bandits, a breezy Chicago-style combo led by swashbuckling trumpet player John Burnett. We found a place for Val with the redoubtable tenor saxophonist Mike Burney and his Quartet which gave her the opportunity to sing her favourite songs – Billie, Anita, Peggy – with a first-class group. We would book her out, whenever the opportunity arose, with visiting jazz stars such as Harry 'Sweets' Edison from the Basie Band, and she always impressed, although on the Edison gig she was ambushed by Duvel, a particularly strong Belgian beer, and fell off her barstool.

The most interesting combination, and the most unlikely one, was with Harlem-style stride piano player, Duncan Swift. I had first worked with Duncan around 1962 when he played trombone, not piano. This was a particularly good version of my band, with singer Roy Everett, Duncan and me on trombone and trumpet respectively, Mike Burney on tenor sax, Roy Fisher on piano, the tragic but brilliant Graham Gallery on bass and Roy Dutton on drums – a formidable swing combo. We held down the Sunday residency at the Tower Ballroom, a stylish lakeside palais with – wonder of wonders! – a revolving stage. Our role was to

Everett's Blueshounds on their regular Sunday date at the Tower Ballroom: (l-r) Roy Fisher, Mike Burney, Tony Caldicott, JS, Duncan Swift, Graham Gallery.

support visiting name bands. It went well for a couple of years, until, firstly, not being the smartest band ever, we borrowed the resident band's striking pink jackets for a lakeside photocall. Reportedly not all the jackets were returned to their proper home, one or two of them certainly not in pristine condition. Of course 'borrowed' implies permission sought and granted, but sadly this was something I had overlooked and I was told that we were lucky to get away with a verbal warning.

Not many weeks later, the featured visiting band was yet another successful, but fairly inept, Trad band whose audience could see or hear no wrong. Always intrigued by gadgets and totally bored with what was being passed off as jazz that night, I found myself experimenting with the buttons that operated the revolving stage. It was wonderful: a touch of the button whisked the band away from the eyes of the audience and left them playing to a blank wall backstage, while a second button whisked them around at speed, back in front of the audience in a state of confusion and disarray. This was getting to be great fun, at least as far as my bandmates and myself were concerned, but surprisingly our enthusiasm was

12. Lady Sings The Blues

not shared, at least openly, by the management and we suddenly found ourselves available for bookings on Sunday evenings.

Not as a direct result of this – in fact he seemed to find this episode the highspot of his time with the band – Duncan relocated to Bristol to join Bill Nile's Delta Jazzmen – on piano, to my bemusement. The Nile band enjoyed a national reputation and were seemingly on the way up. The next I heard of Duncan Swift was when I saw him on television, playing piano, absolutely splendidly, with Kenny Ball's Jazzmen on the Morecambe and Wise Show. This was one of the most coveted chairs in British jazz: a proper salary, excellent conditions and constant touring as well as regular radio and television appearances. Duncan was a man of principle, however, especially when it came to jazz, and, though he served Kenny well, staying with the band from 1977 to 1983, deep down he wanted to develop his passion for the Harlem stride piano style associated with James P. Johnson, Willie 'The Lion' Smith and Fats Waller. When Duncan left Kenny Ball, he did so with the blessing of the boss who never had a bad word to say about him.

The still-missed Harlem Stride piano genius Duncan Swift.

Don't Worry 'Bout The Bear

Fortunately, for us at Big Bear, Duncan moved to rural Bewdley where he installed himself, his wife Faith and daughter Melody and a 6-foot Bechstein piano in a town centre pub. Delighted as I was to have him close at hand, knowing that he enjoyed a pint now and again and had settled the Bechstein in the public bar, I felt some concern that he would spend too much time on the wrong side of the bar, but there was no doubt that the new licensee of The Trumpet made a colourful and uniquely entertaining addition to Bewdley's cultural amenities.

I was delighted to link up again with Duncan after so many years, particularly as he had decided to concentrate on his solo piano playing in a style in which he was indubitably the finest this side of the Atlantic. I wasted no time, programmed him right across the Jazz Festival, arranged a series of performances on BBC *Pebble Mill at One* and started to book him out whenever we could.

Naturally I wanted him to record for Big Bear Records which suited him just fine. To make it worthwhile, he insisted, we had to record on his favourite piano, a Bosendorfer. Not just any Bosendorfer, but a specific one that belonged to a guy in Bristol who Duncan visited solely in order to play the piano. I duly rented specialised piano transportation to bring the Bosendorfer, its stool and its owner, who refused to let it out of his sight, to Zella Studios in Birmingham. Determined to get the best possible recording, I hit upon a friend, a BBC engineer, to borrow their brand new Calrec Soundfield microphone which the corporation had just bought for a cool £14,000 – and we were ready to go.

Or were we? I could hear a distinct, but occasional, click picked up by the Calrec. 'It must be the piano stool,' I insisted, an accusation that seemed to strike at the heart of the piano's owner who clearly took my comment as a wounding personal insult. Over the next hour, we spent time lying on the studio floor, ears pressed to piano leg or stool in attempts to locate the source of the click which by now everyone was hearing. Eventually we worked it out. The vertebrae in Duncan's back were creaking in response to his exuberant pianisms and had been picked up by the super-sensitive microphone – worth every penny of the £14,000. These clicks can still be heard on the opening tracks of the album.

The adventure in recording the album, *Out Looking for the Lion*, didn't end there. In fact Duncan's performance throughout really set the bar for other stride piano players; he even included Jelly Roll Morton's left elbow piano roar – which is exactly that.

For reasons that are, probably fortunately, lost in the mists of time, we decided that the LP sleeve should feature a photograph of the actual piano atop Clent Hill, a nearly-mountain we all loved. I booked longtime pal and top photographer Dave Travis for the session and the piano-shifter didn't blink when I gave him the task and

Duncan Swift, never far from a piano, atop Clent Hills – photographed for Out Looking for the Lion sleeve.

he duly delivered the Bosendorfer as requested. The cherished instrument looked most majestic on top of our hill. Bizarrely, as the photoshoot was in progress, the wife and two daughters of *Birmingham Mail* editor Ian Dowell rode up on their horses. Ian's wife, Caroline, greeted me cheerfully, asked if all was well at Big Bear, then rode off with a friendly wave without, apparently, having noticed the piano.

During the 1989 Birmingham Jazz Festival, Duncan was booked to appear pretty much every day. On about the third day in, he called me to say that an American had turned up at every one of his gigs and seemed very enthusiastic – and would I come down and talk to the guy at his next show? This I duly did. As Duncan had said, the chap was wildly enthusiastic and kept telling me that Duncan was 'the best – the best ever.' Delighted as I was to hear this, I felt obliged to point out that Duncan had learned his craft from the original recordings of Art Tatum, James P. and Willie 'The Lion'. This was his cue to pour scorn on my lack of knowledge. It turned out that he was the biggest restorer and distributor of Pianolas in the Mid West, so he obviously knew what he was talking about. My naïve comment that Duncan reproduced what he heard showed, apparently, that I didn't know what I was talking about. He explained how recordings of piano rolls were done. The blank cylinder was put in place on the Pianola, the technicians would chalk up the piano hammers and the pianist would play his piece as the piano roll turned, leaving a chalk mark to represent every note played. The technicians would then drill a hole at every chalk mark and then continue to drill holes at strategic unchalked spots to enhance the performance.

And that is what Duncan Swift had learned to play in the firm conviction that he could learn to play anything that any other human being had already played.

So the question that has troubled me for years is this: was Duncan Swift the greatest Harlem-style stride piano player?

I rather think that, in the light of expert opinion, he probably was.

The pairing of Duncan and Val was a musical marriage made in Heaven. They both knew and respected the origins of the music whilst eschewing Trad. Individually they were musically excellent and had no fear of awkward keys or terrifying tempos. Furthermore they both listened to what the other was doing and responded appropriately. So many musicians seem to have decided exactly what they are going to play before leaving the house and carry on doggedly, oblivious to anything the other guys are playing. Val and Duncan developed an understanding that allowed them to charge full-tilt at even the most challenging repertoire and deliver it with confidence and evident joy. When I recall Val galloping through the tongue-twisting lyrics of *Wolverine Blues*, which I often do, I can't imagine why I didn't take them into the studio and record them properly. Perhaps, like so many things in life, I thought it would go on forever.

Duncan had the most comprehensive knowledge of verses that I have ever encountered and he always played them properly, giving them his full attention. The verse usually acts as a scene-setter before the main section of the song and, without it, the main lyric can fail to make full sense. The melody of the verse can be as attractive as the chorus which is why it's such a pity that it's become common practice to omit them. Duncan was passionate about playing the verse, arguing that it was written by the composer as part of the whole – and who are we to dismantle a songwriter's work and pick out the parts we like? Or maybe the parts we can play – verses can often be the most complex part of the song.

Duncan's appearance was never conventional, wild long hair atop a lanky, ever-mobile body and a permanently quizzical facial expression. By the time he left the Kenny Ball Band he had acquired the look of a full-blown professorial eccentric, always sporting a bright green or yellow suit and matching winkle-pickers. In full flight at the piano, he was a study in concentration, but with total animation, elbows and knees flying everywhere. His spoken introductions and explanations of the songs were fascinating, an integral part of the performance, a reflection of his wit, intellect, mastery of Harlem stride and knowledge of the Great American Songbook.

We lost Duncan far too early. He died in 1997 of throat cancer, but not before he found time to orchestrate his own funeral service, book the musicians, select the repertoire and write the arrangements. There are some people whose passing you never get over. They include Duncan Swift, the best ever Harlem stride piano player – bar none.

12. Lady Sings The Blues

Lady Sings the Blues was not the only important repertory project that Val Wiseman and I worked on together. Drummer Pete York, resident in Munich, but ever-willing to return to the UK, especially if a tasty gig was at hand, had known Val and me separately since the 1960s. With his passion for the work of drum legend Gene Krupa and Val's for Anita O'Day, who featured with the 1940s Krupa band, it was a logical step to develop a show to re-create the excitement and swing of that band.

We called it *Drummin' Man*, after the Krupa recording, and I again turned to my favourite arranger, Pete Strange, and set about recruiting the band. The other main feature of the Krupa band was trumpet star Roy 'Little Jazz' Eldridge, probably the fieriest and most exciting player of the Swing Era, and there was one obvious choice, close at hand, to take on that exacting role – Bruce Adams, who else? Alan Barnes and the Belgian, Pascal Michaux, were the splendid saxophone section, the immaculate trombone of Roy Williams made up the front line and the Rolls Royce of a rhythm team featured pianist Brian Dee and the Time Lord, Len Skeat, on double bass alongside Pete.

The band was tremendous. We launched *Drummin' Man* at the Messe Frankfurt trade fair where it was the hit of the weekend. I spent a couple of off-duty hours with Bruce, wandering around the brass instrument stands. You have to know that Bruce looks for all the world like the dictator of some East European country, so that, when he shambles up to a display of trumpets, picks one up, fingers the valves and says, 'This looks like a nice wee bebop horn' nobody takes much notice. That's until he inserts the mouthpiece and lets rip. If God were to design the perfect trumpet player, he would probably have pretty much the same dimensions and demeanour as Bruce Adams: six feet tall, barrel chested, imperious manner and power to burn. So, when Bruce muscled his way from a low F sharp through to an F above high C, the world stopped. As Bruce moved on to other companies' stands, playing a little on any horn he fancied, the group following him grew into an enthusiastic crowd. Eventually instrument manufacturers would come up to him, proffer him one of their trumpets and almost beg him to play it. I guess they wanted, just once, to hear their instrument played the way it should be played.

Drummin' Man went on the road and played UK tours as well as events in Holland, Belgium and Luxembourg, including a memorable show for SAAR TV in a derelict, extraordinarily filthy former factory. Nobody dared sit down or touch anything and I wouldn't attempt to describe what passed for the toilet facilities. Despite this the band played brilliantly and somewhere out there is a permanent reminder of *Drummin' Man* in full flight. There is also a recording, deep in the Big

Don't Worry 'Bout The Bear

Bear archives, of that original show in Frankfurt with everyone on the ball and Val Wiseman tackling the difficult repertoire with songs such as *I've Got a Crush on You*, *Street of Dreams* and *Opus One* – material not to be approached by the timid.

I always felt better in the recording studio when Val was there, not only because I enjoyed her company, but because she was my safety net when it came to the accuracy of other musicians' playing. She rarely spoke out, but, if I heard (or thought I heard) dodgy intonation, I would check whether that faint frown of disapproval was crossing her face. Val has perfect pitch, so precise that it seems almost to give her physical pain if something isn't quite accurate. With so much to monitor in the recording studio, it was very reassuring to have Val's ever-acute ear at hand.

One important recording session in which Val played a significant role, both as singer and in terms of quality control, was King Pleasure and the Biscuit Boys' *Blues and Rhythm Revue Volume 1*. Recorded over four sessions between July 1993 and December the following year, the then eight-piece Biscuit Boys, further

Howard McCrary at Ronnie Scott's, Birmingham.

12. Lady Sings The Blues

supplemented by Big Al Nicholls on saxophones, Dave Keech on trombone and alto saxist Paul Clarke, provided the backing for King Pleasure himself as featured singer on four of the 13 tracks and for some extraordinary guests on the remainder.

Howard McCrary, one of the McCrary Five when they toured nationally with the Jackson Five, had stayed in Birmingham when a European tour as singer and pianist with the Phil Upchurch Combo ended. Former Lionel Hampton and Johnny Otis Show stalwart, trombonist Gene 'The Mighty Flea' Connors, from the other Birmingham (Alabama), had already been living in Europe for some years. Probably the most important rhythm and blues singer of them all, Texas-born Charles Brown, stopped over to record when his week at Birmingham's Ronnie Scott's Club was over. And then there was Val, the self-taught singer from West Bromwich. Without any doubt she very much held her own in such august company. Paul Jones, of Manfred Mann and the Blues Band fame and a distinguished BBC presenter, wrote glowingly of the album and singled out 'Val's perfectly lovely take on the Buddy and Ella Johnson classic, *Since I Fell for You*, which she delivered impeccably, complete with verse.' Duncan Swift would have liked that.

Here's another in my long, and still growing, list of regrets. There were to be no more *Blues and Rhythm Revue* albums – probably a classic case of, 'How do you follow that?'

A very special moment for Val was her meeting with one of her three inspirations, Peggy Lee. Peggy, then in her 70s and wheelchair-bound, was on a UK tour, accompanied by a string section, disparagingly referred to by Len Skeat as 'The Gypsies', and a jazz rhythm team, naturally including Len who was, as she often stated, Peggy's favourite double bass player. Len knew how important Peggy was to Val and set up a meeting backstage at Nottingham's Royal Concert Hall as well as arranging guest tickets to the concert for Val and me. The evening, which was not to be without incident, started off on the wrong foot when we entered the Concert Hall to find it full of seemingly thousands of extremely young, and appropriately noisy, children. It transpired the Concert Hall shared a Box Office with the adjacent Theatre Royal and we had been escorted into the room where Dana was appearing in *Snow White and the Seven Dwarfs*.

Peggy was imperious. She made her entrance in her wheelchair, a stage team transferred her to a high swivel chair and suddenly she was in charge, counting in the band, directing the more difficult passages, cuing in the musicians. I never witnessed the famed Benny Goodman 'Ray' with which he fixed erring musicians, but I seriously doubt whether it could have matched Peggy's glare for sheer intensity. Any time a musician made an error, Peggy spotted it and delivered a withering look, most memorably when percussionist Frank Ricotti goofed on the signature timpani figure on *Fever*, of all things the phrase that immediately precedes the song's hook. The look on Frank's face said, 'Please let me be anywhere on earth but here, under the malevolent eye of Peggy Lee, in front of 1500 people and the sneers of those bloody gypsies!'.

Backstage after the show Peggy greeted Val with warmth and a real interest in her and her music. I'm sure that went into Val's diary as a landmark encounter. Looking back at the photographs, Val seemed particularly tickled that there, prominently in the background behind the smiling Peggy and Val, was a bicycle – obviously one of the stage hands preparing to nip off home.

Now, after Val and I have gone our separate ways so far as our personal relationship was concerned, we still work together on music projects.

In 2006 she fulfilled her long held dream and visited New York where a meeting with Annie Ross was surely at the top of her agenda. Annie was playing her regular Monday gig in Greenwich Village. They talked and Val took her photograph. While in New York, Val took the jazz tourist trail, but with a difference: she sang at every opportunity. She started at the legendary Birdland which operated an open mike on Monday nights when the theatres were dark and the show people would turn up to sing. Her travelling companion, a fellow-singer, found an open mike night in Harlem in a club where the young Billie Holiday had made an early appearance. Val made sure that she was photographed under a giant picture of Billie and was delighted to learn that the club was just around the corner from the brownstone steps where the uber-famous photograph *A Great Day in Harlem* was taken by Art Kane in 1958. Naturally a copy of the photograph was hanging in the club.

Among the occasional guest appearances with *Lady Sings the Blues* were those of two former Billie Holiday sidemen. Guitarist Mundell Lowe had played with Billie regularly just after World War II and featured in her last regular show, *Holiday on Broadway*, which had a short run at New York's Mansfield Theatre in 1948.

Mundell appeared with *Lady Sings the Blues* at the Alexandra Theatre as part of the Birmingham Jazz Festival. Unsurprisingly he was a joy to work with and brought something very special to the band. He was an expressive and eloquent soloist and his rhythm playing really did kick. Val, naturally, interrogated him without mercy about Billie, but I also remember I got an extremely rare musical victory over Val. I had long pestered her to include one of my favourite songs, *You Call it Madness*, in her repertoire, if not in *Lady Sings the Blues*, at least on solo gigs. She consistently and steadfastly refused, dismissing it as a song that Billie never did. As he was warming up for the Alexandra gig, I heard Mundell playing *You Call it Madness*. 'Great song,' I said to him. 'Yep,' he replied, 'Billie's favourite.'

12. Lady Sings The Blues

The other musician with Billie Holiday credentials was one of my very favourite people, the wonderful piano player, arranger and bandleader Nat Pierce. Nat performed with Billie on a number of occasions, but most notably he was the Musical Director (which in this case meant putting the whole shooting match together) for the landmark CBS television broadcast, *The Sound of Jazz.* Nat assembled maybe the finest line-up of musicians ever to grace a television studio. For the 1957 transmission, there were nearly 40 of the great names of jazz, including Coleman Hawkins, Ben Webster, Count Basie, Thelonious Monk, Dickie Wells, Roy Eldridge and Jimmy Rushing.

And then there were Billie Holiday and Lester Young whose contributions to *Fine and Mellow* are among my favourite moments. In turn the saxophones solo. Ben is at his finest, all belly as Lester would say, Hawk is forever hip, all over his instrument, then comes Pres with a simple, but overwhelmingly melodic four-bar phrase, repeats it with minor modifications, and then again, almost the same phrase, and the world nearly stops. If you want to know how brilliant that is, look at Billie's expression on film. If ever there was a moment when two musicians were nearly overcome with each other's performance, then this was it. A lot has been written and said about the unique empathy enjoyed by Billie and Pres. In this television show Nat captured it perfectly.

The year he featured in *Lady Sings the Blues*, again at the Alexandra Theatre, he arrived in Birmingham five days early, by arrangement, and we put him to work around the free Jazz Trail. Imagine the legendary Nat Pierce swinging an audience into bad health in a Birmingham pub. He and Val Wiseman did a series of performances together, so that by the time they played the *Lady Sings the Blues* concert, they were totally in step. If only we had recorded it!

When Val left Big Bear and moved back south – to Twickenham this time – *Lady Sings the Blues* continued, but she also devoted herself to other projects, notably developing her long-standing fascination with all things Brontë. Val decided to write a set of songs based on the Brontës, which when completed became the album and concert programme, *Keeper of the Flame.* Val's lyrics, based on the sisters' lives and incidents in their novels, together with a couple of their own poems, were set to music by Brian Dee. The first live performance in 2009 for the Brontë Society at Dewsbury Minster was enthusiastically received and the show has been periodically revived since then.

A few years earlier in 2002, also with Brian Dee, she set about righting a wrong that had existed for decades by recording the first Val Wiseman album under her own name. The band was straight out of the top drawer, with Brian responsible for arrangements and co-producing with Val for release on Mainstem Records. Simon

Thorpe played double bass, Ralph Salmins drums. Guitarist Jim Mullen and trumpet player Bruce Adams both guested. The repertoire is imaginatively selected and the album, *Just for a Thrill*, proves with no doubt at all that, as far as this country's female jazz singers go, Val is at the top of the tree.

Inexplicably, the second *Lady Sings the Blues* album was a long time coming, 2015, in fact. The show was still regularly on the road, as it is today, playing festivals, clubs and concerts, with Val accompanied by a six-piece featuring Digby, Roy and Len from the original band, together with Alan Barnes or Julian Marc Stringle on reeds, Brian Dee on piano and Eric Ford on drums – and the second album was recorded live at the Birmingham Jazz Festival at the Library of Birmingham Theatre in front of a sell-out audience of 300. It was a very special performance and garnered tremendous reviews for the CD.

The album has had a chequered career to date, initially delayed when I was knocked down by a car when crossing the road, breaking enough ribs to keep me out of full action for several months. With a total staff of only four at Big Bear, this was enough to damage productivity, so midway through the release procedure it all ground to a sudden halt.

We were just ready to get back to work on the album release when catastrophe of a much more serious nature struck. We had a 30-date tour in place to promote the album based on its original release date and, by the time we were ready to work on the release, in August 2016 after the Jazz Festival, there was just one date remaining on the tour, at Theatr Brycheinog. Two weeks before the show Val was diagnosed with breast cancer requiring immediate surgery. She seemed more concerned with missing the Brecon date than with the hospital procedure, but eventually I was able to convince her to let me deal with that while she took care of the much more serious business, her surgery.

Frankly everyone was aware that there is no jazz singer who could have replaced Val, but we did have a secret weapon in Debbie Jones, singer and co-leader of Leyland-based Tipitina. Debbie's background is in gospel, particularly the music of New Orleans, but she is a formidable character, determined beyond reason, incredibly musical and an exceptional singer. Debbie didn't hesitate in accepting the challenge and with the support of her husband Justin Randall, the piano-playing co-leader of Tipitina, she set about learning two hours' worth of unfamiliar material in just two weeks.

It was quite a night. The entire band seemed to be waiting in line to give Debbie advice which she accepted with grace even though she didn't need it. By the third number her shoulders visibly relaxed and she began to move about the stage and exchange grins with a very relieved band. Debbie had nailed it; she's the last person to consider herself to be a jazz singer, but she delivered. It's a fair bet that Val, 170 miles away at home in Twickenham, could feel the waves of affection travelling from Brecon towards her on that night.

The issue of Val's health was complicated because, at the time of her diagnosis, she was already waiting for a hip replacement which would have taken her off the road for two months. This operation, deferred because of chemotherapy following her earlier surgery, was finally performed in 2017, but worse was to come. During the procedure the surgeon fractured her femur, leaving her in significant pain and discomfort for many months.

The upshot is that the return to the stage of *Lady Sings the Blues* was delayed until her appearance at The Drill Hall Lincoln in April 2018, nearly two years after the previous concert. The next step was to make our third attempt at a proper release for an important album!

The question that has to be asked is, 'Just how good, compared to the originals, are the performances of *Lady Sings the Blues*?'

Two people who were absolutely qualified to answer that question are Benny Green and Ruby Braff. Benny, probably the foremost jazz critic in the UK, as well as a broadcaster and musician, wrote of the first album, 'What is happening here might even be a shade better than what was being played all those years ago.' Giving consideration to those words, Benny is actually favourably comparing the performances of the British musicians with those of Billie Holiday and such legends as Buck Clayton, Lester Young, Teddy Wilson and Freddy Green.

But Benny was not on his own in this matter. American cornet star Ruby Braff, famous for his irascibility and lack of patience with what he perceived as the shortcomings of his fellow musicians, said, on a blindfold test on BBC's *Jazz Panorama*, 'I think she's wonderful and the musicians sound so beautiful. That's the best jazz singing I've heard in ages. That's just really wonderful.

'Anyone who can sing Billie Holiday that well, with such musicianship and such amazing intelligence – it's such a feat. She sounds so pure and clear, there's no fat on there anywhere.'

Remarkably, as I write, *Lady Sings the Blues* has been performing the repertoire of Billie Holiday for 31 years – just one year longer than Billie's own career. It's been a long and fascinating journey for the former art student from West Bromwich, from shyly asking to be allowed to sing a couple of numbers at a local jazz club to playing alongside the finest musicians of the day and receiving well-deserved accolades from the music media.

Apart from the 1930s Hollywood movie star, Madeleine Carroll, Led Zeppelin's Robert Plant and a wonderful football club, West Bromwich, so far as

I know, doesn't have too much else to celebrate by way of culture. Wouldn't it be neat, I thought, if West Bromwich could honour one of their own?

Sure enough Sandwell Council, home to West Bromwich, once again stepped up to the plate and did the right thing. Libraries boss Barry Clark, already widely respected for mounting all his libraries' bookshelves on wheels, ready to be rolled aside to create concert space, had a plan. He successfully lobbied the council to properly recognise the achievements of Val Wiseman, with the result that in July 2018 the Mayor of Sandwell, Cllr. Joy Edis, and its Culture Chief, Cllr. Steve Trow, made a presentation to La Wiseman 'for her services over many years to music and entertainment'. They also installed a permanent plaque in the Andrew Carnegie-founded West Bromwich Central Library – alongside that of Madeleine Carroll. The celebrations climaxed with a full band performance by Val and *Lady Sings the Blues* – in the library.

Nobody shushed.

Chapter 13

HUMPH: OUR LEADER

I clearly remember the moment when I heard that Humphrey Lyttelton had died. I was eating in our neighbouring and favourite Chinese restaurant with Sarah. It was around 8 o'clock and we had just tumbled out of the office and were starting to relax when Digby Fairweather phoned to tell me the unexpected and devastating news. 'The Leader has gone.' Apparently he was in hospital for a supposedly non-life-threatening operation, but during the procedure had succumbed to an aortic aneurysm.

Humph had been an important part of my life since I was about 12, at arm's length, of course, but through his recordings, concerts, broadcasts and writings. He was my early hero and a great influence in so many ways.

In my teens I would go to Humph's concerts at Birmingham Town Hall at one of which his brilliant and inoffensive alto saxophonist Bruce Turner was the innocent cause of a now-famous incident. Many die-hard fans of Humph, whose original band had been in the revivalist style, thought it near-sacrilege to introduce a saxophone, that symbol of modernism, into the band. The next time Humph brought his splendid band into the Town Hall, a group of traddies held a 30-foot banner from the Lower Gallery, proclaiming, 'GO HOME, DIRTY BOPPER.' Bruce, a sensitive soul, was visibly upset, but Humph found it hilarious and featured the alto sax at every opportunity.

Jazz musicians can be a funny lot, with eccentric ways and a sense of humour incomprehensible to civilians, but by general agreement one of the most eccentric of all was Bruce Turner. He was famously disorganised and, when he formed his Jump Band after leaving Humph, there was many a sharp intake of breath among the jazz fraternity. We didn't have long to wait before our fears were realised. His new band was booked for a gig at Bedford College. Bruce rented a minibus and set off in the best of spirits up the M1, only to find that there was no Bedford College in Bedford. There was one, however, in London, WC1, more or less where they had just driven from.

Bruce always had a problem remembering names which he neatly solved by calling everyone, male or female, 'Dad'. I was with him soon after he moved to

Humphrey Lyttelton, 1960s.

13. Humph: Our Leader

Newport Pagnell where his father lived. Looking genuinely confused, he told me that, on seeing his father approaching on the High Street, he didn't know what to call him.

Many years later, when he began to suffer from arthritis in his hands, he explained that it was God's way of telling him he was playing too much bebop and should slow down. Bruce was a lovely man, a most entertaining companion and a musician of true international status at a time when we didn't have many of those.

I first got to talk to Humph, other than asking for his autograph, that night in 1959 at the unlikely venue of the Derbyshire Miners' Welfare Centre in Ingoldmells, just outside Skegness. He had a tremendous eight-piece band at the time, with Tony Coe, Jimmy Skidmore and Joe Temperley on saxes, John Picard on trombone and a rhythm section of Ian Armit, Pete Blannin and Eddie Taylor. This fell during my stint as a beach photographer and I was in a near-uncontrollable state of excitement for weeks beforehand. Of course all my pals, many of them musicians, promised to come out to support my hero and of course they all found last-minute excuses to bail out. Thus it was that Gwen, the photographic technician, and I found ourselves sharing a bright yellow bike, with the ensuing complications described in Chapter 1.

One of Humph's great bands from the early 1960s: Humph with Tony Coe and Joe Temperley.

Don't Worry 'Bout The Bear

The Derbyshire Miners' Welfare Centre was immense, magnificent and virtually empty. Apart from us, there were just nine people in that huge ballroom. In fairness I have to say they were having a ball, unlikely as it may seem, to some instantly forgettable Joe Loss Orchestra records, utilising every inch of the vast dance floor. I don't know why it is that I am so easily irritated by dancers. Not the tappers, of course, such as Bill 'Bojangles' Robinson, Buck and Bubbles and the Nicholas Brothers, nor indeed the current wave of jitterbuggers and Lindyhoppers, who all share a sense of fun, tremendous technique, a great sense of rhythm and a deep relationship with the music they dance to. It's the posturing and posing of more formal dance styles that get my goat, the dancers whose every step seems to scream out, 'Look at me, look at me!'

The band came on for the first set and were on fire from the start, at least Gwen and I thought so. I'm not so sure about the dancers: they had mostly disappeared into the bar for ice cream sodas and to tell each other how wonderful they looked. Yes, it's true, dancers do irritate me, turning their backs on probably the finest band they would ever hear.

In all the years I knew Humph, I never knew him do a job other than the right way, a man of impeccable standards. That night, in front of an attentive audience of just two people, the eight musicians played two full sets and Humph didn't even skimp on the announcements. Of course I button-holed him for the entire intermission when I'm sure he would have preferred a quiet drink with the chaps. He was attentive, kind, showed me how he did his long-note exercises and told me I should never stop listening to Louis Armstrong. Most of all, he told me I must get serious about reading music. It's fine, he told me, to have fun playing jazz in a pick-up band, but learning to read opens up a whole new world to a musician and removes so many of those barriers that limit the well-meaning and talented amateur. You just don't ignore advice when it comes direct from your hero and from that moment I determined to learn to play properly.

I stayed in touch with Humph as much as I could after that, going to see him whenever his band was in the region, photographing him and his band innumerable times, always hoping he might use one of my images on an album sleeve which he never did. By then I was taking trumpet lessons with an excellent Birmingham-based player, Denis Darlow, and getting immense pleasure playing in his 16-piece student band. Then Humph called to give me the contact details for Dougie Roberts who, Humph thought, could take me up to a better level. Dougie, who really was a bit of a trumpet ace, had played lead with the Johnny Dankworth Big Band as well as taking the trumpet chair in the peppy Dankworth Seven. Dougie's playing had also graced many of the country's most popular big bands such as Eric Delaney's, but his problem was his predilection for taking a taste which, in such high-class musical circles, was the quick way to get labelled as unreliable. As work in London dried up for him, Dougie moved to Birmingham to take the lead trumpet chair in the Colin Hulme Orchestra, resident six nights a week at the City's leading dance hall, the Locarno.

I approached Dougie at the Locarno and asked if he gave lessons. He did and for nearly two years I would go to his tiny Balsall Heath flat once a week, twice when I could afford it, to enjoy learning from, and listening to, a true master close up. Dougie's wife was a fine singer, employed at a different ballroom. Many's the time that Dougie, often short of cash, would ask me for an advance on payment for the next week's lesson. Some things, sadly, never change.

I won't attempt to defend Dougie's drinking habit which he shared with his wife, but being a shared habit must have made it harder to break, not that there was much sign of either of them trying too hard. It goes without saying – but I feel compelled to – that Dougie Roberts, on his day, was one of the finest trumpet players I have ever heard. He had it all: a formidable range, unimpeachable intonation, a dazzling technique and a blistering tone – and he always made it seem so easy. It's a strange thing, but listening to a near-perfect player is inspiring and makes you want to play like that, whereas, when someone is really very good, but has problems that you can recognise as similar to your own, it has the opposite effect.

As well as turning me onto an ideal teacher, about this time Humph had a serious word with me about my instrument. My well-worn Boosey and Hawkes Regent, Humph said, was really not up to the job and I should plan to replace it and, by the way, he told me, my much-loved Rudy Muck 19C mouthpiece also had to go. Back then Birmingham was home to some great music stores, just as it is today, but naturally these days there is less emphasis on brass and reed instruments.

The George Clay Music Centre on Broad Street had enjoyed an earlier life as a motor car showroom. Hence the spacious interior and the wide open spaces of its windows, home to a veritable forest of trumpets, trombones and saxophones. Adopting my usual pose, nose pressed to the window, jaw agape in wonderment, I realised that someone in the store was gesturing for me to enter which of course I did – nobody I knew disobeyed any instruction given by Cecil Viles. Cecil was a man of military bearing, tall, slim, besuited, a grey toothbrush moustache accentuating his authority. He was also an unusually fine trumpet player, featuring with local swing orchestras such as Norman Allen's. He played in the same manner that he conducted his business, with swagger, a fierce self-discipline and unquestionable confidence in his own ability.

Don't Worry 'Bout The Bear

'You still playing that wreck of a Regent trumpet?', he asked, not one to beat about the bush or to waste time on such unnecessary frivolities as a hello or 'How you doing?' I conceded that this was the case, at which point he adopted a conspiratorial tone:

'I've got your new horn. It's a beauty, a French Courtois. I've been holding it for you, waiting until I saw you.' It was actually a done deal the moment I held this splendid, bright-toned, player-friendly instrument. Cecil had almost to prise it from my hand as I left with a promise to return with £70 to claim my new instrument. Of course back home I began to get cold feet, mainly on account of the £70, so I called Humph and started to explain my situation before he halted me. 'Did you say that Cecil Viles recommended this trumpet? You don't need my advice, do what Cecil suggests, that man understands instruments and he knows about musicians.' And that was that!

It wasn't the last time I was summoned into the store as I passed along Broad Street. This was some four years later and I left with my beautiful American Super Olds trumpet which I treasure to this day. It was on this occasion that Cecil converted me from the Vincent Bach mouthpiece to my current Al Cass model. They don't make them like Cecil Viles these days, more's the pity.

It's funny how big a part Broad Street has played in my musical activity, right through to today's bars, restaurants and hotels and their part in the Jazz Festival. It was in Bingley Hall on Broad Street, back in the 1960s a significant exhibition centre, that our band arrived early for what was an important gig. We were to open the show for Kenny Ball and his Jazzmen in six shows over three days of the Ideal Home Exhibition. That was some big deal in those days, with audiences of 1500 for each show. As we came off-stage after our sound-check, I was approached by a cool-looking guy in dark glasses who said, 'Nice band. Are you the leader?' I responded in the affirmative with, I hope, a nice blend of modesty and self-satisfaction. 'What are you doing here?' he asked. A rather dumb question, I thought, but I replied that we were set to open the show for Kenny Ball which I was certain would impress him, even though he'd been too stupid to work it out for himself.

'Sorry, you can't do that,' he told me, 'and, if you do, then I won't be able to let Kenny perform.' It took a while, but it was beginning to dawn on me that I was being addressed by the local Musicians' Union convenor and, yes, he was quite able to pull Kenny and his band out of the gig if we – six out of seven of us not MU members – went onstage. Unsurprisingly, we agreed to join and at that point the convenor demanded our not inconsiderable subscription fees. We emptied our pockets, but fell well short of the required figure. There was only one thing for it: I

13. Humph: Our Leader

had to go to the event organiser and plead for our fee in advance. Rather than disrupt the programme, he paid me the fee with a growled, 'You lot had better be good after all this.' That's how I joined the union. I'm still a member 50 years later and have been on the Midlands Regional Committee for as long as I can remember. I just hope that our current recruitment tactics are less brutal than in those days.

By 1965 the ever-adventurous and indefatigable Humphrey Lyttelton was really indulging himself. I suspect that Wilbur 'Buck' Clayton, born in Parsons, Kansas, had long been Humph's favourite trumpet player, although he would probably always have claimed it was Louis Armstrong. It takes a musician of great courage to invite a player of Buck's quality to play alongside you in your band, but that's exactly what Humph did over and over, on tour, on television and on

Buck Clayton and Humphrey Lyttelton.

record. Not content with bringing over one of the very finest of jazz trumpet players, at various times Humph also brought in and toured my favourite male singer, Little Jimmy Rushing from the Basie band, tenor star Buddy Tate, trombone stylist Vic Dickenson and another Kansas City veteran Big Joe Turner. Here was a man who knew exactly how to have far more fun than is healthy for the average bear.

Buck was a musician of flawless technique and exceptional taste; so many of us tried, with limited success, to model our playing on the finest of Basie trumpet men. In 1934 the 23-year-old Buck Clayton took his 13-piece band, the Harlem Gentlemen, into a three-month residency in Shanghai's Canidrome Ballroom, combining it with his honeymoon, sailing, as he did, the day after the ceremony. The gig was set up by the amazing globe-trotting pianist Teddy Weatherford who, having left the States initially to play in Europe, spent the years from the early 1930s leading bands in China, India, Indonesia and Sri Lanka (then known as Ceylon) before dying of cholera in Calcutta in 1945. After his stint at the Canidrome, Buck was headhunted by the famous Paramount Ballroom, staying in Shanghai until 1936 and playing to such celebrities as the wife of Chiang Kai-shek, the Chinese nationalist leader.

In the late 1960s Buck became almost a fixture in Humph's band: he regularly toured with them and wrote splendid arrangements tailor-made for the band. There was an obvious bond between the two men.

When I again became more closely involved with jazz in the 1980s, this, inevitably, meant becoming more involved with Humph again, at the Cannon Hill Jam Session and, then, as our long-standing Festival Patron.

Humph's weekly Radio 2 show, *The Best of Jazz*, came out of Birmingham's Pebble Mill Studios. He would come to Birmingham every other Monday, record his next week's programme in the afternoon and then go out live for that week's broadcast. He was probably the best broadcaster I ever observed at close range. He was always absolutely relaxed, totally comfortable with his subject, adding comments as they came to him and always seeming to be talking directly to you. We would go to eat Chinese after his show and the same argument always ensued: he insisted that Chung Ying was Birmingham's finest, I preferred Lychee Garden. Most times he had his way. He was Humph.

The other running argument we had was over Sidney Bechet who Humph thought was a terrific player and included some of his material in his own repertoire: Humph's band had even played with Bechet on an illicit recording session in 1949. I hated Bechet – still do – for his insensitive playing, how he trampled over trumpet players' melody lines without regard for what the other

13. Humph: Our Leader

The irreplaceable Humphrey Lyttelton.

musicians were playing. 'Listen to his recordings with Tommy Ladnier,' I would tell Humph. 'You would have hated playing in the same front line as Bechet.' He knew my hackles would always rise when he mentioned Bechet; it was something he did for amusement.

In 1987, with the support and encouragement of another fine broadcaster, Benny Green, and the backing of Mitchells and Butlers, again orchestrated by Malcolm Powell, Big Bear organised the first British Jazz Awards, an event that is now firmly established as the Jazz Oscars – and, of course, Humphrey Lyttelton, the first winner of the Trumpet Award, was to make a memorable contribution to the evening.

I had become increasingly incensed at the lack of opportunities that existed for even our finest jazz musicians to scrape a living. All that was visible was their two hours onstage, clearly having a whale of a time and enjoying an uncommon friendship with their fellow-musicians. Less apparent were the hundreds of miles driven each week, the meals snatched at services and, most worryingly, the regular fight against sleep on the two, three or four-hour drive home. Marriages of musicians have a high mortality rate, not surprising with the extended periods of absence, the daytime recovery hours in bed, the loss of time with the kids as they grow up, not to mention the practice time. Don't think, for a minute, that, when a musician attains a high level of performance, he can relax in the knowledge that he's a good player. Most musicians devote significant time to maintaining or improving their level. Alan Barnes can get exceedingly grumpy if he doesn't manage four hours' practice a day, while Bruce Adams always carries a mouthpiece in his pocket so that he can buzz at every opportunity – that keeps his embouchure strong and is obviously working! All this for an hourly rate less than your average plumber. Not that I've got anything against plumbers: my mate Gary Woodhouse is a plumber and he's one of the nicest folks you could meet.

Wanting to do something about the lack of recognition, I set up the British Jazz Awards. The system has always been straightforward, though the advent of online voting has brought its own problems. We assemble a Nomination Panel of jazz professionals, not academics or politicians, but people who actually work in the business of jazz: club owners, festival directors, journalists, promoters. They each nominate four musicians/bands in each of the categories. Their votes are totalled and the musicians who are selected are put to a public vote alongside a blank space for

Humphrey Lyttelton winning the Schlitz British Jazz Award for Trumpet, with a typically wry Humph comment.

13. Humph: Our Leader

voting for some other preferred name. Where the danger lies in online voting is that internet-savvy musicians can generate votes through, for instance, a Facebook campaign, but we do our best to moderate the effects of this. Some younger bands always did seek to manipulate the voting – a package of voting forms with an unknown's name in one category and all the others left blank was not unknown – but now there seems to be a generally accepted dishonesty in many aspects of the web.

One – actually extremely good – young band were the subject of heavy online voting and phoned me to ask how they were currently placed so they could increase their efforts if necessary. I pointed out that this was not exactly in the spirit of the vote.

Back in 1987 – March 11th, to be exact – the winners of the first British Jazz Awards assembled in Birmingham's finest jazz room, the Grosvenor Suite of the Grand Hotel. Benny Green handled the proceedings with aplomb, memorably saying:

'There is no more deserving a sub-section in the world of art than the jazz musician. He is taken for granted, neglected and under-rated. He is passed by when the goodies of what is laughingly called our civilised world are passed out; he doesn't get his picture in the paper and doesn't become famous.

'Jazz musicians are celebrities only to each other. An occasion like this which pats them on the back and says to them, "We do know what you are up to, we do appreciate it and we do understand how much it is worth" is an auspicious one.'

Benny, with jazz journalist Tony Russell, made the nine presentations – in recent years the number of categories has risen to 16 – before the business end of the evening: the Jam Session. Again, as in our many and various jam sessions over the years, this was not a wild, untidy bash, but a properly organised session planned to get the best from all the musicians and again, we brought in the Manor Mobile recording unit.

It was a night to remember, especially when leading American pianist, Sir Charles Thompson, Count Basie's alter ego, booked to play through dinner (Sir Charles Thompson booked as dinner pianist!), joined Brian Lemon at the piano. All the musicians were on top form – Roy Williams, Peter King, Dick Morrissey, John Barnes, Dave Green, Martin Taylor and Allan Ganley – but, listening to the album even now, I can't help but feel overwhelmed by the simple beauty of Humph's duet with Brian on *If I Could Be With You One Hour Tonight*.

Wherever possible – that is, when we have been successful in securing sponsorship – we have arranged a formal event to announce the Jazz Awards winners with musicians present to accept their awards and take part in what is always an exceptional jam session. Some have been recorded, some broadcast

Winners of the 1987 British Jazz Awards: (front) Allan Ganley, Roy Williams, Humphrey Lyttelton; (middle) Martin Taylor, Dave Green, Brian Lemon, Peter King; (back) John Barnes, Dick Morrissey.

live, and extracts from the inaugural session have been re-released on Big Bear's *Jazz City UK Volume 2* CD. Even when there is no formal event, the process takes place, announcements are made and certificates awarded, and musicians can enhance their CVs and biographies – and their employment prospects – with the fact that they are British Jazz Award winners.

For three years we teamed with the Getzen trumpet company to offer an additional category for the best trumpet performance during the previous Birmingham Jazz Festival, with Getzen endorsee Digby Fairweather making the final decision. Serbian trumpet ace Dusko Goykovich couldn't make the presentation, but recorded a splendid video expressing his regret at not being able to attend; our own Kenny Baker attended, accepted his award with the best of grace before putting on a trademark swinging performance in the Jam Session; Miles Davis simply said to take it to his lawyer's office. Nothing more, not even a

13. Humph: Our Leader

thank you. Now Nina Simone did actually come to Birmingham to be presented with her Platinum Disc for *My Baby Just Cares for Me*, but she seemed to have attended the same School of Charm and Diplomacy as did Miles.

Humph, on the other hand, just didn't know how to behave other than with impeccable taste. On every one of the many occasions we had the pleasure of working with him it was, without exception, pure delight. He was regarded by everyone who understood our music as Our Leader and enjoyed the total respect of all.

It is widely known that, as a true egalitarian and what he described as a 'romantic socialist', Humph turned down honours from the Queen on several occasions, including the offer of a knighthood. That in itself is enough to suggest that he was a little out of the ordinary. He was, in fact, a very private man. I don't recall, for instance, meeting anyone who had met his wife or visited his home, though there is a photograph of him with an early version of his band, taken in his living room with everyone looking extremely uneasy. This, apparently, was the only time the band members were invited to his house. The house, itself, designed to Humph's specification, presented blank walls to the outside world, all the windows opening on to an indoor courtyard.

Spending time with Humph was rather like being granted an audience. He was the most fascinating company, but it was important that you remembered precisely when your allocated time was up. To say that he didn't suffer fools gladly might just be the understatement of the century. He really didn't like the telephone at all, rarely answered it and was known to change his ex-directory number when too many people got to know it. His main channel of communication with the rest of the world was by means of beautifully written letters and via his personal assistant and manager, later his partner, Susan Da Costa.

Humphrey Lyttelton was trumpet player, clarinettist, bandleader, arranger, music broadcaster, comedy presenter, writer of autobiographies and jazz criticism, cartoonist and record company owner (London Records in the 1950s, Calligraph for many years until his death). With his amazing range of activities keeping a grip on his diary must have been the stuff of nightmares, but Sue always handled things calmly and efficiently and was always the person to contact if you wanted anything from Humph.

Beryl Bryden was a decent enough vaudeville-tinged jazz singer who came up in the traditional jazz era. She was somewhat larger than life, overpowering, you might say. Humph, with no little glee, described Beryl as 'descending on one rather in the manner of a Spanish galleon under full sail.' Truth to tell, it was rather more scary than that. One Christmas morning Beryl decided to visit Humph's extremely private home, clutching her Christmas gift for him.

It was a copy of her new CD!

I can find no record of Humph's response.

I read somewhere that Humph excelled at everything he did except ice skating which he blamed on the lack of size 13½ skating boots! During World War II, as a young officer in the Grenadier Guards, he reportedly led his men ashore at Salerno with a pistol in one hand and his trumpet in the other; he wrote storylines for the popular *Daily Mail* cartoon strip *Flook* which was drawn by Trog, aka his clarinet player Wally Fawkes; he featured in the Radio 1 comedy quiz *Jazz Score* and then enjoyed a huge second career as the quizmaster of the immensely successful *I'm Sorry I Haven't a Clue*. I have met people who say they are fans of Humph purely on the strength of *I'm Sorry I Haven't a Clue*, not even knowing that he was a jazz trumpet player.

The last time I saw Humphrey Lyttelton was when he played Birmingham Hippodrome with the stage version of *I'm Sorry I Haven't a Clue*. On stage he was as hilariously irreverent as ever, the funniest man in the show, and he even played some trumpet, splendidly, of course. Sue, Humph, Sarah and I went for a Chinese meal after the show at the Chung Ying – Humph insisted on that. Physically he was beginning to look frail, argumentative, but invariably correct, amusing and, most importantly for me, still on a crusade where jazz was concerned. He quizzed me on the progress of plans for that year's festival and Sarah about her role in organising it. He also told her not to listen to me if I ever criticised Sidney Bechet. Sarah was, unsurprisingly, confused, but utterly overwhelmed by his strength of character.

The train taking me from Birmingham to London en route to the funeral of Humphrey Lyttelton inexplicably developed a fault that left us sitting short of Milton Keynes Station for nearly three hours. The chap sitting opposite to me, noting my obvious agitation over the delay, asked me if it was making me late for an important meeting. I told him no, it was making me late for a funeral. 'A close friend?', he asked, and I replied that it was much more than that, it was the funeral of Humphrey Lyttelton. He looked taken aback and said that Humph was 'our Chairman'. I asked what he meant and he replied, 'He's the Chairman of the British Calligraphy Society.'

Calligraphy! Something else that Humph excelled at!

Chapter 14

THE BOSS IS HOME

When I was about 14 years old, there were two BBC radio programmes that me and my school friends listened to religiously every week. Monday evenings brought *The Goon Show*, with the irrepressible Spike Milligan, Peter Sellers and Harry Secombe with a brand of zany surrealist humour than probably affected us all for the rest of our lives, plus some nicely swinging jazz from harmonica whiz Max Geldray with the Ray Ellington Quartet.

The other essential listening was *Let's Settle for Music*, broadcast every Thursday from the BBC Paris studios in London. Kenny Baker's Dozen, in fact usually 15 pieces, featured the country's finest jazz musicians. Every week Kenny would write new arrangements and the band would gather in the late afternoon for what they termed a rehearsal, but in reality was little more than a run-through of these invariably difficult charts. After that it was down to the pub for a couple of hours, then back to the studio to go live on air at 9 o'clock. Of course there was the occasional clinker, but the excitement of this superb band under the leadership of its mercurial trumpet star was riveting. Kenny Baker's Dozen signposted my taste in jazz for decades. Still does, in fact.

When I got settled in the music business, I was lucky enough to work with Kenny and would book him on every appropriate occasion. When he got to know me better, he would tell me to go ahead and book the musicians to accompany him. 'Go on, surprise me,' he would say. This was a task I took on with more than just enthusiasm. For an early Birmingham Jazz Festival appearance, I put together a six-piece with Kenny, accordionist Jack Emblow, saxophonist Alan Barnes, Brian Dee on piano, Len Skeat on double bass and drummer Ronnie Verrell. Kenny turned up with no arrangements, called the tunes, set the tempos and counted them in. Afterwards Kenny told me that he wanted to take this band home with him!

Another peppy little combo which we organised, this time for the Brouwershaven Festival on an island off the coast of Holland, featured U.S. guitar star Marty Grosz with the Orphan Newsboys. The Newsboys we fielded were

Don't Worry 'Bout The Bear

Kenny, the wonderful, but totally under-rated, Al Gay on tenor sax and Len Skeat on double bass and, reportedly, it was a riot. Marty, a singer in the Fats Waller vein, subsequently always referred to Kenny as 'my Herman Autrey' after the trumpeter with Fats Waller's Rhythm.

Kenny was a small fighting cock of a man, blessed with boundless energy, inexhaustible enthusiasm and a no-nonsense approach to his music. He believed there were only two ways to play music, the right way and the wrong way, and he had neither time nor patience for anyone who couldn't deliver the former.

One of Kenny's particular quirks was that he enjoyed being in a familiar place. He was the only one I knew of, among all the musicians I have worked with, who liked to travel in a camper van. His was no ordinary camper van, but one equipped with all the necessities of life that Kenny deemed important in surviving life on the road. His wife Sue would drive, usually cook a meal on arrival at their destination, Kenny might snatch a few hours sleep before bounding on stage to give everybody hell. There was more than one occasion when Kenny and Sue arrived at the hotel we had booked for them, then ate and slept in their camper van, only using the hotel for the toilet and shower.

Sue Baker was an essential part of Kenny's career as a musician. They met in her role as organiser of the Kenny Baker Fan Club so, unlike too many musicians' marriages, they got off on the right foot with Sue in no doubt as to the importance of his music. She was unshiftingly loyal to Kenny, organising his daily life so that nothing got in the way of his music, and was fiercely protective when she suspected that someone was not acting in Ken's best interests.

They lived in the seaside town of Felpham, not far from Eastleigh near Southampton Airport. Whenever we had a show at the Concorde Club, before club owner Cole Mathieson built his fine Ellington Lodge next door, Kenny would come over to the show and take me back to his house to stay for a couple of days. I was staggered one morning to see him out there at dawn, laying paving on his drive which was clearly extremely physical work. Britain's top trumpet man – a national treasure – laying paving slabs!

One time Kenny began to think that his PRS payments were not getting through to him. PRS checked and found that they had been sent in error to another Kenny Baker who lived in the same village. Kenny, of course, marched straight over to the address they gave him, hammered on the front door and was confronted by a man considerably shorter than himself – and Kenny was not a tall man! The other Kenny Baker, standing a full 3 foot 8 inches, had all the cheques still in their envelopes and said that he had been waiting for him to come round, was delighted to meet him and had always been a fan of his playing.

14. The Boss Is Home

It turned out that this was Kenny Baker the Birmingham-born actor, celebrated for playing R2-D2 in *Star Wars*. They became close, a hilarious twosome who really should have worked up a stage act together. One night, when Kenny's band was featuring in a concert in Preston, the other Kenny showed up. Our Kenny invited him on stage in the second half, pulled up a chair, sat down and perched him on his knee, pretending to work him from behind like a ventriloquist's dummy while still playing hot trumpet. Not a dry eye in the house!

By 1958, when *Let's Settle for Music* came to an end, Kenny Baker's Dozen had appeared outside the BBC Paris studios on only three occasions: two films and one stage appearance which was opposite Billie Holiday on her single appearance at the Royal Festival Hall in 1958.

Throughout my years of working with Kenny Baker I would continually badger him to let me re-form the Dozen with him, this time not as a studio band, but as a live fully functioning on-stage big swing band. Eventually he cracked, instructing me to locate and hire the musicians, a process he wanted nothing to do with, leaving him to dust off the original arrangements and re-write where he thought necessary, which turned out to be most cases. At that time (1993) Big Bear was booking the attractions into Ronnie Scott's in Birmingham, so we slotted in the Dozen for four days and I set about recruiting the band which was pretty much like letting a kid loose in a candy store. One problem I was spared was musicians finding their diaries were full. For Kenny everyone made himself available; the opportunity to feature in the finest swing band outside America was irresistible.

There was, however, one misunderstanding – over the bassist. Not wanting to replicate his previous line-up, Kenny said it was probably better not to book Lennie. At that time there were some tremendous double bass players around, as there still are. Foremost among them were Dave Green and Len Skeat and it was always a difficult decision which one to approach, but this time Ken made it easy and I booked Dave Green. It wasn't until much later that Kenny enlarged on his comment and it became clear that he was referring to Lennie Bush! No matter, Dave's playing, as always, was immaculate and I still live in hope that Len has forgiven me, though he often mentions it – and not in a jocular way.

Dave Green was a school friend of Rolling Stones drummer Charlie Watts. They played together regularly until the Stones offer came along and have continued to do so whenever the opportunity arises. During the 1990s they both featured in the Charlie Watts Quintet, a terrific and unapologetically out-and-out bebop combo.

Ralph Salmins had become my first-choice drummer since Len Skeat had introduced him as a replacement for Eddie Taylor with *Lady Sings the Blues*.

Young Ralph, unknown on the jazz scene at the time, had gigged with, and mightily impressed, Len Skeat, a man known to be extremely particular when it came to drummers. At the rehearsal prior to Ralph's first gig with *Lady Sings*, he was technically on the button, but didn't have the lift needed for the Billie Holiday repertoire. After rehearsal I confided my concerns to Len who asked me, 'Have you told Ralph?' I hadn't, so Len told me I should. I was partway through explaining what I wanted when Ralph asked, 'Do you mean play more Jo Jones?' I replied that playing like the legendary Count Basie drummer would be perfect – and that's exactly what he did.

Around a year before the re-formation of the Dozen, in August 1992, I had a phone call from the normally unflappable Brian Theobald who was in an advanced stage of panic. The Count Basie Band had flown in from New York that morning and were set to appear the following night at the Royal Festival Hall, but David Gibson, the drummer, had damaged his ankle messing around at Heathrow and there was no way he could make the gig. So who on earth could he get to fill the drum chair with the finest swing band on the planet, with no time to rehearse? I told him that Ralph Salmins was the perfect man for the job – after all, he could play like Jo Jones! Brian had never heard of Ralph and took some convincing, but we knew each other well and had worked together for years, so he took my word. I called Ralph who accepted the booking as if calls to play with the Basie Band were an everyday occurrence, only asking what he should wear.

Naturally Ralph took care of business and leader Frank Foster offered him two two-week European tours with the band. I was delighted to see him befriend trombonist Bill Hughes, a really special man who wrote a regular column for our *Jazz Rag* magazine and went on to lead the Basie Band from 2003 to 2010. Bill and Ralph were reunited at the Marbella Jazz Festival in 2004 when the Count Basie Orchestra was headlining and Ralph was with the Alan Barnes All Stars. Ralph remembers, 'I was playing in the lobby and despite the fact that the Basie Band were about to get two hours sleep before leaving for an early flight, Bill came over, said hello and we spent a long time catching up. What a gentleman!'

Joining Ralph and Dave Green in Kenny Baker's rhythm section was pianist Brian Dee who to this day is our first choice for *Lady Sings the Blues*. Brian is a youthful veteran who has worked with most of the great names in the world of jazz and popular music, from such jazz legends as Benny Carter and Ben Webster to famous singers Bing Crosby, Fred Astaire, Peggy Lee, Elton John and – rather more unexpectedly – Cilla Black. Early in his career he had regularly played opposite jazz pianist/comedian/film star Dudley Moore at the Establishment Club.

Kenny Baker was extremely picky when it came to accepting gigs, but, once on stage, always had a ball, especially with his re-formed Dozen.

In the trumpet section, besides Kenny, were the mighty Bruce Adams, Derek Healey, a long-time friend of Kenny's who had served in all the top big bands, notably Ted Heath, and the comparatively youthful Simon Gardner. Legendary trombonist Don Lusher led the trombone section alongside Bill Geldard, an associate of Kenny's for many years, and the amazing Richard Edwards. Richard didn't often venture outside the recording studios, where he is in high demand, but, had he decided his career was to be on stage, he would most certainly have become a household name. The saxophone section, similarly, was a nice mix with the mercurial Alan Barnes alongside four distinguished veterans in Roy Willox, Vic Ash, Dave Willis and Eddie Mordue.

Being there when the musicians congregated for that first rehearsal was one of the most memorable occasions in my musical life. When the orchestrations were passed around, among the 15 musicians were Bill Geldard who had been there the last time they had been played, some 35 years before, and several who had not even been born at that time. There were men in the band right through from their 20s to their 70s. When Kenny counted in the first piece to be rehearsed, Duke Ellington's *What am I here for?*, to say it was an emotional moment would be an understatement.

Kenny Baker was the ideal bandleader. He always led from the front and played exactly what was right, and his every word and gesture made it clear that he expected nothing less from every one of his musicians. His enthusiasm was contagious and inspired everyone to play above themselves.

Unsurprisingly the run at Ronnie Scott's was a sell-out. The ensembles were magnificent, the solos straight out of the top drawer and soon everyone in the band was feeling good. On the second night, in the pub during intermission, trumpet star Bruce Adams said, 'I think we've nailed it now, Kenny.' Walking back to the club, Kenny, clearly seething at what he saw as complacency, asked me several times, 'Did you hear what he said?'. Kenny's remedy was simple. As the band took the stand for the second set, Kenny told them, 'We're going to change the programme,' and called three totally unrehearsed numbers to open with. The band, top men as they were, performed the new material with style and barely an audible glitch, but it was clearly a white-knuckle ride. It was certainly exciting and I saw no further signs of smugness creeping in.

We had agreed to record the final two shows of the Ronnie Scott's run on Richard Branson's wondrous Virgin mobile recording unit. When I went to the Steelhouse Lane Police Station with a request to have the three parking bays at the club's side entrance suspended, I was quizzed by a stern-faced desk sergeant who grunted with seeming disapproval. He perked up just a little when I

14. The Boss Is Home

mentioned it was a jazz recording, but beamed with approval when I mentioned that it was Kenny Baker we were recording. From then it went swimmingly: all the usual charges were waived and I didn't have to press too hard to persuade him to accept guest tickets.

I have always been immensely proud of the subsequent album release, *The Boss is Home*, by Kenny Baker's Dozen. It ticked pretty much all the boxes for me. The reviewers wrote their approval, we got international distribution (by no means a given for a British jazz CD), everyone in the band gave their all and played tremendously. Most important of all, Kenny was satisfied. The recording must stand tall among the best British big band recordings.

Dave Gelly's liner notes say it all:

'Back in the 1950s, before we were all turned into battery chickens and fed on gunk, and something new did not automatically mean something worse, there was a BBC radio producer named Pat Dixon. He made a speciality of devising slightly off-centre ideas for shows on the Light Programme.

'Dixon was a jazz lover, who always slipped some of his favourite music into his productions if he possibly could and, in 1952, he approached Kenny Baker with an idea for a series of informal jazz programmes.

'The show, entitled Let's Settle For Music, went out on Thursday nights and gained a large and loyal following. In fact, it did so well that one series led to another and the whole thing ran for six years, ending only with Pat Dixon's death in 1958. My teenage years, and those of thousands of others, were measured in weekly doses of The Goon Show and Let's Settle For Music, so I take this opportunity to pay a belated tribute to Pat Dixon for being a benign cultural influence on a generation.

'Membership of Baker's Dozen changed over the years, and its ranks gradually swelled from 13 to 16. Among the original members were George Chisholm, Harry Hayes, Tommy McQuater, Freddie Ballerini (doubling on tenor and violin) and the phenomenal E.O. "Poggy" Pogson, who was renowned for being able to play virtually any wind instrument. Each week Kenny would produce an arrangement featuring Pogson on some bizarre item from his vast collection – ophicleide, hot fountain pen, ocarina, musical saw.

'"It had been 35 years since the last Dozen sessions," says Kenny, "and I wasn't at all sure about doing this. But Jim Simpson twisted my arm by promising to do all the work of phoning round and setting it up. All I had to do was search about in the attic for the old scores."

'By any standard the New Dozen is a dream band, containing the cream of three generations of British jazz, and the fact that this is a live recording puts an edge on the music. There is no safety net.

Don't Worry 'Bout The Bear

'My own favourite moments include Alan Barnes' serpentine tenor on *Stumbling*, followed by a completely over the top Bruce Adams (no wonder Kenny says he gets dizzy just listening to him), and Roy Willox on *Squatty Roo*. Although he is one of the country's leading saxophonists, Roy rarely gets a chance to stretch out and play jazz at this length. It was Roy who remarked to Kenny, after the Ronnie Scott's run, that this was one of the best rhythm sections he had ever worked with, and it is indeed phenomenal. The combination of Brian Dee, Dave Green and Ralph Salmins seems to bring out the best in all three.

'As Kenny says, 35 years is too long a time for making sensible comparisons, but the new Kenny Baker's Dozen seems to have everything the old one had. Only one thing is missing: the fun of guessing what monstrosity of musical plumbing Pogson would come up with this week.'

The media reaction to *The Boss is Home* was so encouraging that Kenny agreed that we should take the Dozen out on the road. Booking the band out was pretty straightforward: there was nothing out there remotely like the Dozen so we got the band into good halls and festivals throughout the UK and Europe. Logistically it was another matter entirely, with the diaries of fifteen people to co-ordinate, a bus and hotels for distance gigs to arrange, plus flights into Europe.

The longest schlep we did was to the Imatra Big Band Festival in Eastern Finland, close to the Russian border. The band played a stormer, as usual, but the most memorable bits were the seemingly interminable drive from Helsinki through an almost unbroken avenue of tall trees and Kenny's fixation with St. Petersburg. He had read somewhere that the spires of the former Russian capital were clearly visible from across the Baltic in Finland and kept dragging me out to the terrace where we would peer, without reward, into the distance.

Unusually for a British jazz musician, Kenny's playing was properly valued much further afield. When Harry James died in 1983, rather than go to one of the many fine American trumpeters available, his executors turned to Kenny Baker to lead, and feature with, the Harry James Orchestra, a singular honour as Harry James was one of the most respected of jazz and swing trumpeters of all time. Characteristically, Kenny turned down the lucrative offer.

In the late 1960s, when clarinet king Benny Goodman decided to tour Europe with a band that featured a select few Europeans alongside his American band-members, Kenny was an obvious choice. Benny was notorious as a tough bandleader, a martinet whose steely gaze of disapproval was known among musicians as The Ray. Everyone in Benny's bands, except, of course, Kenny Baker who feared nothing when it came to music, dreaded being fixed by The Ray. On the fourth night of the tour the band played a concert in Brussels. Benny went into the big build-up announcing Kenny's trumpet feature, Bunny Berigan's *I*

14. The Boss Is Home

Can't Get Started, and was just about to count it in when Kenny called out cheerily, 'Get the tempo right this time, will you, Benny?'

A more light-hearted encounter with a jazz legend came during Kenny's years playing the trumpet on *The Muppet Show* where a famous photograph shows him in the company of Kermit the Frog and guest star Dizzy Gillespie!

Kenny and I got to know the playwright Alan Plater and we came up with a neat little plan to present the two of them on stage together. Alan was a jazz fan which showed through in many of his plays such as the BBC television film, *Last of the Blonde Bombshells*, the stage play *Rent Party* and, particularly, the three series he wrote for Yorkshire Television: *The Beiderbecke Affair, The Beiderbecke Tapes* and *The Beiderbecke Connection* which are based around a schoolteacher obsessed with jazz trumpet player, Bix Beiderbecke.

The form of the show that we devised was simplicity itself on the basis of, 'Why complicate things when you've got the immense talents of Kenny and Alan?'

We formed a six-piece band of top musicians built around Kenny and called it Kenny Baker's Half Dozen. Alan gathered together his favourite memories and the show went out as *Beiderbecke – And All that Jazz*. It made for a wonderful, life-affirming evening. The band would play the opener to the obvious delight of Alan, seated onstage at a desk. Alan would then deliver a charming anecdote which would have the band falling about with laughter, then the band would play again – and that's how the show progressed. Two hours never passed more quickly or more enjoyably. *Beiderbecke* played concerts and a radio broadcast and was always a success, only stopping with Kenny's death. Bruce Adams stepped in for the already confirmed dates, but there were no new bookings without Kenny.

In 1999, the year he won his third British Jazz Award for Trumpet, Kenny was deservedly awarded the MBE, but in the same year we lost him in the most unfortunate of circumstances. He had been suffering from a serious viral chest infection and with an upcoming performance of the Best of British, his band that truly warranted that name, he did the sensible thing and put in a dep. I suspect that his decision had much to do with the persuasive qualities of Sue – Kenny was not a man to give up easily. Digby Fairweather was the obvious choice to replace him, leaving Kenny to concentrate on battling back to health. Two days before the show at the Solihull Arts Complex, Digby was attacked while walking home late at night from Westcliff-on-Sea Railway Station. The mugger snatched Digby's trumpet, but more seriously, slashed his hand with a knife, leaving Digby with no alternative but to tell Kenny that he couldn't play the gig.

Kenny, always a man to get things done and avoid any fuss, insisted on doing the show, rather than have Sue phone around for possible replacements. He travelled to Solihull, played the gig perfectly, as he would, but was in obvious discomfort throughout. During the intermission and after the show he was coughing blood. Pianist Brian Lemon offered words intended to comfort: 'You'll be alright, Ken.' Kenny replied, 'Not this time, mate.'

Kenny struggled home, was immediately taken into intensive care in a hospital near to his Felpham home and remained in a coma for several days before passing away.

He was 78. He left his wife Sue and daughter Julie and was mourned by the entire British jazz world. His great friend Jack Parnell, bandleader for the Muppets TV show, said that when he had a show, looked around and saw no Kenny Baker, then he felt that he hadn't got a band. The BBC reported me saying. 'It's not just the passing of a good man and a wonderful musician, it's the end of an era. He is to jazz what The Rolling Stones are to rock.'

Chapter 15

THERE'S NO BUSINESS IN SHOW BUSINESS

The Rep Café Bar, prominently sited on what is now Birmingham's showpiece Centenary Square, had done particularly well from participating in the Jazz Festival. So much so that owners Allan Sartori and Barry Sherwin of Iceford Catering asked Big Bear to organise regular Sunday evening jazz sessions throughout the year which again proved extremely popular.

After a year or so I had a call from Sartori asking me in to a meeting where he had just one question, 'Who *is* this Ronnie Scott fellow then?' Seemingly he had heard the name mentioned at the Sunday jazz shows and wondered if there might just be a business opportunity here. So the idea of Ronnie Scott's in Broad Street, Birmingham, was born.

Undoubtedly the best known jazz club in the UK, Ronnie Scott's in London was owned and operated by BPR, the name made up of the first initials of the three men behind the venture: Brian Theobald, Pete King and Ronnie Scott. I was acquainted with Ronnie from having booked his band and Pete from trying, usually unsuccessfully, to break my bands into his club, but I was very close to Brian. We had worked together on some great musicians, including the Count Basie Orchestra, the Buddy Rich Orchestra, the actual Blues Brothers Band, the Dizzy Gillespie Orchestra and more. Over the years he had become a trusted – and extremely entertaining – friend, so it was only a matter of a phone call to set up a meeting in Ronnie Scott's with Pete King, Ronnie Scott, Allan Sartori, Barry Sherwin – and me, presumably as the chap who knew about putting on jazz events in Birmingham.

Pete and Ronnie showed immense enthusiasm at the prospect of setting up a franchise, clearly seeing it as the first of many, spanning the entire world, if not the universe. Allan and Barry were equally enthusiastic, seeing the club as, in Allan's words, a 'cash cow'. I had very little to contribute to the meeting: all I knew about was music and there was no mention of that.

I wasn't invited to the next, or to any other, meetings, which was explained when Sartori told me unapologetically that he and Pete King had decided that I had outlived any usefulness I may have had and that Pete would look after booking the bands into Birmingham, Allan would handle marketing and I would be kept well away from it all.

Interestingly this wasn't the first Ronnie Scott's Club to open in Birmingham. Back in the early 1960s, the London club operated a regular Monday night at the Mermaid, then an imposing pub on the Stratford Road in Sparkbrook. They did nothing to improve the gloomy aspect of the large upstairs room, but they booked in some tremendous musicians, including top American tenor man Ben Webster. The first time that I met Len Skeat was when he was playing in Webster's quartet at the Mermaid and here we are, still working together nearly 60 years later. The Birmingham club was operated on behalf of Ronnie and Pete by the interestingly named Harry Flick who was someone you really would not like to mess with.

Ronnie Scott's on Broad Street opened in the Autumn of 1991. The main room was a facsimile of Ronnie's in London, right down to the small tables, David Redfern photographs and red and white checked tablecloths. Nothing wrong with that: it looked and felt instantly like a jazz room and, most importantly, had good acoustics.

However, what worried me from the start was the programming. Pete and Allan simply duplicated the bands booked for the London club, headliners and supports, often for a two or even three week run. The audience potential of the Broad Street music venue bore no resemblance to that of the club in the heart of Soho, with its stream of entertainment-seeking tourists. To book expensive artists for a dozen shows or more was totally unrealistic, but even worse was booking costly out-of-town support acts. Clearly it was a way for Pete and Ronnie to subsidise their Frith Street programme, a cynical and short-sighted way to make a saving on their artists' costs, while Sartori and Sherwin simply went along unquestioningly, anticipating untold riches.

When midweek attendances sometimes sank as low as 15 or 20 people in a 340-capacity room, it was obvious that Ronnie's Birmingham was facing an early demise. With virtually no media coverage, little visible marketing effort and highly-priced food and drink of indifferent quality the venture was looking shaky. In its eighth month of operation a near-weepy Sartori (he was good at that) implored me to come in and keep it going until Christmas 1992. We did better than that. We kept it going until the carefully planned and unscrupulous receivership of Ronnie Scott's Birmingham in 2001.

15. There's No Business In Show Business

I suppose it should have been a warning to us all when Sartori's previous company, Iceford Catering Ltd., having for some reason absorbed the building costs of Ronnie Scott's, collapsed in 1996, with debts of £454,000, and inevitably Jazz Enterprises, which ran Ronnie Scott's, Birmingham, followed suit five years later with debts of more than £1.6 million and unsecured creditors including Birmingham City Council which had reputedly poured in £320,000 to help boost the city's image. Sadly the majority of the creditors who lost out were musicians, including the likes of Helen Shapiro and, not surprisingly, Big Bear artists King Pleasure and the Biscuit Boys and *Lady Sings the Blues.* I had been having so much fun booking artists into the club that I had become stupidly blind to the risks involved and supported Ronnie Scott's with substantial loans which were never repaid. This did nothing to improve my mood when Jazz Enterprises, having folded in dubious circumstances, opened the very same night, still as Ronnie Scott's, but with a 'new' operating company.

Ed Bicknell, manager of Dire Straits who at the time of the collapse lost £200,000, summed up Sartori as being not only a crook, but an incompetent crook. He lacked nothing in ingenuity. When Jazz Enterprises collapsed, Broomco (2540) Ltd. bought the company for a mere £78,000 – a good deal for its directors (including, amazingly enough, Sartori and Sherwin) and shareholders (not this time Allan and Barry, but their wives!). Sadly the incompetence kicked in again and Broomco went into liquidation a few months later, only to open again in very short order as a lap-dancing club – with Allan Sartori and his then close friend, Laurence Reddy, in the driving seats.

In 2004 a court case with Barry Sherwin suing Broomco for wrongful dismissal revealed what the *Sunday Mercury* called 'the shambolic inner workings of Ronnie Scott's.'

Judge Caroline Alton showed that gift for the apposite phrase so valued by the judiciary: 'From the early days Mr. Sartori and Mr. Sherwin treated Ronnie Scott's as their own personal piggy bank.' Revealing the 'chaotic truth' behind the club, the *Sunday Mercury* told of unrecorded blank cheques being given to directors, slices of their salaries paid to wives to avoid tax and payslips destroyed, plus 'a life of luxury homes, fast cars and public adulation.'

After the club went into administration, Allan Sartori predictably blamed 'greedy musicians'. Barry Sherwin was dismissed, ironically, for 'putting his hand in the till' (established company policy?) and went on to create a remarkable record, as revealed by the *Sunday Mercury*, of holding directorships in 12 dissolved companies. While Barry was closing various bars in financial disarray, Allan Sartori carried on his tradition of court cases against former friends in a series of long-running, increasingly ridiculous cases with ex-business partner Laurence Reddy over the possession of a strip of pavement with a fast food outlet outside what had been Ronnie Scott's.

If the management team at the club were something of an oddity, then there were also some unusual characters among the staff. Foremost among them was Iain Ross-McKenzie, known universally as Gonzo. A genial and efficient club manager who supported Barry Sherwin in the saner club activities, he raised the role of greeter to something like an art form, so much so that most customers assumed that he was the club's owner. Always impeccably dressed, he was said – and I have no reason to doubt this – to be the nephew of 1940s screen goddess, Olivia De Havilland. He certainly had American connections from his younger days.

An inveterate music fan, he would often dress in the style he imagined appropriate to the featured band. Once, when King Pleasure and the Biscuit Boys were holding sway, he turned up dressed as an American GI, forage cap and all. King Pleasure drew attention to him from the stage before asking him what he was going to dress up as next week when the Spice Girls were booked. (Not that they were!)

Gonzo was married to a stunning girl who was a featured dancer at Birmingham Royal Ballet. After the collapse of Ronnie's, Gonzo appeared as front man at a series of clubs and restaurants, often in cahoots with Barry Sherwin, but ill luck seemed to dog them and, after a failure or two, Gonzo decamped to London and from there to The United Arab Emirates where he is District Manager, Middle East, at Five Guys International. I hope that he's having fun.

Sartori always said that he wanted the club to be the city's biggest top-notch dining experience and be so successful that the music became an incidental – at Ronnie Scott's, for Heaven's sake! To this end he hired the maitre d' from Raymond Blanc's neighbouring posh nosherie. The man was of a tyrannical disposition, the main recipient of his bullying being his assistant, Wagner Carrilho, a kindly and charming Brazilian who loved music and took every opportunity to ask me about the bands.

He told me that all he really wanted was to be a singer. He only lasted about half a year at Ronnie's, hounded out by his immediate boss. I was sad to see him go, but subsequently delighted when he made an impact on *X Factor*.

It has to be said that, as absurdly managed as it was, Ronnie Scott's became a beacon of light on a Broad Street that had yet to develop into the hustling, bustling golden mile of entertainment that it is today. I well remember walking past the barren wastes of demolished buildings with Humphrey Lyttelton on a misty Monday evening in January after he had finished broadcasting *The Best of Jazz* from BBC Pebble Mill. There was scarcely a soul to be seen as we approached Ronnie Scott's, but, when we went into the main room where King Pleasure and the Biscuit Boys were rocking some 300 jumping jiving fans, Humph said, 'It's like walking out of a black and white film into a full Technicolor production.'

There was, briefly, another beacon of culture in Broad Street at that time. There was a splendidly authentic American-style milk bar, situated on a piece of waste ground directly opposite the club. The owners were enthusiastic participants in the Jazz Festival, featuring such attractions as the American bluesman Sherman Robertson. It has never been properly explained just how one night, in the early hours, it exploded and completely burned out.

As inspiring as much of the music we booked into Ronnie Scott's was, the business side of things was equally depressing. The role of Big Bear was to book the artists and handle the PR, an almost impossible task when Sartori was involved. He openly resented paying the musicians properly, even when they attracted a full house, and all he wanted to do was carouse with his friends in the front bar, as far away from the music as he could get, and count the takings at the end of the night. When the club had a good week, Allan would trouser the cash; on a poor week he would plead poverty and do all he could to avoid paying musicians, Big Bear and any tradespeople unfortunate to come within his orbit.

I persuaded them to agree to a weekly business meeting, Wednesdays at 11.00 am. Sherwin understood the value of this and did his best to contribute, but Allan had an extremely short attention span. Habitually, in the middle of making plans to build what was, after all, his business, he would get up from the table, wander over to the cigarette machine and empty out all the cash which he took to the bar and counted out meticulously. He would put the coins into neat piles before telling the barman to change them into folding money which he would then pocket. It was the same routine every week.

Allan's contribution to one of the meetings was to announce that no longer would the press be allowed into the club without paying and certainly there would be no more free drinks for them. As anyone who was around at that time will recall, media coverage of Ronnie's was brilliant and we were doing everything we could to make the club their home from home. I started to justify media activity to Allan, but he simply wouldn't listen. Crying, 'No, no, I knew you would say that!', he left the meeting, backing away from me as he walked, still in reverse, around the club, with me continuing my diatribe and him protesting that he didn't want to hear it. In the end I cracked and told him that he was a disgrace: he didn't want people coming into his club, messing up the ashtrays with cigarette ends, dirtying his cups and glasses by drinking from them, pissing in the toilets and generally cluttering up the club when all he wanted them to do was to walk past without breaking step and throw money in through the door. His response, 'Yes, that's absolutely right,' floored me.

In view of his attitude to the media, it was interesting that one of Allan's many attempts to shift the blame for the collapse of Ronnie Scott's came in a television interview when he claimed that marketing and PR were not up to standard – in other words, it was all Big Bear's fault.

Allan was forever looking for easy money and had long admired the success in obtaining Arts funding of local promoter Birmingham Jazz. He asked me to find out their contact details which I did, and he approached the chairman, Tony Dudley-Evans, with a proposal to set up a company together with the purpose of obtaining funding for Ronnie Scott's. Thus Birmingham International Music was formed, a somewhat grandiose title for a company that, as Allan gleefully told me, was another Sartori cash cow. The Companies House listing gave Tony Dudley-Evans and Allan Sartori as directors based at Dudley-Evans' home address. I've no idea how this panned out, but the company is now listed as defunct.

However, away from the frustration of the backstage machinations and the gross mismanagement, to have such a venue at my fingertips felt like a privilege. It was great to have a stage on which to develop an idea and eventually present it publicly. Without that facility, there are quite a few Big Bear projects that would never have seen the light of day, not that all came to fruition by any means, but we managed a decent success ratio.

Tony Bennett, appearing at Symphony Hall, just across the street, agreed to appear and play an after-hours session without fee at the club to raise money for the Kosovo fund-raising campaign we were conducting. A Kosovan waiter, a really good bloke, worked at the club which gave it special meaning for us. It took about two minutes flat for Tony Bennett to agree to appear and he turned up with his long-time accompanists, the Ralph Sharon Trio, sang a straight one-hour set and then stayed around till the very end, gladhanding and signing autographs. He was amiable and friendly, with nothing of the superstar about him. Clearly one of the good guys!

Ray Charles said that Charles Brown was the inspiration for his choice of stage name and Nat 'King' Cole wrote that Charles was his main influence. Check out Nat's early recordings where he sounds uncannily like Charles Brown. It was a real coup to book Charles Brown into the Birmingham club for a week, the only UK dates he was to play, and I was determined to make the most of it. Charles had long been a particular hero of mine and I had always been amazed – and still am – how little he seemed to be known, even amongst musicians. I pulled

The mighty Charles Brown during his week at the ill-fated Ronnie Scott's in Birmingham.

out all the stops and cashed in every favour I could with the media, so we pretty much got the local and national coverage that Charles deserved.

Blues fans came to the city from Newcastle, Southampton and Exeter – one couple from Cardiff checked into a neighbouring hotel and came in for three nights. Charles was magnificent, his performances riveting and his band on the button. Personally I had a week to remember. I had met Charles Brown the previous year when he played the Notodden Blues Festival in Norway and I was there with King Pleasure and the Biscuit Boys. The first morning of the festival, I was taking breakfast with Buddy Guy and the room was full of American bluesmen when Charles made his entrance. Almost as if rehearsed, the room erupted into a spontaneous version of Charles' hit single, *Merry Christmas Baby*, with Buddy Guy and Junior Wells leading the way. It was extraordinary to see the respect and affection these blues stars, some of them gnarled veterans, had for Charles which makes it even more surprising that he was never a household blues name. The Norwegian promoter introduced me to Charles who gestured towards Buddy and Junior and grunted, 'These boys bothering you?'

I went to his rehearsal that morning with Biscuit Boy Al Nicholls. We were bowled over by the immediate change in Charles' demeanour from amiable and jocular companion to ultra-strict disciplinarian. Where music was concerned,

Charles knew exactly what he wanted from every musician, but he was equally exacting when it came to presentation. Ruth Davies, the attractive bass player, looking all the more feminine in a man's dinner jacket, came in for a tongue-lashing, even though this was just a rehearsal, for not appearing to be totally involved; to Charles every time you played, you put on a show.

'Don't take your eyes off me, bitch,' Charles demanded. 'Look like you're madly in love and can't wait to get me home!' The fact that Charles was famously gay somehow made it all the more ironic.

During the Birmingham run Charles and I laid plans to record him for Big Bear which we did at Chipping Norton Recording Studios, the residential studio owned and operated by Mike and Richard Vernon of Blue Horizon Records fame. Again, once in the studio, Charles became a changed man. Joking and story-telling throughout the journey to Chipping Norton, much to the delight of Val Wiseman and myself, before I had even put the handbrake on he leapt out of the car, bounded up the studio steps, demanding, 'Where's the guitar player?' He grabbed the instrument from the hands of Bullmoose K. Shirley, saying, 'This is what I want you to play' – all before the introductions had been made!

The album, *Blues and Rhythm Revue Volume 1*, featured King Pleasure and the Biscuit Boys with guests Charles, fellow Americans Gene 'Mighty Flea' Connors and Howard McCrary and the always stunning Val Wiseman. It proved to be one of the most satisfying sessions I ever produced. Charles was simply Charles Brown and you can't get better than that.

I had persuaded Charles to revive his lengthy and eloquent piano introductions, asking him to give me a 'Charles Brown Symphony', a phrase which he adopted and used for years. His version of the classic *Fool's Paradise* was a showstopper. A year later he sent me a CD inscribed, 'To Jim Simpson who is so influential in getting myself back to my roots and public.' I rather treasure that.

In the build-up to Charles Brown's week at Ronnie Scott's Allan Sartori, who had a malicious sense of humour, delighted in referring to him as Charlie Brown which to my eternal shame I rose to nearly every time. Allan's lack of respect for musicians always got me going, but sneering at Charles was a step too far, especially as Charles delivered six straight sell-out nights at the club.

Booking attractions into the club gave me the opportunity to indulge myself when it came to some of my favourite artists. Such names as Mose Allison, Ruth Brown and Kenny Baker's Dozen were obvious choices, as was Rolling Stones drummer Charlie Watts with his excellent bebop quintet, more or less dedicated to Bird and Dizzy and, of course, featuring Dave Green, Charlie's pal from childhood.

15. There's No Business In Show Business

We never thought about it at the time, we were having so much music we liked in the club, but apparently Pete King wasn't at all pleased when customers asked him why the Birmingham club had the likes of Ruth Brown, Desmond Dekker and the Phil Upchurch Combo and London didn't.

And it wasn't just musically that we strayed from the party line; we organised events on anything we found interesting. We presented a Mod Weekend where 84 vintage scooters came along to be judged in a Concours d'Elegance while Mod Music fans filled the club. We celebrated an anniversary of the Spanish Civil War with vintage films, talks from the International Brigade Society and a fascinating address by a veteran International Brigader.

We decided to present a *Brum Beat* Revisited event one Sunday, re-forming several combos from the heyday of Birmingham's Beat Era. Danny King headlined and brought the house down. Danny had always delivered the finest vocals I have heard from a British soul singer. The trouble was that Danny never took his career too seriously, didn't pursue pop fame with the near-obligatory single-mindedness, was amused by the girls who hung around the stage door asking for autographs, some of them in the most surprising places. He sang with Locomotive for a year or so, but couldn't be bothered to rehearse. Though he never put a foot wrong in delivering a song, it could be a little chaotic when a seven-piece has never actually played a particular song with the singer. Danny cherished his no doubt complicated private life and also his day job, manager at Dixon's on West Bromwich High Street.

At the Ronnie Scott's event we were enjoying an after-show taste in the bar when someone rushed in, saying, 'Come outside. You have to see this.' We dutifully trooped out to the stage door and, true to form, they were there. We counted 16 girls of various ages, all waiting, anxious to catch a moment with Danny King. He was in his mid-70s at the time.

Like most kids of my generation I developed probably unreasonable passions for obscure American record labels which I guess was the basis for my need to eventually have my own record company. The New York-based Sue Records was one such label. Huey 'Piano' Smith's *Rockin' Pneumonia and the Boogie Woogie Flu* and Harold Betters' *Do Anything You Wanna* were, and still are, on my all-time playlist, as was the wonderful double A side instrumental, on that classic yellow and red label, *You Can't Sit Down*, by the Phil Upchurch Combo. It took some digging around, but eventually I got an offer to the band's agent that he found acceptable. Then I set about convincing Allan and Barry that the Phil Upchurch Combo would be good box office – invariably the most difficult part of any negotiation. The advance ticket sales were fine, resulting in four sell-outs in six nights. These Birmingham dates were the only ones in the UK on the European tour, so fans came from every corner, and Phil and the band were all that anyone could have hoped for. I was interested to see that what was known as a purely instrumental combo now carried a singer, albeit one who also played fine piano. His vocals on his feature spot, *Over the Rainbow*, simply brought down the house every night. Unsurprisingly we got to talking.

His name was Howard McCrary from Youngstown, Ohio. In his early days he had toured as a member of the McCrary family band and later the McCrary Five who co-headlined with the Jackson Five on a coast-to-coast US tour. When the McCrarys moved from gospel to more mainstream music Howard branched out on his own and soon became a major figure on the US gospel scene, picking up a Grammy nomination for his album *So Good* and the Duke Ellington Award for most promising gospel composer. He also worked with Michael Jackson and Quincy Jones on albums, became Musical Director to Chaka Khan and recorded with Diana Ross, Stevie Wonder, Julio Iglesias, Nina Simone, Ringo Starr, Dionne Warwick and Earth, Wind & Fire.

Howard was one of those rare musical chameleons who could almost instantly play – and sing – anything he heard. This only dawned on me when I talked to him, as piano player in this great rhythm and blues band, about the classic recordings and bands of the 1940s and 1950s. He had no knowledge of such things and had simply learned the Upchurch repertoire in order to get hired. From listening to him with that band you would have thought he had spent a lifetime playing that music.

There haven't been enough great singers in jazz and blues in recent years, let alone ones who play piano like McCrary, so I set about introducing him to the music of Jimmy Rushing, Jay McShann, Charles Brown, Willie Mabon, Joe Williams, Ernie Andrews and Big Joe Turner. It was pretty much love at first sight between Howard and these guys and we often spoke of working together if ever the occasion arose.

The week at Ronnie's came to an end by which time a veritable army of Birmingham girls had fallen madly in love with Howard, something he did little – in fact, nothing – to discourage. I was at the band's hotel on the Sunday morning to wave off the taxi taking them to the airport for a flight to Amsterdam for the final concert of their European tour.

I was surprised when Howard phoned me the next morning as I thought by then he would be on the flight back to LA. 'Where are you, Howard, Amsterdam?' I asked. 'I'm at the airport. Birmingham,' was the reply.

Apparently the gig in Amsterdam had been cancelled and Upchurch and the rest of the band had taken the flight back to the States. Quite casually he informed

15. There's No Business In Show Business

Howard McCrary.

Howard McCrary.

me that he had decided to move to Birmingham and pursue a career as a singer and player of jazz and blues with me as his manager. At that point Howard had little knowledge of the jazz and blues repertoire, so I put together a cassette of maybe 14 songs of the type I felt he should consider, just to listen to, to give him a feeling for what I had in mind. Little more than a couple of days later, Howard called me over to the piano and played and sang every single one of the songs perfectly. He had memorised all the lyrics, the melodies and the chord sequences – and, most importantly, delivered them with feeling. Pure genius!

    He moved into my house for a few days while I found him a flat, rented a piano and persuaded Ronnie Scott's to let me organise midnight matinees which I titled The Midnight Slows, Thursdays to Saturdays, featuring just Howard McCrary. Radio and newspaper interviews, set up in a panic, capitalised on the fan base he had built up during his week with Upchurch, and the audiences were there from the start, with the diehards staying on after the feature band finished supplemented by a new, predominantly female midnight audience.

15. There's No Business In Show Business

We recruited a rocking band of Brum's finest, led by saxophonist Mike Burney, with guitarist Josh McCalla, bassist Roger Inniss and Tim Jones on drums, then Tim Jennings and I then set about putting the show on the road. That turned out to be far more straightforward than we could have imagined. The impact McCrary had made at Ronnie's during the Upchurch week and later at his midnight matinees had made him almost a household name across the region. Venues throughout the Midlands booked the band, offers for private parties came in and very soon it made sense to book him into Ronnie's for a week, as the headline act. Through Mitchells and Butlers we arranged a 50-date nationwide tour of M&B pubs sponsored by Budweiser before we set about fixing dates in Belgium, Holland, France, Norway and Germany which also involved radio and television.

The guys in the band were taken aback when, immediately before going on stage at every show, Howard would gather them into an arm-around-each-other huddle, offer up a prayer and ask God to bless the performance. It clearly worked; I don't recall the band ever having a bad gig.

Howard McCrary and Roger Inniss recording the Moments Like This album.

The fact was everyone seemed to love Howard McCrary. Inconveniently for us, so did his wife Tammy, a powerful woman, sister to Chaka Khan and therefore very well connected in the music business. After Howard had been in Birmingham for not much more than a year, Tammy came to visit, and somehow things were never the same again. Understandably Tammy assumed management of Howard and immediately began to think in terms of bigger, and at that stage unrealistic, deals. Her demands became more and more unreasonable and Howard, clearly in awe of her, went along with them. Suddenly what had been a near-meteoric rise in profile, quantity of gigs and level of fees, based on a strong personal friendship built on mutual trust, disintegrated. Then Howard's father was taken ill and Tammy went back to Los Angeles, with Howard firmly in tow. That was the last I heard of him for something like 25 years.

Sadly we never formally recorded his band in the studio – Howard was always worried how Tammy would feel about that – but we made some great quality live recordings at Ronnie Scott's, so there remains something to show for a brief, but fascinating, interlude in the lives of Howard McCrary and Big Bear Records.

Howard and I had lost touch until Birmingham saxophonist Julian Smith, he of *Britain's Got Talent* fame and now starring on luxury cruise ships, called me to say that he had been laying over for three days in Hong Kong waiting for his next ship, when he had met Howard McCrary who was playing in a club. Howard has lived in Hong Kong since 2005, now happily married to a Chinese girl. His career has blossomed in Hong Kong, so no surprise there, and he makes appearances as a feature with the Hong Kong Symphony Orchestra, still the most adept of musical chameleons. He asked Julian to put him back in touch with me.

Howard asked me why I hadn't released our recordings. I told him that we had not had a formal agreement and he said, 'We have now. Go ahead and release.' So the album *Moments like This* was released in January 2019 as part of Big Bear's 50th anniversary celebrations. Meanwhile that leaves me to ponder how I can get him to Birmingham for the next jazz festival. That would be a homecoming to remember!

When Howard left Birmingham, he left behind a lot of good friends. One of them was Mike Burney with whom Howard struck up an intensely productive musical relationship as well as a personal friendship. Dear now-departed Mike, always one to see the bright side, reminded me that at least we had taught Howard to drink. Howard, a lifelong abstainer from all forms of alcohol, had confided to Mike and me during a Belgian tour that he envied us having so much fun when we had enjoyed a taste – or two – so we set about converting him. It took a couple of days, but Howard quickly got the hang of things though his level of restraint was unimpressive. On the final night of the tour, Howard, having drunk several

15. There's No Business In Show Business

Trappist beers too many, was reportedly entertaining the locals in the hotel bar, initially by playing piano, then by dancing on a table, during which process his trousers somehow came off. Mike roomed with Howard and told the tale that, when wakened the next morning, he sprang out of bed and crashed into the wall before apologising profusely to the wall. Howard, with his Gospel background a truly God-fearing man, explained to me that drinking Trappist beers was unlike drinking in the normal sense as they had been brewed by monks and therefore had a religious significance.

Buddy Greco was an internationally known singer of the Great American Songbook, just one level down from Sinatra, Sammy Davis and Dean Martin. He was less well known for his excellent piano playing that graced the Benny Goodman Orchestra when Buddy was still a teenager.

Naturally, when we booked him to play a week at Ronnie Scott's, I wanted to talk to him about his days with Benny. Over recent years Buddy had settled for the less stimulating, but safer and better paid, world of cabaret and had become the archetypal lounge singer, pretty much neglecting his jazz talent. Stimulated, I guess, by talking jazz, he asked me to lunch to discuss a proposal he had in mind: he wanted to know if I could re-establish his jazz career. I prepared well for the meeting which, if not exactly the opportunity of a lifetime, offered me the chance to create and represent a first-class American combo with the finest of jazz credentials. I figured the best plan would be to launch the project at Europe's jazz festivals the following summer; I knew enough of them already to put together ten or a dozen festivals which would pay the proper fees for the band I had in mind. Obviously Buddy was to be the feature, with his vocals and piano playing, but I wanted another soloist to share the load – and that man had to be amongst the best around.

It was a no-brainer. I called Teddy Edwards in Los Angeles which was always a pleasure. Teddy and I went back a long way. He had featured at the Jazz Festival and I had worked with him on other shows, including Cork Jazz Festival. Obviously Teddy knew of Buddy, though he hadn't worked with him, and he was really into the project. We needed a first-class bass player and drummer, not just great musicians, but big jazz names. I asked Teddy to contact drummer Shelly Manne and his own choice of double bass player. No surprise there – he opted for Leroy Vinnegar – and he agreed to make the initial approach to both – which he did. Both expressed interest, so I went to my lunch with Buddy as confident of success as I could be which is so often, as in this case, the build up to a big letdown.

I outlined the strategy to Buddy and he approved. It was only when I got into my stride extolling the virtues of the other musicians that he started to visibly lose interest. Suddenly he held up his hand and told me, 'Hey, wait a minute! Let's talk about me.' It was then that I realised with total clarity that the only thing that would come out of all this planning would be a good lunch at the Lychee Garden. Looking back, maybe my biggest regret was losing the opportunity to work on a major project with that great tenor saxophonist Teddy Edwards.

Apart from the very big names we booked for the club, one local band was always guaranteed a full house at Ronnie Scott's. That was the wild and wacky King Pleasure and the Biscuit Boys who were booked into the club far more times than any other attraction. It was just one of those difficult to explain, but natural, relationships between band and club. Fellow musicians were always in the audience, attracted by that big fat sound, the hot soloists and the turn-on-a-sixpence arrangements. These bookings often led to other work for the band, most notably when a high-flying computer company, having a big office bash at the club, invited the band to perform at their upcoming international convention – in the Scottsdale district of Phoenix, Arizona. With the healthy fee and transatlantic flights covered, we were able to set up the band's first US tour.

Talking to Ed Bicknell about Ronnie Scott's Birmingham was particularly interesting – illuminating even. His association with Ronnie's London, rooted in his love for jazz, began when he moved to London in pursuance of his career as a drummer: Ed could count the great jazz drummer Elvin Jones among his friends. He played with Mogul Thrash, an early version of the Average White Band, before being sacked, he said, for not being Scottish. Ed quickly became a Ronnie's regular soon after Pete King and Ronnie had moved the club from The Old Place in Gerrard Street to its current home on Frith Street and became such a familiar face that it reached the point that he rarely paid to get in, a privilege not afforded to many. Attracted to the business side of music, he went to work for NEMS which Patrick Meehan had bought for £1 and which at that time represented, among others, Black Sabbath, plus other Birmingham bands ELO and Wizzard. What really set Ed on the road to fame and fortune was when he discovered Café Racers with Mark Knopfler. Café Racers became Dire Straits and Ed went on to manage the band. Ed developed an enviable reputation as one of the more important men in the music business, but he never forgot that, at heart, he was a musician. When Mark formed his occasional, though well regarded, Notting Hillbillies, he invited Ed to take the drum chair.

As a Frith Street regular, he struck up what might be loosely described as a friendship with Pete King. In conversation with Ed, it became increasingly obvious how similar his relationship with King was to mine with Sartori. Both of them quickly realised the advantages that were to be taken of the obsession with music that Ed and I shared.

15. There's No Business In Show Business

Just like me Ed allowed himself to be suckered, and like me, he didn't see it coming. We both look back with incredulity at the way we allowed ourselves to be taken, but we both put it down to the same blind spot, our love of the music and the opportunity to be involved in the front line of presenting it. Ed remembers Pete King telling him about the Sartori and Sherwin Birmingham venture and that he had decided to go along with it as it was part of his master plan: to somehow merge the two businesses and then to build a worldwide network of Ronnie Scott's franchises.

By then it was the mid-1990s and the Birmingham club was, in Pete King's words, in need of refinancing. He said he would like to offer Ed Bicknell the opportunity to be involved. Ed, still clearly irked at what he considers to be easily the worst decision he has ever made in all those long years in the music business, paints an all too familiar picture. Initially he was asked only for a relatively modest amount followed by a series of increasingly emotional appeals for more financial help until he found himself more than £200,000 out of pocket. Ed Bicknell is an extremely successful music man and of course he recovered from the blow, but the pain that remains seems to be less to do with the money than being taken for a ride by what he considers to be the scoundrels who operated the Birmingham Ronnie Scott's.

Towards the end of the 1990s the *Sunday Mercury* had been doing its homework and had acquired sufficient background information to be able to ask some awkward questions. Although Allan Sartori told all and sundry that he was the Head of Marketing, he was not at all hands on, so the responsibility of responding to media enquiries, including the awkward ones, fell to me.

I was comfortable with any questions regarding the music and musicians, but, when faced with a seasoned journalist asking if it was true that Ronnie Scott's Birmingham was trading whilst knowingly insolvent, I was pretty much floored. I then would go to Allan, put the question to him and naively accept his denials and explanations. I hoped that the reporter believed that I was being honest just as much as he doubted the words that came from the club, but he persisted. I never shied away from taking calls and well remember one Christmas Eve calling a reporter from a phonebox atop a mountain in the tiny village of Istan in Andalucia, only an hour from Marbella. Subsequently things got somewhat out of hand when reporters decided to beard Allan Sartori in the club, asking questions that he really didn't like and to which he responded by threatening their wellbeing.

It all ended in tears, inevitably with the club going into receivership.

Some months after Ronnie Scott's had ceased to exist, when the dust had more or less settled, I bumped into a pal, Gary Baldwin, on Broad Street. He was one of those people who seemed to know, and be liked by, almost everyone. He had maintained contact with the club, now a strip joint called the Rocket Club, and he insisted that I go with him to see how the venue had changed.

Curious, I went along. Gary was greeted at the door by Cam Sannio who had previously worked as sound engineer at Ronnie Scott's and was now duty manager. I was surprised that Cam greeted me so enthusiastically. Gary bought me a drink that I had hardly had time to taste before Cam stomped over, flanked by two bouncers, and loudly announced that I was to be ejected. He explained that he had phoned Sartori at home to report my presence and had been instructed to have me thrown out. I went quietly, with a fixed, totally insincere smile in place and, I hope, my dignity intact.

Over the years I have read or heard about various enterprises that Barry Sherwin has been involved with. There was Red Bar and McKenzie's, both in the City Centre and both now out of business. He once phoned me from a pub in Euston, the wrong side of too many drinks, telling me that the landlord wanted to book blues artists and that he had recommended Big Bear. The pub's budget was tiny, so that came to nought, but I'm sure that he felt that he was doing a good deed and I like to believe that he meant well. In fact, on the half dozen times we have accidentally encountered each other since the collapse, he always tells me how much he regrets what they did to me. He looks and sounds like he means it so I always take his apology at face value and accept it.

Barry's feelings about Allan in later years were somewhat ambiguous, as an encounter at the funeral of Danny Longstaff indicates.

Danny died far too young. Although his regular schtick was playing with the City of Birmingham Symphony Orchestra he also played fine jazz trombone and seemed to enjoy that rather too much. He and his pal 'Foxy', actually CBSO violinist Mark Robinson, decided that in light of their own and the orchestra's significant consumption of good ale, they might be distinctly better off financially if they opened their own pub, which they did. It was a pleasure to see what appeared to be the entire CBSO scuttling along the canal towpath during the Symphony Hall intermission for a quick drink or two at their chums' canalside pub, the cunningly named Fiddle and Bone.

Danny came to Big Bear to book his jazz and blues into the pub, and it did rather well for a number of years. It was not without character as a venue. Situated canalside with a huge open-air terrace, the venue itself was an attraction and we booked an interesting programme, including four consecutive Saturdays featuring the pre-hit Jamie Cullum – admission free.

Danny was a most genial host and Foxy, presumably tiring of the project, left him to take care of business. Increasingly Danny seemed to spend more and more

15. There's No Business In Show Business

time the wrong side of the bar. There was also a widely reported kerfuffle when a resident of a neighbouring apartment threatened legal action over alleged noise pollution, which everyone thought was a little rich as the apartments were built quite a while after The Fiddle and Bone opened.

Whatever, The Fiddle and Bone went bust, going down owing Big Bear £3,500. That may not appear to be a huge amount of money, but coming hot on the heels of the former Mitchells & Butlers pub, The James Brindley, folding owing us £7,500, it hit us hard. Danny and I had been pals for years and remained so, still seeing each other regularly through our Musicians Union activities: he was Chair of the Executive Committee and I am on the Regional Board.

Danny was delightful company and his death at the age of 63 was really unexpected. Sarah Yang and I had enjoyed a Chinese meal with him and his girlfriend only a few days earlier. At Danny's funeral I spotted Barry Sherwin in the church congregation and determined to keep my distance, but when we all repaired to the pub he made a beeline for me. Again he said how sorry he was, but seemed flush enough to buy me a few glasses of wine, which I figured was the very least he owed me. Inevitably the conversation turned to Sartori, as Barry had only recently won a court case against him, a pyrrhic victory as Barry was awarded £12,000 which more or less covered his legal costs. We were both agreeing what a shameless and deeply unpleasant character Allan Sartori was when Barry said, 'Everything people say against Allan Sartori is true, but if he now walked through that door I would go over and hug him.' I find it amazing, but Barry is actually just one of a handful of people I know who readily admit what an unpleasant man Sartori was, but still profess affection for him. Inexplicable!

As I write, Barry Sherwin seems to have gone to ground after a short-lived spell as General Manager of the swish Birmingham Hotel du Vin. He has changed his name to Bhagwant Sing Sherwin and is probably planning his next venture. I really hope that he can make a good fist of it, whatever it is, as he is a man not without talent. He has a lively mind, presents himself well, certainly doesn't lack in intelligence, has an irrepressible sense of humour and in actual fact is very good company. During the Ronnie Scott's years, almost everything we achieved was in cahoots with Barry, who really did understand the value of the music we organised – although it has to be said that he remains an incurable fan of heavy metal.

With the demise of Ronnie's, Allan Sartori continued in his self-styled role as The Baron of Broad Street, moving seamlessly into his role as manager of the prominent Rocket Club. By 2009 he had embarked on the ill-fated quest to wrest ownership of the strip of land outside the club from the grasp of club owner Laurence Reddy. The value of this land was the fast food caravan that occupied the space and generated some £1200 a week rent, which Allan coveted and described as his pension. He elaborately prepared for the first High Court case, building the fiction that his Italian father had, for many a year, operated an open air food outlet on the site, complete with white picket fence, and Allan was simply continuing the tradition.

Laurence Reddy contested the case in The High Court in 2011, apparently relaxed in the belief that the truth would be clear to all and that Allan's case had no merit. However, it appeared that he was taken by surprise by Allan's presentation, which was not remotely true, and lost the case, which he immediately appealed. The Appeal Court judges ordered a retrial during which it was decided that this now-famous strip of land should revert to Birmingham City Council, hopefully along with the not-inconsiderable weekly income. The end of a four year battle.

As Mr Justice Morgan said in a High Court hearing, 'Mr Sartori had a real difficulty in distinguishing what actually happened from what he would have like to have happened.' The fact that first Her Majesty's Stationery Office and then an Allied Carpets store had previously occupied what became Ronnie Scott's premises was in itself a bit of a giveaway. It can't be imagined that either of these businesses would have appreciated an Italian pop-up café on their front doorstep.

The saga continued. In 2013, the headlines read 'Former Pubwatch Chairman Allan Sartori Banned From Broad Street Pubs'. He then surfaced briefly, handling the marketing for another Broad Street strip venue, before becoming the focus of the TV programme *Can't Pay, We'll Take It Away*. The Channel 5 TV cameras followed the bailiffs to his Bearwood home in an attempt to retrieve some £25,000 of alleged unpaid solicitor's fees. Ironically one of the bailiffs was a former security man at Ronnie Scott's and clearly remembered Allan from those seemingly far-off days. The programme reported seeing Allan through the front door, crawling on all fours in order to avoid detection. Once the bailiffs were inside, Sartori pleaded poverty and claimed to be only a lodger at which point the bailiffs appeared to give up.

Allan Sartori had one more headline to come. On Thursday 26th July 2018, in the middle of the Jazz Festival, I was at a performance of the Alan Barnes Quartet at Lee Longlands on Broad Street, some two minutes walk from what had been Ronnie Scott's, when I received a phone call. It was a now-retired newspaper reporter phoning to tell me that Allan Sartori had died that day. He was 68.

Chapter 16

KING PLEASURE AND THE BISCUIT BOYS

Way back in the mists of time – well, 1984, to be exact – five mid-teenage boys huddled deep in conversation in a Darlaston milk bar. They had bunked off early from school because they had something of cosmic importance to discuss.

They had decided to form a rock and roll band.

As kids they had been won over by local wild men of rock, Slade and Roy Wood's Wizzard in particular, but they had also delved back in time to discover Bill Haley and The Comets before becoming captivated by the black musicians who were responsible for rhythm and blues as we know it today.

So first things first – the band needed a name. Their choice was not an inspired one, probably just the name they all disliked the least, The Satellites – which was sort of reminiscent of The Comets. The really important thing to agree was their individual stage names. They did rather better in this department, coming up with Scratch the Man Skirving, Bullmoose K. Shirley, P. Popps Martin, the Dixie Prince and Crusher Page, aka Mad Pagey.

The next topic on the agenda was The Music. It should be understood that at this point not one of them could actually play, nor even owned, a musical instrument. This seems to have presented no barrier as they quickly allocated the as yet non-existent instruments before expressing themselves well satisfied with their afternoon's work.

They had a band.

The next years were chaotic with school study relegated to the position of also-ran alongside the overwhelming need to learn to play their instruments and rehearse. They had little else on their minds than to be part of a proper, full-time working band.

This they finally achieved in 1987. Their previous experience was limited to busking on the streets of Walsall, but, on their first appearance before an audience in a formal setting they won a talent competition in Birmingham which I happened to be judging. I immediately signed the band to Big Bear for recording, agency and management.

First of all we had to do something about the name. By then they had namechanged from The Satellites to Some Like It Hot. When I insisted on changing their name again, the leader, Mark Skirving, didn't disagree, but asked what name I would suggest. 'Why not come up with something like King Pleasure…', I suggested, borrowing the working name of the singer Clarence Beeks, '…and The Biscuit Boys?', loosely referring to the blues radio programme broadcast on Radio KFFA out of Helena, Arkansas.

'That's brilliant,' he said. 'We'll use that, King Pleasure and the Biscuit Boys.'

I tried to explain that I had only suggested it as the type of name he could work on, not wishing to purloin someone else's identity. To no avail: he was adamant and that has been the name of the band for over 30 years and more than 6500 performances across every country in Europe as well as the USA, Russia and the Middle East.

From the outset we had fun with the band. The jokey names and the hilarious, but extremely silly, stage show were obvious, but this was underpinned by a pretty good, quickly improving musicianship which was the only area taken

An early King Pleasure and the Biscuit Boys line-up: (l-r) Bullmoose K. Shirley, Lisa Sugar Lee, Piano Man Skan, King Pleasure, Bam Bam Beresford, Slap Happy, P Popps Martin.

16. King Pleasure And The Biscuit Boys

seriously by the band. By the time King Pleasure and the Biscuit Boys had been with Big Bear for a few months they had settled down as a seven-piece with a handful of changes. Only Mark, previously known as Scratch the Man Skirving, now King Pleasure, Bullmoose K. Shirley and P. Popps Martin remained, now joined by Piano Man Skan, Slap Happy, Bam Bam Beresford and the impossibly glamorous Miss Lisa Sugar Lee as band singer.

Their first album, entitled *King Pleasure and The Biscuit Boys*, released on 12 inch vinyl and cassette, the norm in those days, was not only a good recording, but a masterpiece of hokum. The sleeve notes, written in conjunction with Big Bear staffer and music business veteran Rowdy Yeats, were a surreal fiction, claiming that 'King Pleasure and the Biscuit Boys are the fastest rising combo to emerge from the Mid West since Little Jimmy Thompson took the bus from Houston, signed up with Chuck Liggins and started a fire on the coast that still burns today.' For Mid West read West Midlands. Miss Lee's vocal coach was credited as Wilma Vanse (anagram of Val Wiseman) and my credit for production read Buddy Bryant, derived from Mother's maiden name. We produced a new Dancing (Big) Bear logo just for this band's recordings and we even printed the album cover slightly out of register to give it a 1940s look.

By the time the second album, *This is It*, came along, the music was something to reckon with. The rhythm section was thunderous, the horn ensembles a powerhouse and King Pleasure's vocals really the business. Now we toured twelve Mitchells and Butlers pubs in Birmingham in one day in a 1948 Bedford Deluxe charabanc, playing a 30-minute set in each, promoting the album and raising money for the brewery's favourite charity. The spinoffs were totally unexpected. After seeing news coverage of the event on local television, Ragdoll Productions invited the band to appear, in a cut down version, on five of their Teletubbies programmes; Malcolm Powell, M&B Projects Manager, was so impressed that he arranged a series of 30-day tours of M&B pubs throughout the UK; and, most bizarrely of all, Belgian promoter Paul Ambach booked the band for the Oostende Blues Festival where they opened the show for B. B. King. This was the first of several KP performances opening for the Beale Street Blues Boy, and, just as on all the subsequent shows, he came to the boys' dressing room, thanked them and presented each of them with a gold lapel badge, a facsimile of Lucille, his guitar. Ever the gentleman!

At that time Belgium, and later Holland, became almost a second home for the band, playing clubs, culture centres and festivals on a regular basis. My pal Tony Gallen, married to a Belgian girl, owned the Hotel Memling which overlooked the main square of the somewhat strait-laced, but extremely pleasant,

Flemish village of Aalter. Neatly placed on Belgium's main East-West motorway, it was an ideal base from which to tour. The first sign of any problem came when, in a bout of innocent high jinks, the band changed over the contents of two rooms – bed, furniture, pictures on the walls, reading lamps – before checking out. I had to pacify an irate Tony Gallen on the phone and assure him that this wouldn't happen again. It didn't, at least not at the Memling, but it did become an integral part of the band's hotel culture. The manager of a country hotel, close to Nuremberg, when confronted with a similar situation, was heard to declare, 'This isn't one of our rooms!'

Things hadn't long settled down at the Memling when, in just a 'normal pillow fight', two fire extinguishers were somehow set off. Tony confronted the band and threatened to tell me what had happened unless they agreed to pay cash compensation there and then. The band never mentioned the incident to me; I only found out about it when having a drink with Tony some time later.

All was quiet around the Memling for a year or so, then on a day off (beware a band on tour when they have a day off) the band partied a touch over-enthusiastically and 'did get a little carried away,' as Mark admitted later. How it got to this stage I've no idea, but around 10 o'clock at night, Slap Happy and Bullmoose, for reasons known only to themselves, decided to drop their trousers and poke their naked bottoms out of the hotel windows overlooking the town square at a time when there were still plenty of people about. Not the most outrageous behaviour, you might think, especially as the band did apologise profusely when complaints were made, but by next morning it was an entirely more critical matter. The rumour had gone around the village and back to Marie Elise, Tony's rather severe wife, that their two teenage daughters had been seen mooning out of the hotel windows the previous evening. This put a completely different spin on things and I was told in no uncertain terms that King Pleasure and the Biscuit Boys were no longer welcome at the Hotel Memling. It was a good few years before Tony began to see the funny side of it. Marie Elise never did.

By now the band had settled into a line-up that was to undergo little change over the coming years. The delectable Lisa Sugar Lee was finding life on the road with half a dozen near-certifiable hooligans just a little too exacting and announced at a band meeting that she had decided to quit the band. Her parting speech ran along the lines of, 'You're just a no-good bunch of male chauvinist pigs.' Which was fair enough.

During a BBC interview Mark was asked about Lisa's departure and her possible replacement and, without giving the matter too much thought, he said that it would be nice to have a trumpet player in the band. Within minutes I took a

Taking a break from recording at Chipping Norton Studios, Charles Brown, flanked by King Pleasure and the Biscuit Boys.

phone call from Cootie Alexander (aka Paul Allin), a trumpet player whose day job was in the brass renovation department of a Halesowen musical instrument store. We chatted, he auditioned the next day, quit the day job the day after, and by the next week was a fully accredited Biscuit Boy, electric blue zoot suit and all. Cootie was an impressive figure and a tremendous player, big-toned, with a stratospheric range and impeccable technique. Well versed in big band jazz, he provided the lead to the imperious horn section that took the band up to another level, as can be heard on their third album, the enthusiastically received *Better Beware*.

The band's first trip to Russia (and mine) was in 1991 when the Iron Curtain was still in place. It all came about through an encounter I had with an eccentric Englishman called David Benton who worked for the Arctic Riga Hotel in Kirkenes, Norway's most northerly town and well within the Arctic Circle. David buttonholed me at the annual Silda Jazz Festival in Haugesund and seemed to know all about Big Bear, from the Birmingham Festival to individual artists we were working with. He wanted help and advice in organising a travelling blues festival that would first appear in the hotel where he was marketing manager and then play shows in Russia. Originally he was talking of 10 to 14 days in Russia which seemed out of balance to me as Norway has always been fertile territory for the blues and I had enough contacts to arrange five or six shows in what was, after all, far more familiar – and hospitable – terrain than behind-the-Iron-Curtain Russia.

We agreed that he would feature King Pleasure and the Biscuit Boys as second on the bill behind Texas blues singer Lou Ann Barton and her band. I never mind deferring to known acts on the bill; it's far better to be a surprise packet and blow them off the stage than to be in top spot to be popped at. Because of my support David wanted to feature the Big Bear logo on the tour poster, but the King Pleasure version, the Boogaloo Bear. I supplied art work accordingly.

Come the day, we flew London to Oslo to Tromso to Kirkenes – that was pretty standard for gadding about Norway in the 1990s. My first surprise was when David proudly took us down to the hotel's basement bar which gloried in the name Gorby's Discotheque (after the then Russian leader) – and also in my King Pleasure logo. Not only did it stand six feet tall on the entrance door, but also it was prominently displayed on the traditional Russian shirts of the dozen or so staff.

The next day was clear until the evening's routining session, so Val Wiseman and I decided to explore the locality which was volcanic, a hard climb, but affording spectacular views. We strolled around, spent a nice afternoon in deserted surroundings and came back relaxed. That was until the locals began to question us about where exactly we had been, which we did our best to indicate on a map of the locality on the hotel's wall. In response we were asked, 'Didn't you know about the bears?' and 'Are you crazy?'. We got the picture, but I comforted a clearly distressed Val with the assurance that, although it might have been dangerous, it didn't compare with spending an afternoon in the bar with King Pleasure.

The show David had assembled was actually pretty good. Lou Ann Barton is always good value, a straightahead rocking blues singer from Fort Worth, Texas, who has served with Stevie Ray Vaughn and Roomful of Blues, and she always sports a good band. Fellow Americans Texas Harmonica Rumble with Greg 'Fingers' Taylor were also on board, together with a couple of very decent Norwegian blues bands.

The routining session went smoothly, although there was a lot of muttering when the bands checked the poster – which sported not one, but three bears, though I wasn't complaining – and found that the tour was billed as a seven day event in Kirkenes, Nikel and Murmansk when we had all been booked for just three days. Just another flaky Bentonism – he had already been nicknamed Big Bad Benton!

The Kirkenes concert was fine. It rocked along nicely in front of a decent crowd and it goes without saying that King Pleasure stole the show. There were enough paying customers to satisfy David who was actually not a bad man, just a fantasist who seemed to think that he only had to wish for something hard

16. King Pleasure And The Biscuit Boys

enough and it would happen. But he was careless, paid little attention to detail and was ever-ready to throw up his arms in despair and cry for help.

The next day the tour bus turned up on time at the Hotel Arctic Riga, the 25-strong party boarded and we set off for the Russian border post.

Which wasn't yet open.

When eventually it opened, we lined up to be processed, except of course for the sillier of the Biscuit Boys who amused themselves by sneaking up on the Russian border guards and snatching a photograph or two with the officials who had made it quite clear that they did not want to be photographed. Any worries I might have had about the imminent arrest of Biscuit Boys were dispelled by an outbreak of shouting by the Russians, screaming at Lou Ann Barton and threats and a stream of colourful epithets from the American contingent.

It transpired that, between applying for a Russian entry visa and actually getting to the border, Lou Ann had changed boyfriends and couldn't understand why the border guards wouldn't accept that one American boyfriend was much the same as another as far as passports were concerned. So Lou Ann Barton, her band, her boyfriend and their equipment were abandoned on the Norwegian side of the border and they were left to fend for themselves, clearly no longer any responsibility of David Benton's.

Eventually managing to get into Russia, I sat next to David on the bus and was interested to learn that he knew about the boyfriend switch, but didn't consider it important enough to reapply. The fact that he was now without his headline act was apparently of no concern to him because he was agog at the immediate prospect of reuniting with his Russian girlfriend. Slowly it all became clear: he had an ulterior motive in organising this shambles of a tour. His girlfriend lived in Nikel and was unable to get the papers necessary to leave the Soviet Union and relocate to Norway, just as he was not allowed to cross into Russia without a legitimate reason, such as a blues tour. The original plan, as advertised on the tour poster, was for a seven-day festival, but this was just wishful thinking gone mad. In the end the tour didn't even get to Murmansk, just Kirkenes and Nikel. He also confided that he hoped his girlfriend would be able to sit unnoticed on the band bus and travel back to Norway where they could live happily ever after. There's misguided and there's misguided: anyone who believed that anything more noticeable than an ant could evade Russian border control was out of his mind!

I did meet the object of David's affections in Nikel when Val and I had coffee with her. She proved to be a pretty, sweet and charming girl, a schoolteacher who spoke excellent English and who, we realised, was determined to get over to the

West. I hope she made it and managed to exert some much-needed control over David. It would be nice to think that things finally turned out well for them.

Nikel, named after the mineral, was just that, a town devoted to the mining of nickel: people living in garage courts, no shops, no apparent leisure facilities, but a fine display of statuary of Russian heroes from Papa Joe onwards – nothing pre-Stalin, of course. The concert hall was large, maybe 1,500 capacity, and, with deserted streets in every direction, it was difficult to imagine where the audience would come from. Then a van screeched to a halt adjacent to the concert hall. The back dropped and, before it was in place, some 50 or so people descended on what turned out to be an illegal mobile shop carrying items that were in demand, but otherwise unobtainable. Some 20 minutes of brisk trading and the van was away. During the day we saw three or four such incursions.

We were taken by the local commissar – a pretty decent chap, as so many of the people we met proved to be – to a museum-cum-souvenir shop that was opening for just 30 minutes in our honour. Try as we might, there really wasn't anything that we wanted to buy.

As the time for our concert approached, there appeared, as if by magic, crowds of smartly dressed people, seemingly very much in a holiday mood, gathering outside the concert hall. By the time the show was ready to hit, the hall was overflowing. Then came the speeches which seemed to go on forever, with the audience politely clapping every now and then without any apparent enthusiasm. The feeling that I had was that they were humouring the speakers, simply waiting until it was over.

Their response to the music – every band, in fact – was something different. Wild applause greeted every solo, nobody was sitting still and pockets of dancing were breaking out. This was the ideal setting for a King Pleasure and the Biscuit Boys performance: the boys delivered a show of pure rock and roll mayhem that is probably still talked about in those parts.

The town hosted an after-party, with half bottles of an eminently drinkable vodka dished out along with a local delicacy which for all the world seemed like rock cakes. The folks were really welcoming to us, some struggling to make conversation in English, most of them coming up to us with a big grin and a handshake before just standing with us, nothing to say, but with that grin still in place. It left us all with a very special feeling.

Then it was their turn. We were invited to return to the hall and ushered to seats near the front to enjoy an impressive performance of regional music, song and dance. The quality of the performance, the costumes and the sheer verve of the performers would have graced the stage of any theatre I've ever been to.

16. King Pleasure And The Biscuit Boys

At the end, when all of the bows had been taken, the vodka and the rock-cakes reappeared and the party resumed. Who knows, or can remember, what went on that night? However, I do have some recollection of a not very musical jam session, then we retired to our hotel, bleak, bare, more like an army barracks than a hotel, with a disconcertingly brown trickle of water the only result of turning on the taps. Reportedly, at around 3 in the morning, I stomped out of my room to remonstrate with a group of Americans who were carrying on the jam session in the corridor. They say I behaved with dignity, asking them to desist, but apparently the Americans collapsed, helpless with laughter, because I just happened to be naked.

The schedule called for a 5.30 am departure for the Biscuit Boys' party to get us across the border and into Kirkenes Airport in time to check in at 8.00 am for the flight to Oslo which then connected with our onward journey to London. Not feeling too good after the previous night's excesses, I had yet more reason to curse David Benton and his amateurish organisation when we found that, instead of our rustbox of a 50-seater bus, we were to be taken to Kirkenes in what was actually a seven-seater – yes, nine of us, our baggage and instrument cases. It wasn't possible to complain to the driver as he spoke absolutely no English.

There was no alternative to finding a way to squeeze our already battered selves into the van and, in doing so, I realised that we were a man short, Piano Man Skan. Now I had been aware for some time of the general ill-feeling towards Skan from the rest of the band, but I had no idea how intense it had become until that moment when Mark told me – and I think he meant it reassuringly – that it was OK, I should relax, they had decided to sack Skan and leave him in Russia.

When Skan first joined the band, his playing wasn't too strong, but he could hold his own musically with a bit of sleight of hand. Furthermore he was a good showman and a decent singer and he looked and behaved as a Biscuit Boy should. The problem was that he didn't work on his technique, as did the rest of the band, and he began to slip behind until it was felt he was hindering the band's development. There were personal issues, too, which in such a small community as a band just got worse until constant bickering became the order of the day.

So there was Val, who always tried to stay out of the band's business, attempting to reason with half a dozen badly hungover rock and roll hooligans, pre-dawn in a forgotten corner of Soviet Russia as the time to our check-in in neighbouring Norway steadily ticked by. Frankly, I did see the merits of making the grand gesture, though I wasn't sure it was quite fair to take his passport, as Mark had done. I figured that this might get the band into the Rock and Roll Hall of Fame as the most characterful, colourful sacking ever; on the other hand we might get to feeling pretty bad about the whole thing if this passport-less itinerant piano player found himself slammed up in some gulag or other. So, between us, Val and I managed to persuade P. Popps, always too much the nice guy, to go and retrieve the bedraggled and bewildered Skan.

The next – and, in retrospect, predictable – hitch came when we approached the Russian border and our driver refused to go any closer. It slowly dawned on us that he was trying to tell us that he hadn't the right papers and he could be arrested if he was questioned by a border guard. Accepting the inevitable, and again cursing David Benton, we unloaded the gear and made our way to the border post, where a sleepily uninterested guard did little more than glance at our passports, and then we plodded the mile or so down the road to the Norwegian border.

Which was closed until 8 o'clock.

That scuppered any chance that we ever had of catching our flight and the connection to London. As soon as the border opened, I borrowed their phone and called the hotel in Kirkenes, insisting that they immediately despatch their courtesy bus to the border post to collect our party and take us to the hotel where we could clean up and have breakfast. I convinced the Duty Manager that David Benton, unavoidably detained in Nikel, had authorised this to be put on his bill. It transpired that there were no other connecting flights to London that day, so we overnighted in an Oslo hotel, flights and hotel on my American Express, and flew out to London a day later than expected.

Piano Man Skan duly got the boot on our return to England, to be replaced by a wide-eyed innocent teenaged near-genius piano player from Middlesbrough whose parents were not at all comfortable with him leaving home at such a tender age. As usual, parents tend to be right about these things.

Danny McCormack, aged 16 at the time, was already a King Pleasure fan and had persuaded his father to drive him to the band's North East gigs. Classically trained and armed with familiarity with the Biscuit Boys' repertoire, he was smoothly assimilated into the band. Musically on the button, his initial on-stage awkwardness was quickly replaced by gross over-acting which, of course, was just what was expected of a Biscuit Boy. The band then set about teaching him to drink which, again, he took to with alacrity.

There is a footnote to this tale of incompetence and misadventure. Two or three years later, when Big Bear was booking the bands and doing the PR for Ronnie Scott's, Birmingham, I had a phone call from somebody who told me that Steve Firman of Kodak International, a particularly good friend of mine, had asked him to phone me. When he told me he was David Benton, I greeted him with something like, 'Benton, you incompetent bastard, you owe me £700 and I want it now!' – that's very much a sanitised version of my response. When my anger had subsided, it began to dawn on me that this was indeed David Benton, but not the one I knew. This one was a personal friend of George Melly who was resident at Ronnie Scott's that week and he was phoning to invite me for lunch with George, Steve and himself – at which I was able to entertain them with the Norwegian and Russian odyssey of the other David Benton.

King Pleasure's first venture to the other great super-power was a rather more comfortable experience. Initially invited to play at a computer convention in Scottsdale, near Phoenix, Arizona, we added to this anchor date, opened in San Jose and played three nights in Boz Scaggs' San Francisco club where the most amazing one-man act, Bud E. Luv, opened the show. We then drove to Los Angeles to play the Brown Derby, the legendary 1940s rhythm and blues venue where Big Jay McNeely was famed for his bar-walking. KP's tenor man, Jonny Boston, naturally couldn't miss the opportunity to do his own bar-walking, only to be cussed out by the management and fined 100 dollars.

Despite my initial hesitation I had soon forgotten that we had shamelessly borrowed the stage name of Clarence Beeks and with the passage of time had begun to consider it our own. The one time that this caused embarrassment was

The real Blues Brothers Band, Duck Dunn, Steve Cropper, Mr. Fabulous and all, with King Pleasure and the Biscuit Boys.

that night at The Brown Derby. A smartly dressed man with his two young daughters arrived early and took a table directly in front of the stage. The band came on and began swinging the room into bad health much to the evident delight of the two girls. About 20 minutes in, he came over to me and enquired, 'When is he coming on?' I asked him who and he replied, 'King Pleasure, of course.' I explained the situation, saying that I was sure that he would enjoy the show, but to no avail. Collecting his daughters, who protested volubly, he made his grand exit.

As Clarence Beeks had died a dozen or so years previously, booking him that night would have been a real coup for The Brown Derby!

In Phoenix we stayed at a modest roadside hotel; Scottsdale was way too ritzy for the likes of us. The hotel bar was near-deserted, but the pianist sounded tremendous, both his playing and his singing. I asked at the bar what the pianist drank, got him a whisky and shambled over to listen more closely and to get talking. It turned out that he was Gaynel Hodge, pianist with the Penguins who had enjoyed a huge hit with *Earth Angel* which Gaynel co-wrote. I quickly roused the Biscuit Boys and we enjoyed a memorable night with a true rock and roll star.

The next stop was Cambridge, across the river from Boston, Massachusetts, where the band was booked in for five nights at the original House of Blues, the first of several owned by Blues Brother Dan Aykroyd and Hard Rock Café's Isaac Tigrett. Sited just off Harvard Square of Jimmy Rushing and Count Basie fame, the House of Blues was one of the finest music venues I have ever seen. The recorded music was all anyone could wish for, but it was linked to a series of monitor screens that carried biographical details and photographs of the featured artist. At 6.00 pm the room was re-configured, trestle tables came out of the walls and chairs were lowered from the ceiling – suddenly the room was a saloon of the Wild West variety. The audiences were terrific and loved the band who found themselves absolutely at home; *Atomic* magazine of New York wrote, 'To those who say that swing is a musical form best left to Americans, prepare to be proven wrong. This British combo is bullet-proof!'

I'm still not sure where we found the will-power from to leave town when the stint was finished.

Then there was the time when Lugano Jazz Festival in Switzerland invited King Pleasure and the Biscuit Boys to perform for a one-hour live TV show as a big band. The then seven piece added top tenor sax men Willie Garnett and Mike Burney, Birmingham trumpet star John Burnett and Duncan Swift on trombone. There's a video still on YouTube of admittedly terrible quality which nonetheless captures a remarkable performance which drove the 5,000 crowd wild.

16. King Pleasure And The Biscuit Boys

This fine festival consisted of five stages set in the town's picturesque squares. Willie Garnett quickly discovered that each backstage area had a refrigerator for the band's use – filled with beer. When King Pleasure's fridge was emptied, quite quickly, Willie was spotted on several occasions making his way surreptitiously, methodically emptying the other fridges which earned him his lifelong nickname, Willie 'The Fridge' Garnett.

Apart from assorted international adventures (and a few at home) King Pleasure and the Biscuit Boys are a serious musical proposition. Without the luxury of any significant sales success on record, wildly enthusiastic reviews certainly, but nothing to make the tills ring out of control, the band has carved out a remarkable career. To date, it's more than 30 years non-stop on the road and it shows no sign of coming to an end. Of course, over such a long period of time, there have been the inevitable changes. Only King Pleasure himself and guitarist Bullmoose K. Shirley remain of the original band, but the current line-up are anything but newcomers. As I write, tenor and alto saxist John 'Boysey' Battrum has clocked up 19 years, pianist Mighty Matt Foundling 12 years and double bassist and clown extraordinaire Shark van Schtoop 18 years, while drummer Gary 'The Enforcer' Barber joined from fellow-Big Bear artists Tipitina in 2007.

One day someone will write the book on King Pleasure and the Biscuit Boys and properly compile the family tree. Pianist Danny McCormack reports that he last played with Cootie Alexander in 2012 and he still played like a monster. We all live in hope, Cootie more so than most. He's married to a school head teacher and has his own business in the small town of Hope, smack in the middle of The Peak

A typically formal King Pleasure and the Biscuit Boys, snapped in the mid-1990s.

District National Park. He seems inordinately cheerful, and I'm sure that he is, but I was saddened to hear that this imperious trumpet man is no longer enjoying a stellar musical career. I really do hope that he is having a ball playing when he wants to and what he wants to, but I must admit to a moment of extreme sadness when he answered the phone with 'Hello, this is Paul Allin Property Maintenance'. I'm pleased of course that he's eating regularly, takes proper holidays, whatever they are, and has a nice home, but I despair that what we laughingly refer to as our civilised society cannot provide a decent living for such an excellent musician.

Singer Lisa Sugar Lee, still looking as if she had just stepped out of a 1950s Hollywood movie, is now Lisa Zdravkovic, married to guitarist Dragan Zac Zdravkovic and working as a Liaison Manager and photographer where she is producing some splendid work.

As for that unstoppable steamroller of a rhythm team, Ivory Dan McCormack, no longer the slightest bit the wide-eyed innocent, is lecturing in Music at Derby University and letting his hair down on tour with Roy Wood's Band; double bass player Alan 'Slap Happy' Gare, after a successful stint with Imelda May, has re-located to Glasgow where his wife has taken a proper job and where he is certain to find a rocking band; the ever-swinging drummer Dean 'Bam Bam' Beresford, rated by those who know as alongside his hero and inspiration, Kansas City's Gus Johnson, has a regular gig with Sheffield-based singer/songwriter Richard Hawley and is still picking up rave reviews.

Paul P Popps Martin, a far better musician than he ever realised, apparently gave up playing and sold off his saxophones within a month of leaving the band, to settle a tax bill which was later found to be incorrect and the payment refunded. But not the saxophones. He married and moved to Prestwick in Scotland where he has been teaching saxophone, running an online sheet music business and playing saxophone mostly for fun. He has also built himself a home recording studio which he clearly enjoys. As if that's not enough, he has taken up photography and enjoys portraiture and landscapes, but his long term plan is to save enough to retire and live in Spain. Noting that Slap Happy has recently moved to Glasgow, P Popps is planning a get-together, and who knows what that could lead to?

He was a particularly good man, a most loyal band member, and is a real loss to music. He's particularly missed by guitarist Bullmoose K. Shirley who was his best pal since the age of twelve.

King Pleasure always did surprisingly well when it came to filling the tenor saxophone chair. Martin Winning was a Godsend, but so was Jonny Boston, earlier with Phil Mason's band and the Pasadena Roof Orchestra. For a few idyllic

16. King Pleasure And The Biscuit Boys

months the band went up to a nine-piece and really became the undisputed Number 1 rhythm and blues band on this, or any other, planet. Of that band Paul Jones said that it was 'the hardest act to follow since the parting of the Red Sea' and the ever-perceptive Dave Gelly of the *Observer* wrote, 'Beneath the fun and rollicking good times lies an outfit skilled enough for the horns to come on with the bite and precision of the Basie Band.'

When Mart Winning left to join Van Morrison and Boston re-located to Holland where he now leads his own band, the Jazzuits, another extremely influential player Big Al Nicholls took their place and brought with him the ability to write hot-shot arrangements that really raised the band's game, bringing a class and style that was the envy of their so-called competitors. Al now leads his own band, the no doubt immaculate Blue Harlem, features with the T.J. Johnson Band and has a full datesheet of one-nighters.

Looking back at that great band, it's impossible not to think about the band's roadie, the near-legendary Terry The Toupe (pronounced Toop). Not a tall man, he was blessed with the strength of two separate gorillas. Terry had a heart of gold and a sense of loyalty way beyond reason, but it would not be unfair to say that he was inclined to be a little impetuous.

The Irish Centre in Birmingham's Digbeth was, and probably still is, a cracking 400-capacity gig room seemingly unaltered since the 1960s. King Pleasure and the Biscuit Boys always delivered the goods there, but one particular night, as they went onstage, I spotted two unfamiliar figures sidling into the band's dressing room. Without giving the matter any thought as they were clearly up to no good, I charged in after them.

Not a clever move. There were two unpleasant-looking characters, both looking exceedingly displeased at being interrupted while rolling what appeared to be herbs of some sort, into silver foil packages. Just as they began to respond, not totally pleasantly, to my intrusion, someone pushed me aside, rushed up to the intruders and yanked them out of the club into the street with an arm around the neck of each of them. The ever-aware Terry The Toupe had spotted the activity, realised what was happening far more quickly than I did, and acted appropriately. No fuss, he just took care of business.

It has to be understood that Terry's toupee was not a particularly good fit, all the more obvious because of the colour of the hairpiece. It was a bright orange. To any sensible person it was obvious that you only drew attention to this at your peril, which is exactly what two Birmingham doormen did. The entrance to Rebecca's nightclub was at the top of a long flight of stairs, and, as Terry was leaving, one of the doormen, most unwisely, snatched his hairpiece and threw it down the stairs.

Terry's response was immediate. He dashed down the stairs, carefully putting the toupee in place before he ran back and smacked both doormen before throwing them downstairs and strolling off nonchalantly into the night.

There was another occasion that could well have had far more serious consequences. The Adam and Eve pub was a regular music venue with a nicely relaxed attitude to licensing hours. Pianist Big Man Clayton was well into his stride on his final set when, absolutely unprovoked, a local hooligan came up behind him and held what appeared to be a gun to his head. Not your regular Saturday night occurrence at this particular pub. The entire room froze.

That is, all except Terry The Toupe, who crept out of the side door, along the street and re-entered through the front door, behind the miscreant. Picking up one of those big heavy old-fashioned pub ashtrays, he smacked the man alongside the head, rendering him unconscious and standing by to restrain him until the police arrived. He then went straight to the bar and asked, 'Is that worth a pint?'

Not long ago King Pleasure talked to Terry's son – Stephen Brown has grown up to be as well-built as his dad, but taller. They were both extremely amused when Stephen recounted a recent fracas between Terry and a 30-something-year-old neighbour. Terry The Toupe lost it, laid out the neighbour with one whack and was led away by two highly amused policemen. Terry is now in his eighties!

For nigh on ten years King Pleasure and the Biscuit Boys were easily the leading attraction at Ronnie Scott's on Broad Street where the HOUSE FULL signs went up for a remarkable five or six weeks every year. Now, 35 years after the meeting in the Darlaston milkbar, the band is still on the road through the UK and Europe, still knocking them dead with their own particular brand of Kansas City-based rocking rhythm and blues.

Chapter 17

MARBELLA: FIESTA AND FIASCO

The 1992 Birmingham Jazz Festival was well under way when I received a phone call from a Spanish man who was in Birmingham en route to Rugby to visit his then girlfriend. The reason for his call was simple.

'What is a wonderful festival doing in such a rubbish town?', he enquired, apparently in all seriousness. I learned, at the outset of what was to develop into a durable friendship, that tact and diplomacy were not among the attributes possessed by Jose Maria Gomez Iglesias. We agreed to meet and discuss his viewpoint in a little more depth. Anyway, with my interest in all things Spanish, I thought we might have an interesting conversation.

Jose, a native of Marbella in Andalucia, worked for that city's council. He was at that time in no position to do anything about it, but he insisted that the festival would be far more at home in the glamorous coastal setting of Marbella. Apart from that topic, we had a lot to talk about and even found we had friends in common on the Costa del Sol. We agreed to keep in touch and get together when Val, my brother and I visited the Coast that Christmas.

This went on for several years as Jose steadily moved up through the ranks at Marbella Council. Eventually, one Christmas, Jose asked me to stay over for a few days to discuss a festival project he had in mind and to view potential venues. This was music to my ears and I found myself regularly visiting Marbella over the coming months to put the festival in place. Our plans reached fruition in May 2003 when we took over the Marbella International Jazz Festival after an unsuccessful first attempt by a Marbella-based, Russian-funded company the previous year.

Little did I imagine in those far-off optimistic halcyon days the pitfalls, triumphs and times of sheer farce over the four years of this manic festival.

When I became involved with Marbella Jazz Festival, Jesus Gil y Gil had just come to the end of a tempestuous 11 years as Mayor of Marbella. He had rebuilt his business and political career following a criminally disastrous start when an apartment complex he was building near Segovia collapsed, killing 58 people. It was later found that the cement hadn't been allowed to set and no architects, surveyors or plans had been anywhere near the project. Gil received a jail sentence of 5 years, but was pardoned after 18 months by the then Spanish dictator Francisco Franco whose memory Gil later perpetuated by displaying his bust in his mayoral office.

When he became Mayor of Marbella in 1991, he had already been President of Atletico Madrid for four years, one of the many scandals and court cases of his career involving the unauthorised display of Marbella's logo on Atletico's shirts, Gil y Gil funding his football club through his day job. As Mayor he did indeed cut crime rates and reduce obvious begging and homelessness, but at the expense of civil liberties: prostitutes were beaten, foreigners with too little money deported and homeless citizens bribed to go somewhere else. British, Italian and Russian gangsters were, however, welcome, as were former Nazis on the run. Gil y Gil's power spread further than Marbella with his son installed as Mayor of Estepona and other members of his political party in power in the North African enclaves of Ceuta and Melilla. His position seemed secure, but eventually the authorities took action on the corruption of his regime.

In April 2002, a year before our first festival, Jesus Gil was removed as Mayor and banned from all public office and briefly jailed, but by then corruption was endemic and even now the shadow of Jesus Gil still hangs over Marbella city politics. He was replaced as Mayor by Julian Munoz, who didn't try too hard to disassociate himself from his predecessor, as he represented the new political party Grupo Independiente Liberal which, by coincidence I'm sure, has the acronym GIL. He did, however, faithfully follow in Gil's footsteps by being jailed for corruption.

In 2013 it was estimated that the mayoralties of Gil and his successor, Julian Munoz, resulted in looting 81.19 million euros from Marbella city funds – which could buy you an awful lot of jazz festivals! – and Gil's heirs are responsible for refunding it. Meanwhile, though officially absent from the scene, Gil's influence never wavered, though it was not by his own choice that, in 2004, he brought about the most chaotic of many chaotic days at the Marbella Jazz Festival.

After waiting in the wings, not always patiently, for a number of years, I was somewhat disconcerted to find that, when given the green light to launch a jazz festival in 2002, Jose passed us by and engaged the services of Victor O'Gilvie and Louis de Vries of International Concert Promotions. Apparently it didn't work out too well – disaster is how Jose summed it up. He has always maintained

17. Marbella: Fiesta And Fiasco

that the decision to go with Victor was not his; he claimed it came from the top. That would be the redoubtable Jesus Gil y Gil, about to be banned from office, but still not to be opposed in Marbella.

For the following year we were given the go-ahead at Christmas and put a full programme in place by the end of February.

Before we were officially engaged to get to work, Jose told me I needed to meet with councillors to get their approval. The meeting was set for a late evening in November. I was to drive my hire car up a mountain by an obscure road until I reached a pull-in directly after a certain kilometre sign and wait to be contacted. I did as I was told, exactly as I was told in fact, because the needle was wavering somewhere between extremely apprehensive and terrified. I arrived at the designated spot and from somewhere in the gloom headlights flashed and a large black sedan moved slowly off up a dirt-track. Figuring that I was expected to follow, I did. We parked up quietly in what appeared to be a large farmyard. My car door was opened for me and I followed dutifully. How else?

The farmhouse was large and the room I was taken to was comfortably shabby, seemingly full of children who were polite and calm and dogs who were not. I was seated in a comfortable chair and handed a large glass of very dry sherry within sight of half a dozen shirt-sleeved men around a large table. They were arguing or just talking boisterously, I couldn't tell which, but either way they seemed unaware of my presence.

After what felt like an inordinate wait I was invited to sit at the table. The loud and impenetrable Spanish continued apace, now with a series of gestures in my direction, before I was asked, in very formal stilted English: Was I well? Did I like Marbella? Was this my first time in Spain? How was the weather in England? I was then thanked profusely for being kind enough to visit them, presented with a bottle of Manzanilla de San Lucar de Barrameda and led back to the road to Marbella.

The next day Jose, whom I had expected to be present (but wasn't), told me that we should start work immediately on the festival. For reasons I cannot even begin to fathom, the previous evening's gathering had somehow discerned that I might be the man for the job, but I'll never know how or why. Maybe the fact that I didn't nod off – fear does that to a man – or didn't sing, dance, smack any of the children or kick any of the dogs did the trick. I have often wondered if I was in the presence of Jesus Gil y Gil himself. In retrospect I doubt it – there was too much equality among the men at the table – but I have little doubt that, after the previous year's failure, he had ordered his henchmen to run the rule over this ambitious foreigner.

I had a shared office in the smartly modern Palacio de Ferias y Congresos, just off the main street, the Avenida Ricardo de Sorriano, and a mere spit to the beach. I had a desk and a phone, but no computer. Jose's staff were a mixed bunch. I would get to work a little before the prescribed time of 9 o'clock, but it was often a fair wait before anyone else arrived, giving me the use of someone else's computer and time to prepare the Big Bear office in Birmingham for the day's work.

Jose was never an ever-present. Apparently he wasn't expected to be. He was, after all, the Boss and he had other demands on his time, such as taking his young daughter to her dance lessons. When he did find time to discuss – if that's not too strong a word – the jazz festival, he found it difficult to concentrate, giving me the feeling that I was being a bit of a nuisance bothering him like this. His media relations girl, Carolina Esteban, was a different matter: diligent, sharp as a tack and totally taken with the idea of organising a jazz festival. After a while she began to come in early and stay late and even wanted to listen to the music of the artists we were booking. The girl in charge of marketing was another hard worker. Married to an Irishman and having lived in Ireland, she spoke totally fluent English with a strong Irish accent which seemed strange coming from someone so patently Spanish. We worked out a double act for when we approached potential sponsors, a formula that yielded a good success rate. I would stumble through a general introduction about the significance of the festival in my dodgy Spanish and then she would faithfully translate our sales pitch and their response.

We landed some good sponsorship, notably from the Junta de Andalucia, the regional tourist board based in Malaga. They funded a programme of performances in the area around Marbella, invariably in the fascinating *pueblos blancos* idyllically situated in the mountains. Not only was it a thrill to organise these shows in such stunning settings, but the performers took the festival to a new audience with the intention of funnelling them back into the events in Marbella.

Jose's office manager, an aristocratic and elegant woman with a serene manner, was deceptively astute at ensuring I met the right – that is influential – people, most of them politicians. However, there was one occasion when a newly-formed political friendship led to embarrassment. This councillor prevailed upon me to hire his nephew as the driver of the festival bus, picking up musicians from the airport or their hotels and taking them to their shows. Apparently this seemingly polite and pleasant young man had found it difficult to hold down a job and needed this work to build his confidence. He started off nicely enough, but the musicians told me that a couple of times he had to be dragged out of the bar, reluctantly, to drive them to their hotel. I mentioned my unease to Jose's right

17. Marbella: Fiesta And Fiasco

hand girl, Maria Felix, and she assured me she knew him well and he was reliable. Further incidents culminated in a scheduled 7.00 am pick-up to take the New York funksters, The Fatback Band, to the airport. He was there early, waiting for the band outside the hotel, looking a little battered, and it was only when he closed the passenger door and tried to open the driver's door that he collapsed, slid down the side of the bus and lay there on the pavement in sweet oblivion. Dead drunk. Apparently he had been on an all-night drinking session since dropping the band off the previous night.

Clive Johnson, the manager of the Fatbacks, had him loaded onto the bus, still unconscious, while Clive drove to Malaga Airport with no insurance, but determined that the band would make their flight to Madrid and the ongoing connection to New York – which they did. Clive left the bus at the short-stay, therefore hideously expensive, airport car park complete with its resident drunk. Inevitably Maria Felix gave me a hard time for allowing no less a person than the nephew of a councillor to be treated in such a disrespectful manner.

There were some wonderful times, mainly as a direct consequence of the music, in the four years that we organised the Marbella Jazz Festival, but equally there were some not so good moments, most of them connected with Maria Felix. In retrospect she clearly resented others – in this case, me – having the attention of Jose. That belonged to her. From the start she positioned herself firmly between him and me, invariably with a problem as the direct result.

Jose's English was good, more fluent than hers, but, when we were compiling the printed programme, she insisted that my notes, including artists' biographies, went to her for translation – and not only into Spanish. For some reason she altered my English notes, whether deliberately or by re-typing without understanding, a typical error being her translation of Archie Shepp into Archie Sheep on the extremely large posters, a version of his name which he found amusing enough to repeat on stage several times.

One year, without discussing it or even telling me, supposedly in the interests of saving money, she cancelled all my drivers and thereby destroyed my travel plan. I didn't discover this until I arrived in Marbella on the eve of the festival to find that she had arranged for some of her louche friends to work as volunteer drivers – paid, of course! The fact that Maria Felix never got what the festival was all about was demonstrated on the first day when, having designated herself as a driver, she went to Mike Burney and his band at the end of their second of three sets to pick them up and take them back to their hotel. It was, she explained to Mike, better to do it like this as she was on her way to lunch and it saved her returning at the end of the performance. Mike, to his eternal credit, refused to budge, played the full performance and the band took cabs back to their hotel. Normal service was resumed the following day after a series of frantic – and apologetic – phone calls to my original drivers.

Although the staff at the Palacio were sometimes found wanting, Carolina Esteban always delivered the goods. Her press conferences were the like of nothing I had ever experienced in the UK. At every media call we were confronted by an apparently eager array of reporters, photographers and film cameramen, pretty much like in 1950s Hollywood movies. And it wasn't just for show: the subsequent coverage always exceeded reasonable expectations.

What really helped was the Council's enthusiasm in promoting the festival. Every lamp-post sported a banner, every billboard was devoted to the festival. Interestingly, bearing in mind that this was Marbella's tourism shoulder period, the audiences were more or less 50% Spanish and 50% tourists and expats.

Unsurprisingly, all this created significant interest in the event, and not just the ticketed concerts in the Palacio de Ferias. At an unadvertised 3.00 pm soundcheck for an evening performance on the Beach Stage – one area where Birmingham can't compete – The Fatback Band found themselves routing to a 400-strong audience, simply attracted by the music.

We had a string of memorable performances in Marbella. Many newly arrived tourists were delighted to find themselves surrounded by music in such an idyllic setting. The basic plan for the Marbella Jazz Festival was, strange to say, not terribly different from that of Birmingham. Marbella has the advantage of a nice mid-size concert hall with a 1560 capacity which the council willingly turned over to the festival for the ticketed events, three evenings of concerts, mostly double bills, each year. We employed the tried and trusted Big Bear formula of interrupting the daily routines of folk by presenting fine music in often unusual public settings in the hope that they would pick up a programme and maybe attend a ticketed concert.

In the Palacio we presented a nicely balanced, sensibly priced programme with American artists such as the Count Basie Orchestra, Arturo Sandoval, Dianne Schuur, Joey De-Francesco, the Sun Ra Arkestra, Annie Ross, Roy Ayers' Ubiquity, Larry Coryell, Archie Shepp, Billy Cobham, Johnny Griffin, Kyle Eastwood and Benny Golson, plus UK attractions *Lady Sings the Blues* and King Pleasure and the Biscuit Boys. Many of the shows were sell-out, none at less than 80% capacity.

The daytime events were all free admission and featured a real mix of bands: a couple of good local bands, British musicians who had made their home on the Coast, the occasional American star such as Roomful of Blues' Al Copley, Continental bands that we knew from the Birmingham festival such as the Lazy

17. Marbella: Fiesta And Fiasco

Jumpers from Barcelona, Germany's Bourbon Street Stompers and the Miskolc Jazz Band from Hungary. Booking the support bands was actually very easy. We were spoilt for choice with the many good European bands we had booked for Birmingham who all fell over themselves to play in Marbella.

Pound for pound, probably the most successful musician on the Jazz Trail was the straightahead tenor saxophone player from Birmingham, my friend Mike Burney. After the first year he was always the most requested act. There were many bigger, smarter, more exotic, more visually entertaining combos, but Mike cut it every time with his uncomplicated Texas-style tenor – somehow the audiences just got it. Bruce Adams always tells me how important it is to 'play the truth'. Satch did, Lester and Billie did, and so did Mike Burney.

I have to admit that, wonderful as the music was, the settings were invariably the co-stars. The opportunities to present unusual events in Marbella were legion. We featured the top American funk outfit, The Fatback Band, free on the beach to some 3,000 people; held New Orleans Parades on the Avenida Ricardo Soriano, Marbella's main street; had pop-up shows throughout the Casco Antiguo and in beach bars galore, and from the second year, when funding from the Junta de Andalucia kicked in, we were able to go out to the *pueblos blancos*. We even had the run of an elderly three-masted schooner, the *Velero Amorina*, which we sailed out of Puerto Banus, adjacent to Marbella. I had long admired it in its home mooring in the harbour at Malaga and now put it to work taking jazz out into the Mediterranean.

The events of the weekend of May 14th to 16th, 2004 were certainly the most difficult in the festival's four years. It didn't take long, particularly in the eyes of the Count Basie Band, for the Saturday to begin to disintegrate. The band's previous night's performance in Rotterdam had over-run, so they were late back to the hotel. They had a 5.00 am call to enable an 8.00 am check-in at Amsterdam Schiphol for the 10.00 am flight to Malaga. They were due to arrive in Marbella about 2 o'clock which would give time for a few hours' sleep before the 6.00 pm sound-check. At least that was the plan. A tough schedule, but, when you're on the road (and this band had been on the road in one form or another since 1936), this is what you expect.

What you do not expect, after only four hours' sleep, is to have to hang around the airport for some five hours because your flight is delayed. Eventually, around 5 o'clock, the bus from Malaga Airport deposited them at the Guadalpin Hotel in the middle of the Marbella Jazz Festival. Things didn't get much better at hotel reception with 18 extremely grumpy musicians all demanding to be checked in at once. They weren't all grumpy, however. Bandleader Bill Hughes found himself a

The sax section of the Count Basie Orchestra directed by Bill Hughes headlining at the Marbella Jazz Festival.

comfortable place to sit and a pot of tea and we set about salvaging what could have remained a fractious situation. Showtime was 8.00 pm, only a few steps away at the Palacio de Ferias. We agreed to hold back the sell-out audience until 7.30, simply do a line-check and dispense with the soundcheck, and get the band in place for 7.00, allowing a brief two hours for them to rest, clean up and have something to eat.

I undertook responsibility for setting up the music stands onstage and allocating the orchestration books to the appropriate players. If anyone thinks this could be an onerous task, then I have to own up that I couldn't have been more delighted to take it on. It was, in fact, pretty much the thrill of a lifetime. Some of these orks had been in the Basie book since 1957, many of them originals actually written in the hand of Neal Hefti. These pages had actually been handled and played by generations of famous musicians in what I believe to be the finest of the big bands: Franks Foster and Wess, Joe Newman, Wendell Culley – the fourth trumpet part for *Li'l Darlin'* had a hand-written instruction, just before the trumpet solo, 'Wendell down front' – Thad Jones, Lockjaw Davis, Marshall Royal, Freddy Green, Bill Hughes himself. Notes such as 'Snooky to fourth', indicating that Snooky Young was moved from the demanding first trumpet chair to fourth to give his lip a bit of a rest, were the stuff of dreams to me. I was there, wishing the process could last a week, when my reverie was broken with a, 'What the fuck do you think you're doing?' The invariably irascible Scotty Barnhart was clearly unaware that Bill Hughes had asked me to distribute the arrangements, although in fairness he hadn't invited me to browse the entire pad. Scotty was not only first trumpet in the band, but also the straw boss, the band member tasked with making things work. Scotty took his role seriously, here sacrificing his meal to come in early and make sure everything had been done properly – which he grudgingly admitted it had.

The Count Basie Orchestra at the Marbella Jazz Festival went out live on radio that night, a remarkable two-hour session. I sat in the front row with saxophonist Alan Barnes who knows all about such things and he told me with no uncertainty, 'We will never again hear a saxophone section as good as that.'

82-year-old altoist Jackie Kelso had returned to the Basie band in 1995 at the age of 73. Asked by Alan when he intended to retire, he replied, 'Retire? From this band? You'd have to be crazy.'

From its beginnings in the 1930s the Count Basie Band has always featured great drummers. Butch Miles in the Bill Hughes-led Basie outfit at Marbella was right there in the great tradition.

As the band came offstage, exhausted but triumphant, Scotty growled at me, 'How was that?' I replied, 'Tremendous, straight out of the top drawer,' to which he said, 'This band always plays best when it's angry. Where can we get a drink?'

That weekend didn't go too well for me, either, and even less so for Jesus Gil y Gil, the former Mayor of Marbella, who died in hospital, still under arrest, in Madrid on the Friday.

The Festival had been running smoothly. Marbella City Council had declared a Brotherhood (*Hermanidad*) with Birmingham Jazz Festival and Birmingham Lord Mayor-to-be Councillor John Hood had come to Marbella with Festival Board members Derek Inman and John James. We had been presented with commemorative plaques and the Thursday night concert had celebrated the links between the two cities and their festivals.

Jose had asked if I would like to put together a band of my favourite musicians to feature at Marbella – I can't imagine being given a more pleasurable task. Then the offer of the *Hermanidad* came up and I got to thinking that it would be appropriate to do something special to celebrate it. Thus the *Marbella Jazz Suite* came into being. I wrote eight short stories based on Marbella and donated them to the city in perpetuity and commissioned Alan Barnes to compose and arrange a piece of music to reflect each story. Then I selected my eight hot-shot jazz musicians to rehearse, perform and record Alan's new material. Wednesday afternoon and evening were spent rehearsing, the band played a stomping photocall on Thursday morning and really took care of business in front of an audience of 1,200 at the Palacio in the evening. We did a live radio broadcast and recorded an album to go on general release in the UK and Europe. The band consisted of eight outstanding British jazzers: Alan himself, Bruce Adams, Simon Gardner, Alex Garnett, Mark Nightingale, John Donaldson, Matt Miles and Ralph Salmins.

The mixing session, the following week was a special one. We had recorded on the Loasur mobile recording unit, so it made sense to mix on the same gear. Their studio was near Coin, a dramatic 30-minute drive through the mountains from Marbella to a remote walled compound that housed the high-tech recording and television unit. The mix took three days and I wished I could have stayed longer. I have rarely arrived at work in such a stimulated state of mind.

The *Marbella Jazz Suite* performance was on Thursday, but any hopes we had of a nice straightforward festival were dissipated on Friday with the death of Senor Gil. At around 11 o'clock on the Friday evening I was told that my presence was required at the Town Hall at midnight. I had heard the rumours that Jesus Gil y Gil had died, but, as he had been in prison for some time, and therefore presumably in some sort of disgrace, it hadn't occurred to me that his passing would affect the festival in any way.

17. Marbella: Fiesta And Fiasco

How wrong I was!

The stern-faced gathering in the inner chamber of the Town Hall, spookily lit only by candle-light, told me that I was to cancel the entire festival for the following day out of respect for the man who had spent his last years imprisoned for corruption. I put forward a series of suggestions for compromise, reminding them that Saturday's programme had more events than any other day, that musicians who were already in town would need to be paid, whether or not they performed, that the bars and restaurants would certainly not make their agreed contributions if their bands were not allowed to perform. Then there was the not inconsequential matter of the performances arranged for the neighbouring *pueblos blancos* and paid for by the sponsorship of the Junta de Andalucia, Malaga-based and surely not crying over the passing of this particular Marbella criminal.

The response was mainly a collective shrug of the shoulders, as if they were all driven by some unseen power. As it were. My pitch wasn't helped by my limited Spanish, nor by their sudden loss of any familiarity with the English language. The only point they were able to concede was the appearance of the Count Basie Orchestra which had sold out days before. Maybe the thought of 1560 irate ticket holders, seen by them as potential votes, was what did it, but there it was: cancel the entire programme except for the Basie band. It took an age, but, when I emerged onto the Plaza de Naranjas at 2.00 am, I had been given permission to proceed with the Basie concert, but with strict instructions to cancel everything else.

There was clearly going to be a lot more work to be done than would have been the case had the shows not been cancelled. Venues, musicians and the media had to be informed, all the scheduled artists' transport needed to be cancelled, and, inevitably, there would be a flood of public enquiries. Realising that I would need additional back-up the following day, I was considering how John Hood, John James and Derek Inman would feel if I woke them to ask if they would lend a hand. I needn't have worried: at the Guadalpin I found all three of them still in full flight at the bar with Bruce, Alan and the chaps, having far too much fun. They agreed to my proposition that they would help me man the phones and explain the situation to the many English-speaking bands involved.

We trooped into the office at 8 o'clock. With not a lot of Spanish between the four of us, it was a bit of a struggle, but we only had to hold the fort until 9.00 when Jose and the Spanish staff would start to drift in.

Come 9.30 and I was really starting to worry. None of them regularly came to work on time, but for all eight to be late on the same day was not normal, so I began phoning around. Jose wasn't answering his phone and it wasn't until I had called four or five of them that I got a response which was not what I expected and certainly not what I wanted: the Festival was cancelled, so naturally nobody was coming to work on a Saturday. Somebody, almost certainly Maria Felix, had picked up the information and phoned round the staff with the news that they could take the day off – which they did with alacrity.

Eventually Carolina, the press officer, turned up to help us, as did a few of the musicians, but that was it. The boss, Jose Gomez Iglesias, didn't even appear for the Basie concert which was being broadcast live on radio from his venue. Derek and the two Johns worked splendidly and I think we just about got away with it. Nobody was happy about the cancellation, particularly the venues that were anticipating a busy and profitable last day of the festival and the musicians for whom playing this wonderful music compensates for all the hours hanging about in airports and train stations, but at least one of the musicians made the most of it.

Stuck by the telephones, we saw nothing of this, but the indefatigable Bruce Adams, having enjoyed a taste or two during the day, decided to serenade the folk by the pool at the excellent Guadalpin Hotel. Reportedly he was easily persuaded to wade into the pool up to his chest, fully clothed, while still playing his trumpet – impeccably, I'm sure. Needless to say, many people considered this the highspot of the festival and clearly it gave Bruce inordinate pleasure. However, the coda came as a bit of a shock when sobriety returned and Bruce realised that the contents of his pocket, including flight ticket and passport, were more or less destroyed. I never found out how he handled that and wasn't really aware of that detail until his co-conspirator Alan Barnes confided in me some years later. Apparently Bruce had sworn him to secrecy at the time, but there exists a splendid photograph taken by Merlin of Bruce caught red-handed in the pool. Merlin has often denied being the person who encouraged Bruce, but I still believe he had a hand in the affair – what photographers will do to get a good shot! Regardless, it's a great photograph that I have used on several occasions.

And what of Jesus Gil? There's not exactly a mystery about his death; it's more like a theory that you still hear repeated throughout Marbella which suggests that many seemingly reasonable people don't actually believe that he is dead. There are three basic reasons for this disbelief. Firstly, apparently, it is normal in Andalucia for men of prominence, when they pass, to lie in state to allow people to pay their respects. Then there's the question of inheritance. They will tell you that, because of Andalucian laws on the matter, when a man of substance dies, his estate is broken up among the claimants. And thirdly? With a knowing look they will point out that he owned the hospital in which he died.

Argentina, they say, is the forwarding address.

17. Marbella: Fiesta And Fiasco

Though the death of a much-venerated criminal is, even in the world of jazz festivals, a touch uncommon, the Marbella years were never short of drama, the visit of the Sun Ra Arkestra to Marbella, suddenly, on the eve of the festival, for instance. Their European tour was organised by Gaby Kleinschmidt, a long respected German agent from Freiburg. Gaby was to have had the 11-piece Arkestra playing one-nighters through Germany for ten days before they went into a club in Rome for a week, then flying into Marbella to finish the tour on the Saturday. However, as they started their German tour, Gaby heard from Rome that the nightclub was cancelling. If that sounds outrageous, that's exactly what it is. Fortunately this sort of thing rarely happens, but, when it does, it's devastating.

Who was going to pay the band's salary for that week or reimburse the cost of flights for the legs Stuttgart to Rome to Malaga, who was going to feed them and, most importantly, where were they going to stay for a week? Most of these questions were, I'm sure, put later into the hands of Gaby's lawyer, but she came up with a nifty plan to take care of the immediate problems. She asked me if I could arrange for the band to be looked after in Marbella for three days instead of the scheduled one while she accommodated them in her house for the remaining

Sun Ra Arkestra's Charles Davis running his scales in the paradise that is Marbella.

The Sun Ra Arkestra gathering for a photocall at Marbella.

days – now that must have been some wild experience! To ease the burden on Marbella, Gaby assured me that the group would do all they could to help promote the event over those days. I took all of five seconds to agree. What a blast to have the Sun Ra Arkestra around and at a loose end for a few days, a rare and very welcome opportunity!

The first problem, to find accommodation and meals, was easily solved. I cancelled the 11 single rooms for one night at the 5-star Guadalpin and re-booked five twin rooms and one single at my regular Marbella hotel, the far more modest 3-star El Faro. The savings from the Guadalpin covered the entire stay at El Faro. Next I put the arm on the jazz-loving owners of two festival venues, telling them how cool it would be to have the Sun Ra Arkestra eating and conversing in their bars. I arranged a press photo-call on the beach which was a riot. The band played, simply because they wanted to, for an hour, a crowd gathered, dancing broke out and the subsequent photographs appeared like a rash all over the Andalucia media. It was even picked up on television and aired that evening.

Come the night of the concert and I figured that by then I had become pretty much accepted as one of the gang. Pre-show, sitting in the dressing room, ready to go on stage, just waiting for the end of the intolerably lengthy speeches by local politicians, they unexpectedly asked me to leave the room which I did, albeit a little grudgingly. As I left, I saw them all gathering in a circle to pray. I lurked outside the dressing room, waiting for the cue from the radio producer that the speeches were about to end and the band should make their way to side stage.

17. Marbella: Fiesta And Fiasco

Suddenly the dressing room door burst open: the prayers had now been replaced with a strange chant and the line of musicians began dancing their way towards me. I quickly decided to let things roll as, quite frankly, I might as well have tried to stop an advance by the entire Sioux Nation. It was beautiful: suddenly the pontificating politicians were surrounded by a chanting, strangely attired mob of musicians, live on radio. They did the only thing possible in the circumstances, they slunk off into the night, leaving the stage to one of the most original of jazz attractions to deliver a tremendous live broadcast with three encores for which the broadcaster, wisely, stayed on air.

I was sorry to have to wave them off to Malaga Airport the next day. It had been such an enlightening experience having them around. To a man they were co-operative, helpful and patient beyond belief, posing for photographs wherever they went and for an hour after the show. The Sun Ra Arkestra don't always get the acknowledgement they deserve from the Jazz Mafia. One thing is certain, they are all fine musicians; the orchestrations are not straightforward, but the discipline is there and they play them impeccably. Maybe some folk shy away, put off by the nutty background story that was circulated when they first came to notice. Perhaps some were discouraged by Sun Ra's assertion that he was not born on this planet, but came from Saturn, and some media comment, true or not, that there is no record of his birth anywhere in the United States. Maybe not, but they should really be checking out pianist Herman 'Sonny' Blount who recorded with Wynonie Harris and played with such luminaries as Fletcher Henderson and Coleman Hawkins before changing his name and forming the Arkestra.

Sun Ra died in 1993 and, when his successor, Arkestra stalwart John Gilmore, also died, founder member Marshall Allen assumed the leadership of the Arkestra, a task which, in 2019, he is still doing in exemplary fashion at the age of 94.

Marshall proved an extremely bright and kindly man and I am grateful to have worked with him in Marbella. He told me something that I found fascinating and that strangely had a pay-off for me a few years later. The Arkestra was on a lengthy tour of the US and Canada back in the 1970s when the band bus broke down in Toronto. Now a breakdown is always a nuisance, but this one had particularly far-reaching effects. The result was a three-year stay for the band in Toronto where they found enough gigs to sustain them. Marshall found nothing remarkable in staying away from home for three years. Fast forward to the 2006 Birmingham Jazz Festival where I was delighted to present those crazy Canucks, the irrepressible Shuffle Demons, famous for their *Spadina Bus* recording. Interested in what inspired their off-the-wall, but extremely musical, performance, I was chatting with drummer/leader Stich Wynston when all became dazzlingly clear.

The Shuffle Demons are from Toronto where, all those years earlier, the Sun Ra Arkestra had left their indelible mark. Stich is openly proud of his musical debt to Sun Ra, though he has taken it off in his own personal direction. One thing is clear. What Louis Armstrong is to most of us, Sun Ra is to Stich Wynston. I find it profoundly moving that a band or musician can leave such an identifiable mark on a city, just like Buck Clayton on 1930s Shanghai or Professor Longhair and James Booker on 1950s New Orleans.

I firmly believe that the two most important UK-born female jazz singers are Annie Ross and Val Wiseman. About Annie Ross' status among jazz singers there is no doubt. She swings like mad, has perfect intonation and interprets a lyric with far more sensitivity than most. Her work on Lambert, Hendricks and Ross' groundbreaking *Sing a Song of Basie* is the very peak of vocalese. Just listen to Annie's vocal version of Basie's piano introduction to *Avenue C* or her interpretation of Buck Clayton's trumpet solo on the same song – no, that's ridiculous! Just buy the album and listen to it all the way through. Many times. Intently.

Born in England to a Scottish show business family, niece of the singer Ella Logan and sister of the comedian Jimmy Logan, Annie went to the States, worked as a child film star and stayed there, initially living with her Aunt Ella. In Marbella she told me that she had been writing her book, but had decided not to pursue it. I begged her not to give up on it and have since nagged her at every opportunity, but I've heard nothing to suggest that she's taking notice – which is a great pity.

Annie was one of Val's three favourite singers, so the prospect of opening the show for her in Marbella was a source of much excitement and quite a lot of panic. The plan had been for Val's *Lady Sings the Blues* to open the show, followed by Oscar Brown Jr from Chicago – singer/songwriter/civil rights activist/politician/playwright, famed, among other things, for the vocal setting of *Work Song* – and Annie Ross, both accompanied by Annie's regular band, the Tardo Hammer Trio. When, to my delight, I was able to persuade Oscar to co-star with Annie, I believed we had something very special on our hands. Sadly Oscar was taken ill only days before his scheduled departure for Spain and died later that month. The resolute Annie Ross, 74 years old at that time, was unfazed and said that she would handle the show herself.

To give Annie a chance to recover from her transatlantic travel, we flew her in a few days early. She flew the New York-Madrid Red Eye, transferred to Malaga and showed up in my office in the early afternoon, looking immaculate and relaxed, but very frail. I was surprised and not pleased because I thought that our driver had brought her there by mistake when the plan had been for her to rest up in her hotel, recover from the effects of an overnight flight with no sleep and be

17. Marbella: Fiesta And Fiasco

prepared for the next day's photocall and performance. It transpired that Annie had taken charge and altered the plans. Having booked her for a week at Ronnie Scott's in Birmingham some years earlier and spent a lot of time with her, I knew resistance was futile in the face of a determined Annie Ross.

'What's happening?' she demanded. I explained the plans for her to rest and she responded with, 'This is a jazz festival, isn't it? What's happening?' This diminutive lady, no longer young, without sleep, wanted to know where the action was – and she also wanted to meet Val Wiseman who she knew all about.

Concerned as I was at her frail appearance, I realised that there was no point in arguing and capitulated, telling our driver to take her to see a couple of bands I thought she would like.

In the early evening, checking around that performances were going as planned, I arrived at the Paseo de Mar stage to find the audience rocking to Hungary's Miskolc Jazz Band, with the indefatigable Annie Ross taking control, singing and swinging, having accumulated a crowd of nearly 300. A Spanish jazz fan rushed up to me with, 'This is Annie Ross. Isn't she wonderful? I've just been listening to her with Mike Burney in the Alameda Gardens.'

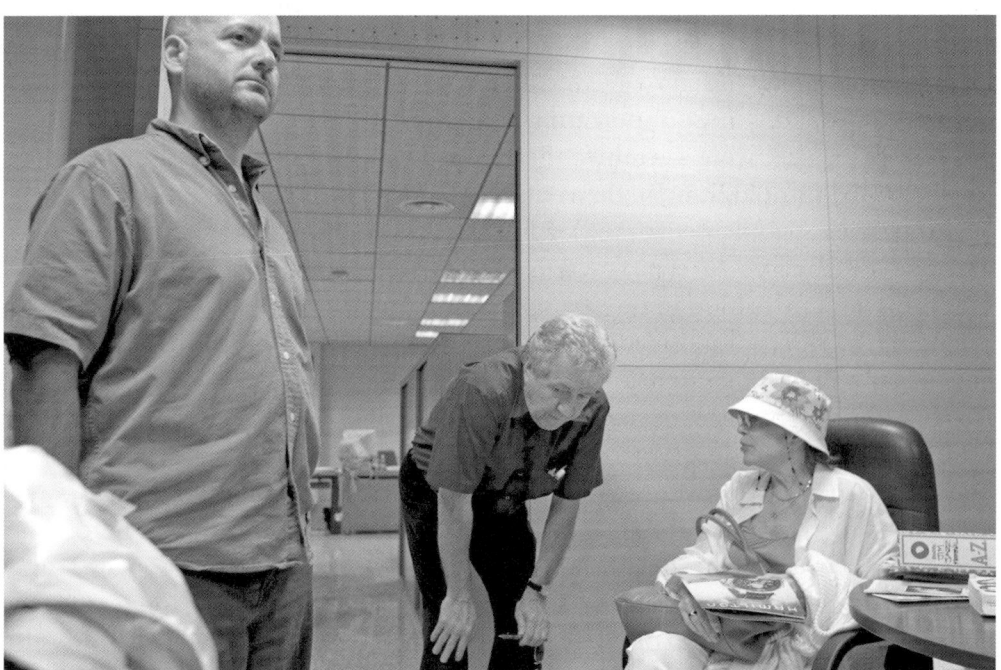

Annie Ross and pianist Tardo Hammer in my Marbella office, with Annie clearly in charge.

It goes without saying that she was stunning, clearly having a ball. 'Is she OK?' I asked her driver. 'I'll say,' he said, 'this is the third band she has sung with today. The audience is just following her around.'

That's how Annie Ross spent her rest day. Needless to say, the following night's concert was a sell-out.

The performance at the Palacio was a stunner. Val and the band were on top form, pulling out all the stops for the sell-out audience – and one audience member in particular. Annie Ross sat in the middle of the front row throughout the *Lady Sings the Blues* performance, mouthing all the lyrics originally performed in the 1930s, 1940s and 1950s by Annie's very good friend, Billie Holiday, now long dead. It's very hard to imagine what was going through her mind as she listened to that wonderful repertoire performed pretty much as it would have been by Billie. I don't know what she said to Val in the intermission, but she hugged her for what seemed like an age. The emotions on display backstage were so memorable I felt that I was in the middle of one of the greatest jazz movies ever.

Annie's performance was imperious. She was in total control of her band and the audience was mesmerised. Val sat in the middle of the front row, in the seat vacated by Annie, for the entire performance.

It's an enduring regret that the Marbella Jazz Festival ended as it did. Its achievements in only four years were significant and it was being referred to as one of Spain's three most important jazz festivals.

The audiences were certainly there, musicians were delighted to come to Marbella (who wouldn't be?), the venues and hotels were all keen to be involved. It's just that the people we worked with at the Palacio didn't understand what they had and the bosses in the Town Hall appreciated the festival, but left the Council's administration in the wrong hands.

Apart from the administration being inept, they hadn't even bothered to put the basics in place. The Palacio had no credit card. When I asked how they expected to pay for artists' flights, I got the usual communal shrug of the shoulders. So the flights were put on my credit cards and, after the collapse of Marbella council, there was no one around to give me any suggestion of how I could recoup my 12,000 euros.

The balloon finally went up on March 29th, 2006, just a few weeks before the Jazz Festival was set to start when the Police Operacion Malaya swung into action with the arrest of Mayor Marisol Yague along with some 22 city councillors on charges of bribery, embezzlement and corruption. On consideration her arrest should not have been too much of a surprise. Marisol could simply be seen as treading in the footsteps of her immediate predecessors, Jesus Gil y Gil and Julian Munoz, both earlier imprisoned on similar charges.

17. Marbella: Fiesta And Fiasco

The following week the situation took a turn for the worse when Marbella City Council was dissolved. In the ensuing chaos almost everyone I needed to talk to seemed to have run for the hills; for several days none of the Palacio management team could be found with the exception of Carolina, the Press Officer. We somehow got through the Jazz Festival as most of the venues remained on board and, outside of Marbella, things appeared to be normal. In this situation it was no surprise that several companies, including ourselves, took a financial hit.

The result of all this was Spain's biggest corruption trial with 53 convictions and 42 acquittals. Marisol received a six-year sentence, Julian Munoz a two-year sentence as a result of Malaya, but that was on top of the 45 years he was already serving for corruption and real estate offences. The so-called Mr Big, Juan Antonio Roca, was handed an 11-year stretch.

Anyone who thinks that being the subject of Spain's Biggest Corruption Trial was just a flash in the pan for Marbella should remember that in 2005 the city was also home to Europe's Biggest Money Laundering Network.

Amongst the many crimes committed by the Marbella officials and their cronies was one that, in the greater scheme of things, might have been of minor importance, but to me was a cause of great disappointment. That was to squander all the effort that was put in to make Marbella one of Spain's best jazz festivals. Which it undoubtedly was in its short life and, developed properly, would surely have become one of the most important in Europe.

After all the tribulations, would I do it again? Of course! Who would turn away an opportunity to promote jazz in Paradise?

Anyway, the buggers have still got my jazz and blues photography exhibition and I would like it back together with those 12,000 euros.

Chapter 18

THE MIDEM YEARS

Drummer Pete York often quips, 'There's no business in show business' or 'Learn to play an instrument, be a professional musician, you know it makes cents,' which sometimes brings a wry smile, more often a grunted, 'That's too true to be funny.' It wasn't always this way. Some of us remember things called 'record stores' – it's true, ask your dad! Placed prominently on the High Streets throughout the civilised world, they were well-stocked emporiums selling music in its many forms. This may be hard to believe, but the staff were invariably well-informed and passionate about music and – brace yourself – were pleased to see customers and discuss music.

Thanks in the main to the French music business convention, Midem, held annually in Cannes, Big Bear had steadily built up a network of distribution partners throughout Europe as well as Australasia, sometimes South Africa, and occasional individual release partners in South American countries as well as Singapore and the Pacific Rim. I tried to visit the most active of the European distributors every month to discuss upcoming releases and marketing and talk to the Press Office and the sales force. I know it's a far cry from what passes for the music business these days, but it actually worked. We sold records, had releases played on radio and reviewed in newspapers, artists' tours were arranged and there was the occasional television spot.

One of our most active territories was the Benelux countries where we were represented by Johnny Hoes Benelux Music Industries and Telstar Records in Weert in the Netherlands. On one of my visits label manager Bert Salden was very excited about an upcoming domestic Telstar release of his which, he was pleased to tell me, was available for the UK. This meant that we could have the rights, pay an agreed royalty, and release it on Big Bear in the UK. With customary British snobbishness regarding any music not from the UK or USA, I listened to the record before telling him – pompously, I'm sure – that the British record-buying public was far too sophisticated to go for that sort of music.

Not many weeks later I had a yet more excited Bert on the phone telling me that his record had gone into the Top 20 on release in Holland and he already had

18. The Midem Years

lease deals in place for Germany, Spain and France. It was, he insisted, still available to Big Bear for the UK, so I asked him to post me a copy which he did. My reaction was precisely as before. Three weeks later he called with even hotter news. The record was in the Dutch Top Ten, it was Number 3 in Germany and top five in France. He asked for the last time if I wanted the record for Big Bear – no conditions, no advance payment, just a rush release. I explained again, doubtless at great length, that the UK would not buy music as infantile as that.

Not many weeks later the single was like a rash all over the UK charts, with no fewer than three versions of the same song simultaneously in the Top 20.

The song in question was *The Birdie Song*, with the Tweets peaking at Number 2 in October 1981 and Telstar's original version, by the Electronicas, making the charts on its release through Polydor.

Without doubt it would have changed the fortunes of Big Bear Records beyond recognition, but pause and consider the other side of the coin. Imagine we had had that hit on Big Bear. I would not have been able to walk down Hagley Road without people stopping, pointing and saying, 'Look over there! That's Jim Simpson – he's the Birdie Song Man!'

My first Midem was an introduction to a world that I never dreamt existed and one that I find as wondrous to contemplate now as I did when I first discovered it. Of course I had heard about Midem, we all had, but we knew it wasn't for the likes of us. It was for Phonogram, Polydor, EMI, CBS, and the rest, not for small independents, least of all small independents from Birmingham! By 1973 I had produced the first Eddie Burns album, *Bottle Up and Go*, and didn't really feel ready to take the leap and release an album on Big Bear, so I leased it to B&C Records on their Action label. I had followed that with a series of four albums as the Big Bear series on Polydor, introduced somewhat over-colourfully by Mike Leadbitter:

'A lack of Living Blues forced a starving Big Bear out of the Birmingham woods four years ago. The hunting was good – already that lean, hungry look had been replaced by one of well-fed contentment. More good news – he not only had food enough to satisfy himself, but there was plenty left over for his friends. The Big Bear needs Big Blues to survive and so do you. Get yours now.'

Those Polydor releases were *Let the Good Times Roll* by The Mighty Flea with Mickey Baker, *Live at Montreux* by Doctor Ross, *American Blues Legends '73* and *Blues From Mars* by Johnny Mars. The next Big Bear album was the eponymously titled *Homesick James and Snooky Pryor*, recorded in March 1973. The Big Bear four-album deal was complete and here comes Richard Branson offering a lease deal on his Virgin Records subsidiary, Caroline Records, headed by well-respected record biz man Simon Draper – and part of the deal was to fund a Midem visit for me to market the album to record companies worldwide. Although by then I was keen to start releasing albums on the Big Bear label, this was an offer that was too good to turn down.

Branson's company funded my flight and registration. That was the expensive part – all I had to do was find my living costs. Of course I was expected to attend any social events. That was no hardship, but they didn't all pass without incident. Richard in those days was what you might call flamboyant! He seemed to like being surrounded by people having a good time, no bad thing in my book.

For whatever reason, following one of Richard's generously funded dinner parties at a ritzy harbourside restaurant, he put out a call for anyone who would like to go to the casino. At that point I had never been inside a casino and, if I was ever to experience such a thing, I could do a lot worse than a casino in Cannes along with Richard Branson. Surprisingly there were no other takers, so we two set off along the Croisette to the Casino de Cannes.

En route I tried to explain to Richard that this would be my first time in a casino and my first wager, except for one time, laid up with a broken ankle and bored beyond belief, I had ventured into a bookie's on what happened to be Derby Day. I saw that one of the horses was named Psidium which seemed too much of a coincidence to ignore as my favourite comedian at the time was Sid James. I placed my 10 shilling bet convinced that Psidium would win which he duly did at 66-1. Pocketing more than £30, I deemed that would be the beginning and the end of my betting career. So there I was in the cab with Richard who was not in the least impressed by my perfect history playing the horses, only interested in how we were going to break the bank at Cannes Casino.

He cashed £400 into gambling chips and gave me half with strict instructions to follow my instincts – and no pussy-footing around playing on red or black. 'Pick good numbers', he instructed me as he wafted off into the perfumed depths of the casino, leaving me by the roulette table – probably all I could handle, he correctly surmised.

I did little at first other than try to work out if there was any pattern – there wasn't – before opting for 23, my parents' house number, no doubt a sure-fire winner. I think I lost about £10, certainly enough to convince me this was a mug's game, and waited for Richard to return, weighed down by bucketloads of chips. It must have been a couple of hours before he came back, looking disconsolate and telling me we were leaving. I managed to drag out of him that he had lost all of his stake. 'But it wasn't like that all of the time,' he said. 'I was well ahead a couple of times.' Thinking to cheer him, I handed him my almost-intact stake with what I took to be some words of comfort. Richard exploded, asking me why I couldn't understand that this was designated gambling money, part of a twin assault on the bank, not to be carried around in my pocket and meekly handed back. Where, he demanded, was the excitement in that? Still fuming, he jumped into a cab, leaving me to walk back to my hotel. The next morning on the stand he was his normal cheery self, but he obviously found me too boring to invite out on the town again.

Midem was always a very special time for me. It was a reminder of why we got involved in the music business in the first place, an opportunity to play your music to folk who understood, to place your recordings across the world and to discover new bands. Most importantly it was an opportunity to make and sustain friendships and partnerships, some of which would last half a lifetime.

Raymond Gonzalez from Paris, for instance, is a promoter, agent, manager and general man about music who knows pretty much every contact in Europe you might ever need. Raymond helped me with European promoter contacts for King Pleasure and the Biscuit Boys when they were young and wild, but on stage all was forgivable – they were mustard-hot! Way back in 1988 over an early morning coffee in the old town of Cannes, Raymond was nearly exploding with excitement. He had received a telegram confirming that the Dan Aykroyd office had given him the European touring rights to The Blues Brothers Band. Now this was no tribute band, this was the real deal, the proper Blues Brothers Band, minus front men John Belushi and Dan Aykroyd. It was a dream band straight from my favourite movie, with Steve 'The Colonel' Cropper, Al 'Mr. Fabulous' Rubin, Blue Lou Marini, Tom 'Bones' Malone, Leon 'The Lion' Pendarvis, Donald 'Duck' Dunn, Matt 'Guitar' Murphy and Danny Gottlieb. Before Raymond and I had finished our coffee, we had shaken hands on a deal to bring The Blues Brothers Band to feature in that Summer's Birmingham Jazz Festival, playing two shows at the Alexandra Theatre.

Unsurprisingly I booked King Pleasure and the Biscuit Boys to open on what were sell-out shows. That still looks good on King Pleasure's CV, especially as Raymond was so impressed he booked them for other Blues Brothers tour dates. Raymond and I repeated the formula for another two years, The Blues Brothers Band making a total of six appearances in the festival.

I got to know Al Rubin well over the years – what is it with trumpet players? – though I knew him a little before that as a fine New York-based jazz trumpeter, playing sessions with everyone from Cab Calloway to Peggy Lee. Steve Cropper had long been a hero of mine as guitar man with Booker T and the MGs and as Otis Redding's record producer. It was Cropper who completed, whistling and all, the wonderful *Dock of the Bay* after Redding's death in that plane crash.

Don't Worry 'Bout The Bear

Cropper was patience itself, with me pestering him over breakfast and supper with questions on production – he really was a master.

Some five months later I was holidaying in Andalucia with my brother Ron and Val Wiseman and it seemed to rain non-stop. We tried to outrun the weather, leaving Marbella, driving across the mountains to Sevilla, then down the Atlantic coast to Tarifa, but the rain didn't let up. We found what we thought was an appropriate hotel in Algeciras, but changed our minds on learning that parking was 15 minutes walk away and resumed our journey round the coast. Somewhere, in the barren land between Sotogrande and Manilva, we spotted an isolated hotel next to a roadhouse bar and decided to opt for warm beds, a decent meal and possibly a glass or two of wine. We checked in, but, preferring to eat in its noisily convivial atmosphere, scuttled between the raindrops to the roadhouse.

In fact it was a lot noisier than we had bargained for, mainly attributable to a large party of extremely vocal Americans a few tables away, for whom the manager apologised. The food was good, the wine was doing its job and we were feeling better as one of the Americans passed our table en route to the toilet. On his return he caught my eye. 'Jim Simpson!' he shouted. 'Blue Lou Marini!' I responded. The noisy Americans were in fact The Blues Brothers Band who had been staying at the same hotel and were due to play midnight to 2.00 am at an aircraft hangar of a venue on the other side of the motorway before getting straight onto the tour bus to Madrid Airport, a good six hour journey, for a 10.00 am flight to Rome. Some slavedriver, that Raymond Gonzalez! We snatched a little sleep, enjoyed a tremendous performance and did our best to scoff the rider as the band embussed for Madrid.

For much longer than I care to remember Raymond Gonzalez has been one of my favourite people and certainly he was the man to be with in Paris when I had a few days off between tours. Whenever we chat, inevitably I ask him about the terrifying Nina.

Raymond took care of business for Nina Simone for the last 15 or 16 years of her life. During that time she was apparently unable to return to the USA owing to a misunderstanding with the Internal Revenue, in as much as she was reluctant to pay taxes on her earnings. Having re-located in rapid succession to Barbados, Liberia, Switzerland and the Netherlands, she settled near Aix-en-Provence. Raymond tells of bottle upon bottle of pills, the second to counteract the effects of the first, and so on, and his stories of life on the road with Miss Simone are incredible. The most memorable for me was of the time Nina was playing a weeklong engagement at a Rome nightclub. She was getting more fractious by the day and, by the time Saturday came around, she was flying. The story goes that the club manager, concerned that Nina hadn't hit the stage by the appointed time, entered the dressing room, only to find that Nina had Raymond pinned against the wall with a knife at his throat. Raymond tells that the manager, thrown into an immediate panic, yelled at Nina, 'No, not in here, not in here!' to which Raymond countered, through gritted teeth, 'Not in fucking anywhere!'

By the time I got to know Raymond, I had had a couple of encounters with Nina, neither of them totally pleasant. Talking to him, things tended to fall into place, the causes of her bitterness became clearer. As a girl, she aspired to be a classical pianist, but was turned down by the Curtis Institute of Music in Philadelphia despite a well-received audition. A rejection she always attributed, improbably, to racism. Her desire to be a famous classical pianist remained and she now took private lessons. To fund these she played piano in an Atlantic City bar where the owner insisted she must sing as well. She was so successful that she was offered a recording contract by Bethlehem Records. She wasn't interested in a recording contract – she was going to be a classical pianist – but she did agree to make one album, *Little Girl Blue*, recorded in 1957, released in 1958. She insisted on being paid in cash, $3,000, for which she signed away all rights to the music on the album, thereby sowing the seeds of even more resentment in the future. At the time she reasoned that no one in their right mind would buy this sort of music – and $3,000 would help her on her way to becoming a great classical pianist.

That never happened and she soon embarked on a long-standing relationship with Colpix Records, singing and playing 'the Devil's music'. Years passed and some Florida-based company claimed to have bought the rights to that first album. They sold the European rights – at Midem, of course – to Jean-Luc Young and Joop Visser of the UK-based Charly Records. They in turn placed one of the tracks with a London advertising agency to use on an upcoming television commercial for Chanel Number 5. The rest is history. In 1987, over 30 years after it was recorded, *My Baby Just Cares for Me* hit Number 5 in the UK and featured on most European charts, including Number 1 in the Netherlands.

Nina never forgave Bethlehem, the Florida company, Charly Records and pretty much the entire world because she had sold her rights for what in hindsight proved to be pennies, forfeiting over a million dollars in royalties. But she had done it willingly, so there was nothing she could do but complain – which she did, constantly and vociferously. On the other hand the success of *My Baby Just Cares for Me* gave a massive boost to her profile which served her rather more than well for the rest of her days.

While organising the 1991 British Jazz Awards, I was invited to a Midem meeting by Jean-Luc Young and Joop Visser. They wanted to know if I would incorporate the presentation to them of Nina Simone's platinum disc for *My*

Baby Just Cares for Me into that year's Awards ceremony. It took me almost two seconds to decide because, unknown to Jean-Luc and Joop, I was going to try to involve Raymond.

The upshot was that Nina agreed to appear at The British Jazz Awards at Birmingham's Grand Hotel to receive her platinum disc. She was to pay air fares for herself and her female companion from Amsterdam; we were to supply ground transport, dinner, hotel and breakfast. That must have been the deal of the century, but Nina was happy with it.

On the day a smartly-suited Tim Jennings met the duo at the airport and organised a black cab with the ladies comfortably reclining in the back seats while Tim perched on the pull-down – still, it was only 25 minutes to the city. Reportedly Nina was sweetness and charm throughout the journey; Tim was quite taken with her affability. I met the party outside the Grand Hotel, checked them in and invited Nina to take tea with me in the faded elegance of that great Birmingham hotel. Surprised and delighted that Nina was turning out to be a reasonable, even pleasant human being, I was beginning to question the accuracy of her terrifying reputation.

8.00 pm: 300 hundred guests were seated, happily waiting for dinner to be served and being entertained by guests of honour Humphrey Lyttelton and Benny Green, while I was in a third floor corridor of the Grand Hotel, my anxiety increasing every moment that I had no response to my knocking on the door of Miss Nina Simone who was due to make her entrance. By 8.30 I was on my hands and knees shouting under the door, trying to make conversation with Nina and at the same time fielding a series of questions and problems from downstairs: 'Humph wants to know how much longer you want him to waffle on,' 'Would Miss Simone like to be introduced to the Lord Mayor?' and, most worryingly, 'Chef says he can't hold dinner back any longer and he is going to start serving in five minutes.'

Shortly before 9.00 pm Nina came out of her room, seemingly calm and relaxed, which I most certainly was not, wished me a good evening and asked me to lead the way. As she entered, the room erupted in sustained applause. She made her way to her table, nodding occasionally, saying nothing and going nowhere near cracking a smile. As she sat, the applause subsided, very slowly, but the atmosphere remained electric. The chef came to her table, saying he would be happy to prepare whatever she wished. Nina went for soup and a sandwich; at least her companion opted for the three-course.

The awards presentations were greeted with the enthusiasm one would expect, other than by Miss Simone who didn't appear to notice, or to care about, what was going on. And so we came to the big one, Benny Green announcing the

18. The Midem Years

presentation of a platinum disc to Nina Simone. Again the room erupted and this time it seemed that the applause never would subside. When eventually it did, it seemed that Nina was asleep. She wasn't; she was just working hard to display her indifference to the room. Benny cajoled in the kindest of ways, the audience repeatedly raised cheers and eventually Nina Simone took centre stage in the Grosvenor Suite of the Grand Hotel and delivered her speech of thanks which I remember, word for word, with total clarity.

She had flown in from Amsterdam at her own expense, clearly enjoyed very little of what went on around her and didn't even give herself the satisfaction of delivering her usual rant, bad-mouthing 'those thieving record companies'. All she could bring herself to say to the 300 people who were overjoyed to spend the evening with her, was:

'Thank you very much.'

No smile, no indication that she even meant what she said.

This was the second occasion when I had been exposed to Nina's very personal approach to public relations. My first encounter with her was backstage at Birmingham Town Hall in 1967 when she was on tour with comedian Dick

Nina Simone barely concealing her hostility towards the cameraman (JS).

Gregory. My dear friend, Max Jones, asked me to take photographs of Nina for *Melody Maker* where he was in charge of the substantial jazz content. The tour manager cleared it with Nina. After I waited for a while, when I entered her dressing room, I was greeted with open hostility. She didn't say much, but her body language screamed, 'Get out of my dressing room!'. The photographs were fine; she just glared at me throughout which actually helped to bring out her personality. When she had had enough, she just went and sat in a corner with her back turned to me.

While they don't have quite as colourful a back-story as Raymond, I am always delighted to hear from my Midem friends; Holger Petersen, for example, the owner of the award-winning Canadian label Stony Plain Records, a real music man. Early on we agreed never to do business together as we valued our friendship too much to put it at risk over a deal that might go wrong. Nevertheless we have exchanged music for many years and we always pass on any interesting business leads and support each other in every way we can. At Midem ours was always the first meeting in our diaries and he was always a pleasure to be with, a top man whose impressive Stony Plain catalogue includes such names as Maria Muldaur, Asleep at the Wheel, Jay McShann and Jimmy Witherspoon.

Your Midem identity badge is important and should be worn with pride. It bears your photograph, name, company name and area of business, but at one of the first Midems I attended, someone used his badge to indicate the depth of his arrogance. His badge carried his photograph and the statement, 'If you don't recognise this face, then you should not be in the music business.'

That was Jonathan King.

MIDEM is a French acronym for Marché International du Disque et de l'Edition Musicale, International Market for Recording and Music Publishing. It has been held in Cannes since 1967 and is our business' equivalent to the Cannes Film Festival. Traditionally it was held over a week every January, then reduced to four days and in 2014 it switched to June 'in order to give delegates a better experience of Cannes.' If that meant that delegates might be attracted by the city's beauties, beaches and summer sun, then that's fine as far as it goes, but many of the real music folk gave up attending as sunshine and sand are categorically not what brought us to Cannes. To have representatives of the music business and media of pretty much every country on earth in one building, all there to share their music and do business, was an opportunity only a little short of Heaven-sent.

Our small independent record company, Big Bear Records, still has distribution and label representation in Holland, Belgium, Luxembourg, Germany, Austria, Switzerland, Sweden, France and China as well as online where we did our deals face to face at Midem with iTunes, YouTube and our aggregator, San Francisco-based

18. The Midem Years

Sarah Yang at Midem.

INgrooves. Where INgrooves were concerned, there was a waiting list to meet MD Alex Branson, but he happened to be staying at the same hotel as us, so at breakfast we talked trumpets – again, he was a trumpet player! – for an hour and did the on-line aggregator deal in about ten minutes. The current Big Bear Records UK distributor deal with the excellent RSK Records was also done at Midem – and why not? The alternative was to schlep around the Home Counties meeting as many distributors as possible. At Midem, on Day 1, I met separately with four UK distributors, made the pitch, met two of them informally for a second time over coffee and opted for RSK who agreed the deal which we both signed the following day.

Midem was the perfect way for me to do business; there's no way we could have set up our existing distribution network without it. However, June is an impossible time for me to get out of Birmingham, with last-minute preparations for a July Jazz Festival. So 2013 had to be the last of a total of 31 Midems for me. For our last nine, particularly successful years I was partnered by Sarah Yang and we had honed our approach to near-perfection by the time they moved the dates. We still believe that, if we had been able to attend, we wouldn't have lost our deals in Scandinavia, Spain, Poland, USA and Italy when they expired.

Midem always came up with unexpected spin-offs. A chance meeting in a Cannes supermarket with Rimante Sodeikiene of Music Export Lithuania led to six consecutive years of support from the Republic of Lithuania to enable bands from that country to play at the Birmingham Jazz Festival. Our favourite eating place was La Farigoule on the Rue de Meynadier in the old town, managed by a not-so-crazy, but totally wacky, Moroccan called Lily. She would virtually hoist Midem-badged passers-by into her tiny restaurant where, as a matter of course, you were seated at long tables in close proximity to total strangers with whom you were about to rapidly become better acquainted. One time we sat next to a woman who worked for Polish Radio which quickly aroused my interest only to have it fade when it became clear that her schtick was classical music whereas ours was jazz. Then she told us that her brother worked for a jazz label in Warsaw. Contact was made and that was the start of our association with Magic Records.

We also got into conversation in La Farigoule with representatives of an Argentinian television company, Fansworld TV, who were planning to film music videos over 20 days in Europe later that year. They had allocated one day to London and asked me to advise them as to where they should film on a second day in the UK. Naturally I got on my soapbox with my 'Birmingham is the UK Capital of Rock and Roll' spiel. It must have worked. I had a phone call that summer from the company, telling me they were going to produce six six-minute films about music in Birmingham – and would I like to suggest topics and introduce them? They are still available on Fansworld TV, Argentina.

Restaurants play a significant role in the Midem culture, especially where the older hands are concerned. Many Midem rookies, when day is done at the Palais des Festivals, think that they are off the leash and entitled to live it up in Cannes' undeniably exciting night life. The more experienced Midemista won't eat anywhere that doesn't have a significant number of diners with Midem badges. We got lucky one year and were able to go a step further than the average bear.

The most picturesque street in Cannes is the Rue du Suquet in the heart of the old town. The top of this steep, but fascinating, climb is home to the finest pizza we had ever eaten. Bear in mind that Cannes was at one time part of Northern Italy and naturally memorable pizza places abound, but the Don Camillo is a step ahead of the rest. The first time we ate there, we talked music with the owner and left him with a couple of CDs. The following day in the Palais Christoph Jess, Head of Product Management at H'Art Records, Big Bear's distributor in Germany, Austria and Switzerland, was clearly impressed that the previous evening he had been eating in a pizzeria where they played Big Bear CDs.

18. The Midem Years

That got me thinking. We ate at Don Camillo every night for the rest of that Midem, really got to know the owner and agreed a plan for the next year's Midem. We would go into Don Camillo the day before Midem with our new CDs, posters and booklets about our product. They would put posters in the windows, play our CDs and display our publicity while we carried the line, 'The Bear Eats at Don Camillo' on our business cards and Midem print, and stickered on our CDs. I can't say we ever knowingly landed a deal as a result of this, but it gave Big Bear a good profile and elicited a lot of comment and Don Camillo became a place to go for jazz- and blues-inclined Midemistas. Stony Plain boss Holger Peterson once hosted a dinner there for eight of his overseas distributors. We did this for three years until Don Camillo decided to close in January owing to lack of trade in the rest of the month.

There is so much that I miss now that Big Bear no longer attends Midem, not least the sense of worth you get from doing a good job properly. Sarah and I would fill my meeting diary and half of hers, starting two or three months in advance, always ensuring that the other person knew exactly why we wanted to meet them. Sarah would ensure that they heard our music in advance – if they were not going to like it, better find out early and cancel the meeting than waste valuable Midem time. We found our ideal hotel, arrived a day early and spent that day scouring the Midem Guide for other people we would like to meet and writing notes to them. As the doors to the Palais opened on the first day, we would place the notes in the appropriate pigeon holes. Sarah would follow up, filling up her diary with new meetings while I started to wade through my meetings.

Faced with diminishing attendance figures, unprepared to accept that this was simply a reflection of the worldwide music business, the organisers of Midem failed to realise that getting over 8,000 delegates in one building, ready and willing to do business over four days, was something of a triumph. Instead of rationalising the event to reflect the new reality, they followed the line of letting delegates 'enjoy Cannes when it is open.'

But it's the business of music that does it every time. That's why Midem was so wonderful and why the clientele has changed and numbers are steadily decreasing. It really isn't rocket science. Beaches, sea cruises and niteries are the stuff of summer vacations. The small matter of survival in the music business is now tougher and riskier than ever before. It's such a pity that Midem, once one of the business' most important, valuable and inspiring pillars, just didn't get it.

Chapter 19

JAGGER, THE KILLER AND THE PRETTIEST MAN IN ROCK AND ROLL

In the 1960s journalist Dennis Detheridge set up *Midland Beat*, a monthly newspaper inspired by Bill Harry's *Mersey Beat* which had launched on a tide of Beatlemania. The area Dennis defined as the Midlands somewhat exceeded the definition most folk would recognise, stretching from East Anglia to Gloucester and from Oxford to Sheffield. In truth the editorial coverage of groups in the area was impressive. A *Midland Beat* survey registered no fewer than 5,500 groups: to qualify for registration a group had to have its own PA and van and a band uniform. No mention of haircuts.

I provided the photographs and was grandiosely titled Photographic Editor at a salary of £12 a month, to include all expenses. The real perk of the job was getting press tickets for almost any club or concert I wanted – Dennis Detheridge was certainly well connected. He also allowed me to contribute a jazz and blues column and review gigs, so it worked well for me.

It was a period when Birmingham was well blessed with musical talent, some of it breaking through nationally and internationally. An early success was *Tell Me When* by Solihull's The Applejacks, all a bit cutesy, but nevertheless a big seller for Polydor who instantly set up a Birmingham office under the guidance of Arthur Smith, manager of The Applejacks. Arthur was kind enough to provide an office for me in exchange for the odd photo session and I got particularly lucky when Polydor asked him to arrange a cine photographer to publicise one of their emerging acts. The only person Arthur knew who was even vaguely in that field was me. He might have considered it something of a drawback that I had never used a cine camera in my life, but he didn't let it show.

I borrowed the College of Technology 16mm Bolex and set off to rendezvous in London's Highgate Cemetery to film The Slender Plenty whose debut single,

19. Jagger, The Killer And The Prettiest Man In Rock And Roll

Silver Tree Top School for Boys, had been written by David Bowie. In truth the film wasn't a poor piece of work. I kept it simple and filched a couple of ideas from a then-current Beatles film and, when it was synchronised with the recording, I think it did the job. Arthur told me later that Bowie had been present, but how was I to know? I'd not heard of him at the time. I always wonder if a copy of that film has survived, but I would probably cringe if I were to see it now.

Back in Brum things were hotting up. Having apparently exhausted the potential for undiscovered talent in Liverpool, EMI A&R man, Norrie Paramor, turned his attention to Birmingham, as did, at more or less the same time, Decca Records, Dial Records and no doubt several other companies. Two separate albums, both entitled *Brum Beat*, were released almost simultaneously, some good bands and many not so good waited in line outside London recording studios and I got lucky when every man and his dog seemed to need photographs of Birmingham bands.

In the real world proper talent was emerging. The Moody Blues, an early Birmingham supergroup featuring Denny Laine of The Diplomats alongside former members of The Krew Kats, had a huge hit with their version of Bessie Banks' *Go Now* and overnight became a name band. Things hadn't always gone smoothly for them. When they first formed, they signed management with Phil Myatt, one of the owners of the popular Carlton Club, later to be re-named Mothers, in Edgbaston. Phil, always on the lookout for a quick buck, thought he had a sponsorship deal in place with Mitchells and Butlers brewery. So confident was he that he clothed the band in (admittedly smart) hound's tooth suits with MB embroidered on the pockets, had the same letters painted on the outer skin of the bass drum, sat back and waited for the brewery's sponsorship – which somehow failed to materialise!

In desperation Phil sought to find a strong name for what was clearly an important group, a name that utilised the letters MB, which was how The Moody Blues, one of the finest groups to emerge from the city, came to be named.

Hot on the heels of the Moodies came a band built around a folk-singing guitarist from South Wales who was at the University of Birmingham studying German. Spencer Davis, whose repertoire included blues-ish material from Leadbelly and the like, had a Monday residency at the Golden Eagle in Hill Street. Promoter David Postle thought he needed to beef up Spencer's act, brought in the Winwood brothers, bass player Muff and 15-year-old pianist-singer Steve from Muff's mainstream jazz band, nicked Pete York from my band, Locomotive, and the rest is history. Pete actually jumped ship after a couple of weeks, saying he couldn't stand having to play what he considered to be pop

An early publicity photograph of The Spencer Davis Group: Muff Winwood, Spencer, Pete York and Steve Winwood at the wheel of my 1954 MG TF.

music, rejoined Locomotive, but only lasted a few days, the thought of a regular pay cheque irresistible, as it would be to most of us. The group was originally called The Rhythm and Blues Quartette and Muff told me that, at the band meeting to decide on a better name, he had suggested The Spencer Davis Group as Spence was the oldest and, anyway, the name sounded good. Privately he confided in Steve and Pete, saying, 'If we use Spence's name, we can lie in bed in the mornings while Spence has to get up and do the press interviews.' Whatever, despite their short career, from 1963 to 1968, I believe The Spencer Davis Group

19. Jagger, The Killer And The Prettiest Man In Rock And Roll

to be the finest band to come out of Birmingham, with hits like *Keep on Running*, *I'm a Man*, *Gimme Some Lovin'* and *Somebody Help Me*. The Blues Brothers recorded a fine version of *Gimme Some Lovin'* which featured in that best of all movies. After that hit bands from Birmingham came thick and fast.

Somehow *Melody Maker* came across my photographs in *Midland Beat*, leading to the legendary journalist and former editor of *Melody Maker*, Max Jones, giving me a call. I was pretty much overwhelmed. Max was a personal hero and Louis Armstrong's biographer for Heaven's sake! Max later told me a nice tale about being on the road with Satch, preparing for the biography. Louis was always a little tentative with a white man he didn't know well and for the first few days kept a little distance between them. Max said he knew the moment when Satch accepted him. There was a rustle outside Max's hotel room door, then a joint appeared, pushed under the door.

Max asked if I would like to cover *Melody Maker's* work in the Midlands. There was no direct pay as such, but I would take on their assignments, they would file the photographs and pay me the princely sum of £3.50 each time one was used. The upside was that I got to retain the copyright. Not a life-changing arrangement by any means, but I was delighted and jumped at the chance, though I was a touch disconcerted when Max put the phone down while he was in mid-sentence.

Over the following years I got to know Max and his wife Betty, whom he called Betsy, very well and soon became accustomed to his strange habit of putting down the phone whenever he decided that a conversation had reached the end of its usefulness, regardless of who was speaking at the time. It was one of his many idiosyncrasies that I found charming and came to anticipate with pleasure. This reached its climax when Val and I went to stay for a few days with them in their home at Elmer Sands. The English Channel was just over a bank at the bottom of their garden, with the spray of the waves invariably coming over the bank. As we arrived, the road was teeming with the Coastal Defence team as the sea had risen alarmingly. They were going round knocking on doors and distributing sand bags. Max said he was just going to move the car, explaining that, in a previous flood, he had left it in the garage. When the waters rushed through, they had lifted up the car, bumped it against the garage walls before returning it to solid ground, scratched and a little battered. Max had evolved a policy of leaving both the front and back doors of the garage open so that the sea could rush through unimpaired, while the car was parked at the front, out of harm's way.

This seemed eminently sensible to me, so we all sat down at an upstairs window, whisky in hand, watching the sea put on a show for our entertainment. It wasn't until the next day, when Max offered to show me his archive, an irreplaceable collection of photographs and letters from the likes of Leonard Feather – even Billie Holiday! – that I found it was housed in the very same garage through which the water had surged. 'Don't worry,' said Max, 'the sea never comes up that high.'

As we left, Max and Betty came out front to see us off, then, mid-farewell, he just went back inside, still talking. He had obviously decided that there was nothing more to say and departed the scene. I still chuckle over that.

When Big Bear was getting more heavily involved with American bluesmen, Max was supportive way beyond the call of duty. He would always place features and interviews prominently in *Melody Maker* and increasingly asked me to write items. As part of the American Blues Legends '73 tour, the guys played an early show in Zurich before dashing across town to catch the direct train to Hamburg where we were to deliver three performances in three days. Meanwhile the road crew drove to Hamburg with our equipment, not under any time pressure, as the venue was providing equipment, so we would not need our gear until the next stage of the tour. We left Zurich at midnight, arriving at 6.00 pm the next day, ready to hit at 8.00 pm. Max had asked me to keep a diary of that epic rail journey with Lightnin' Slim, Whispering Smith, Homesick James, Snooky Pryor, Boogie Woogie Red and Washboard Willie which he published as a full-page feature in *MM*. To say I was delighted is to put it mildly. I hardly had to write a word, these great blues players said it all and I just wrote it down before putting it in some sort of order and phoning it in to the features desk.

I still miss Max. He was the archetypal hard-bitten journalist, cynical, tough as steel – think Damon Runyon – but he taught me such a lot. I'll never forget his phone calls. 'Bear,' he'd say, 'Max,' and he'd launch without ado into whatever he had in mind. Through him I got to meet, photograph and sometimes interview Muddy Waters, Howlin' Wolf, Chuck Berry, Otis Spann, Jerry Lee Lewis and many more. The first time I interviewed and photographed Little Richard, I apologised for taking so many photographs and so much of his time. 'Don't you mind, boy,' he said. 'Just go ahead, I'm the prettiest man in rock'n'roll.'

Much as I enjoyed photographing Richard, I can't say that any of my several encounters with Chuck Berry were remotely the same. I spent probably 30 minutes in his dressing room at the Hippodrome without him once looking in my direction, let alone looking at the camera. When I submitted the photographs to the *Melody Maker*, Max wanted to know why they were all of Chuck's profile, none full-face.

One another occasion, this time at a smaller venue, Barbarella's, a Birmingham night club that presented some very interesting bands, he was in similar mode before the show. Contracted to play one set of 75 minutes, he delivered his usual

Little Richard, self-styled Prettiest Man in Rock and Roll.

brilliant show-stopping performance, but inexplicably left the stage after 30 minutes, went out and sat in his car, ignoring all pleas to go back and finish the performance. The crowd was going wild, naturally enough. The management, worrying that things might get out of hand, asked me to go out and reason with him as we had enjoyed (no, not the right word!) a previous acquaintance. This time he did speak to me, 'Gimme 500 pounds cash now or I'm out of here.'

Don't Worry 'Bout The Bear

I passed on the message, the management paid him the £500, though they had already paid the agreed fee in full, and Chuck came on and did what he did best, put on yet another of his amazing, almost unequalled performances.

One of the nicest, sweetest and most co-operative people I ever photographed was supposed 1960s posh girl gone bad, Marianne Faithfull. The job went

Chuck Berry, one of the three most influential men in Rock and Roll. The others? Little Richard and Jerry Lee Lewis, of course.

19. Jagger, The Killer And The Prettiest Man In Rock And Roll

without incident, but some 30 or so years later I booked her into Ronnie Scott's for a week. Thinking it might get things off to a nice start, I printed enlargements of my favourite three 1960s images of her, had them framed and presented them to her on opening night. She accepted them graciously, examined them carefully and announced, 'I think your photographs are lovely, but your delivery's terrible!'

During the 1960s we were blessed by the American Folk Blues Festival tours organised by Horst Lippman and Fritz Rau out of Frankfurt. Every year the tour would appear before a capacity audience at Birmingham Town Hall, presenting a wondrous collection of some of the best blues artists around, including Muddy Waters, Howlin' Wolf, Sister Rosetta Tharpe, Otis Spann, Lightnin' Hopkins, Sugar Pie DeSanto and many more. We were the rock and roll generation, but Lippman and Rau opened the door to the real roots of that, and many other music forms. To this day I find it hard to believe that I actually got to meet, spend time with, photograph and listen to these giants of the blues, not knowing what an important part that music would play in the rest of my life. I kept in touch with some of them, including Muddy, Sonny Terry and Brownie McGhee, Buddy Guy and Cousin Joe.

As I write this, we have a touring exhibition of some of my dodgy 1960s black and whites entitled *Jagger, The Killer and the Prettiest Man in Rock and Roll*. The

Muddy Waters with JS.

Don't Worry 'Bout The Bear

Hitmaker with Hi Heel Sneakers, Tommy Tucker later recorded for Big Bear Records.

question I am asked most frequently is, 'How did you get so close to those artists?' The answer is simple. Even with the biggest names in the business – Little Richard, Chuck, Jerry Lee, Count Basie, Mick Jagger, Muddy Waters et al. – there was an almost total lack of formality. They – or, at least, most of them – appreciated the subsequent press coverage, were often interested enough to want to chat and considered it as just another part of being on the road. Security was minimal and pretty much unnecessary.

As I became involved in managing, and later recording, bands, photography took a back seat. The only times that my trusty Mamiya C3 got dusted off was when we needed publicity shots for our own bands – after all, I was the least expensive photographer I knew of.

19. Jagger, The Killer And The Prettiest Man In Rock And Roll

There came a point when I decided that we had to produce our own publication. Frustrated at the continuing lack of London-based media interest in the stable of Big Bear artists and believing that they all – Tea & Symphony, Bakerloo, Locomotive and Black Sabbath – deserved to be heard, I re-entered the world of journalism.

So in January 1969 the first edition of *Big Bear* hit the streets with a print run of 20,000 copies. The first edition's front page headlines blared, 'SEX CHANGE SNAKE IN DRUG PROBE SCANDAL', subtitled 'REPTILE RAPE ON RUNWAY'. The story had nothing to do with the headline, simply telling the readers about our four fine bands. I had taken advice from veteran Brum jazz journalist Fred Norris, asking him what headline in his experience would be most attention-grabbing. The paper contained a nicely-written reflection on Black Sabbath written by my long-time chum, Pete York of The Spencer Davis Group. He drew attention to their upcoming appearance on John Peel's *Top Gear* programme and publicised the release of their first single, *Evil Woman*, which in fact sank without trace. The choice of song probably had something to do with Tony Hall's lack of belief in the band's own original material, insisting on covering a recording by a little-known group from Minneapolis.

Big Bear was a free sheet, looked and smelled like a real newspaper, and was incurably irreverent. Folk seemed to like it, so much so that all copies of issue 1 were snapped up. Thus encouraged, issue 2 saw an increase in pagination to an impressive (to us) six-page publication. One-man blues band Duster Bennett contributed a blues column; Bobby Lamm and Terry Kath of Chicago Transit Authority, later shortened simply to Chicago, fellow blues fans, provided a lengthy interview; Terry reviewed the new Locomotive album and Willie Dixon and Howlin' Wolf each wrote a column – so you can see where we were coming from. There was also an advertisement for the upcoming programme at Henry's Blueshouse, including Duster Bennett supported by Black Sabbath. Ticket price? Four shillings and sixpence, that's nearly 25 pence in today's money.

Big Bear 3 expanded yet again, up to eight pages. By now we were taking advertising, the publication was in demand and had become financially viable, much to the surprise of one and all – it wasn't intended to be that way. Producer of the *Black Sabbath* album, Rodger Bain, wrote a perceptive piece on that recording, Chicago's latest LP was previewed, Film and Music Editor of *I.T.* Mark Williams (later of *Time Out* and *Rolling Stone*) had been so tickled by our previous efforts that he donated a fascinating feature defining exactly what 'underground' music was. At least, in his opinion! Another blues buddy, Bob Hite of Canned Heat, wrote a full-page feature and we continued to get a sizeable mail bag in response to our scurrilous gossip column, *Stoned Gnome*.

Inside we placed a message from Black Sabbath, reproducing a review in *Disc and Music Echo* magazine that read, 'Philips Records have only missed out on one gimmick as far as this Black Magic Music for the Sick Masses offering is concerned. Surely it should have been advertised with the following slogan: "Children under sixteen will not be permitted to buy this album. We strongly advise those of a nervous disposition NOT, repeat NOT, to listen alone." My advice would be not to listen at all if you like your albums to contain something new and fresh musically. To me all this stuff has been done a million times before.' *Melody Maker* wrote, 'There's a diabolically pretentious poem inside the cover and the music made by this trio is the sort that you've heard a million times before. Sadly unoriginal. (* – one star).' We reproduced the *Sounds* magazine Underground chart for that week, with the album placed at Number 3, with the message: '…but you obviously thought otherwise. Thanks! Ozzy, Geezer, Tony and Bill.'

This was the beginning of our fight-back in what Warner Brothers, on their recent Sabbath re-release, referred to as the Ten Years War between Sabs and the popular music media.

The response to our first three issues made it clear that, unwittingly, we were doing something right. That realisation, coupled with the fact that Big Bear's bands were not the only ones in town, demanded a re-think. As a result what would have been *Big Bear* Number 4 saw the light of day as *Brum Beat* Number 1, a broadsheet publication that demanded attention for the great music coming out of this city.

Brum Beat filled a niche, welcomed without hesitation by the region's music industry: record stores, recording studios, music instrument retailers and manufacturers, promoters and venues willingly gave support by placing advertising, there was a clear demand from fans and, most importantly, bands and musicians got involved from issue 1.

It wasn't long before the paper became more widely known, with a number of London-based music industry figures subscribing. When UB40 emerged in 1979, signed to David Virr's tiny Dudley-based Graduate Records, it was obvious to all who heard them that this band was special, in attitude as well as music. For several issues UB40 dominated the front page of *Brum Beat* as we went on a crusade to support yet another fine Birmingham band. Their first album, *Signing Off*, produced by former Locomotive drummer Bob Lamb in his bedsit even before he founded Highbury Studios, started UB40 on their path to world domination. Within minutes, so it seemed, no fewer than five A&R men from major recording companies were on the phone, each with the same crass question, 'Are there any unsigned Birmingham bands that sound like UB40?'

19. Jagger, The Killer And The Prettiest Man In Rock And Roll

Brum Beat became an integral part of the region's music business. We organised the annual Pernod Hottest Band in Town talent contest which operated on a knock-out basis with two bands going head-to-head in matches at different venues on different nights and the winners progressing to the next round – the whole competition lasted almost as long as the football World Cup!

We also produced a double album, *Brum Beat: Live at the Barrel Organ*, which was, I believe, unique in selling advertising across the double gatefold sleeve which was designed as a facsimile of the *Brum Beat* newspaper. The recordings were made over a ten-day period in June 1980. We recorded every night and lunchtimes at weekends and selected the best 12 bands out of 16 involved. From these three subsequently tasted national success. Carol Decker and the Lazers became T'Pau, The Quads hit with the single *There Must be Thousands* on Big Bear and the Playthings' Rick Jones and Maggie Edmond (later known as Maggie De Monde) had hits later in the 1980s with two separate groups, Swan's Way and Scarlet Fantastic. We rented the caravan that was the Buzz Mobile recording unit and put it on the Barrel Organ car park where it virtually became my home for ten days. I would record every evening, go home to sleep and come back the next morning to mix the previous day's recording, have breakfast, lunch and dinner at the pub and then start again. It really became a way of life for those few idyllic days.

By the mid-1980s *Brum Beat* was prospering, so much so that we were able to employ an editor, Steve Morris, but I was getting bored with most of what passed for popular music at the time. Fortunately Steve retained his enthusiasm, so I sold him *Brum Beat* for the princely sum of £1,000, retaining the copyright on all publications up to that point. *Brum Beat* still exists as an online publication, approaching its 50-year landmark at the time of writing.

Apart from music magazines I have always enjoyed writing about local affairs, so, when Big Bear last re-located its office, some 30 years ago, and moved all of 40 yards to a position adjacent to the Ivy Bush pub, naturally we decided to produce a four-pager called the *Ivy Bush Telegraph.* This printed 1,000 copies each month, paid for by exceedingly local advertising, and covered topics of national interest such as a new restaurant opening on the Hagley Road.

For the last four years I've been able to write about local affairs without the responsibility of editorship. The editor of the local free newspaper *HEM Life* kindly indulges me by giving me a column with no editorial restrictions whatever. I have fun writing features on such topics as the Scottish Communist Bob Cooney, a hero of the Spanish Civil War and a celebrated folk singer who moved to Birmingham to meet up with his old pal David Campbell whose grand-children filled the ranks of UB40 – I write about them, too, and Andy de Comyn who recently sculpted a

Not the Entire Sioux Nation, but the twelve fine Birmingham bands that graced the Big Bear double album, Live at the Barrel Organ.

statue of local man Frank Foley, a spy for MI5, who was responsible for the rescue of more Jewish children from the Holocaust than Oskar Schindler.

Big Bear's next foray into the world of newsprint came in 1987 and was inspired by the company's re-entry into the world of jazz. *Jazz Rag* began as a small-scale black and white publication relating mainly to Big Bear's activities, but soon enlarged and broadened its scope and, 30-plus years later, is a glossy, full colour, nationally distributed bimonthly magazine.

Sold by subscription and through jazz venues, festivals and retailers nationwide, *Jazz Rag* stands alongside *Jazz Journal*, *Just Jazz* and *Jazzwise* in keeping the jazz audience informed and (possibly) entertained. My brother Ron now writes much of the editorial and we have a valued team of reviewers, several of whom have been with us from the outset. In recent years we have been lucky enough to carry regular features from one of the United States' most esteemed jazz writers, Scott Yanow. Many of the UK's top jazz musicians, such as Digby Fairweather, Alan Barnes, Val Wiseman and Simon Spillett, are frequent contributors. For some time

we carried the feature, *The View from the Back of the Basie Bus*, written by the long-term Count Basie trombonist, Bill Hughes, later leader of the Basie band. An extraordinary man and a good friend, Bill retired from the band in 2010 and died in 2018, but the Basie Band lives on, now fronted by trumpet man Scotty Barnhart. Former Basie alto saxophone player Preston Love also contributed a regular column to *Jazz Rag* based on his monthly feature in *The Omaha Star*.

At a time when my 1960s photographs are getting much more attention than ever before, I'm still photographing seriously, but infrequently. I have reluctantly abandoned my Mamiyaflex C3 film camera in favour of a Canon digital single lens reflex. I did this under unreasonable pressure from my photographer son who sweetened the deal immensely by giving me a splendid lens, the value of a small car, that he had discarded in an upgrade.

Merlin Daleman, my son, was born in 1977 in what at that time was a serious relationship with Marja Daleman, a music teacher from South Holland. As a child Merlin seemed to enjoy everything that he did, especially photography, and he had his first photograph printed in a nationally distributed music paper when he was only 12. It was extremely disappointing when Marja decided to move back to Holland with Merlin.

Throughout his childhood Marja was totally co-operative about Merlin staying with me in England during holidays and me visiting them whenever I was able. This led to me getting involved in an unexpected business venture. I was driving to Tilburg in the South of Holland every four weeks and the loss of working days in the UK, coupled with the travel costs, was beginning to affect my finances. I had long been a fan of Belgian beers, particularly those brewed by Trappist monks, so the solution presented itself. I sold my Jensen Healey two-seater sports car and replaced it with a six-seater Peugeot estate which neatly converted to a van capable of carrying some 35 cases of beer.

I registered the company name 'Belgian Frank' and set about meeting the brewers of my favourite beers. My first arrangement was with Liefmans of Oudenaarde who produced only two beers: a brown beer and the same beer laid down for three months with raspberries which macerated and turned to alcohol. Both came in unlabelled champagne-style bottles complete with cork and metal clasp. They were provisie beers which meant that they could be stored and would improve for at least 14 years. The brewery was over 300 years old and still obtained its water from the original well.

The Westmalle Trappist was my favourite Trappist beer, brewed by monks who, although trading with the outside world, still had to abide by the rules of their order. I discovered this when I was running late for a pick-up at another Trappist brewery, De Schaapskooi (now De Koningshoeven), near Tilburg. I asked Marja to ring up and explain that I was delayed. For some reason she couldn't make contact. When I arrived and duly apologised, they asked if a woman had been calling on my behalf. That explained all. They were fully computerised, used modern machinery in their brewery and adjacent farm, but were still not allowed to speak to a woman.

I contacted a number of specialist beer shop customers in the UK, taking the Dover-Calais ferry and dropping off in London, Northampton, Solihull and then Birmingham, arriving home with almost no stock and a carload of empties. It was hard work, but at least it enabled me to spend time with Merlin regularly.

Now Merlin makes the Birmingham Festival a regular port of call in an international schedule that has taken him on major photojournalistic projects to such diverse places as Cuba, Ukraine and Kentucky, plus an ongoing series of photographs highlighting the effects of Brexit in the UK for his Dutch daily newspaper, *NRC*. Photographing jazz musicians and events is no doubt a welcome break from the gritty realism of many of his assignments and his stunning images of the Birmingham Jazz Festival reach a wider public through annual exhibitions at New Street Station and the *Jazz Rag* magazine which enjoys a constant supply of high-quality photographs.

Chapter 20

IN THE CONFIDENT HOPE OF A MIRACLE

So what about the next 50 years?

Right now Big Bear is simply doing what Big Bear always has done. Stumbling across talented singers and musicians and finding ourselves unable to resist involvement, continuing to develop our ongoing recording, artist management and festival activities and generally proceeding in the confident hope of a miracle. Alongside the redoubtable King Pleasure and the Biscuit Boys and *Lady Sings the Blues*, wherein, by some miracle, Val Wiseman is actually singing better than ever, we are involved with Tipitina, The Whiskey Brothers and the, as yet, non-existent Wang Dang Doodle.

Tipitina are spiritually direct from New Orleans, though their postcode would indicate Leyland in Lancashire as their home. Debbie Jones, now Randall, is a singer and musician of such startling ability that it's near inexplicable that her

The extraordinary Debbie Jones of Tipitina.

A true New Orleans piano professor, Justin Randall.

name is not on the lips of every fan of the blues, gospel and barrelhouse of New Orleans. Pianist Justin Randall is, I contend, the finest exponent of New Orleans piano on this planet. Think Professor Longhair, James Booker, Henry Butler, Fats Domino, Dr. John and you are on the right track.

The title of their first Big Bear album is a bit of a giveaway, *I Wish I Was in New Orleans.* Justin takes it a step further with 11 short interludes in tribute to the great New Orleans piano players, from Three Finger Mamie Desdunes to Jelly Roll Morton, and way beyond.

Their second album, *Taking Care of Business*, is a far more sophisticated affair recorded live at Birmingham's Hotel du Vin. Listen to Debbie's take on Randy Newman's *Louisiana 1927* to get some idea of what they deliver. We had a bit of a surprise when it came to the final song. Justin wanted something calm and reflective to finish off the often wildly rocking album, and he came up with *Sweet Louisiana*, a piano instrumental that filled the bill, but nobody knew its provenance. We assumed that some old-time Louisiana piano professor had penned it around the dawn of the 20th century, so Justin went ahead and did a capital job on it. Later, when checking copyrights for the album's release, we were a little surprised to find that it had been written by one Albert Ketelbey who had lived in Newtown, Birmingham, little more than a mile from where we recorded his song. It made, of course, the perfect end to the album. The third album is in discussion as I write.

The Whiskey Brothers are another combo whose sound belies their origins. They're from the Kings Heath suburb of Birmingham, but the music they deliver comes at you straight out of 1930s Mississippi juke joints. Richard Heath has the best blues voice I've heard in an age and his mandolin playing is ideal for their take on early blues. The seemingly understated piano playing of Gerry Smith perfectly fits what Richard gets up to – and he is also a formidable exponent of the piano accordion. As I write, we are deep into the planning of their second album. The first, *Bottle Up and Go*, was recorded at what now seems to be our spiritual home, Gospel Oak Studios. Situated on an isolated farm in deepest Warwickshire, it's a splendid place in which to record. The songs for the second album are all taken from early Big Bear recordings by American bluesmen re-worked to fit The Whiskey Brothers' style and it's proving to be a bunch of fun.

Wang Dang Doodle, nicked from the title of the Koko Taylor hit single on Chess Records, is the name accorded to a floating group of blues musicians of the rural variety, what might be referred to as a spasm band. The plan has been to edge towards an album featuring good songs from unexpected sources, with lyrics sung and played beautifully, but rocking along with a bit of a rumble. I have long wanted to record together the contrasting voices of Debbie Jones and Richard Heath, underpinned by Justin Randall's piano, Gerry Smith on piano accordion, with the addition of Bullmoose K. Shirley of King Pleasure and the Biscuit Boys, possibly the UK's finest rhythm and blues guitar man. The final piece of the jigsaw is the blues journalist Stuart Constable who fronts The Shufflepack. Stuart has a fine, authoritative blues voice and is a tremendous harmonica player of the Little Walter/Sonny Boy Williamson school.

It's always a pleasure to work with the extremely wacky Bob Kerr and his Whoopee Band whose music is rooted in that of the hilarious American combo, Spike Jones and the City Slickers. When I was a kid I was mesmerised by Spike Jones devotee Freddy Mirfield and his Garbage Men while the similar Sid Millward and his Nitwits and Dr. Crock and the Crackpots were famous in their time. The stage shows and the outfits were madness itself, but the standard of musicianship was straight out of the top drawer.

Bob was a member of the Bonzo Dog Doodah Band and then became leader of the New Vaudeville Band who had a hit with *Winchester Cathedral* which led to their touring the USA as support, bizarrely enough, to The Rolling Stones. In the event they were just too nutty for American audiences and were not invited back. Truth to tell, not all British audiences get it either, but the band, now metamorphosed into the Whoopee Band, is wonderful.

Any professional musician will tell you that life on the road is not in the slightest bit as glamorous as it might appear, but it's harder for the Whoopee Band than most. They carry so many props – there are around 90 hat changes, for instance – that, when they play Europe, the guys in the band fly while Bob drives the tour bus with all their weird and wonderful gear.

Bob tells of the week they did in a St. Petersburg club. He took the band bus on the ferry from Harwich to the Hook of Holland, drove through Germany and took another ferry to Denmark, crossed into Sweden and then on the Aland ferry into Finland, finally taking another ferry into Russia. Eventually he arrived in St. Petersburg and pulled up outside the club, to be welcomed effusively by the owner:

'Welcome to St. Petersburg. Welcome! You're on stage in 60 minutes.'

We also have a lot of fun working with the seriously eccentric Ricky Cool and the In Crowd. Over the last three decades Ricky has fronted a series of fine rhythm and blues combos, all with interesting names: The Texas Turkeys, The Rialtos, The Icebergs. Musically the band is rooted in 1960s Wardour Street, London, specifically The Flamingo Club where rhythm and blues and Jamaican Ska were the order of the day.

The Birmingham, Sandwell and Westside Jazz Festival is looking in good shape as we approach our 35th year. Councillor Ian Ward, leader of Birmingham City Council, asked me, as a 'favour', to move the dates of the 2022 Festival to coincide with the Commonwealth Games in Birmingham. A favour? I see it as a fabulous opportunity to demonstrate to the world how life-affirming beautifully played music can be, to showcase the many excellent venues across the region that have supported us for, in some cases, as long as 30 years, and to show the multitude of visitors just how much Birmingham audiences appreciate good music.

So, too, do Birmingham musicians: one of their great qualities is the way they stick together. When one of their number falls on hard times, which is sadly far too often, there's a queue of fellow-musicians offering to play without fee to raise funds. When Mike Burney became terminally ill, everyone pulled out the stops. Roy Wood brought his full Rock & Roll Band at his own expense, King Pleasure and the Biscuit Boys and the Steve Gibbons Band freely donated their services, Roy Davis provided his Asylum venue for nothing and a veritable Who's Who of Birmingham musicians made up the majority of the capacity audience. We all hope that it made the last months of this formidable musician just a little more comfortable.

Thanks to the jazz festival, Big Bear has encountered a bunch of interesting bands playing in the older styles of jazz. They are invariably from Europe and seem gloriously unaware of the stigma normally accorded to such music in the UK by jazz academics, the highbrow elements of the media and, sadly, too many young musicians only too ready to dismiss anything before John Coltrane as Trad.

Bands such as the Bourbon Street Stompers from Germany, the Hotsy Totsy Five from Moravia, the quaintly named Pepper and the Jellies from Teramo, Italy, Les Zauto Stompers de Paris, the Lithuanian Schwings and Hungarian Budapest Ragtime Orchestra – excellent musicians performing the music with the same verve and understanding that first made jazz a worldwide popular music, and there's nothing wrong with that.

Potato Head Jazz Band are a cracking, anachronistic six piece Dixieland band from Granada in Spain. How these young musicians, drawn in the main from Andalucia, have become so steeped in the freewheeling Chicago style of the 1940s remains a mystery, but they not only deliver it with style and flair, but with a clear understanding of the tradition. This is no British-style Trad band, more like the breezy, musically accomplished Freddy Randall Dixielanders. We're currently trying to find a way to fund a British tour and to record their second album.

Those who employ such terms as Improv to refer to a jazz style, who dismiss the Count Basie Orchestra as old-fashioned, who think it laudable that the UK's jazz colleges turn out hundreds of tenor saxophone players each year who all sound like Michael Brecker would naturally disagree, but I believe that there's nothing wrong with jazz that swings healthily, features great arrangements and inspired soloists, is perfectly played and entertains an audience of ordinary folk.

David Platz of Essex Music gave me valuable guidance in my early ventures into recording, distribution and publishing. If I was ever disappointed at singles sales figures, he would always tell me that there was no such thing as a failed single. It was simply that it hadn't yet become a seller.

Many a time over the years I comforted myself with this advice when the folk who controlled the airwaves did not share my enthusiasm for some of the admittedly quirky Big Bear product. David Platz held Big Bear Records in high regard as well as being amused at our lack of conformity. Many's the time at an industry function that he introduced me to people, adding that we were the only recording company he knew who did not record music with the object of making money. He found it laudable as well as foolish to record simply because we thought it important to capture the music.

David Platz died in 1994 and did not witness the one blatant attempt I made to release a CD specifically to generate income. I was approached by Richard Newman on behalf of a guitarist and singer who, he insisted, was a rock superstar just waiting to be recognised. He was the son of the near-legendary model and girl about music

Don't Worry 'Bout The Bear

Paula Boyd and Andy Johns, the producer of The Rolling Stones and Led Zeppelin. His uncles were Mick Fleetwood, George Harrison and Eric Clapton.

The artist was Will Johns who had already produced his CD *Hooks and Lines*. It was a perfectly good production, but with nothing really distinctive about it. I totally overlooked this in the euphoria of having an album on Big Bear by such rock and roll royalty. The media would certainly be falling over themselves to write about it and to play it on air. I set about the release in 2012 with the confidence of a man who already had a hit on his hands, manufactured it in the more expensive digipak format complete with on-body printing and put into place a promotion plan that far exceeded anything we had done before. And why not? I had a surefire hit on my hands.

In the event, no media of any consequence picked up on the back story, we had only a few BBC radio plays, the enthusiasm of the fans queuing up to see and hear The Will Johns Band did not materialise and here I sit surrounded by a mountain of unsold Will Johns albums.

As I write this, in the early months of 2019, Big Bear is careering out of control as usual, into its 51st year in what we laughingly call the music business –

JS pondering his next move amid the chaos of what passes for the Big Bear office.

20. In The Confident Hope Of A Miracle

and, in this respect at least, we have learned our lesson. None of the projects we considered to mark our 50th birthday came remotely near the 'specifically to generate income' category, but they certainly made an ambitious list. Some we decided were unaffordable, some would have required a workforce far greater than ours, while others have been spiked for future consideration. I have to keep reminding myself that there are only four of us working full-time: Tim, Sarah, Nick and myself, plus our freelance design star Nerys James and my brother Ron who almost single-handedly produces all the *Jazz Rag* editorial as well as offering all the help he can from his West Yorkshire home.

However, plenty of the projects are under way. Over the last 12 months I've been digitising and remastering earlier Big Bear recordings with Barry Bayliss at Gospel Oak Studios and we have been repeatedly surprised at just how good some of those recordings are. These go back to the 1970s, many of them unreleased. The blues material in particular stands out, probably because that generation of mainly Mississippi blues singers simply has not been replaced. Those huge booming voices that grew out of the cotton field hollers are no more. Musicians play the blues as well as they were ever played, but emerging singers have either evolved their own ways of interpreting the blues or, in most cases, they just haven't got the equipment. There are exceptions, but they are few and far between.

As a result we are readying a series of albums, spearheaded by Chick Willis, 'The Stoop Down Man', and Shuggie Otis, plus a new compilation of our 1970s recordings with Homesick James, Eddie 'Guitar' Burns, Tommy Tucker, Mickey Baker and the gang. It's a sad comment on how subdued the human spirit can become when striving to conform, but it took a moment of clarity for me to realise an important fact about this last set of recordings.

Remember that most of these old guys were hooligans and nobody subdued them when it came to their music. That's why the blues worked its magic as a relief from the pressures of 20th century life, most especially for America's black minority. I had a title in place for the compilation, *Blues and the Bear – A Road Well Travelled*, which was cute and cuddly, but during the 2018 Jazz Festival I saw the light.

We had a band from Newcastle-under-Lyme, Dirk Diggler's Blues Revue, playing at our Water's Edge stage on Brindleyplace. We'd been discussing ways we could work together, so I was giving them my full attention and, when they started playing, they were far too loud. I decided to get them to turn down after the first number, but then I became aware that nobody was leaving and people were clearly enjoying it. To be honest, I did receive one complaint. A young lady with a violin case over her shoulder called me over imperiously to say, 'I'm a musician. This band is too loud and there is distortion on the guitar.'

Blues hooligans Dirk Diggler's Blues Revue from Stoke-on-Trent.

I found myself remembering that this music is supposed to have attitude, to believe in itself and to do it like it should be done. At that moment I decided to change our album title to *Damn Right I Got the Blues* and get back to manning the barricades in the spirit of those old hooligans.

So now the plan is for an additional Birmingham festival, *If This Ain't the Blues*, kicking off in May 2020.

In the jazz world, I'm convinced that the next wave of popularity will be based on the music of Django Reinhardt. Big Bear's excursions into gypsy jazz have so far resulted in fine albums by Nomy Rosenberg, Remi Harris and Barcelona's Pere Soto and Django's Castle. There are so many young gypsy-style bands of tremendous quality coming through in recent years that they are bound to bring their own audience with them.

My hope is that Big Bear's contribution to the inevitable breakthrough will be through the Dutch Sinti gypsy, Nomy Rosenberg. The Rosenbergs and the Reinhardts have family links going back into the mists of time and Nomy is related in some distant way to Django. Nomy's elder brother Jimmy is considered by many to be one of the finest guitar players ever, though his offstage problems have limited his career.

20. In The Confident Hope Of A Miracle

There is a famous photograph from the Samois-sur-Seine Gypsy Jazz Festival showing the three-year-old Nomy playing a guitar as big as he is. At the age of 15 he shared the Carnegie Hall stage with Les Paul and George Benson and I'm certain that he didn't feel over-awed. Nomy cannot read or write, but plays guitar as naturally as you or I breathe. It was a delight to see and hear Nomy and his rhythm guitarist Ringo Steinbach relaxing together. They seemed never to be without their guitars, calling key changes mid-song, laughing aloud when confronted with difficult chord changes or impossible tempos.

Big Bear released a Nomy Rosenberg album on CD in 2009. Nomy picked Sarah and me up at Eindhoven railway station in his mobile home and took us to his village which was all mobile homes. It wasn't plain sailing, mainly because of his heavy-handed father. The album negotiations were conducted in English, translated by a Dutch friend of the Rosenbergs. The father's expression lurched in an instant from a charming smile to fierce anger – then back again. I had no idea what he was saying and I guessed the translations were modified somewhat for my benefit. After agreement was reached, he shook my hand and spoke to me in perfect English!

We decided to hold the album launch event in De Lantaren in Rotterdam in conjunction with Big Bear's longtime Benelux distributor, Dee 2 Records. The label boss of Dee 2 is Rob Ebbers and he was yet another of the contacts we made at Midem. When I first met him at Cannes, years before, he told me he had met his wife at a King Pleasure and the Biscuit Boys show in De Melkweg in Amsterdam. Once he had told me that, settling the deal was a formality.

When we arrived at De Lantaren, newly manufactured CDs from England in hand, I was met at the door by a concerned and puzzled Rob Ebbers. Apparently Nomy's father was already behind a desk, selling copies of our album, with a totally different cover design. He had bootlegged his own son's album from under our nose! It has to be remembered that Nomy's father had form and was certainly not a man to be confronted in a club at night, so my protestations were of the milder variety.

The problems with Rosenberg Senior didn't end there. We arranged to bring Nomy's trio to the UK to promote the album and feature at the Jazz Festival. I had asked Nomy not to bring his father which he agreed to immediately, but a couple of days before the shows I received a phone call from his Dad which made it clear: No Dad, no Nomy. The trio was splendid, all I could have hoped for, and Nomy was undoubtedly the hit of the festival, but his Dad behaved true to form, storming on stage at every imagined wrong move by his son, loudly berating him. Try as we did, he was uncontrollable.

Don't Worry 'Bout The Bear

Subsequently on several occasions I tried to contact Nomy, keen to work on a second album as well as to make sure he was all right, but I got little, and then no, response. I've tried every possible avenue to re-make contact and the search for Nomy Rosenberg is an important element in our 50th anniversary plans. I have been told, but don't want to believe, that he has stopped playing and is now working on the roads. I can't help but wonder if his father's behaviour has something to do with Nomy's apparent decision to quit playing music. Finding Nomy and reviving his career is on my mind for the immediate future.

And it's not only Nomy.

We despaired, back in the 1960s, when we heard of important jazz and blues musicians in America reduced to driving trucks, sweeping up in factories or building swimming pools. 50 years later, in the UK, we tolerate a similar situation: the outstanding piano player driving a delivery truck, the trumpet ace going to college to learn to be a carpenter and the tremendous blues singer working 40 hours a week selling white goods in an electrical store.

That's progress, I guess.

If This Ain't The Blues.

Appendix 1

DISCOGRAPHY

Big Bear Records Albums

The Dog That Bit People: The Dog That Bit People
Eddie Guitar Burns: Bottle Up And Go
Doctor Ross with Lafayette Leake & The Chicago Aces: Live At Montreux
Johnny Mars: Blues From Mars
The Mighty Flea with Mickey Baker: Let The Good Times Roll
Lightnin' Slim, Whispering Smith, Homesick James, Snooky Pryor, Boogie Woogie Red, Washboard Willie: American Blues Legends '73
Homesick James & Snooky Pryor: Homesick James & Snooky Pryor
Eddie Playboy Taylor, Doctor Ross, Big John Wrencher, Cousin Joe, G P Jackson: American Blues Legends '74
Doctor Ross: The Harmonica Boss
Cousin Joe: Gospel-Wailing Jazz-Playing Rock'n'Rolling Soul-Shouting Tap-Dancing Bluesman From New Orleans
Big John Wrencher with Eddie Playboy Taylor & The Blueshounds: Big John's Boogie
Mickey Baker: Take A Look Inside
Eddie Playboy Taylor & The Blueshounds: Ready For Eddie
Eddie Guitar Burns: Detroit Blackbottom
Homesick James, Tommy Tucker, Little Joe Blue, Eddie Guitar Burns, Lonesome Jimmie Lee Robinson, Billy Boy Arnold: American Blues Legends '75
Willie Mabon: The Comeback
Homesick James: Home Sweet Homesick James
Erwin Helfer: Boogie Piano Chicago Style
Johnny Mars: The Oakland Boogie
Clark Terry's Big Bad Band: Live on 57th Street
Snooky Pryor: Shake Your Boogie
Doctor Ross: Jivin' The Blues
Eddie Playboy Taylor, Mickey Baker, Eddie Guitar Burns, Washboard Willie, Homesick James, Snooky Pryor, Doctor Ross, Boogie Woogie Red, Johnny Mars, Tommy Tucker, Cousin Joe, Whispering Smith: The Blues Volume 3

Johnny Mars, Eddie Guitar Burns, Billie Boy Arnold, Little Joe Blue, Lonesome Jimmie Lee Robinson, Eddie Playboy Taylor, Mickey Baker, Big John Wrencher, Cousin Joe, G P Jackson, Doctor Ross, Snooky Pryor, Washboard Willie, Homesick James, Boogie Woogie Red: The Blues Volume 4
Mickey Baker, Snooky Pryor, Homesick James, Johnny Mars, Doctor Ross, Big John Wrencher, Cousin Joe: The Blues Volume 5
Eddie C Campbell, Good Rockin' Charles, Billy The Kid Emerson, Lester Davenport, Chico Chism, Little Smokey Smothers, Jimmy Dawkins, Willie Black: American Blues Legends '79
Muscles: Muscles
Claude Williams: Kansas City Giants
Bright Eyes, The Lazers, Willy & The Poor Boys, The Quads, Rockers, Speed Limit, Dansette Damage, Mayday, Dangerous Girls, The Playthings, The Thrillers, Spoonful, Eclipse: Brum Beat: Live At The Barrel Organ
Humphrey Lyttelton, Digby Fairweather, Roy Williams, Roy Crimmins, Bruce Turner, Dick Morrissey, Randy Colville, Dave Shepherd, Mick Pyne, Jim Douglas, Harvey Weston, Johnny Richardson: The M&B Jam Session
Humphrey Lyttelton, Roy Williams, Peter King, Dick Morrissey, John Barnes, Brian Lemon, Dave Green, Martin Taylor, Allan Ganley, Sir Charles Thompson: British Jazz Awards 1987
Duncan Swift: Out Looking For The Lion
Groove Juice Special: Groove Juice Comin' To Town
King Pleasure & The Biscuit Boys: King Pleasure & The Biscuit Boys
Bill Allred's Goodtime Jazz Band: Swing That Music
King Pleasure & The Biscuit Boys: This Is It!
Lady Sings The Blues: Lady Sings The Blues
Duncan Swift: The Broadwood Concert
King Pleasure & The Biscuit Boys: Better Beware!
Bruce Adams Quartet: One Foot In The Gutter
King Pleasure & The Biscuit Boys: Live At Ronnie Scott's Birmingham
Bruce Adams/Alan Barnes Quintet: Side-Steppin'
Kenny Baker's Dozen: The Boss Is Home
King Pleasure & The Biscuit Boys with Charles Brown, Gene The Mighty Flea Connors, Val Wiseman & Howard McCrary: Blues & Rhythm Revue, Volume 1
Bruce Adams/Alan Barnes Quintet: Let's Face The Music
King Pleasure & The Biscuit Boys: Smack Dab In The Middle
King Pleasure & The Biscuit Boys: Hop, Skip & Jump
Eddie Playboy Taylor: Ready For Eddie Plus [2CD]

King Pleasure & The Biscuit Boys: Let 'Em Roll
Various: American Blues Legends '73/'74 [2CD]
Big John Wrencher: Big John's Boogie Plus [2CD]
Homesick James and Snooky Pryor: The Big Bear Sessions [2CD]
Alan Barnes All Stars: The Marbella Jazz Suite
The Doctor Teeth Big Band: Rhythm Is Our Business
King Pleasure & The Biscuit Boys: Hey Puerto Rico!
Tipitina: I Wish I Was In New Orleans
Various: Don't Worry 'Bout The Bear [2CD]
Django's Castle with Bruce Adams: Swing Hotel du Vin
Nomy Rosenberg Trio: Nomy Rosenberg Trio
King Pleasure & The Biscuit Boys: Live At Last
Tipitina: Taking Care of Business
The Will Johns Band: Hooks & Lines
Remi Harris: Ninick
The Whiskey Brothers: Bottle Up And Go
Lady Sings The Blues: Laughing At Life
King Pleasure & The Biscuit Boys, Bruce Adams Quartet, Bruce Adams/ Alan Barnes Quintet, The Whiskey Brothers, Tipitina, Nomy Rosenberg Trio, Lady Sings The Blues, Alan Barnes All Stars: Jazz City UK Volume 1
Humphrey Lyttelton, Digby Fairweather, Roy Williams, Roy Crimmins, Bruce Turner, Peter King, Dick Morrissey, John Barnes, Randy Colville, Dave Shepherd, Brian Lemon, Mick Pyne, Dave Green, Martin Taylor, Jim Douglas, Allan Ganley, Sir Charles Thompson, Harvey Weston, Johnny Richardson: Jazz City UK Volume 2: The Jam Sessions
Howard McCrary: Moments Like This
Chick Willis: Things I Used To Do
Shuggie Otis: Long Time Coming

Other albums recorded under Big Bear management

Tea & Symphony: An Asylum For The Musically Insane [EMI Harvest]
Bakerloo: Bakerloo [EMI Harvest]
Black Sabbath: Black Sabbath [Vertigo]
Locomotive: We Are Everything You See [EMI Parlophone]
Tea & Symphony: Jo Sago [EMI Harvest]
Black Sabbath: Paranoid [Vertigo]
Indian Summer: Indian Summer [RCA Neon]
Hannibal: Hannibal [B&C Records]
Brewers Droop: Opening Time [RCA Victor]

Appendix 2

BANDS THAT APPEARED AT HENRY'S BLUESHOUSE

Alexis Korner	John Hammond Jr [USA]
Angus	Judas Priest
Anno Domini	Jude
Arthur Big Boy Crudup [USA]	Kansas Hook
Bakerloo [Blues Line]	King Biscuit Boy [Canada]
Barabas	Larry Johnson [USA]
Barclay James Harvest	Lightnin' Slim [USA]
BB Blunder	Locomotive
Beggars Opera	Mainland Dreamboat
Black Sabbath	Man
Blonde on Blonde	Mark Almond
Brewers Droop	Medicine Head
Bronco	Mighty Baby
Budgie	Mogul Thrash
Carol Grimes with Uncle Dog	Open Road
Champion Jack Dupree [USA]	Open Country
Chicken Shack	Paladin
Children	The Pahanna
Clarke Hutchinson	Patto
Colin Staples Blues Band	Pete Brown & Piblokto
Creation	Rainbow
Curtis Jones [USA]	Reverend Gary Davis [USA]

Appendix 2

Dando Shaft	Road
Duster Bennett	Robert Plant
Earth	Rock Rebellion
Eddie Guitar Burns [USA]	Roger Ruskin Spear & His Kinetic Wardrobe
Flying Hat Band	Rory Gallagher and Taste
Fred Athens Wood	Satisfaction
Gasoline	Shuffling Hungarians
Gass	Shy Wolf
Gerry Lockran	Simon Prager & Steve Rye
Ginger	Skin Alley
Glen Cornick's Wild Turkey	Son House [USA]
Good Habit	Sonny Terry & Brownie McGhee [USA]
Gracious	Spider John Koerner [USA]
Gravy Train	Stackridge
Groundhogs	Status Quo
Gypsy	Tea & Symphony
Hannibal	Ten Years After
Help Yourself	The Dog That Bit People
Home	Thin Lizzy
Idle Race	Thunderclap Newman
Indian Summer	Trapeze
J.B. Hutto [USA]	UFO
James Litherland & Million	Ulysses
Jameson Raid	Village
Jellybread	Walrus Gumboot
Jethro Tull	Warhorse
Jimmy Fastfingers Dawkins [USA]	Whispering Smith [USA]
John Bonham	White Rabbit
	Zoot Money

Appendix 3

AMERICAN BLUESMEN TOURED / RECORDED BY BIG BEAR

Baby Boy Warren [Robert Henry Warren]	b. August 1919 Lake Providence, Louisiana d. July 1977 Detroit, Michigan
Big John Wrencher	b. February 1923 Sunflower, Mississippi d. July 1977 Clarksdale, Mississippi
Billy Boy Arnold	b. September 1935 Chicago, Illinois
Billy The Kid Emerson [William Robert Emerson]	b. December 1925 Tarpon Springs, Florida
Boogie Woogie Red [Vernon Harrison]	b. October 1925 Rayville, Louisiana d. July 1992 Detroit, Michigan
Charles Brown	b. September 1922 Texas City, Texas d. January 1999 Oakland, California
Chick Willis [Robert Lee Willis]	b. September 1934 Cabannis, Georgia d. December 2013 Forsyth, Georgia
Chico Chism [Napoleon Chism]	b. May 1927 Shreveport, Louisiana d. January 2007 Phoenix, Arizona
Cousin Joe [Pleasant Joseph]	b. December 1907 New Orleans, Louisiana d. October 1989 New Orleans, Louisiana
Doctor Ross [Charles Isaiah Ross]	b. October 1925 Tunica, Mississippi d. May 1993 Flint, Michigan
Eddie C. Campbell	b. May 1939 Duncan, Mississippi d. November 2018 Oak Park, Illinois
Eddie Guitar Burns	b. February 1928 Belzoni, Mississippi d. December 2012 Detroit, Michigan
Eddie Playboy Taylor	b. January 1923 Benoit, Mississippi d. December 1985 Chicago, Illinois
Erwin Helfer	b. January 1936 Chicago, Illinois

Appendix 3

Gene 'The Mighty Flea' Connors [Eugene Conners]	b. December 1930 Birmingham, Alabama d. June 2010 Prescott Valley, Arizona
Good Rockin' Charles [Henry Lee Bester]	b. March 1933 Tuscaloosa, Alabama d. May 1989 Chicago, Illinois
G.P. Jackson	b. August 1920 Alligator, Mississippi d. February 1990 Kansas City, Missouri
Homesick James [John William Henderson or James Williamson]	b. April 1910 Somerville, Tennessee d. December 2006 Springfield, Missouri
Howard McCrary	b. September 1954 Youngstown, Ohio
Jimmy Dawkins	b. October 1936 Opelousa, Louisiana d. April 2013 Chicago, Illinois
Johnny Mars	b. December 1942, Laurens, South Carolina
Lester Davenport	b. January 1932 Tchula, Mississippi d. March 2009 Chicago, Illinois
Lightnin' Slim [Otis Hicks]	b. March 1913 St Louis, Missouri d. July 1974 Detroit, Michigan
Little Joe Blue [Joseph Valery Jr]	b. September 1934 Vicksburg, Mississippi d. April 1990 Reno, Nevada
Little Smokey Smothers [Abraham Smothers]	b. January 1939 Tchula, Mississippi d. November 2010 Chicago, Illinois
Lonesome Jimmy Lee Robinson	b. April 1931 Chicago, Illinois d. July 2002 Chicago, Illinois
The King Biscuit Boy [Richard Alfred Newell]	b. March 1944 Hamilton, Ontario, Canada d. January 2003 Hamilton, Ontario, Canada
Mickey Baker [McHouston Baker]	b. October 1925 Louisville, Kentucky d. November 2012 Montastruc-la-Conseillere, France
Nolan Struck	b. June 1940 Dunson, Louisiana
Shuggie Otis [Johnny Alexander Veliotes Jr]	b. November 1953 Los Angeles, California
Snooky Pryor [James Edward Pryor]	b. September 1919 or 1921 Lambert, Mississippi d. October 2006 Cape Girardeau, Missouri
Tommy Tucker [Robert Higginbotham]	b. March 1933 Springfield, Ohio d. January 1982 Newark, New Jersey
Washboard Willie [William Paden Hensley]	b. July 1909 Bullock County, Alabama d. August 1991 Detroit, Michigan
Whispering Smith [Moses Smith]	b. January 1932 Union Church, Mississippi d. April 1984 Baton Rouge, Louisiana
Willie Mabon	b. October 1925 Hollywood, Tennessee d. April 1985 Paris, France

Appendix 4

EVENTS ORGANISED BY BIG BEAR MUSIC (PARTIAL LIST)

Arctic Border Blues Festival: Kirkenes [Norway]
Nikel and Murmansk [Soviet Union]
Big City Blues Festival
Birmingham Blues Summit 1992
Birmingham Country Music Festival
Birmingham, Sandwell & Westside Jazz Festival
Birmingham Super Prix street entertainment
British Jazz Awards
Coventry Jazz Festival
The Great Rock and Roll Weekend
Highgate Brewery Festival
Marbella Jazz Festival
Music Takeover Birmingham City Centre
National Jazz Festival [21 cities from Durham to Basildon, Bristol to Barking]
Newcastle Under Lyme Jazz & Blues Festival
New York Non Stop – British Airways
Shrewsbury Jazz Festival
Soho Jazz Festival
Stourbridge Jazz Break
Sugnall Jazz & Blues Festival
Walsall Jazz & Blues Festival
Welcome Home Festival
Wolverhampton Jazz & Blues Festival

ACKNOWLEDGEMENTS

We gratefully acknowledge the assistance of the following who generously helped with information, encouragement and advice, and supported us in different ways on the long road to publication:

Sarah Yue Yang, Tim Jennings, Nick Hart, Merlin Daleman, Barry Clark, Ed Bicknell, Jasper Carrott, John James, Derek Inman, Digby Fairweather, Mark Skirving, Val Wiseman, Mike Olley, James Black, Jill Hitchman, Peter Suddock, Stuart Constable, Raymond Gonzales, Rob Sealey, Dave Travis, Gerv Havill, Steve Firman, Debbie and Justin Jones-Randall, Dan Cole, Jon Welch, Ralph Salmins, John Patrick, Julian Smith, Pete York, Dee Askew of the Count Basie office.

PHOTO CREDITS

Text:
Merlin Daleman: 174, 180, 262, 263, 266, 268, 271, 294, 298, 299, 301, 302, 306, 308. Jim Simpson: 23, 46, 47, 58, 49, 65, 70, 71, 96, 112, 115 bottom, 131, 133, 137, 139, 153, 166, 183, 196, 197, 201, 203, 225, 240, 243, 251, 281, 283, 288, 291, 292. Alan Johnson: 42, 44, 98, 99, 101, 105, 111, 114, 115 top, 122, 146, 156, 293. Kate Munn: 28, 31, 32, 141, 182. Brian Steel: 188, 229, 230, 231. Jim O'Neal: 126, 127. Roger Howes: 22, 56. Birmingham Mail: 7, 206. Dave Travis: 185. Bill Smallshire: 213. Maria de los Dolores Bacasrese: 11. Dave Hunt: 18. Wendy Dutton: 24, 26. Ivanhoe Photography: 160 top. Lorentz Gollachsen: 163. Harry Siviter: 179. Birmingham City Council: 161 middle. Yann Flood-Page: 95. Wrates Photography: 17.

Gallery section:
Merlin Daleman: I lower, II middle and lower, III upper and lower, IV and V all except Kenny Baker, VI all, VII upper and lower, VIII all. Val Wiseman: V bottom. Bill Smallshire: IV Kenny Baker. Jim Simpson: I top, II top, V top, VII middle.

INDEX

Index Notes: *italicized* locators refer to photographs; roman numeral locators refer to gallery photographs; some subheadings are ordered chronologically.

A
Aarons, Al 177-8
Abbey Road Studios 39
Abbott, Andy 140
Adam and Eve pub, Birmingham 254
Adams, Bruce IV, VI, *163*, 187, 204, 214, 260, 264, 266
Alain Braine 151
Alex Welsh Band 22, 178, 180
Allen, Marshall 269
Allen, Pete *28*, *31*
American Blues Legends 125, 316-17
    '72 tour 43
    '73 tour 94-9, 118, 290
    '79 tour 125-7, 134-5
    see also Big Bear Records
American Federation of Musicians, Kansas City 136-7, *137*
American Folk Blues Festival 293
Applejacks 27, 286
Arden, David 80-81
Arden, Don 72-3, 75, 78-81
Armit, Ian 16-17, 197
Armstrong, Louis 6-7, 289
Arrival 116
Art Blakey's Jazz Messengers, 159
Ash, Vic 214
Astronaut's Journey and *UFO* 152-3
An Asylum for the Musically Insane 45
Atlantic Records 106
Aykroyd, Dan 250, 277

B
B.B. King 241
B&C Records 52, 275
Bagot, Tony 178
Bain, Rodger 51, 52, 62-3, 295
Baker, Chet 173
Baker, Keith 51, 52
Baker, Kenny IV, 5, 206, 209-11, 212-17, *213*, 226
Baker, Kenny (actor) 210-11
Baker, McHouston 'Mickey' 91, 99, 103, 104-9, *105*, 113, 116, 172, 275, 307, 317
Baker, Sue 210, 218
Bakerloo (formerly Bakerloo Blues Line) 40-41, 51-2, *56*, 60, 62, 295
Baldwin, Gary 235-6
Barbarella's, Birmingham 190-91
Barber, Chris 177
Barber, Gary 'The Enforcer' 251
Barclay, Eddie 107
Barnes, Alan IV, *163*, *163*, 170, 187, 192, 204, 214, 238-9, 263, 264, 298
Barnes, John 205, *206*
Barnett, Dave 162
Barnhart, Scotty 263-4, 299
Barry, John *31*
Barton, Lou Ann 244, 245
Basie, William James, the Count 60, 90
    orchestra see Count Basie Orchestra/Band
Basso, Gianni 172-3
Battrum, John 'Boysey' 251

321

BBC
- *The Best of Jazz* 202
- *The Goon Show* 209
- *Jazz Club* 178
- John Peel 37, 152
- *Let's Settle for Music* 209, 211
- Paul Jones 189, 253
- Tony Blackburn 143, 147

The Beatles 24
Bechet, Sidney 202-3
Beeks, Clarence 249-50
Beiderbecke – And All that Jazz 217
Bennet, Tony "Duster" *44*, 44-5, 124, 295
Bennett, Tony 224
Benton, David 243-4, 245-8
Benton, David (friend of George Melly) 248-9
Beresford, 'Bam Bam' Dean *240*, 252
Bester, Henry Lee (Good Rockin' Charles) *127*, 128
Betteridge, David 37
Bicknell, Ed 221, 234-5
Big Bear 295-6
Big Bear Music *see* American Blues Legends; Black Sabbath; Henry's Blueshouse; Locomotive; Simpson, Jim; *and* individual musicians' names
Big Bear personnel 162, 173-4, 241, 307
Big Bear Records
- in 2019 306-7
- American performers 91, 316-17
  - Charles Brown 226
  - at Chess Studios, Chicago 127-8
  - Clark Terry 117-18
  - Claude Williams 135
  - Cousin Joe 113-16
  - Doctor Ross 123-4
  - Eddie Burns 92-3, 109
  - Gene 'The Mighty Flea' Connors 172
  - Howard McCrary 232
  - Mickey Baker 108
  - Tommy Tucker 102
  - Willie Mabon 103
- British/European performers
  - Bob Catley 151-2
  - Bullets 148
  - Celluloid Heroes 147
  - Duncan Swift 184-5
  - Garbo 145-7
  - gypsy jazz albums 308
  - Hans Dulfer 151
  - *Jazz City UK Volume 2* 206
  - Kenny Baker's Dozen *The Boss is Home* 215-16
  - King Pleasure and the Biscuit Boys 154, 188-9, 312
    - *Blues and Rhythm Revue Vol 1* 172, 188, 226
    - *King Pleasure and the Biscuit Boys* 241
    - *This is It* 241
  - *Live at the Barrel Organ* 297, 298, 299
  - *The M&B Jam Session Volume One* 157
  - *Marbella Jazz Suite* 264
  - Muscles 140-44
  - Nomy Rosenberg 309
  - Quads 152-3
  - Roy G. Hemmings 149-50
  - singles and West Bromwich Albion anthem 149
  - Tipitina 302-3
  - Tjens Couter and Alain Braine 151
  - Val Wiseman *Lady Sings the Blues* 181, 192
  - Whiskey Brothers 303
  - Will Johns Band 306
- discography 311-13
- distribution and label representation 274-6, 282-3
- EMI's Licenced Repertoire Division 142, 143-4
- formation and first release 37-8
- at Midem *see* Midem
- reputation 100, 148, 154, 304
- *see also* American Blues Legends

Big Bill Broonzy 4-5

Index

Big John Wrencher 99, 113, *118*, 316
Billy 'The Kid' Emerson *127*, 128-9, 316
Billy Boy Arnold 91, *101*, 102
Bingley Hall, Birmingham 200
The Birdie Song 274-5
Birmingham City Council Leisure Department 158
Birmingham College of Technology 19-20
Birmingham Jazz Festival III, 5, 138, 148, 284
   origination (1984) 155-8, 173
   inaugural festival (1985) 158-9
   (1986 and 1990) 159, 161, 178
   (1989) 185
   (2006) 269-70
   (2018) 238-9
   as Birmingham, Sandwell and Westside Jazz Festival 174-5, 304
   bomb scare 165-6
   guide dog scheme 161-2, 170
   Lady Sings the Blues 162, 181, 190
   performers 159-61, 163-4, 166-8, 172-3, 175, 209, 277, 304-5
   the Spiegeltent 163-4, 165
   Swinging Down Broad Street 7, 162-4
Birmingham Mail 89
Birmingham music scene (1960s) 18-19, 27, 286-9
Birmingham Odeon *160*
Birmingham pubs and clubs *see* individual venue names
Birmingham Town Hall 4-5, *31*, 45, 155
Birmingham, Sandwell and Westside Jazz Festival 174-5, 304
Black Barn Studios, Surrey 181
Black Sabbath I, 50, 51, 53-69, *56, 58-9, 64-6, 70-71*, 74, 295-6
   Black Sabbath 62-3, 295
   The End Tour 88-9
   legal case and aftermath 72-3, 75-9, 84
   Paranoid 72-4
   Sabotage 84
Black Sabbath bench 86-7
Black Widow 73

Black, Willie 128
Blackburn, Tony 143, 147
Blaine, Esther 162
Blakey, Art 159-61, *160*
Blannin, Pete 17, 197
Blount, Herman 'Sonny' (Sun Ra) 268
Blue Magnolia Jazz Band 21
Blues and Gospel Train (1964) 112
Blues at the Bear, Bearwood 125
Blues Brothers Band 161, *249*, 277-8, 289
Blueshounds 26, *182*
Bonham, John 39, 45, 63
Boogie Woogie Red 94, *95*, 95-6, 118-19, 290, 316
The Booze Brothers 49
Bottle Up and Go 92
Boyce, Alex 52
Braff, Ruby 193
Branson, Alex 283
Branson, Richard 275-6
Brewers Droop 48-50
British Jazz Awards 164, 203-7, 217, 279-81
Broad Street, Birmingham 199-200, 238
   Ronnie Scott's 189, 211, 214-28, 230, 233-5, 254, 293
A Broken Heart 34-5
Brouwershaven Festival 209-10
Brown, Charles 189, 224-6, *225, 243*, 316
Brown, Geoff 113, 140-45, *141*, 172
Brown, Oscar Jr 270
Brown, Ruth 226-7
Brown, Stephen 254
Brown, Terry The Toupe 253-4
Bruce Turner Jump Band 22
Bruce, Adams 192
Brum Beat 61, 148, 296-7
Brum Beat albums 287
Brunning, Bob 92
Bruton, Paddy 9
Bruynoghe, Yannick 4
Bryden, Beryl 207-8
Buckner, Milt 130
Buddy Rich Orchestra 159
Bullets 148

Burnard, Ron 5
Burnett, John 181, 250
Burney, Mike 19, 25, *26*, 30, 39, 172, 181-2, *182*, 231, 232-3, 250, 259-60, 261, 304
Burns, Eddie *see* Eddie Guitar Burns
Butler, Terry 'Geezer' 54-7, 76, 84, 85-7, *86*, 296
Byrd, Henry Roeland 48

C
Caldicott, Tony *182*
Campbell, Eddie C. *127*, 128, 316
Campbell, Ian 26, 27
Cannonball pub, Birmingham 155
Caroline Records 275-6
Carrilho, Wagner 222
Carrott, Jasper 87
Carter, Frank (Lord Mayor of Birmingham 1985) 159
Carter, Stephen 157
Casey, Al 159
The Casuals 145
Caswell, John 38-9
Cat Squirrel 119-20
Catley, Bob 151-2
Cattini, Clem 145
CBS 34-5, 73, 79
   The Sound of Jazz broadcast 191
Cedar Club, Birmingham 35
Celluloid Heroes 147
Chalk Farm Recording Studios 92-3, 114-15, 124
Champion Jack Dupree 22, *42*, 43, 159-61, *160*
Chandler, Chas 79
The Chapel jam session 19
Charlie Daniels Band 135-6
Charly Records 279-80
chart returns 66-7
Checker 102
Chess Records and Recording Studios 102-3, 127-8
Chicago Aces 120-21

Chico Chism 128, 316
Chipping Norton Recording Studios 149-50, 226
Chism, Napoleon 128, 316
Chuck Berry 109, 190-92, *192*
City of Birmingham Symphony Orchestra 236
Clancey's factory, Halesowen 16
Clark, Barry 194
Clark, Paul 189
Clayton, Big Man 254
Clayton, Wilbur 'Buck' 10, *131*, *201*, 201-2
Clempson, Clem 51
Clyne, Jeff *168*
Coe, Tony 197, *197*
Cole, Dan 89
Colosseum 51, 66
Complete Course in Jazz Guitar, The 104
Connors, Gene 'The Mighty Flea' IV, *158*, 159, 171-2, 189, 317
Constable, Stuart 53, 303
Cooney, Bob 52
Cootie Alexander (aka Paul Allin) 243, 251-2
Cork Jazz Festival 169
Count Basie 60, 90
Count Basie Orchestra/Band 130, 131-2, 167, 181, 201-2, 212, 299
  at Birmingham *159*, 160, 177-8
  at Marbella 261-4, *262*
Cousin Joe 99, 110-18, *111*, 130, 131-2, 151, 293, 316
Cowlyn, Rob 94
Cream 120
Cropper, Steve 277-8
Crown Hotel, Station Street *see* Henry's Blueshouse
Crudup, Arthur Big Boy 41
Crusher Page (aka Mad Pagey) 239
Cummings, Tony 124

D
Daleman, Marja 87-8, 299-30
Daleman, Merlin 87, 175, 266, 299-300

Index

Daley, Ron 25
Dankworth, Johnny 198
Darlow, Denis 19, 198
Darrington, Steve 48, 49
Davenport, Lester *127*, 128, 317
Davidson, Gordon 21, *22*
Davies, Ruth 226
Davis, Miles 161, 206
Davis, Roy 304
Daw, Jef *46*, 46-7, *47*
Dawkins, Jimmy 'Fastfingers' 125-8, *127*, 317
de Comyn, Andy 297-8
Dee 2 Records 309
Dee, Brian 187, 191, 192
deFrancesco, Joey 165
Delta Jazzmen 183
Den of Iniquity 38
Derbyshire Miners' Welfare Centre 197-8
Desmond Dekker 227
Detheridge, Dennis 286
Detroit Blackbottom 109
The Devil Went Down to Georgia 136
Dickenson, Vic 202
Dickins, Barry 67-8
Dickinson, Ken 21, *22*, 25
Dire Straits 234
Dirk Diggler's Blues Revue 307-8, *308*
Dixie Prince 239
Doctor Ross 41, 91, *99*, 100, 107-8, *118*, 118-25, 145, 275, 316
The Dog That Bit People 38, 39, 92
Don't Worry 'Bout the Bear 124
Donaldson, John 264
Douglas, Jim 180
Draper, Simon 276
Drummin' Man show 187-8
Dudgeon, Gus 35, 45-6
The Duel 168
Dust My Broom 94-5

E
Earl Bostic 112
Earth 54-5

Earth Angel 250
Ebbers, Rob 309
Eddie 'Playboy' Taylor 99, 100, *118*, 311-12, 316
Eddie Guitar Burns 41, 91-3, 102, 109, 307, 316
Edison, Harry 'Sweets' 159, 181
Edmond, Maggie (later Maggie De Monde) 297
Edmunds, Dave 49, 50
Edwards, Richard 214
Edwards, Teddy *168*, 168-70, *169*, 233-4
Eggy Ley's Hotshots 178, 179
Eldridge, Roy 'Little Jazz' 187
Elliot, Ken 116
Ellis, Joe 32
Elsdon, Alan 178
Elwell, Sue 162
Embassy Sportsdrome, Walford Road 6-7
Emerson, William Robert *127*, 128-9, 316
EMI
  Harvest Records 45, 51
  licencing and distribution *142*, 143-4, 147
  Parlophone 35, 39
Equity VAEC contracts 91
Essex Music *see* Platz, David
Essex Music Studio 145-6
Esteban, Carolina 260, 266, 273
Evans, Chris 145-8, *146*
Everett, Roy *see* Taylor, Roy

F
Fairport Convention 152
Fairweather, Digby 11, 170, 173, *179*, 180, 192, 206, 217, 298
Faithfull, Marianne 292-3
Fame, Georgie 29, 159, 161
Fansworld TV 284
Farlowe, Chris 51
The Fatback Band 259, 260
Felix, Maria 259, 266
Fendick, Lazy Ade 21
Fewtrell, Eddie 140
Fimister, Dave 9-10

325

Finch, Brian 'Monk' 28, 30, 31, *31*
Fisher, Roy 180, 181-2, *182*
Flamingo Club, Wardour Street, London 29, 34
The Flamingo, Redruth 27-8
Flowers, Herbie 145
Food for Thought 61
Ford, Eric 192
Ford, Richard *141*, 143-4, *144*
Foster, Frank *161*
Foundling, Mighty Matt 251
Freddy Mirfield and his Garbage Men 4
Freddy Randall Dixielanders 304
Fuller, Jesse 22-3

G
Gallen, Tony and Marie Elise 241-2
Gallery, Graham 33, 181-2, *182*
Ganley, Allan 205, *206*
Garbo 145-8, *146*
Gardner, Simon IV, 214, 264
Gare, Alan 'Slap Happy' *240*, 242, 252
Garner, Erroll 177
Garnett, Alex IV, 264
Garnett, Willie 250-51
Gay, Al 180, 210
Gaye, Marvin 100
Gayle, Crystal 168
Gaynor, Mel 143, *144*
Geldard, Bill 214
Gelly, Dave 92, 132, 215-16, 252
Gene 'The Mighty Flea' Connors IV, *158*, 159, 171-2, 189, 317
George Clay Music Centre, Birmingham 199-200
Gibbons, Steve 304
Gilbert, Jerry 39, 124
Girl on Page 3 148
Gomez Iglesias, Jose Maria 255, 256-9, 264, 265-6
Gonzales 150
Gonzales, Babs 117
Gonzalez, Raymond 277, 278-9
Good Rockin' Charles *127*, 128, 317

Goodbye Country/Lovely Lady 39
Goodman, Benny 216, 233
Gospel Oak Studios 303, 307
Gotta Get a Job 153
Goykovich, Dusko *166*, 166-7, *168*, 206
Grand Hotel, Birmingham 164, 205, 280
Grand Theatre (later the Plaza), 4
Grappelli, Stephane 138-9
Greco, Buddy 233-4
Green, Benny 167, 193, 205, 280-81
Green, Dave 205, *206*, 211
Grosz, Marty II, 170, 209-10
Guy, Buddy 22, 23, 23-4, 225

H
Haines, Norman 29, 31-3, *32*, 35, 37, 38, 59, 77
Hall, Bob 92, 124, 172
Hall, Tony 33-4, 37, 38, 46, 51, 62, 116
Hannibal (formerly Bakerloo) 52
Harlem Gentlemen 202
Harris, Keith 24
Harrison, George 39
Harrison, Vernon *see* Boogie Woogie Red
Harry James Orchestra 216
Hart, Nick 174
Hartley, Pete 138
Harvest Records 45, 51
Hawkins, Coleman 131
Hawkins, Johnny 34-5
Healey, Derek 214
Heath, Richard 303
Helfer, Erwin 92, 316
Hemmings, Roy G. 149-50
Henry's Blueshouse 40-45, 48, 50-53, 83, 86, 295
  bands and musicians 41-2, 44, 54, 314-15
  Blueshounds line-up *26*, *182*
  fate of Crown Hotel 52-3
Hensley, William Paden *see* Washboard Willie
Herbie Goins and the Nightimers 29
Hi Heel Sneakers 101

Index

Hicks, Otis *see* Lightnin' Slim
Higginbotham, Robert *see* Tucker, Tommy
Hill, Roger 172
Hincks, John 51
Hincks, Mick 38, *47*
Hiseman, Jon 51
Hite, Bobby 295
Hodge, Gaynel 250
Hodge, Pete 25, 31, *31*
Holiday, Billie 190-91, 211, 272
Homesick James Williamson 91, 94, 97, 98, *101*, 275, 290, 307, 313, 317
Hood, John 265-6
Hooper, Paul 51
Hopkins, Lightnin' 293
Hounslow, Chas 10, *11*
House of Blues 250
Howlin' Wolf 295
Hoy, Andy 50
Huggins, Cilla 48, 124
Hughes, Bill VII, 212, 261-2, *262*, 299
Hunt, Bill 52
Hunt, David 20
Hunt, John 92
Hutto, J.B. 41

I
I Don't Know 102
I Live for your Love 147
I'm For Real c/w *Jump Up* 150
Ian Campbell Folk Group 26, 30, 52
Idle Race 43
If I Could Be With You One Hour Tonight 205
Indian Summer 50-51
Ingram, Adrian 51-2
Inman, Derek 265-6
Inniss, Roger 231, *231*
International Concert Promotions 256
Iommi, Tony 54, 57, 84, *86*, 86-7, 89
The Irish Centre, Birmingham 253
Island Records and Studios 37, 52
It's Over 147
ITB Management 26

Ivy Bush pub, Birmingham 156
Ivy Bush Telegraph 297

J
J.A.L.N. Band 149
Jackson, Bob 51
Jackson, George G.P. *99*, *118*
Jagger, The Killer and the Prettiest Man in Rock and Roll exhibition 293-4
James, John 265-6
James, Nerys 307
James, Steve 140, *141*
Jazz Enterprises 221
Jazz Festival *see* Birmingham Jazz Festival
Jazz Rag magazine 212, 298-9, 307
Jennings, Tim 162, 163, 231, 280
Jepson-Homer, Clare 162
Jeremy, John 138
Jet Records 81
Jo Jones 130-31
Jo Sago 45-6
Johns, Will 306
Johnson, Clive 259
Johnson, Gus 131
Johnson, Larry 41
Jones, Curtis 41
Jones, Debbie VIII, 192, *301*, 301-2, 303
Jones, Max 282, 289-90
Jones, Paul 189, 252
Jones, Rick 297
Jones, Tim 231
Joseph, Pleasant *see* Cousin Joe

K
Kansas City Seven 21, 25
Kansas City, USA 130-1, 133-9
Kath, Terry 295
Keech, Dave 189
Keef, Marcus 65-6, 73-4
Keeley, Stan 176, *177*
Kellie, Mike 28, 30, 39
Kelso, Jacky 263
Kennedy, Joe Jr 138
Kenny Ball's Jazzmen 22, 183, 200

Kerr, Bob 303-4
Ketelbey, Albert 302-3
King Biscuit Boy 43-4, 91, 317
King Pleasure and the Biscuit Boys V, 160, 221, 222, 223, 225, 234, *240*, 249, 277
    band members *240*, 251-3
    Belgium tour 241-2
    formation and signing with Big Bear 159, 239-41
    at Lugano Jazz Festival, Switzerland 250-51
    Norway and Russia tour (1991) 243-8
    recordings 154, 188-9, 312
        Blues and Rhythm Revue Vol 1 172, 188-9, 226
        King Pleasure and the Biscuit Boys 241
        This is It 241
    Terry The Toupe 253-4
    US tour 249-50
King, Danny *28*, 30-31, 39, 227
King, Jonathan 282
King, Pete 220, 227, 234-5
King, Peter 205, *206*
King, Ray 149
Kleinschmidt, Gaby 267-8
Knopfler, Mark 49, 234
Kruger, Jeff 29
Krupa, Gene 187

L
Lady Sings the Blues show 160, 162, 179-81, 190, 191-3, 211-12, 221
Lamb, Bob 37, 38, *47*, 296
Lamm, Bobby 295
Lang, Harry 148
Langston, James *46*, 46-7
Leadbitter, Mike 43, 48, 91, 92, 93, 124, 275
Led Zeppelin 45, 63
Lee, Peggy 189-90
Lee, Ron 151
Leckie, James, QC 76-7
Lemon, Brian 180, 205, 218

Leonard, Gerry 135
Lewis, Reg 82-3
Lightnin' Slim 91, 93, 94-6, *96*, 97, 100, 109, 119, 290, 317
Lightning Struck the Poorhouse 112
Lights Went Out 151-2
Lippman, Horst 293
Lipstick Traces 116
Little Joe Blue *101*, 102, 317
Little Richard 290, *291*
Little Smokey Smothers *127*, 128, 317
Live at Monterey 171
Locomotive 56, 59, 60, 62, 63, 173, 295
    formation 21-2, 26-7
    members and later careers 28, 30-33, *32*, 37, 38-9, 45, 47, 77, 227, 287-8, 296
    recordings 34-9
Lonesome Lee Robinson *101*, 102, 317
Longstaff, Danny 236-7
Louise 49
Love is Strange 106
Love, Preston 299
Lowe, Mundell 190
Lucas, Geoff 75
Lusher, Don 214
Luv, Bud E. 249
Lynam, John 140
Lyttelton, Humphrey 6, 7, 16, 22, 25, 90, *139*, 157-8, 159, 163, 173, 178, 195-208, 222-3, 280

M
Mabon, Willie 91, 102-4, 317
Mace, Ralph 43
Madge, Billy *32*, 38
Magic Records 284
Magnum 151
Manfred Mann 66, 189
Manne, Shelley 233
Marbella Jazz Festival 255-73
    (2006) 272-3
    Festival office politics 258-60
    2004 last day cancellation 260, 265-6

Index

Gil y Gil and Marbella councillors 255-7, 264-5, 266-7, 272-3
Marbella Jazz Suite 264
performers 260-64, 267-72
press officer Carolina Esteban 260, 266, 273
Marini, Blue Lou 277, 278
Marquee Martin 68, 78
Marquee, Wardour Street, London 51
Martin, John 68
Martin, Paul P Popps 239, *240*, 248, 252
May Blitz 52
Mazzone, Mooney 32
McCalla, Josh 231
McCormack, Danny 163, 248, 252
McCrary, Howard *188*, 189, 228-33, *229-30*, 317
McCrary, Tammy 232
McIntyre, Joe 25
McKay, John 48, 49
McShann, Jay 131
Meehan, Patrick 73, 75-8, 84, 87
Melly, George 4, 164-5, 249
Melody Maker 5, 41, 112, 282, 289, 290
Mermaid pub, Birmingham 220
Messe Frankfurt trade fair 187
Mezzrow/Bechet Septet 110-12
Michaux, Pascal 187
Mick Mulligan's Magnolia Jazz Band 4-5
Midem 274-7, 282-5, 309
Midland Beat 18, 27, 112, 286
Midland Jazz Club 176-8
Miles, Butch *263*
Miles, Matt 264
Millar, Keith 38-9
Mirams, Andrew 75, 76
Miskolc Jazz Band 271
Mitchell and Butlers *see* Powell, Malcolm
Molbeck, Jonas III
Moments Like This 232
Monkton, Joe 151-2
The Monty Sunshine Jazz Band 177, 178
Moody Blues 27, 287
Mordue, Eddie 214

Morris, Steve 297
Morris, Johnny 10
Morrissey-Mullen 159
Morrissey, Dick *169*, 205, *206*
Moseley, Birmingham 45-6
The Move 72
Mr. Armageddon 37
Muddy Waters 112, 120-21, 293, *293*
Mullen, Jim 192
Muscles 113, 140-44, *142*, 151, 172
Music Week 159
Musicians' Union 200-201, 237
 Exchange System 90-91
Mussolini, Romano 173
My Baby Just Cares for Me 279-80
Myatt, Phil 287
Myers, Louis 123

N
Nancy Jazz Festival 106
Napier, Simon 48
NEMS 234
Neon Records 50-51
Never Gonna Let You Go 38
New Magnolia Jazz Band 21, *22*
Newell, Richard (King Biscuit Boy) 43-4, 91, 317
Nicholls, Big Al 189, 225, 253
Nightingale, Mark IV, 264
Norris, Fred 295
North Sea Jazz Festival 131-2
Notodden Blues Festival, Norway 225

O
O'Day, Anita 187
Old Crown jazz club, Digbeth 5
100 Club, London 48, 91, 92, 102, 124-5, 171
Oostende Blues Festival 241
Orphan Newsboys 170-71, 209-10
Osbourne, John Michael 'Ozzy' 53, 54-60, 75, 76, 79-81, 84-5, 87-8, 296
Osbourne, Sharon 80-81
Otis, Johnny 171-2

Otis, Shuggie 171
Out Looking for the Lion 184-5

P
Palacio de Ferias y Congresos, Marbella IV, VI
Paramount Records 43
Parnell, Jack *158*, 163
Parnell, Jack (bandleader) 218
Parsons, 'Pissy' (RAF Flight Lieutenant) 13
Pee Wee Hunt, *12th Street Rag* 4
Peel, John 37, 147, 152
Peg Leg Bates 7-8
Pegg, Dave 30
Pesky Gee! 73
Petersen, Holger 282, 285
Phil Upchurch Combo 227-8
Phillips, Nigel *46*, 46-7
Phillips, Sam 119
Phonogram 64, 66, 68
Picard, John 197
Pierce, Nat 167-8, *168*, 191
Pine, Wilf 73, 75-6, 78, 84, 87
Plant, Robert 45
Plater, Alan 217
Platz, David 34-5, 45, 61, 62, 84-5, 304
Playthings 297
Polydor Records 33, 275, 286
Ponomarev, Valery IV
Poole, Terry 51, 52
Potato Head Jazz Band 305
Powell, Cozy 51
Powell, Malcolm 155-9, *156*, 161, 203, 241
Presley, Elvis 119
Pryor, James Edward (Snooky) 94-5, *95*, 97, 275, 290, 317

Q
Quads 152-4, *153*, 297

R
Ragdoll Productions 241
Ramey, Gene 131
Randall, Justin VIII, 192, *302*, 302-3

Rattenbury, Ken 179-80
Rau, Fritz 293
Ray King Band 149
RCA Records 49-50
Rebecca's nightclub, Birmingham 140, 253-4
The Rebel 59
Record Collector 51
Red Lightnin' Records 49
Red Red Libanon 151
Reeves, Marc 53
Regent Sound Studios, Denmark Street, London 62
Reid, Billy 3
Reid, Sleepy 21
Reif, Fred 93
Rep Cafe Bar, Birmingham 219
Richard, Cliff 14
Ricky Cool and the In Crowd *172*, 304
Ricotti, Frank 189-90
Rideout, Derek *17*, 17-18
Roberts, Dougie 19, 20, 198-9
Robinson, Lonesome Jimmie Lee *101*, 102, 317
Robinson, Mark 236
Robinson, Matthew 162
Rocket Club 236, 237-8
Rockin' Berries 27
Roll Over Mary 39
Ronnie Scott's Birmingham 189, 211, 214-28, 230, 233-5, 254, 293
Ronnie Scott's London 130, 234
Rooker, Jeff 21
Rooster Blues 93
Rosenberg, Nomy 308-40
Ross-McKenzie, Iain 222
Ross, Annie VI, 178, 190, 270-72, *271*
Ross, Charles Isaiah *see* Doctor Ross
Ross, Richard 135
Rowe, Mike 48, 124
Roy Gee and the Dictionary of Soul 150
Royal Concert Hall, Nottingham 189
Rubin, Al 277-8
Rudi the Red-Nosed Reindeer 37

Rudi's in Love 35-6, 173
Rushing, Jimmy 57, 191, 201
Ruskin Spear, Roger 45
Russell, Tony 205

S
Sacrifice 38
Salmins, Ralph 170, 192, 211-12, 264
Sandwell Council 194
Sandy Brown's Jazzmen 178
Sannio, Cam 236
Sartori, Allan 219-24, 226, 235-8
Savage, Mike and Angela 83
Saw Mill Man Blues 112
Scott, Ronnie 34
    clubs *see* Ronnie Scott's Birmingham; Ronnie Scott's London
Scott, Stuart *141*, 143, *144*
Sealey, Paul 178
Second City Jazzmen 76, 78
Sex Pistols 48
Shapiro, Helen 221
Sherwin, Barry 219, 221-2, 227, 236, 237
Shirley, Bullmoose K. 226, *240*, 241, 242, 251, 303
Shuffle Demons 269-70
The Shufflepack 53, 303
Shuttleworth, Speedy 21
Sid Phillips Band 6
Simone, Nina 207, 278-82
Simpson, Jim II, IV, VIII, *306*
    great-grandfather 27-8
    childhood and parents 1-4, 209
    introduction to live theatre 4-5
    discovers rhythm and blues 6-7, 227
    National Service, forms station band 8-13, *11*
    works in Skegness 14-17, *17*
    Humphrey Lyttelton advises 197-200
    buys new horn 199-200
    works as photographer *19*, 19-20, 286-7, 290-94
    runs student Tek City Jazz Club 21-4
    tours with Locomotive 27-9
    records with Locomotive 33-6
    stops playing, manages Locomotive 36-7
    founds Big Bear Records 37-8
    see also Big Bear Records; Midem
    opens Henry's Blueshouse, manages Bakerloo 40-42
    writes to Andy Hoy of RCA 50
    relationship with bank 82-3
    naming of Black Sabbath 54-5
    seeks Black Sabbath recording deal 60-66
    launches *Big Bear* paper 294-5
    management pressures 68-9
    Black Sabbath legal case 72, 75-9
    Montreux (1972) 120-23
    gambling at Cannes with Richard Branson 276-7
    British tours of American jazz musicians 90-94, 125
    driving with Uncle Joe 112-13
    life with Marja Daleman and son 87, 299-300
    trades in beers 300
    North Sea Jazz Festival (1979) 131-2
    visits Chicago and records there 125-8
    visits Kansas City and records there 134-9
    turns down Birdie Song 274-5
    inaugurates Birmingham Jazz Festival *see* Birmingham Jazz Festival
    relationship with Humphrey Lyttelton 202-3, 207-8
    relationship with Val Wiseman 178-9, 181
    gets out of Russia 247-8
    plans *Lady Sings the Blues* project 179-81
    sets up British Jazz Awards 203-7
    business difficulties at Ronnie Scott's 223-4, 235-6
    encounters Nina Simone 279-82
    Marbella Jazz Festival organisation 256-60, 264-73
    sets out Count Basie orchestration books 261-2

works with Howard McCrary 228-33
　　plans *Drummin' Man* show 187-8
　　Rock and Roll museum campaign 52-3
　　at Black Sabbath The End Tour 88-9
　　see also Big Bear Records
Simpson, Kate 49, 83, 87, 100
Simpson, Ron II, 132, 298, 307
Sing A Song of Basie 167
Skeat, Len *158*, 170, 180, 187, 189, 210,
　　211-12, 220
Skidmore, Jimmy 197
Skirving, Mark 240-41, 242-3, 247
Slater, John *17*, 17-18
Smith, Arthur 286-7
Smith, Frank 135
Smith, Gerry 303
Smith, Joe 68, 78
Smith, Julian 232
Smith, Moses 'Whispering' 43, 91, 94, *95*,
　　96, *96*, 290, 317
Smothers, Abraham *127*, 128, 317
Snooky Pryor 94-5, *95*, 97, 275, 290, 317
Sodeikiene, Rimante 284
songwriting 186
Soprano Summit 170
Sounds 39, 144
Spann, Otis 293
Spedding, Chris 145
Spencer Davis Group 27, 161, 287-9, *289*
Spillett, Simon 298
Squires, Dorothy 3
Star Club, Hamburg 59-60
Stewart-Grayson, Jack 143-4
Stewart, Rod 66
Stony Plain Records 282, 285
Storey, Rick 28
Strange, Pete *168*, 179, 187
The Stringbeats 149
Stringle, Julian Marc 192
Struck, Nolan 128, 317
Sugar Pie DeSanto 293
Sun Ra Arkestra 267-70
Sun Records 119
Sunday Mercury 221, 235

Swift, Duncan 30, 181-6, *182*, *183*, 250
Swinging Down Broad Street suite 7, 162-4
Sylvester, Charlie 149

T
T-Bone Walker 121
T'Pau 297
Takin' Care of Business VIII
Tate, Buddy 131, 202
Taylor, Eddie 180, 181, 197
Taylor, Eddie 'Playboy' 99, 100, *118*, 316
Taylor, Martin 205, *206*
Taylor, Mick 38
Taylor, Roy (aka Roy Everett) 18, 26, *26*,
　　30, 39, 181, *182*
Tea and Symphony 45-8, *46*, 60, 62
Teagarden, Jack 1
Tek City Jazz Club 21
Telephone Blues 94
Telstar Records 274-5
Temperley, Joe 197, *197*
Terry The Toupe 253-4
Terry, Clark 117-18, 135
Tharpe, Sister Rosetta 112, 293
The Longest Running Disco in the World 149
The Rebel 59
Theobald, Brian 212
There Must Be Thousands 153
There's Never Been a Night 152
Thompson, Charles 205
Thorpe, Simon 192
Tiny Grimes Band 112
Tipitina VIII, 192, 301-2
Tjens Couter 151
Topic Records 53
Tower Ballroom 181-2, *182*
Transatlantic 143
Trident Studios, London 51
Trojan Records 92
Tucker, Tommy 91, 100-103, *101*, 294,
　　307, 317
Turner, Big Joe 202
Twiby, Biz 21

Index

U
UB40 27, 37, 61, 296, 297

V
Valery, Joseph Jn (Little Joe Blue) *101*, 102, 317
van Schtoop, Shark 251
Vas, Olaf IV
Vaughan, Sarah 177
Venue, London *112*, *115*
Verrell, Ronnie 159
Vertigo 64-6
Viles, Cecil 199-200
Vinnegar, Leroy 233

W
Waits, Tom 168
Walk of Stars 86, 88
Walt Disney Corporation 38
Wang Dang Doodle 303
Ward, Bill 54-5, 76, 85, 87
Ward, Ian 53, 304
Ward, Phil *22*
Warner Brothers 68, 78, 84
Warwick Castle pub, Birmingham 24-5
Washboard Willie 94, 95, *95*, 96, 118, 290, 317
Waters, Muddy 293, *293*
Watts, Charlie 211, 226
Watts, Ron 48-9, 50
Wayne, Charlie (Carl Wayne) 72-3
Weatherford, Teddy 202
Webster, Ben 191, 220
West Side Jazz Band 177
Westside BID 85, 88, 162, 174
What am I here for? 214
The Whiskey Brothers VIII, 303
Whispering Smith 43, 91, 94, *95*, 96, 290, 317
Whoopee Band 303-4
Wild Bill Davison 22
Wilde, Marty 29
William, Mark 295
Williams, Claude 131-9, *133*, *139*

Williams, Cliff 52
Williams, Mary Lou 130-31
Williams, Roy II, *158*, 159, 180, 187, 205, *206*
Williamson, James *see* Homesick James Williamson
Willis, Chick I
Willis, Dave 214
Willox, Roy 214
Winkelman, Pete 162
Winning, Martin 16, 253
Winwood, Steve 25, 30
Wiseman, Pete 176-7
Wiseman, Val III, VI, 159, 172, *179*, *180*, 241, 244, 247-8, 298
  career 176-81, 186-94, 270-72
Wood, Roy 304
Woodhouse, Barry 203
Woods, Chris 28, 30, 39
Wynston, Stich 269-70
Wyper, Olav 50-51, 64-6

Y
Yang, Sarah VII, 174, 175, 237, 283, *283*, 285
Yanow, Scott 298
Yardbirds 63
Ye Olde Foundry, Dudley 89
Yeats, Rowdy 241
York, Pete 27, 51, 172, 187, 295
You Call It Madness 190
Young, Graham 89
Young, Lester 131

Z
Zdravkovic, Lisa Sugar Lee 241, 242, 252
Zella Studios 35, 37, 60, 152, 184